Visual Basic™ Programming
A Laboratory Approach

COMPUTER SCIENCE PRESS

Alfred V. Aho, Columbia University
Jeffrey D Ullman, Stanford University
Foundations of Computer Science: Pascal Edition
Foundations of Computer Science: C Edition

Michael J. Clancy, University of California at Berkeley
Marcia C. Linn, University of California at Berkeley
Designing Pascal Solutions: A Case Study Approach
Designing Pascal Solutions: Case Studies Using Data Structures

A. K. Dewdney, University of Western Ontario
The New Turing Omnibus: 66 Excursions in Computer Science
Introductory Computer Science: Bits of Theory, Bytes of Practice

Robert Floyd, Stanford University
Richard Beigel, Yale University
The Language of Machines: An Introduction to Computability and Formal Languages

Michael R. Garey, Bell Laboratories
David S. Johnson, Bell Laboratories
Computers and Intractability: A Guide to the Theory of NP-Completeness

Judith L. Gersting, University of Hawaii at Hilo
Mathematical Structures for Computer Science, Third Edition
Visual Basic™ Programming: A Laboratory Approach

Ellis Horowitz, University of Southern California
Sartaj Sahni, University of Florida
Fundamentals of Data Structures in Pascal, Fourth Edition

Ellis Horowitz, University of Southern California
Sartaj Sahni, University of Florida
Susan Anderson-Freed, Illinois Wesleyan University
Fundamentals of Data Structures in C

Ellis Horowitz, University of Southern California
Sartaj Sahni, University of Florida
Dinesh Mehta, University of Tennessee Space Institute
Fundamentals of Data Structures in C++

Ellis Horowitz, University of Southern California
Sartaj Sahni, University of Florida
Sanguthevar Rajasekaran, University of Florida
Computer Algorithms

Thomas W. Parsons, Hofstra University
Introduction to Compiler Construction

Gregory J. E. Rawlins, Indiana University
Compared to What?: An Introduction to the Analysis of Algorithms

Wei-Min Shen, Microelectronics and Computer Technology Corporation
Autonomous Learning from the Environment

James A. Storer, Brandeis University
Data Compression: Methods and Theory

Steven Tanimoto, University of Washington
Elements of Artificial Intelligence Using Common Lisp, Second Edition

Kim W. Tracy, AT&T Bell Laboratories
Peter Bouthoorn, Gröningen University
Object-Oriented Artificial Intelligence Using C++

Jeffrey D. Ullman, Stanford University
Principles of Database and Knowledge-Base Systems, Vol I: Classical Database Systems
Principles of Database and Knowledge-Base Systems, Vol II: The New Technologies

Visual Basic™ Programming

A Laboratory Approach

Judith L. Gersting
University of Hawaii at Hilo

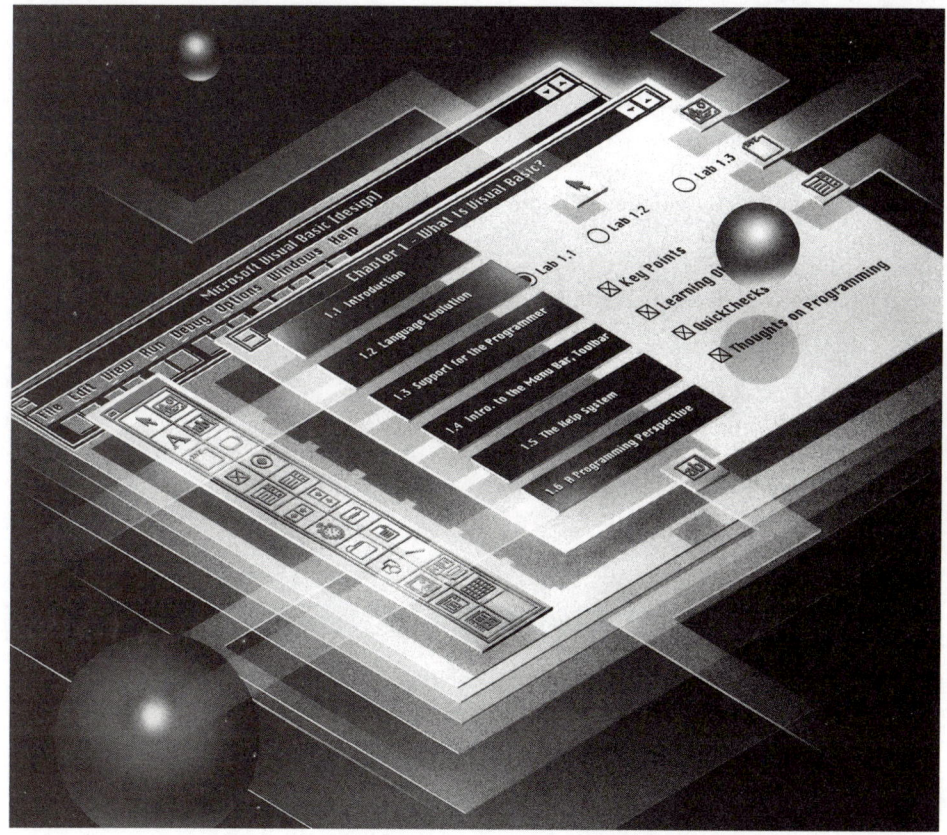

Computer Science Press
An imprint of W. H. Freeman and Company
New York

Visual Basic and Windows are trademarks of Microsoft Corporation.

Library of Congress Cataloging-in-Publication Data

Gersting, Judith L.
    Visual Basic programming : a laboratory approach / Judith L. Gersting
       p.   c.m.
    Includes index.
    ISBN 0-7167-8317-7 (soft cover)
    1. BASIC (Computer program language) 2. Microsoft Visual BASIC.
I. Title.
QA76.73.B3G48   1996
005.265—DC20   96-33933
                                                                                   CIP

© 1996 by W. H. Freeman and Company

No part of this book may be reproduced by any mechanical, photographic, or electronic process, or in the form of a phonographic recording, nor may it be stored in a retrieval system, transmitted, or otherwise copied for public or private use, without written permission from the publisher.

Printed in the United States of America

Computer Science Press
An imprint of W. H. Freeman and Company
41 Madison Avenue, New York, NY 10010
Houndmills, Basingstoke RG21 6XS, England

First printing 1996, SEM

DEDICATION

Dedicated fondly to Dr. Gene Medlin of Stetson University, whose MAD (Medlin's Automatic Device) was our mutual introduction to computers in the early years.

CONTENTS

To the Teacher xiii
To the Student xiv

1 What Is Visual Basic?   1

Key Points 1
1.1 Introduction 1
1.2 Language evolution 2
Lab 1.1 5
QuickCheck 1.1 11
1.3 Support for the programmer 11
1.4 Visual Basic menu bar and toolbar 12
Lab 1.2 15
QuickCheck 1.2 19
1.5 Visual Basic Help system 19
1.6 A programming perspective 21
Lab 1.3 25
QuickCheck 1.3 29
Review Questions 29
Exercises 30
Projects 30

2 How Visual Basic Programs Work   32

Key Points 32
2.1 Objects and properties 32
Lab 2.1 35
QuickCheck 2.1 39
2.2 Objects, events, and code 39
Thoughts on Programming: Event-Driven Programming 40
Lab 2.2 47
QuickCheck 2.2 53
2.3 Big picture of event-driven programming 53
2.4 Modest program design 54
Lab 2.3 57
QuickCheck 2.3 59
Review Questions 59
Exercises 60
Projects 61

3 User Interface; Project Management   63

Key Points 63
3.1 What is "the user interface"? 63

3.2 Visual Basic Toolbox 64
3.3 Common properties 65
3.4 Text Box 68
Lab 3.1 71
QuickCheck 3.1 77
3.5 Project management 77
3.6 Printing a project 79
3.7 Methods 80
Lab 3.2 83
QuickCheck 3.2 89
3.8 Editing code 89
3.9 Control Arrays 91
Thoughts on Programming: User Interface Design 92
Lab 3.3 95
QuickCheck 3.3 101
Review Questions 101
Exercises 102
Projects 103

Data Storage; Input and Output   105

Key Points 105
4.1 Building the pieces 105
4.2 Identifiers 110
4.3 Assignment statement 111
4.4 Print method 112
Lab 4.1 113
QuickCheck 4.1 119
4.5 Declarations 119
4.6 Constants 124
4.7 *Val* and *Str$* functions 124
4.8 Implementing an algorithm 128
Lab 4.2 131
QuickCheck 4.2 135
4.9 Input box 135
4.10 Modal forms 138
Thoughts on Programming: Documentation 140
Lab 4.3 145
QuickCheck 4.3 151
Review Questions 151
Exercises 152
Projects 153

Data Manipulation   155

Key Points 155
5.1 More on decimal numbers 155

5.2 Arithmetic expressions 157
5.3 String expressions 161
Lab 5.1 163
QuickCheck 5.1 167
5.4 Intrinsic functions 167
Lab 5.2 173
QuickCheck 5.2 179
Thoughts on Programming: Requirements Analysis and Specification 180
5.5 More on the Print method 179
Lab 5.3 187
QuickCheck 5.3 191
Review Questions 191
Exercises 192
Projects 193

6 Procedures   196

Key Points 196
6.1 Introduction 196
6.2 What is scope? 196
6.3 Scope of procedures 197
6.4 Scope of variables and control objects 199
Lab 6.1 205
QuickCheck 6.1 211
6.5 Argument passing 211
Lab 6.2 217
QuickCheck 6.2 221
6.6 User-defined functions 221
Thoughts on Programming: Top-Down Design 223
6.7 A program design example 224
Lab 6.3 229
QuickCheck 6.3 231
Review Questions 231
Exercises 232
Projects 234

7 Conditional Processing   236

Key Points 236
7.1 Viewpoint 236
7.2 Boolean expressions 237
7.3 If-Then-Else statement 240
7.4 Select-Case statement 243
Lab 7.1 247
QuickCheck 7.1 253
7.5 Control objects for making choices 253
Lab 7.2 257

QuickCheck 7.2 261
Thoughts on Programming: Design Representation 261
7.6 Still another program design 267
7.7 Visual Basic debugger 271
7.8 Guiding the order of user actions 277
Lab 7.3 281
QuickCheck 7.3 283
Review Questions 283
Exercises 284
Projects 286

8 Looping 289

Key Points 289
8.1 Visual Basic statements for looping 289
Lab 8.1 301
QuickCheck 8.1 305
8.2 Still more control objects: List boxes and combo boxes 305
8.3 Scroll bar 310
Lab 8.2 313
QuickCheck 8.2 317
Thoughts on Programming: Prototyping 317
8.4 Searching 318
Lab 8.3 321
QuickCheck 8.3 325
Review Questions 325
Exercises 326
Projects 328

9 Menus; Graphics 330

Key Points 330
9.1 Pull-down menus 330
9.2 Pop-up menus 333
Lab 9.1 335
QuickCheck 9.1 337
9.3 General information about graphics 337
9.4 Picture file images 337
9.5 Design-time artwork 338
9.6 Custom toolbars 340
Thoughts on Programming: Reusability 342
Lab 9.2 345
QuickCheck 9.2 349
9.7 Run-time artwork 349
9.8 Simple animation 351
Lab 9.3 353

QuickCheck 9.3 357
Review Questions 357
Exercises 358
Projects 359

10 Data Structures   360

Key Points 360
10.1 Arrays—something old, something new 360
10.2 Array declarations 362
10.3 Array usage 365
10.4 Two-dimensional arrays 367
Lab 10.1 369
QuickCheck 10.1 373
10.5 Sorting 373
10.6 Searching 376
Thoughts on Programming: Algorithm Efficiency 380
Lab 10.2 383
QuickCheck 10.2 387
10.7 Parallel arrays 387
10.8 User-defined types 389
Lab 10.3 393
QuickCheck 10.3 397
Review Questions 397
Exercises 398
Projects 400

11 Files; Message Boxes   403

Key Points 403
11.1 Why use files? 403
11.2 Types of Visual Basic files 404
11.3 Opening and closing sequential files 405
11.4 Common Dialog control 406
11.5 Writing to a sequential file 408
11.6 Reading from a sequential file 401
Lab 11.1 415
QuickCheck 11.1 419
11.7 About random-access files 419
11.8 Writing to and reading from random-access files 420
11.9 File type comparisons 422
Lab 11.2 425
QuickCheck 11.2 431
11.10 Message boxes 431
11.11 Error handling 435
Thoughts on Programming: Program Testing and Reliability 440

Lab 11.3 445
QuickCheck 11.3 447
Review Questions 447
Exercises 448
Projects 451

12 Communicating with Other Applications — 453

Key Points 453
12.1 Evolving communication 453
12.2 Object Linking and Embedding 457
Lab 12.1 459
QuickCheck 12.1 465
12.3 Interacting with databases 465
12.4 Adding, deleting, and searching records 467
Lab 12.2 469
QuickCheck 12.2 473
12.5 Querying a database 473
12.6 A disclaimer 474
Thoughts on Programming: System Integration 475
Lab 12.3 477
QuickCheck 12.3 481
Review Questions 481
Exercises 482
Projects 483

Appendixes — 485

A Windows—Once Over Lightly 485
B Managing Files 489
C Windows 95 491
D Visual Basic Toolbar and Toolbox 498
E Visual Basic Version 4.0 499
F Hot Keys 503
G Alternate Type Declarations 504
H Project Files 505

Index 506

TO THE TEACHER

This textbook is the direct result of my search for the most workable environment for teaching an introductory computer programming course for nonmajors. I want students to acquire a useful skill and master fundamental concepts in programming. The pedagogy and organization are the result of these two objectives.

Exploration Approach

The book is intended as an introduction to programming using Visual Basic. No prior computer experience is assumed. The unique feature of the book is its emphasis on a laboratory-based, "exploration" approach. What students do has far more impact as a learning experience than what they hear or read. Visual Basic is dynamic and exciting for the students, and they can learn best by active involvement with Visual Basic.

The laboratory exercises, found throughout the book, are carefully designed to allow students to explore, experiment, and think. Instead of long text discussions of "when you do a, b will happen," the idea is to have students try to observe for themselves what happens. Instead of "type in these lines of code," the idea is to have them design the code they need to solve increasingly more difficult tasks. Gaining confidence with this sort of exploration enables students to continue to use Visual Basic in new situations after the course has ended, an essential goal of the text. Even within the semester, student transformations from total novice to knowledgeable computer user able to produce quite sophisticated and useful windows-based programs—thanks to the power of Visual Basic—are rather impressive.

This experiment-based philosophy has required a new way of thinking on my part in teaching the course and in writing this book. I have tried to resist the old, ingrained lecture approach of "tell them everything they need to know" but rather to create the book—and the course—in a guided discovery mode. There are many laboratory sessions within the text that are structured to explore certain topics that have been introduced but not completely explained, and many sessions explore new topics not previously introduced. In other words, the laboratory experiences are an integral part of the book, not an add-on or a supplement. New information is introduced in the lab sections, and I make no apology for this. It is in keeping with how I think a programming course should be taught. Once we as teachers accept a change in our role from fount of knowledge to knowledgeable facilitator, this approach becomes a viable and interesting alternative to a traditional class. Students not only learn more; they have fun doing so.

In terms of course mechanics, I spend much of the class time in a closed laboratory environment. I assign each of the three labs in each chapter, but not all the laboratory work can be finished in the time allotted for class. Students complete the labs as homework and submit their completed worksheets and electronic files for grading. They put the graded lab sheets back into their notebooks for future reference, and their graded files are returned with comments. I give few, if any, programming assignments beyond those required in the labs, but the book provides a variety of additional assignments for flexibility with different approaches. If workstations are at a premium or if collaborative learning is desired, students can work on the labs in pairs or small teams. The book can also be used in a more traditional classroom format by using the labs for in-class demonstrations, with homework and programming assignments selected from the exercises and projects.

The intended audience for this book is primarily people who want to learn about windows programming. Visual Basic is used as a mechanism to support this goal, not as an end in itself. I am striving for a middle road. I do not want to simply present a "gee-whiz" look at the bells and whistles of Visual Basic, engaging as those may be. On the other hand, this book is not for the experienced Windows programmer who will be writing low-level applications. Again, no programming experience whatsoever is assumed. Familiarity with Windows is helpful, but not essential; material in appendixes covers everything needed. Version 3.0 of Visual Basic is assumed. Appendixes give an introduction to Visual Basic version 4.0 and to Windows 95.

High-Level Program Design

Visual Basic should not be taught as simply an enhancement of some earlier version of BASIC with some graphical screen controls thrown in. It is inappropriate, for example, to begin Visual Basic programming with a study of the control structures of the language. With its event-driven nature, good Visual Basic program development requires a higher level of abstraction first. There is a lot of emphasis early in the book on high-level program design. We do get to "traditional programming" topics in due time. This early emphasis on high-level design, forms layout, division of tasks among control objects, and so on, has three advantages:

1. It's the "right" way to present Visual Basic, consistent with an event-driven and somewhat object-oriented language.

2. It starts with topics that are easy and fun for the students and reinforces success early, giving them confidence.

3. It sends a message right away to the occasional high school BASIC hacker that this is not the same old stuff!

Program development practices and philosophy are further emphasized in Thoughts on Programming sections throughout the book. These cover such topics as event-driven programming, user interface design, design representation, prototyping, and so on.

Chapter Overview

In Chapter 1 students run a multiform Visual Basic project and look at the Visual Basic environment, including the Help system. The steps of the program development process are introduced. Chapter 2 discusses the nature of event-driven programming and explains that objects have associated properties and recognize certain events. The multiform example is examined to see how code can be written to respond to these events. The Object Task Card, a tool for high-level program design, is introduced.[1]

The emphasis in Chapter 3 is on user interface design, with an examination of the most common Visual Basic controls and their properties. The details of managing the files that make up a project are discussed. Control arrays are introduced. Even though this seems early for such a topic, students have little difficulty with an array of control objects, perhaps because

---

[1] The OTC is based loosely on the CRC card idea, introduced by Kent Beck and Ward Cunningham in "A laboratory for teaching object-oriented thinking," 1989 proceedings of OOPSLA.

it is rather tangible. This is the simplest way I've seen in any programming language to ease into the topic of arrays.

Chapter 4 presents some of the low-level features of Visual Basic programming, namely, how to begin constructing algorithms for individual procedures. Conditional and iterative processing are discussed briefly in the abstract just to introduce the needed ideas. Variables, data types, the assignment statement, and the input box are covered. Chapter 5 is a bit of a lull after the details introduced in Chapter 4 and before the more difficult topics in Chapter 6. Chapter 5 explains how expressions are processed and goes over the most useful Visual Basic intrinsic functions.

Chapter 6 is probably the most conceptually difficult chapter. It discusses the various types of procedures in Visual Basic, the details of passing arguments, and the extremely important topic in Visual Basic of scope—of procedures, of variables, and of control objects.

Chapter 7 covers Visual Basic conditional statements and the use of control objects that indicate choices (option buttons and check boxes). It also discusses a number of design representation techniques and applies them to a fairly complex programming project. Iteration is discussed in Chapter 8, along with list boxes and combo boxes on which iterative processing is often useful. List boxes are used as additional examples of arrays. Chapter 9 discusses Visual Basic menus. It also discusses basic graphics and animation techniques.

Chapter 10 deals with one-dimensional and two-dimensional arrays. By this time, students have seen lots of arraylike things, so this topic goes more smoothly than in a traditional programming course. Algorithms for sorting and searching are provided. Chapter 11 presents Visual Basic file handling for both sequential and random-access files. It also discusses message boxes and error handling.

Chapter 12 discusses interaction of Visual Basic with other applications through OLE and with databases through the use of bound data controls.

Some flexibility is possible in the order of topics covered. For example, both menus and message boxes can be introduced much earlier if desired.

Pedagogy

The laboratory exercises are self-contained. Each begins with Learning Objectives and is followed by a QuickCheck to review concepts introduced in the text and the lab. The step-by-step working format of the labs is enhanced with marginal notes keyed to the Learning Objectives. Aside from the labs themselves, pedagogical features of the text include:

- Key Points that highlight important concepts in programming and features of Visual Basic

- Extensive use of illustrations and computer screens to help students visualize material being discussed

End-of-chapter exercises are categorized (after Chapter 1) as:

- Review Questions, to reinforce concepts learned

- Reading Code and Writing Code, to hone detailed coding skills

- Exploring Further (often additional enhancements to or modifications of an existing program), to expand on certain topics or pursue new ideas without having to do an entire project from scratch
- Projects, in which students bring together their developing skills in program design, implementation, and testing to produce complete, interesting applications

Supplements

The disk bound into the back of the textbook includes all the files students need to carry out the lab activities. An instructor's manual, available from the publisher, contains suggested solutions to the written lab pages and answers to QuickChecks, Review Questions, and Reading Code, Writing Code, and Exploring Further exercises, as well as a disk with sample programming solutions for the lab assignments.

Acknowledgments

Many people contributed talent and expertise in the creation of this textbook. In addition to my book team at W. H. Freeman, I would like to thank the following reviewers, whose detailed and helpful comments improved this book:

Alan Cook, Jefferson State Community College
Tom Danieli, Instructional Designer, Lansing Computer Institute
Andrew J. Harris, Coordinator of Service Courses, Indiana University/
    Purdue University, Indianapolis
Richard A. Hatch, San Diego State University
Jim Hightower, Department of Management Science/Information Systems,
    California State University, Fullerton
Dara Lee Howard
Kieran Mathieson, Oakland University
George S. Nezlek, Loyola University of Chicago
Margaret Anne Pierce, Georgia Southern University
Oskars Rieksts, Kutztown University
Hilbert Schultz, University of Wisconsin, Oshkosh
Maureen C. Thommes, Bemidji State University
Michael J. Walton, Miami-Dade Community College

    Remaining flaws and errors are, of course, entirely my fault. And, finally, thanks go to the people at Microsoft for the Visual Basic product, an innovative and powerful tool for windows programming.

TO THE STUDENT

Welcome to the exciting world of windows-based programming. Through a series of explorations and laboratory sessions, you will learn a powerful and practical computer tool, Visual Basic programming.

This textbook has been designed with you in mind. You'll learn a very useful skill; I also hope you'll find the process fun. Each chapter is organized to make mastering Visual Basic programming as easy as possible.

Chapter Organization

Each chapter begins with Key Points, which highlight the programming concepts and Visual Basic features you'll encounter in the chapter. You'll find them useful not only as a road map to where you're going when you begin the chapter but also as a quick review of where you've been when you are finished.

Throughout each chapter are illustrations and computer screens to help you find your way around in Visual Basic's graphical user interface. The more comfortable you are with this icon- and menu-driven environment, the more enjoyable your explorations in Visual Basic will be. You'll be able to create interesting screen displays early on with the powerful tools Visual Basic supplies.

But programming is much more than creating visual presentations. You must be able to design a plan for the program to carry out its task. Several design tools are presented. One such tool is the Object Task Card. Make using it a habit. If you use the OTC to help you assign each task an object when you are designing your program, you'll save time later when actually writing the program.

You also need to understand some of the underlying concepts essential to good programming, regardless of the environment or language used. I've put these concepts in boxes called "Thoughts on Programming," not because I consider them secondary but to emphasize how fundamental they are. Read and understand them; they're important!

Laboratory Exercises

Acquiring the skills to be an effective programmer in Visual Basic requires hands-on computer experience and the ability to explore on your own. Much of what you need to learn cannot be found in a lecture; it needs to be discovered and reinforced by practice. It is for that reason that the laboratory exercises are an integrated and essential part of each chapter. They are unique in many ways, including format, and are an important feature of this textbook. Your success in the course depends on how thoughtfully and systematically you perform the lab exercises.

Each lab is self-contained to provide you with a useful guide while performing the exercise and a valuable resource when you return to it for study. You may not remember everything you originally saw and learned, so check off each step as you finish it and write down the results in pencil in the space provided. Use the Learning Objectives, marginal notes, and QuickChecks to review the points each lab exercise covers and to ensure that your explorations produce the results intended.

End-of-Chapter Exercises

Whether formally assigned or not, these exercises will reinforce everything you've learned in each chapter. Use the open-ended and fill-in-the-blank Review Questions to test your mastery of the chapter material.

Of course, one programs by doing, and to help develop the skills you need to become a good programmer, a series of Exercises—Reading Code, Writing Code, and Exploring Further—is provided; all give opportunities for practice.

Above all, programming is a problem-solving skill, and the Projects developed as homework assignments, either individually or in teams, are meant to show you how Visual Basic is used to solve the real problems you'll encounter as a student or later in your career. Some appear entertaining, others more practical, but all will lead you further on your adventure of discovery of the power of Visual Basic.

CHAPTER 1

What Is Visual Basic?

KEY POINTS

- Visual Basic uses the Windows operating system to allow windows-based application programs to be written.
- Programming languages have evolved over the years from low-level machine languages to languages with sophisticated and user-friendly graphical user interfaces.
- The Visual Basic menu bar and toolbar allow you to use the facilities of the Visual Basic environment.
- You should make the Visual Basic Help system your best friend!
- Programming involves much more than merely writing code. In particular, the design of a program progresses through a series of representations of the problem.

1.1 Introduction

This book introduces you to computer programming by using Visual Basic,[1] a relatively new and quite powerful programming language. Visual Basic is a computer program that allows you to write other computer programs. A **computer program** is a set of instructions to a computer that direct it to carry out some activity. A program is often called **software** to distinguish it from the machine, which is called **hardware**. One of the key pieces of software in any computer is its **operating system**. The operating system, as one of its many functions, accepts instructions from the computer user to run other programs. A program you write using Visual Basic (or any other programming language) to perform some particular task is called an **application program** to distinguish it from more general programs like operating systems or Visual Basic itself that serve as support systems for writing and running application programs.

Visual Basic uses the Windows operating system to allow you to write windows-based programs. So the word "windows" is being used in two different ways. The word **Windows**[1] (with a capital W) refers to the operating system in which Visual Basic runs. The Windows operating system presents the computer user with screens or panes of information known as **windows** (with a small w). There are certain standard features that all windows have. For example, windows can be moved about on the computer screen by the user. An application program created by Visual Basic also presents the user of the program with one or more windows that share these standard features. Hence Visual Basic programs are called windows-based programs.

Figure 1.1 shows the three levels of programs mentioned. Windows allows Visual Basic to run, which in turn makes it possible for you to create

---

[1] Visual Basic and Windows are trademarks of Microsoft Corporation.

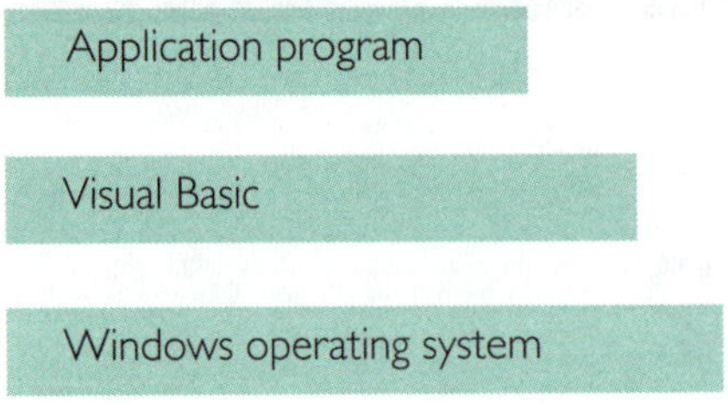

Figure 1.1
Hierarchy of computer programs

- Application program
- Visual Basic
- Windows operating system

and run windows-based application programs. It is important to distinguish between the Visual Basic program and application programs that are written using Visual Basic.

You don't need to know much about Windows to run Visual Basic. However, because Visual Basic is a windows-based program and the application programs you will write with Visual Basic are windows-based, you should be familiar with the standard windows features. Check the list of terms in Table 1.1; if some are not familiar to you or if you just want to review working with windows, read Appendix A. (If your system is running Windows 95,[2] then read Appendix C.)

Table 1.1
Terminology for working with windows

Active window	Icon
Click	Maximize, minimize buttons
Control-menu box	Mouse
Cursor	Pop-up menu
Double-click	Pull-down menu
Drag-and-drop	Resizing a window
Dragging	Scroll bar
Hourglass	Title bar

1.2 Language evolution

As stated earlier, Visual Basic is a programming language. A brief history of the evolution of programming languages may give you some appreciation of the power and appeal of Visual Basic.

Computers store all information internally using only the symbols 0 and 1. That's because computers are electronic devices and can use "low voltage" and "high voltage" to represent these two symbols. Our familiar digits 0, 1, 2, ..., 9, and letters of the alphabet, are all encoded into strings of 0s and 1s when stored in a computer. For example, in the most widely used encoding scheme, B is represented by 01000010. Words, and even entire computer programs, are represented in the computer by combining such strings.

In the earliest days of writing computer programs (late 1940s), all instructions—and all data on which those instructions operated—had to be written using these strings of 0s and 1s, the only language the computer understands. Such **machine language programming** was tedious in the extreme. Imagine having to get long sequences of 0s and 1s exactly right! The early 1950s brought improvement with the introduction of **assembly language programming**. In assembly language, the programmer can use words

---

[2] Windows 95 is a trademark of Microsoft Corporation.

like STORE X instead of some sequence of 0s and 1s to give very simple instructions to the computer. However, because the computer still understands only machine language, a computer program called an **assembler** is required; the assembler translates assembly language into machine language.

By the mid 1950s, the first **high-level programming language** had been invented. A high-level language allows much more powerful and humanlike computer instructions, such as

```
If Temperature > 100 Then Print "Hot"
```

Each such instruction may require many machine language instructions to carry it out. Because of this additional expressive power, the programmer can concentrate more on the big picture of what needs to be done. But ultimately, a program in a high-level language still has to be translated into its machine language equivalent. A piece of software called a **compiler** or an **interpreter** does this translation.

The first high-level language was **FORTRAN**, standing for Formula Translation. Introduced in 1957, this was a language designed primarily for engineering and scientific problems. Engineers and scientists were the heaviest users of the big, expensive computers then available. Shortly thereafter (1960), a language called **COBOL** (Common Business Oriented Language) was developed for the business data-processing world. The original **BASIC** (Beginner's All-purpose Symbolic Instruction Code) programming language was developed in 1963, making it also one of the earliest high-level languages. The intention of BASIC, reflected in its name, was to make it an easy language so that programming could be done by less technical people, even by school children. BASIC was the language supplied with many of the early microcomputers that first appeared in the late 1970s.

Over the years BASIC has gone through a number of transformations to make it a more modern and powerful language. Visual Basic, introduced in 1991, is the latest incarnation. This book assumes that you are using the Standard Edition of Visual Basic Version 3.0. (If you are using Visual Basic Version 4.0, you can do everything we will discuss plus even more; see Appendix E.)

Figure 1.2 sums up the thumbnail sketch of programming language evolution provided here. (There are many programming languages not shown; don't imagine that nothing happened between 1963 and 1990.)

The primary innovation of Visual Basic is its use of a **graphical user interface** or **GUI**. Visual Basic application programs are windows based, and the user can make things happen by clicking on icons or buttons, picking menu items, and so on. The programmer's working environment while writing the program also has a graphical component in which he or she designs the application program's user interface. Using Visual Basic, it is possible to create sophisticated windows-based application programs complete with multiple windows, menus, buttons, icons, scroll bars, graphical effects, color, and so on. These visual effects were undreamed of in the early days of computing, and even until recently, they were impossible or very difficult to achieve. Now they are relatively easy, and you will learn how to do them.

The programming language part of Visual Basic is a modern form of BASIC. The statement at the beginning of this chapter that Visual Basic is a new language is only partly correct. The "Visual" part is new, but the "Basic" part is not. If you have any experience with BASIC programming, you will find much that is familiar when you begin to write code.

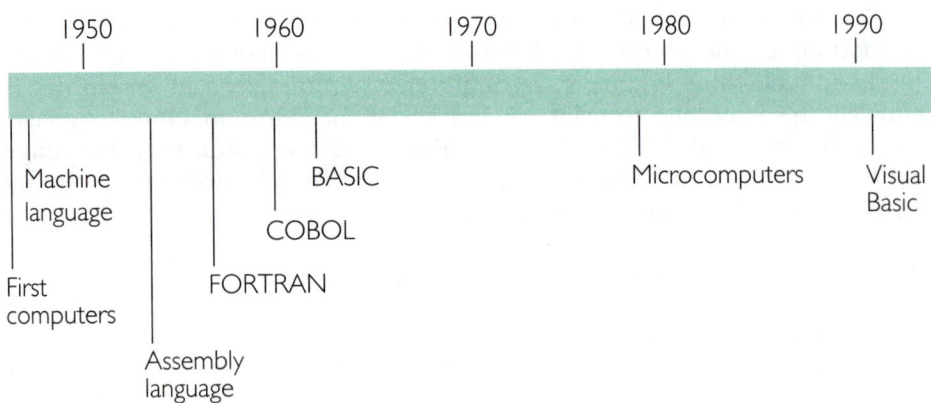

Figure 1.2
Programming language timeline

Visual Basic has so many capabilities that this book can't begin to cover them all. However, by the end of the book you will be able to do further explorations on your own if you need to learn more.

In the meantime, running a Visual Basic application program will illustrate the kind of windows-based, graphical user interfaces Visual Basic allows you (the programmer) to create. Running Visual Basic itself will illustrate the windows that assist the programmer in the task of writing an application program.

Name: _____ Date Due: _____

LAB 1.1

LEARNING OBJECTIVES

- Running a Visual Basic application program
- Using buttons and a pull-down menu
- Identifying windows in the Visual Basic environment
- Using Command Button and Label icons on the Toolbox

Perform the following activities. You may want to check off each step as you complete it so that you don't lose your place. Space is also provided in which to write your answers to questions.

1. ____ Bring up Windows on your system.

   ____ Open the File Manager in Windows by double-clicking on the icon.

   ____ Locate the file called **lab1.exe**. This file is a Visual Basic application program. (Your instructor may need to tell you where to look for this file; if you are using the diskette that comes with this book, the file will be on a diskette drive, which is A or B.)

2. ____ Run the **lab1.exe** program by double-clicking on the file name. You will see a window with instructions, a box for your first name, and two buttons. What appears in the title bar of this window?

   | **Running a Visual Basic application**

3. ____ Type your name in the box, then click one of the two buttons. Describe what happens.

   | **Using buttons**

4. ____ Click the other button. Describe what happens.

5. ____ Exit the program by double-clicking on the control-menu box on the Opening Screen window.

6. ____ Run the *lab1.exe* program again. Can the two buttons be clicked in either order?

Using a pull-down menu

7. To exit the program this time, select File below the title bar on the Opening Screen window. This will cause a pull-down menu to appear. What are the menu choices?

____ Exit the program.

____ Close the file manager.

8. ____ Now you are going to run Visual Basic itself, as opposed to running a Visual Basic application. Double-click on the Visual Basic icon in Windows.

Identifying windows in the programming environment

9. ____ What you see is the Visual Basic **programming environment**, the facilities Visual Basic provides for you to write programs. Initially, this environment may seem confusing because so many windows are present. Eventually, you'll see what they are all for.

____ Find four windows associated with Visual Basic that have descriptions in their title bars. Some windows probably overlap others, so you may have to "click around" on the screen a bit to make each window active. What are these four windows?

____ Resize these windows so that none overlaps another. Note that a window can be resized both horizontally and vertically at the same time by dragging on a corner of the window frame.

10. ____ The **Form window**, shown here in miniature, is where you design the window the user will see when your application program runs. The grid of dots is present to make it easier to align buttons and other objects on the form. It does not show when the program is running.

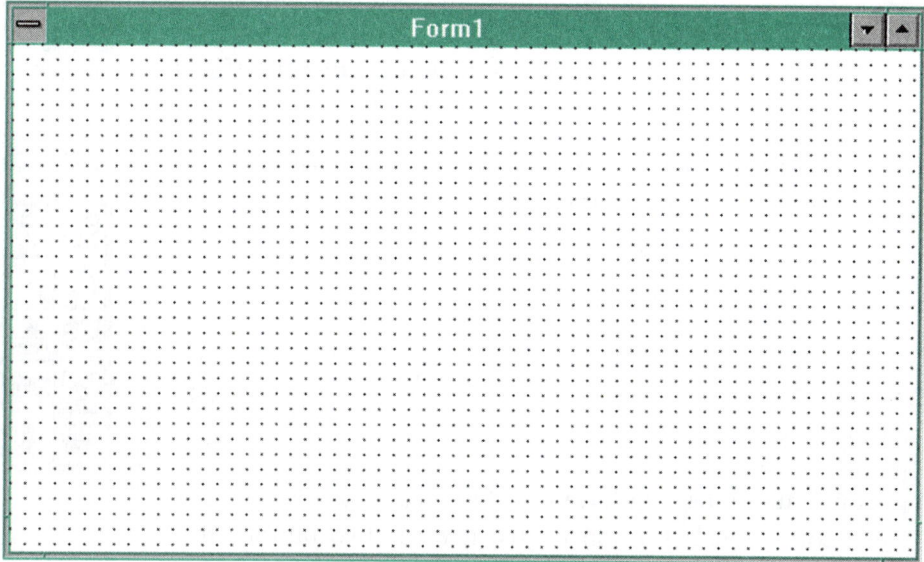

An application program can present multiple windows by having the programmer use multiple Form windows in developing the program. How many Form windows do you think were used in developing the program *lab1.exe*? Explain your answer.

11. ____ A fifth window in the Visual Basic environment has nothing written in the title bar, but it is called the Visual Basic **Toolbox window**, shown in miniature here, and consists of a selection of icons.

Using the command button icon

To put a Command Button on the form:

____ Click on the Toolbox icon for the **Command Button**, the one that shows a rounded rectangle

____ Move the cursor to anywhere in the Form window, and click and drag. What happens?

Congratulations, you have just designed a form with a single command button on it, just like the two buttons that were on the opening form of *lab1.exe*.

12. To put a Command Button on the form another way:
____ Double-click on the Command Button icon on the Toolbox. What happens?

____ Drag and drop the button to position it on the form (place the mouse pointer inside the button to move it).

____ Resize the button by dragging on the **sizing handles** (the black dots on the edge of the button).

Using the label icon

13. ____ Now put a label on the form. The Toolbox icon for a **Label** shows the letter A. Labels are often used to display instructions or other information.

14. ____ An object (like a label or a command button) that is displaying sizing handles is an **active object**. Only one object on a form or the form itself can be active at any one time.

____ To make the Form window active, click inside the Form window (but not inside any of the objects on the form).

____ In the Microsoft Visual Basic [design] window, click on Window. This opens a pull-down menu. The first menu choice (menu choices are also called **menu picks**) is Color Palette. It should be highlighted.

____ Select this menu pick either by pressing the Enter key or by clicking on the menu pick. This opens yet another window in the Visual Basic environment.

____ Click on any of the colored squares in the Color Palette. What happens?

15. ____ On the right end of the Microsoft Visual Basic [design] window, after a row of icons, there are two little squares, each with a pair of numbers beside it. Explore until you figure out what the number pairs mean. (Hint: Make the Form window active, then try moving the Form window about on the screen. Try resizing the Form window.)

16. ____ To close Visual Basic, double-click on the control-menu box (left end of the title bar) on the Microsoft Visual Basic [design] window. You do *not* want to save changes to ***Form1.frm***.

> **QuickCheck 1.1**
> 1. Visual Basic uses the _____ operating system.
> 2. What's the difference between the Visual Basic program and a Visual Basic application program?
> 3. What is new about Visual Basic compared to earlier versions of BASIC is its use of a _____.
> 4. How do you start up Visual Basic?
> 5. Name two ways to put a Command Button on a form.

1.3 Support for the programmer

In Lab 1.1 you saw the sort of graphical user interface that a Visual Basic application program can present to the *program user* and some of the windows it supplies for the *programmer* to use. Visual Basic provides further support to the programmer. Again, a brief historical perspective may be useful.

For many years, software for most programming languages consisted simply of the necessary compiler to translate a program written in the particular programming language into a machine language version. In order to write the program (also called **program code** or simply **code**), you (the programmer) had to use a totally different piece of software, like a text editor. After writing the program, you exited the text editor (saving your work, of course) and then invoked the compiler. If the program could not be successfully compiled because you had used some incorrect programming statement, you might get a list of one or more error messages giving the line in the program at which the error first became apparent. You then had to go back to the text editor, make changes to your code, get out of the text editor, and run the compiler again.

Once the program successfully compiled, you asked the operating system to execute the compiled (machine language) version. If further errors occurred—for example, the answers when the program executed were not those expected—you had to find the problem, go back to the text editor, make changes, get out of the text editor, run the compiler again, and then execute the program again using the new compiled version.

As you can see, there was much going into and out of various pieces of software. Eventually, however, software developers began to provide programmers with an **integrated development environment (IDE)** or **programming environment**. In an IDE, all these various steps can be done within the framework of the environment. In other words, the environment package includes a text editor for writing a program and the ability to compile the program and to execute the program simply by choosing different options within the environment. Additional options within the environment allow the programmer to more easily **debug** (find and correct the errors in) a program by, for example, stopping the program at any particular statement and examining the current value of the quantities the program is working with.

The programming environment's purpose is to make the programmer's task as easy as possible. The Visual Basic programming environment does this by presenting the programmer with a graphical user interface consistent with the windows philosophy: a mouse-controlled cursor, icons, pull-down menus, resizable windows, the "drag-and-drop" method to position items, and so on. The programmer can "pick-and-click" both to design the visual aspects of the windows-based program he or she is developing and to simplify the work of editing, testing, and debugging code.

1.4 Visual Basic menu bar and toolbar

One of the windows in the Visual Basic environment that you saw in Lab 1.1 is the Microsoft Visual Basic window. This window, shown in Figure 1.3, contains the Visual Basic title bar, with standard windows maximize and minimize buttons and a control-menu box. What interests us here are the toolbar and the menu bar. They provide access to the many features of the environment.

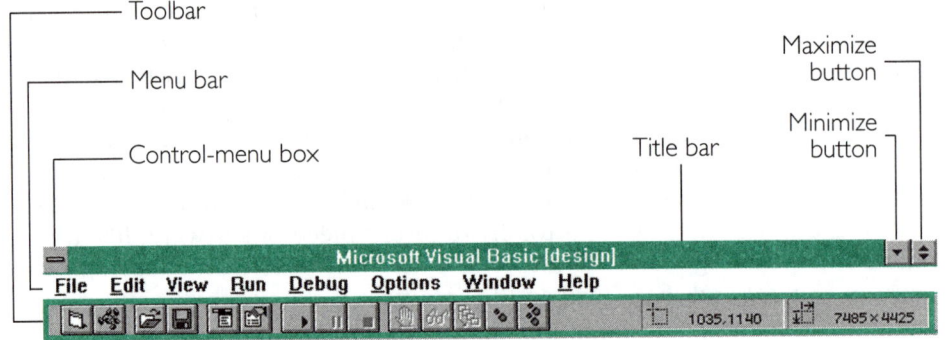

Figure 1.3
Visual Basic toolbar and menu bar

Each item in the menu bar represents the title of a pull-down menu that allows you to choose one of a set of related tasks. Suppose you want to access a particular menu. In Visual Basic (or any windows setting) there are often multiple ways to accomplish something. The icon below is used whenever alternate ways to do the same thing are presented.

To access a menu, either

OPTIONS
▶ Click on its title in the menu bar.
▶ Hold down the "Alt" key and type the underlined letter (also called the **access key**) in the menu title.

Thus to pull down the File menu, as shown in Figure 1.4, you can either click on the word "File" or use the Alt-F combination of keys; "F" is the access key for the File menu. (Note that this option gives a choice between using a mouse and using the keyboard. The keyboard option provides a faster means of access for those who are good typists and who don't mind learning all the keyboard equivalents.)

1.4 VISUAL BASIC MENU BAR AND TOOLBAR • 13

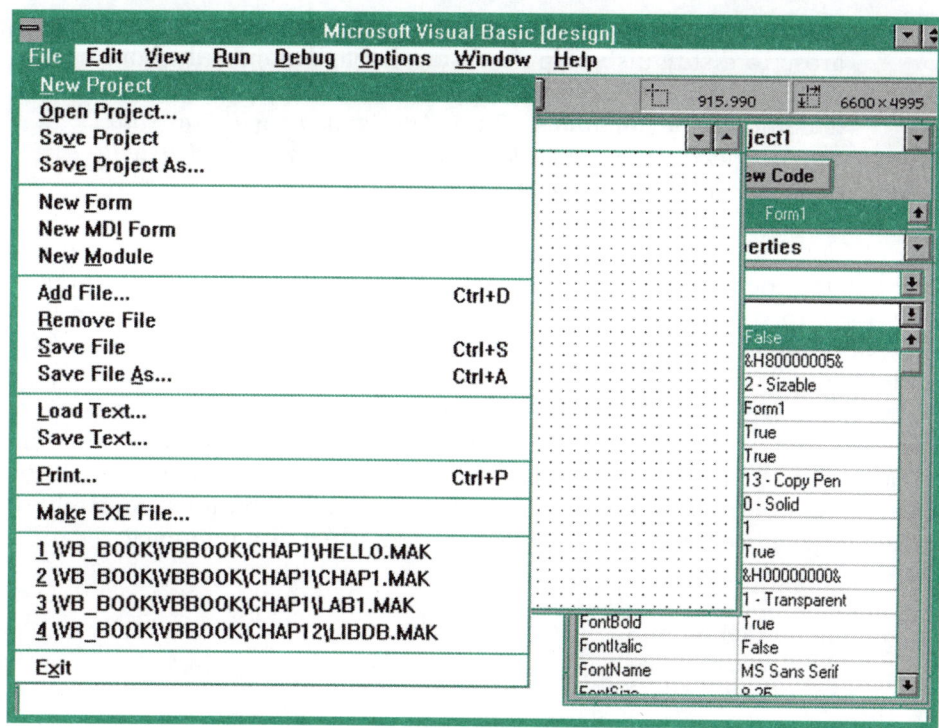

Figure 1.4
File pull-down menu in Visual Basic

Here's a brief description of the kinds of jobs each menu attends to. Don't memorize these lists; you'll work with the menus in detail as time goes on and you'll quickly become familiar with what they do.

File menu: A Visual Basic application program is called a **project**, and a project is made up of several "files." The File menu handles the tasks of managing a project, such as starting a new project, opening an existing project, adding files to or removing files from a project, and saving a project.

Edit menu: The Edit menu handles text-editing tasks when writing program code.

View menu: The View menu allows you to move quickly from one part of the code to another.

Run menu: The Run menu allows you to run (execute) a program, or stop execution.

Debug menu: The Debug menu allows you to control various features useful in debugging your code.

Options menu: The Options menu allows you to set various properties of the environment (and of the project), such as color schemes and whether the project should be automatically saved before it is run.

Window menu: The Window menu allows a particular window in the Visual Basic environment to become the active window.

Help menu: The Help menu brings up various aspects of the Visual Basic on-line help system. **On-line help** means that you can access the help system while you are on-line, that is, from within the Visual Basic environment. This term arose to distinguish help that is available dynamically from within a piece of software from help available in printed documentation manuals. *The Help system will be your biggest friend in successfully using Visual Basic, and it will pay you many times over to become familiar with it.*

Not all options of a menu apply to any given situation. When you pull down a menu, items in dark print are **enabled**; the actions they represent apply to your present situation and you can select them. Items in light print are **disabled**; the actions they represent don't apply to your current situation and you cannot select them.

The toolbar contains buttons that can be clicked to perform some of the more frequently done tasks in the menus, and thereby provide a shortcut to accessing the menu. If the user wishes to use only the menus, the toolbar can be removed. Figure 1.5 describes the toolbar buttons. Appendix D includes the same information so that you can use it as a reference.

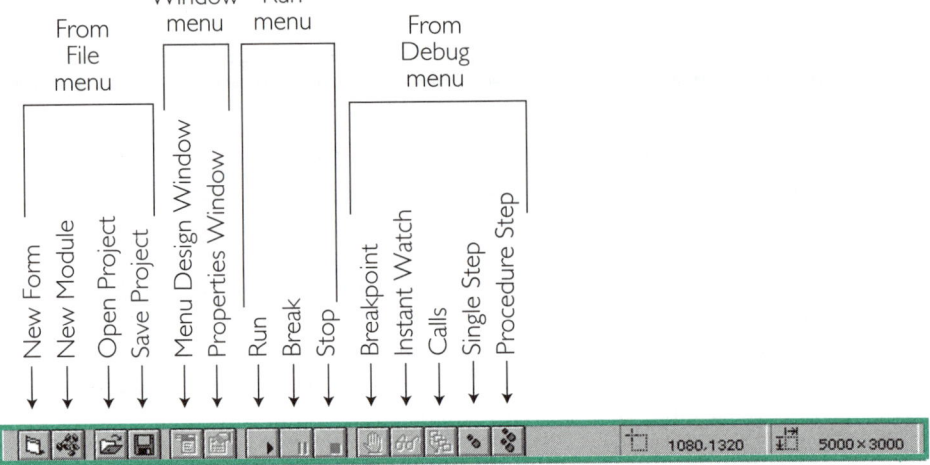

Figure 1.5
The Visual Basic toolbar buttons

At the right end of the toolbar are two sets of number pairs. (Did you figure out their meanings in Lab 1.1?) From Lab 1.1, you know that the Visual Basic environment contains a Form window, simply called a form. Suppose the form is the active object. Then the first pair of numbers on the toolbar gives the location of the upper left corner of the form using the upper left corner of the screen as a reference point. In Figure 1.5, the first pair of numbers is 1080, 1320. These numbers mean that at the moment the toolbar was observed, the left edge of the form was 1080 units away from the left edge of the screen, and the top edge of the form was 1320 units below the top edge of the screen. The second pair of numbers gives the width and height of the form. Figure 1.5 shows that the form at that time was 5000 units wide and 3000 units high. But what are the units? They are *twips*. A **twip** stands for one twentieth of a point. The **point** is a unit used to represent type size; one point is 1/72 of an inch. A type size of 12-points is therefore 12/72 = 1/6 of an inch. A twip equals 1/1440 of an inch.

If an object on the form is the active object, then these number pairs give, respectively, the left and top position of the object from the upper left corner of the form, and the width and height of the object.

Name: _____ Date Due: _____

LEARNING OBJECTIVES

- Using the Visual Basic File and Run menus
- Using the Visual Basic Project window

LAB 1.2

1. ____ To bring up the Visual Basic environment, double-click on the Visual Basic icon in Windows. Visual Basic assumes by default that you want to work on a new project and presents you with a new, blank form.

2. ____ Click on the Project window (which may initially be partly hidden by the form) in order to make it the active window. The title bar of the Project window says Project 1, the default name for a new project. Within the Project window are listed the various files that are part of the current project. However, here you want to work with the project that produced the *lab1.exe* program.

3. ____ To open an existing project from within the Visual Basic environment, do one of the following:

Using the File menu

OPTIONS
- Click on File on the menu bar and select Open Project.
- Use the access keys: Alt-F (for File) followed by Alt-O (for Open Project).
- Click on the Open Project toolbar button.

After any of these actions, a *dialog box* opens asking you to select the project file (Figure 1.6). (A **dialog box** is a pop-up window—a small window that suddenly pops up somewhere on the screen—that asks the user for

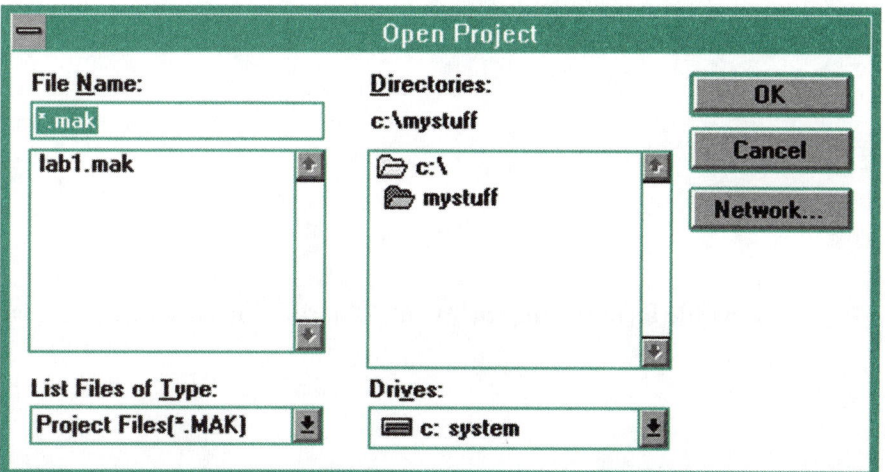

Figure 1.6
Dialog box for selecting project file

some information.) If you used the File menu, you may have noted that the choice Open Project was written

>Open Project...

The presence of the ellipses (three dots) following the menu choice is a standard windows notation to show that a dialog box will appear to which you must react before the action you chose can be carried out.

In response to this particular dialog box, you want to open the project given by the file name **lab1.mak**; again, your instructor may have to help you locate this file.

____ Select the file name by clicking on it, and press the Enter key or click on the OK button.

Using the Project window

4. ____ Look at the Project window again. What appears in the title bar now?

5. ____ Scroll through the Project window. What are the files that are part of the **lab1** project?

6. ____ Select **lab1.frm** in the Project window and then click the View Form button. You see essentially the same form you saw when you ran **lab1.exe** in Lab 1.1. The difference is that you are not executing the completed application program; you are looking at it within the Visual Basic environment, where the program was developed and can be modified. What "objects" do you see on this form?

7. ____ View the form **lab1a.frm**. What "objects" do you see on the form?

8. ___ View the form *lab 1b.frm*. Describe the "objects" you see.

9. ___ Note that the title bar of the main Visual Basic window says "[design]." When you are in **design mode**, you are writing the program. You can also test your program by running it within the Visual Basic environment.

Using the Run menu

___ Run the program by doing one of the following:

OPTIONS
- Click on Run on the menu bar and select Start.
- Use the access keys: Alt-R (for Run) followed by Alt-S (for Start).
- Press the shortcut key (also known as a **hot key**) F5.
- Click on the Run toolbar button.

The program should run just as before. Note, however, that you are still within the Visual Basic environment. The main title bar indicates that you are in **run mode**; the notation [design] has been replaced by [run]. To exit the application program and get back to design mode, select Exit from the *application program's* File menu, or use the *application program's* control-menu box.

10. ___ Rerun the program, using a different way to start it up than the way you used in the previous step.

___ To stop execution this time and get back to design mode, do either of the following (you may have to move the form window in order to see the menu bar or toolbar):

OPTIONS
- Click on Run and select End (the access keys won't work here as long as the application form is the active window because they apply to the application form's menu, not the environment menu).
- Click on the Stop toolbar button.

These methods allow you to stop the execution of any application program by using the Visual Basic environment rather than the program itself.

___ Exit Visual Basic. You do *not* want to save any changes.

QuickCheck 1.2

1. True or false: Visual Basic gives the programmer an IDE.
2. How do you tell when a menu item is enabled?
3. Describe a sequence of steps to open an existing Visual Basic project.
4. When you have opened a Visual Basic project, what information can you get from the Project window?
5. Describe how you could stop a running Visual Basic application program.

1.5 Visual Basic Help system

Increasingly, modern software relies on on-line help systems rather than printed manuals to aid the user. The Visual Basic Help system is your best source of information if you have a question about some aspect of Visual Basic. Through the Help system, you can:

- Refresh your memory on some point covered in this book.
- Get information on details not covered in this book.
- Explore new Visual Basic topics.

Think of the Help system as your personal Visual Basic tutor, ready to answer any question. Note, however, that the Help system can provide only information about Visual Basic; it cannot tell you how to write a particular program. That's why much of the page space in this book is used to talk about programming, while omitting many of the details of Visual Basic per se.

Figure 1.7 shows the Help menu from the Visual Basic menu bar. The choices

    Obtaining Technical Support...
    About Microsoft Visual Basic...

access some messages from Microsoft. If it is available, the choice

    Learning Microsoft Visual Basic

brings up a short tutorial that gives an overview of Visual Basic. Selecting Contents opens a pop-up Help window, shown in Figure 1.8.

The Visual Basic Help system is organized as a **hypertext** document; this means that you can follow links from place to place within the document by clicking on any underlined words highlighted in color. The cursor shape

Figure 1.7
Help pull-down menu in Visual Basic

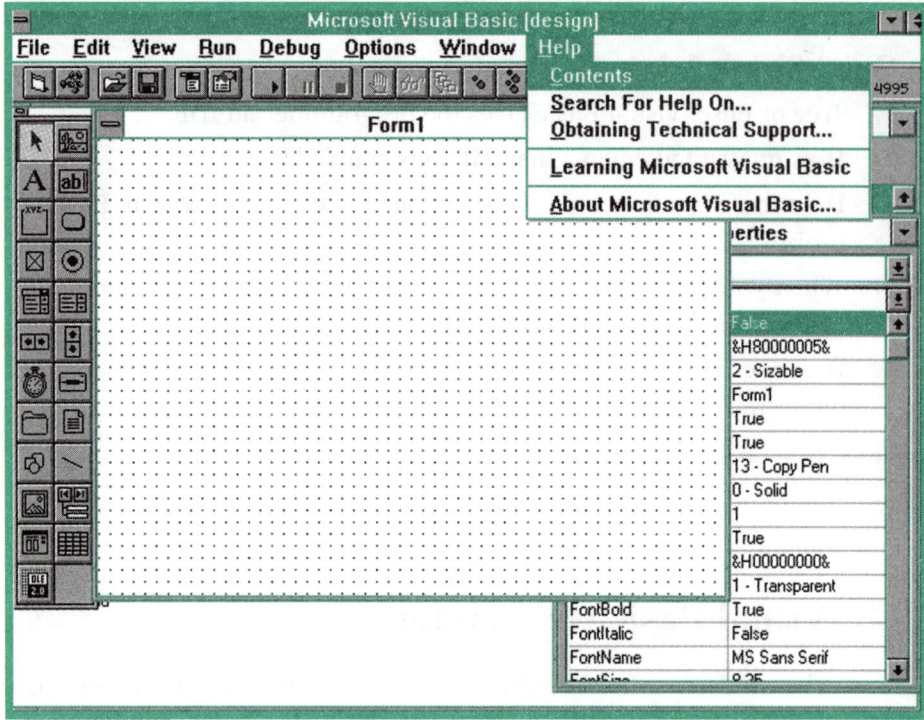

also changes to a pointing finger over any word that represents a link to another part of the document. This allows you to browse through the Help document and look at topics of interest. A word underlined with a dotted line represents a link to a definition of the word.

For example, clicking on Programming Environment in the screen shown in Figure 1.8 brings up another screen with a link to Toolbar. Clicking on Toolbar brings up still another screen that shows an image of the Visual

Figure 1.8
Help Contents window

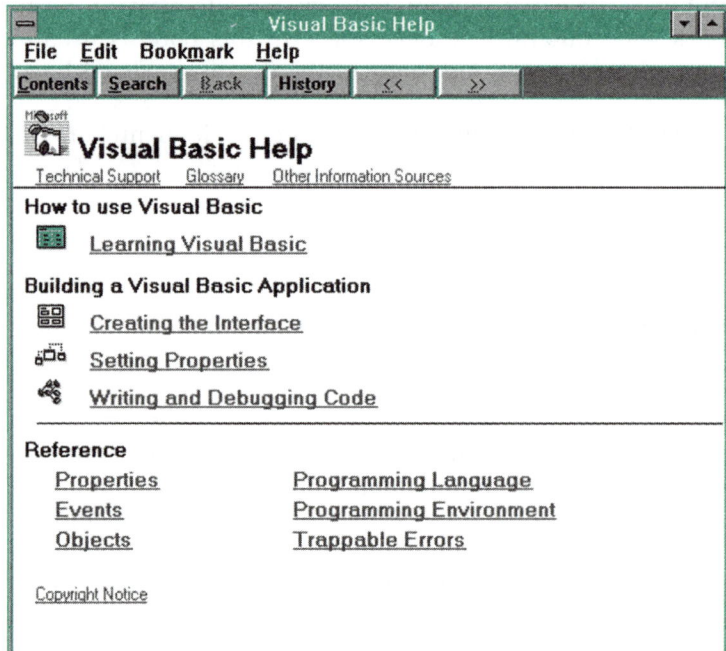

Basic Toolbar. Clicking on the File menu in this image opens another screen with a link to Open Project, and clicking on Open Project brings up a screen describing how to open a Visual Basic project.

Figure 1.8 shows that the Help window has its own menu bar and toolbar. Again, each item in the menu bar represents the title of a pull-down menu. The *File* menu allows you to print a Help screen. The *Edit* menu allows you to make an electronic copy of a help screen so it can be inserted in a document, or to make your own personal notes on a particular help topic. The *Bookmark* menu lets you mark places in the help system you frequently visit and want to be able to reach quickly. (If you are using a networked version of Visual Basic, you may not be allowed to permanently "personalize" the system in this way.) And the *Help* menu leads to information on how to use Help.

The toolbar of Figure 1.8 provides various ways of navigating through the Help system, such as going *Back* to the previous screen you viewed or seeing a *History* of screens you have recently viewed in order to select one to which to return.

The Help Contents window in Figure 1.8 was accessed by choosing Contents in the basic Help menu of Figure 1.7. As useful as the Contents option is, the Search For Help On... option is even more useful. Usually you want information on some specific thing. Choosing Search For Help On... brings up a dialog box in which you can enter a specific topic on which you want information. Visual Basic then shows a list of subtopics for that topic for which Help screens are available. From a selected subtopic, the click of a button takes you to the Help screen for that subtopic. You need to become comfortable with using the Search For Help On... option. If you don't know exactly what you want information about, a scroll bar in the dialog box lets you scroll through topics until you find one that seems as if it might apply.

The final way to use the Help system is to take advantage of its **context-sensitive** feature. This involves using the hot key F1. Whenever you press this key, Visual Basic does its best to figure out where you are and what help screen might apply to your present situation. It then automatically brings up the appropriate help screen.

At the risk of being repetitious, *the Help system will be your biggest friend in successfully using Visual Basic, and it will pay you many times over to become familiar with it.* After a bit of experience using the Help system, you'll be a pro!

1.6 A programming perspective

Although the **lab1** program was just for fun, it will be looked at again to see the code that makes it work and to illustrate certain aspects of Visual Basic programs. However, real-world programs are usually written to do tasks that would be difficult, tedious, or impossible without the computer's help. A program is intended to solve a certain problem, whether that problem consists of processing the employee payroll in a business or of entertaining the computer user with a video game. The primary skill needed for programming is that of problem solving.

To solve a problem, you must clearly describe the problem to be solved and figure out what actions will bring about a solution. Then you must carry out these actions, and, as a precaution, check the resulting solution to be sure the problem has been satisfactorily solved. These steps apply to any type of problem—building a bridge, planning a dinner party, tuning up your car engine, or looking for a job. In very broad terms, the steps in solving any problem can be summarized as:

1. ***Describe what*** the problem is.
2. ***Figure out how*** to solve the problem.
3. ***Carry out*** your solution plan.
4. ***Check*** the solution.

If the problem is an appropriate one to be solved by a computer program, that will become evident at step 1. Steps 2, 3, and 4 then consist of planning the solution in terms of a computer program, implementing this plan using some programming language, and testing the resulting program to be sure that it does what it is supposed to do. The program may exist for a long period of time, and someone may eventually want to change it to solve a slightly different problem. Therefore it is important to keep a record of how the program solves the problem. Hence for programming, as well as for solutions to other recurring or long-lived problems, there is a fifth step to the problem-solving process:

5. ***Keep a record*** of how your solution works.

These problem-solving steps have special names in the context of programming:

1. **Requirements analysis and specification**
2. **Program design**
3. **Program implementation (coding)**
4. **Testing**
5. **Documentation**

These steps will be discussed further in the Thoughts on Programming sections throughout the book.

A few comments can be made now, however. The programming process is *not* as sequential as the numbered steps may suggest. The steps may overlap one another, or an earlier step may have to be revisited later. An initial understanding of the problem requirements must come first, but a preliminary design may reveal questions that require further clarification of the problem requirements. Implementation may begin on some parts of the program while the design of other parts is still being completed, and the implementation process may reveal problems that require reconsideration of the design. Testing or at least plans on how to test can begin as soon as the problem is well understood. Documentation is not the last step but rather an ongoing record-keeping process throughout all the other steps.

Step 3, program implementation, is the process of writing instructions in a programming language, also known as **coding**. Coding is the task that most people think of when they hear "computer programming." But it is only one task out of five. Furthermore, it is far from being the central task. If steps 1 and 2 have been done correctly, then step 3 is somewhat mechanical and not terribly creative. Programming teams typically budget only 15 to 20 percent of the total program development time to coding.

On the other hand, step 2, program design, is a highly creative process. The design must bridge the gap between what the program is supposed to do, as determined in step 1, and the program instructions to do it, step 3. What the program is supposed to do is a high-level concept expressed in terms of what people want to have happen. Program instructions—even in a high-level programming language—represent a much lower level of thinking, closer to what a machine has been wired to do. The design must begin with the abstract program requirements and end with something very close to code. The design process thus consists of a series of representations of the problem spiraling down through various levels of abstraction. Figure 1.9 illustrates this idea, although there is nothing fixed about the number of levels. Also, while the overall progress of the design is in the top-to-bottom direction of the arrow in Figure 1.9, it is often accomplished by occasional backtracking to an earlier level, making some changes, and then moving forward again

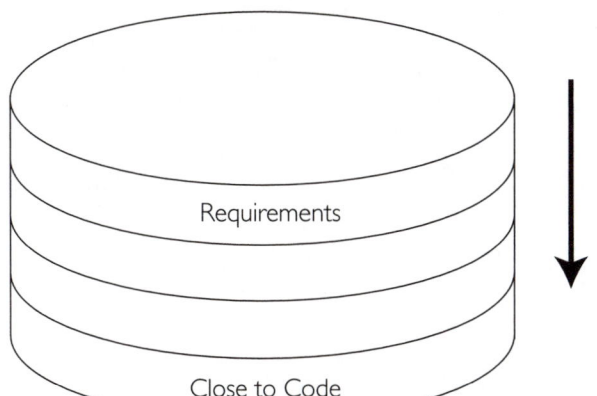

Figure 1.9
Levels of abstraction in program design

The steps in programming are relatively independent of the particular programming language that will be used to implement the solution, but the number of layers in the design process is not. The advent of a graphical user interface adds to the design effort in the following sense. While Visual Basic provides nifty mechanisms like windows, buttons, scroll bars, and menus for effective user interaction, the design process must include a plan for how those tools are to be used. This requires design work at a higher level of abstraction than with a more traditional programming language, where managing communication with the program user often takes up a large part of the code. Visual Basic removes a lot of effort from a low level of design (close to code) and adds some effort at a higher level of design (the graphical user interface). Original BASIC was introduced before there were even video screens; output came only in the form of a printed page of text. Later versions of BASIC—before Visual Basic—treated the screen just like a page of text. So the design process for Visual Basic programming is bound to be different.

Another difference in the design process occurs because of the event-driven nature of how a Visual Basic program runs, which is quite different from how a standard BASIC program runs. This will be explained in the next chapter.

Name: _____   Date Due: _____

LEARNING OBJECTIVES

- Implementing a simple form design
- Saving a Visual Basic project
- Using the Visual Basic Help system

LAB 1.3

Implementing a form design

1. ____ Start Visual Basic by double-clicking on its icon. A new blank form is ready for you to work on.

2. ____ Below are the specifications for what the form should look like for a simple Visual Basic program. (Most form specifications would not be this detailed.) Apply each of these specifications to your form:

   ____ The background color should be light green. (Hint: Try the first pick on the Visual Basic Window menu.)

   ____ The form itself should be 8025 twips wide and 5055 twips high.

   ____ There should be one command button on the form of size 1455 twips wide by 735 twips high at location 2880 twips from the left of the form and 2280 twips from the top of the form.

   ____ There should be one label on the form with size 3015 × 615 and position 2160 × 480.

3. ____ Run this program. What happens when you click the button? Why?

   ____ Go back to design mode.

4. ____ Although this Visual Basic program doesn't do anything yet, it is the basis for future work, so you should save the files that are part of this project. This is a new project that you are saving for the first time, and you need to name the files.

   To save the project and give it a name:

   Saving a project

   ____ From the Visual Basic File menu, choose Save Project As... . You will be asked whether you want to save the changes to the form (you do), and you will be asked to give a file name.

   ____ Save the file in the appropriate directory (ask your instructor) with the name *message.frm*.

___ Then you will be asked for the name under which to save the project. Use the name ***message.mak***.

___ Exit Visual Basic.

5. ___ Just to show that everything has been saved:

___ Start Visual Basic again.

___ Open the ***message.mak*** project (use the File menu, the access keys, or the toolbar button and look for that file wherever you just saved it).

___ Use the Project window to view the form. It should look the same as before.

6. ___ Resize the command button so that it is approximately square. Because you have now changed the form, you should save your work again. You are saving it under the same name as before, so you can use Save Project instead of Save Project As... .

___ Save your work.

Using the Help system

7. ___ Suppose you want to use the Visual Basic Help system to learn more about command buttons. Command buttons are examples of control objects.

___ From the Help/Contents window, follow the links Objects, Controls, Controls List, and Command button.

___ Then follow the link to Caption property. The Help window for the Caption Property tells you, among other things, the kinds of objects to which the Caption property applies and gives you a description of what the Caption property represents. What does the Caption property represent on a form?

___ Click on the Back button. What happens?

___ Use the History button to go directly back to the Controls screen. Then click on the definition of "event." Briefly, what is an event?

___ Close the Help window.

1.6 A PROGRAMMING PERSPECTIVE • 27

8. ____ Pull down the Help menu and choose Search For Help On.... In the dialog box, type "Caption"; then click Show Topics. In this case there is only one subtopic, called Caption Property, so click on Go To. This brings you to the same screen as before.

   ____ Be sure your machine is connected to a printer, and use the File menu to print information on the Caption property.

   ____ Close the Help window.

9. ____ To illustrate context-sensitive help, make the command button the active object on the form and then press the F1 key. What happens?

10. ____ Suppose you want to know about a programming statement called an If-Then-Else statement.

    ____ Use the Help system to find information on this statement (don't worry if the resulting information means nothing to you right now). The Help system provides examples of the use of any particular programming statement.

    ____ Bring up the example of how to use the If-Then-Else statement. In this example, the user will supply a number for X. If the user supplies the number 35, what value does the example code give to Y?

    ____ Close the example.

    ____ To return directly to this Help entry at any time, you can set a bookmark. Use the Help Bookmark button to define a bookmark for this Help entry.

    ____ Use the Help Contents button to go back to the Contents screen.

    ____ Use your Bookmark to get directly back to the If-Then-Else entry.

    ____ Close the Help system and exit Visual Basic.

QuickCheck 1.3

1. How do you tell when a word in a Help topic is a link to another topic?
2. Why might you want a Help Bookmark?
3. What key activates context-sensitive help in Visual Basic?
4. One of the most creative parts of the programming process is _____.
5. How do you save a new Visual Basic project?

Review Questions

1. A computer program is _____.
2. What is the difference between "Windows" and "windows"?
3. When you write a program using Visual Basic, will the result be an application program or an operating system?
4. All information is stored internally in a computer using the symbols _____ and _____.
5. Programs written in high-level programming languages must be translated into _____ before they can be executed on a computer.
6. The earliest high-level programming languages first appeared around _____.
7. Visual Basic programs have a GUI ("gooey") interface. What does this mean?
8. An active object on a Visual Basic form will display _____ by which its size can be adjusted.
9. Name three activities a programmer can do within an integrated programming environment.
10. Describe a quick way to open a menu with an underlined letter in its name.
11. What does it mean when an item shows in light print on a menu?
12. What is a twip? Where will you encounter one in Visual Basic?
13. What is a dialog box?
14. Explain how you would use the hypertext feature of the Visual Basic Help system.
15. What does it mean to say that Visual Basic Help is context sensitive?
16. What's the difference between Visual Basic design mode and Visual Basic run mode?
17. True or false: Coding is the central task in computer programming.
18. List the five problem-solving steps in programming and give a very brief description in your own words of what each one means.

19. Explain what is meant by "Program design must bridge the gap between requirements and implementation."
20. Explain why documentation of a program is important.

Exercises

1. You are planning a cross-country trip by automobile, and you don't want to drive too far on any one day. Apply the five informal problem-solving steps of Section 1.6 to your problem.

2. An architect and designer of custom houses advertises with a flyer containing the following information:

> Mr. Tackhammer is a graduate of the prestigious Hard Knox School of Architecture. He is well known for beautiful architectural designs that make the best use of the natural beauty of both the site and the materials. A satisfied client reports, "Mr. Tackhammer worked closely with us to understand what we really wanted. He talked over each phase of the design with us, from the overall floor plan to the details of the kitchen cabinets." A well-known builder reports, "It is always a pleasure to build a home from Mr. Tackhammer's designs. They are well thought-out and accurate. Each home goes together smoothly during the building process, so building inspections are met on schedule and within budget, resulting in a satisfied customer." Another client affirms, "We were very pleased with our original Tackhammer home; when it came time to add an extra room, it was easy to tie it in to the overall architectural plan, thanks to the detailed drawings Mr. Tackhammer had left with us."

Explain how this information ties in with the five steps involved in programming.

Projects

1. Open project *chap1.mak* (this file will be found wherever you found *lab1.exe*). What you see is someone's first attempt at a form design. Rearrange the objects and change the background color so that the effect is more pleasing. (The functionality of these objects would also affect how they should be placed, but because you don't have that information, just base your decision on pure aesthetics.) Be sure to save your project when you are done.

2. Your boss has sketched the layout for the form for a new Visual Basic application. Figure 1.10 shows the sketch plus some instructions. Create the form your boss is looking for. To learn how to use the Color Palette to set the colors of the labels, consult the Help system. Theoretically, the technique described there works for all other objects on the form that display text, which would include command buttons. However, Visual Basic does not allow you to change command button colors.

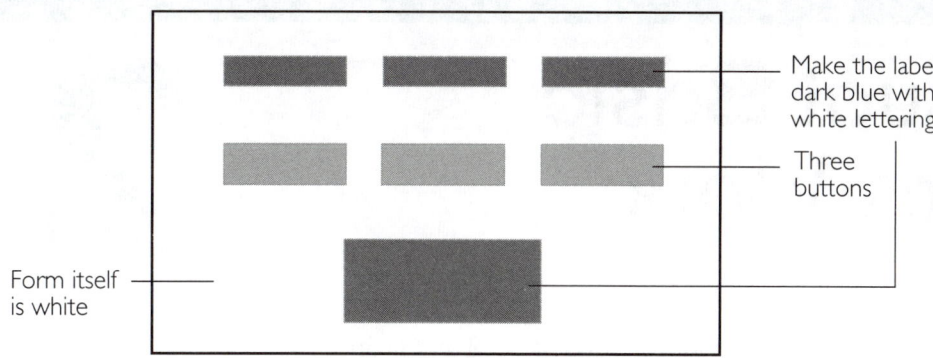

Figure 1.10
Form for new Visual Basic application

3. Open the Visual Basic project **hello.mak**. Run this program and click on the "Click Here" command button. Then go back to Visual Basic design mode. Double-click on the "Click Here" button. This will bring up a window called the Code window. Here you see the program code that tells the label what to display when the button is clicked. Change this message so that the label displays "Goodbye" when the button is clicked. Run the program again to see if this change works properly. Save your files when you exit Visual Basic.

CHAPTER 2

How Visual Basic Programs Work

KEY POINTS

- Objects have properties; the Properties window allows most object properties to be set at design time.
- Objects recognize events; Visual Basic is event-driven programming.
- The Code window allows you to view, edit, or create program code.
- Event-driven programs, once started, run in a continuous wait loop until interrupted by an event.
- Simple Visual Basic applications can be designed using the OTC (Object Task Card) representation.
- Skipping the design phase for a program in order to save time does not, in the long run, save time.

2.1 Objects and properties

To understand how Visual Basic programs work, a review of the anatomy of the *lab1* program is useful. In Lab 1.2, you loaded *lab1.mak* into the Visual Basic environment and used the Project window to view each of the three forms of that project. Each form corresponds to one of the windows the user of the program sees when the program executes. Each form has one or more command buttons; when the program runs, the user clicks on these buttons to make something happen. (Often just the term "button" is used to mean "command button.") The Opening Screen form has a label displaying instructions to the user and a "text box" for the user to enter text consisting of the user's first name. The Greeting Screen form has a label in which some text is displayed when the program runs; it also has a decorative horizontal line. The Picture Screen form uses two "image controls" to store two different pictures, two labels, and a "timer" that looks like a little clock. When the program runs, the timer controls the timing of how the two pictures are displayed in succession, and the two labels hold the text information that appears under each picture.

The *lab1* program is typical. The primary ingredients of any Visual Basic application program are **objects**. A form is an object. Command buttons are objects that reside on forms. Labels that can display text or image controls that can display pictures are objects that reside on forms. Text boxes in which the user can enter text are objects that reside on forms. So are timers and artwork such as lines. Objects on forms are called **control objects** or just **controls.** Command buttons, labels, image controls, text boxes, timers, and lines are therefore control objects.

Each type of object, including forms and all the different control objects, has certain properties associated with it. An object's **properties** are characteristics or attributes, usually affecting the physical appearance of the object. For example, in Lab 1.1, you brought up the Color Palette window and used it to change the **BackColor property** of the form. Most objects have a BackColor property, but some do not. Image controls, like the ones in which the two pictures are stored, do not have a BackColor property because a picture brings its own background with it. Lines also do not have a BackColor property because they have no background area.

The point here is not to memorize the details of which objects have which properties, but simply to understand the idea illustrated in Figure 2.1—there are different kinds of objects and there is a different set of properties that apply to each kind.

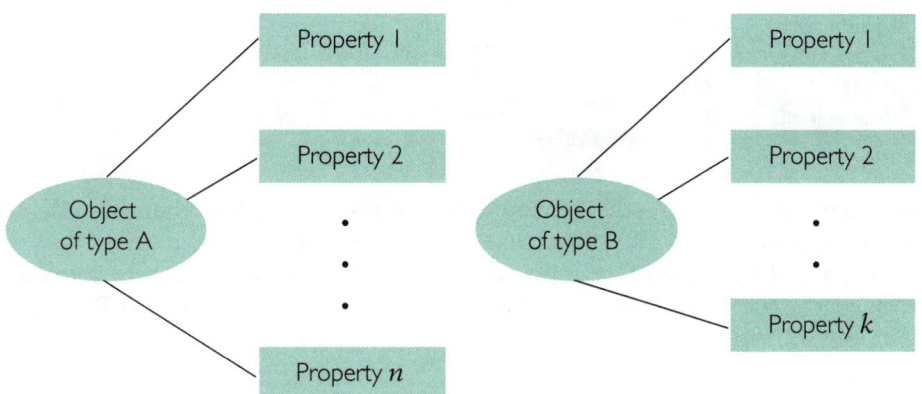

Figure 2.1
Each type of object has its own set of properties.

The Properties window in the Visual Basic environment is used to set the properties of objects at **design time**, that is, when the program is being developed in the Visual Basic design mode. Each object has its own associated Properties window that shows just the properties that apply to that kind of object. A few object properties can be set only at **run time**, that is, when the program is being executed. These run-time properties do not appear in the Properties window.

Figure 2.2 shows the Properties window for a command button on the first form of the *lab1.mak* project. In the Object box at the top of the Properties window, the name of the current object is given in boldface type, along with the type of object it is. Here the button is named cmdGreeting, and it is a CommandButton object. (The prefix *cmd* in the button name is an indication that the object is a command button.) In the properties list, one particular property is highlighted (in Figure 2.2 it is the Caption property), and the current setting for that property is given in the Settings box. Figure 2.2 shows that the current setting for the Caption property is the string of characters "Click here for greeting". Different properties can be selected by clicking on the appropriate row of the Properties list, and the information in the Settings box will change accordingly. The scroll bar beside the Properties list indicates that there are more properties than can be seen in the current window size.

Each new object comes with default settings for each of its properties. The Settings box of the Properties window is where the setting for a

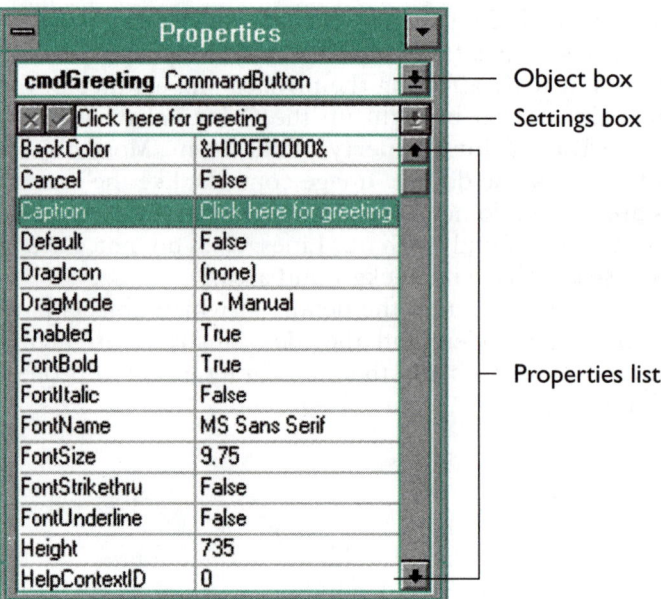

Figure 2.2
Example of the Properties window

property can be changed. The new value of the setting will then be reflected in the appearance of the object itself. For a few properties, namely those of location and size, the reverse process also works; the object can be moved or resized on the form, and the changes are then reflected in the Properties window settings.

Name: _____ *Date Due:* _____

LEARNING OBJECTIVES

- Becoming familiar with the Properties window
- Changing property settings for objects

LAB 2.1

1. ____ Open the **lab1.mak** project in Visual Basic.

   ____ View the **lab1.frm** form.

   ____ Click the rightmost button on the form to select it.

   ____ To make the Properties window active, do one of the following:

   Properties window

   OPTIONS
   - Click on any visible portion of the Properties window.
   - Click on Window on the menu bar and select Properties.
   - Use the access keys: Alt-W (Window) followed by Alt-O (Properties).
   - Click on the Properties Window toolbar button.
   - Press the shortcut key F4.

2. ____ What is the current Caption setting?

   The Settings box operates like a word processor, allowing the current setting to be edited. When you move the cursor over the Settings box, it changes into an I-beam shape, typical for word processing.

   Changing property settings

   ____ Position the cursor in front of the word "here" in the Caption setting. Hold down the mouse button and drag over the word "here" to highlight it. Then press the Delete key. Look on the form; what is the effect on the button?

3. ____ In the Properties window for this button, what are the current values of Left and Top?

___ Drag the button to move it to the upper left corner of the form. What happens to the Left and Top settings?

4. ___ What are the current values of Height and Width?

___ Change the Height value in the Settings box to 2000. Note the change in the button on the form.

___ Resize the button on the form to make it wider. What is the new value of the Width property shown in the Properties window?

5. ___ Highlight the Visible property for this button. Note that the down arrow at the end of the Settings box is now enabled.

___ To drop down a list of choices for this setting, click on this arrow.

___ Select False. Note that nothing changes on the form.

___ Now execute the program; what happens?

6. ___ Go back to design mode. Because there are only two choices for the Visible setting, you can also change the setting by double-clicking on the Visible property name. (Double-clicking "toggles" the property back and forth between True and False.)

___ Set the property back to True.

7. ___ Click the down arrow at the end of the Object box. This drops down a list of all the control objects on the current form.

___ Select the cmdGreeting button.

___ Change the Caption to remove the word "here."

8. ___ Select the label containing the instructions.

___ Put a border around this label. (Hint: Look at the BorderStyle property.)

9. ___ Use the Project window to view form *lab1a*.

___ Select the horizontal line and change it to a dashed line.

10. ___ Select the label. What property should you set to change the background color of the label?

___ To bring up the Color Palette, do one of the following:

OPTIONS
- Use the Visual Basic Window menu.
- Double-click on the property in the Properties window.
- Select the ... at the end of the Settings box for that property in the Properties window.

___ Change the background color of the label.

What property should you set to change the color of the text in the label? (Hint: You already changed the background color; the text is in the foreground.)

___ Change the color of the label text.

11. ___ Change the text in the title bar of each of the three forms to read:

    ```
    <yourname>    Form 1
    <yourname>    Form 2
    <yourname>    Form 3
    ```

    where `<yourname>` stands for your name. (Recall what Form property you need to set.)

12. ___ Use the Project window to view form **lab1b**.

    ___ Select the timer object.

    ___ Change the setting for the Interval property and run the program. You may have to do this several times to answer the next question. What is the effect in this program of the setting of the timer Interval property?

13. Exit Visual Basic. This time you *do* want to save the changes to all the forms, so answer Yes to everything.

> **QuickCheck 2.1**
>
> 1. Name three kinds of control objects.
> 2. The physical appearance of an object is controlled by the settings of its _____.
> 3. True or false: The Properties window is different for each type of object.
> 4. Name a property whose setting can be anything the programmer chooses.
> 5. Name a property whose setting must be chosen from a fixed list provided by Visual Basic.

2.2 Objects, events, and code

All the objects artfully placed on forms, all the various properties set to present a pleasing appearance, won't do anything but sit there when an application program is executed. Without program instructions—code—nothing will happen.

Just as each object type has an associated set of properties, each object type has an associated set of events that it can recognize. Any command button, for example, can recognize a **Click event** when the user clicks on that button. In order for something to happen, code must be written to respond to this event. A button can recognize a number of other events. For example, a **MouseMove event** occurs whenever the user moves the mouse pointer anywhere within the button. These other events are less commonly used; that is, the button still recognizes these events, but usually there is no code written for them, so nothing happens when they take place. On the other hand, a button cannot recognize a **DblClick event** (when the user double-clicks with the left mouse button), but a label can.

So each kind of object has its own set of recognizable events. As with properties, you don't want to memorize which objects recognize which events, but just get the idea of Figure 2.3 that different kinds of objects recognize different events.

In the *lab1* program, code has been written to cause the program to respond when certain events occur on certain objects. Figure 2.4 illustrates how the user triggers events and how the program responds. Although Figure 2.4 at first glance appears somewhat daunting, it is not that complicated. The three dotted boxes represent the three forms of the project. At the top, the user starts the program. This causes a Form Load event for the Opening form; code has been written so that this event displays and positions the form on the user's screen. The program then waits for some user action. The user can click on the Continue menu, or enter a name; while these actions initiate events, no code has been written to respond to these events, so nothing happens and the program continues to wait. The user can click on the Exit menu; in response to this Click event, the program terminates.

THOUGHTS ON PROGRAMMING

Event-Driven Programming

Most traditional programming was done using **imperative languages**, also known as **procedural languages**. Imperative languages include FORTRAN (mentioned in Chapter 1) and BASIC (except for Visual Basic). Other well-known imperative languages are Pascal, C, COBOL, and Ada.

In an imperative language, the statements in the program give the computer step-by-step instructions, or "imperative commands." If the programmer did his or her job correctly, then when the computer carries out these instructions, in the order dictated by the program code, the intended results will be obtained. When a program written in an imperative language is executed, the program code takes control. The program begins to do whatever the code dictates is the first thing to be done. The program may occasionally stop and ask the user for data before it proceeds further, but after the user supplies what is requested, the program once again resumes its inexorable march without the user having any say about what happens next.

Visual Basic, on the other hand, employs **event-driven programming**. Here the overall sequence of events is not driven by the program code, but by external events over which the program itself may have little or no control. As an example, when you, the user, execute *lab1.exe*, you can click first on either of the two buttons on the opening screen. Indeed, from the opening screen you can repeatedly click on either one of the two buttons or order your button-clicking in any way you choose. Each time you click on a button, a "Click event" takes place for that button. Program code is written to react to that specific Click event in a particular way. Thus, once the user has generated an event, the program takes control of what happens next. However, once the activity programmed in response to that event is complete, you, the user, again control the program. In *lab1*, nothing further will happen until you click on another button.

Code in event-driven programming is therefore activated by the occurrence of an event. Events can be caused by the user performing some action, such as clicking on a button. A program instruction to generate an event can also be written; when that instruction is executed, the event occurs, and any code that exists to respond to that event is executed next.

Event-driven programming is the model for how all programs work in a windows environment, so event-driven programming is a popular theme in computer science today. Another such theme is **object-oriented programming**. While Visual Basic lacks some of the features necessary to make it a truly object-oriented programming language, it does have an object-oriented flavor. Visual Basic programs are designed around objects—forms and controls, for example. When developing a program in Visual Basic, the programmer plans what objects should be present, and also what small subtask each object should perform in order to carry out the overall task of the program as a whole. This will dictate the program code to associate with each object-event combination. (Visual Basic denotes an event occurring on an object by giving the object name, an underscore, and the event name.)

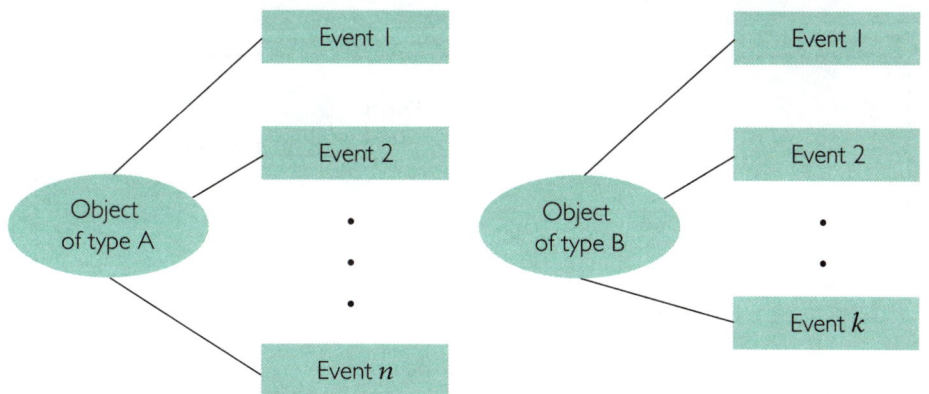

Figure 2.3
Each type of object recognizes its own set of events.

When the user clicks on the Greeting button, code for this Click event causes the computer to read the name that was entered in the text box and to display the Greeting form, which in turn triggers a Form Load event and a Form Activate event that, respectively, position the Greeting form and fill in the Greeting label. The program then waits (lower left of Figure 2.4) until the user clicks on the OK button; code for this Click event hides the Greeting form and returns the program to the wait condition on the Opening Screen form.

If the user clicks the Picture button on the opening form, much the same things happen in bringing up the Picture form. However, the Timer object on this form is set up to initiate a Timer event shortly after the timer object is turned on (lower right of Figure 2.4), which causes the pictures and labels displayed on the form to change. When the user clicks the OK button, the Opening form again appears, waiting for the next user action.

In a large program, the dynamics of possible interactions between user, events, forms, control objects, and code can be difficult to keep in mind, even for the programmer. Diagrams like Figure 2.4, although they need not be this formal, help document how a program will behave.

Until now, program code hasn't been discussed except to note that nothing interesting happens without it. Where, indeed, are the instructions—the programming language statements—in a Visual Basic program? A "program" in most other programming languages means code and nothing else. In a Visual Basic program, code is only part of the story, but a very essential part; it's the engine behind the GUI, the thing that brings the GUI to life.

In the Visual Basic environment, program code resides in another window that hasn't been mentioned yet. Not surprisingly, it is called the Code window. The Code window allows you to view the code that has already been written for a program or to write new code. Much of the code, as has already been mentioned, is designed to respond to an event that has been recognized by some object. Each such parcel of code is called an **event procedure**. An event procedure is therefore associated with an object-event pair, namely the particular object and the particular event on that object to which this procedure is the programmed response.

Figure 2.5 shows form *lab1b* from the *lab1* project. The single command button on this form is named cmdOK1B. When the program is running and the user clicks this button, the program returns to the opening screen, form *lab1*.

Figure 2.4
How the *lab1* program responds to events

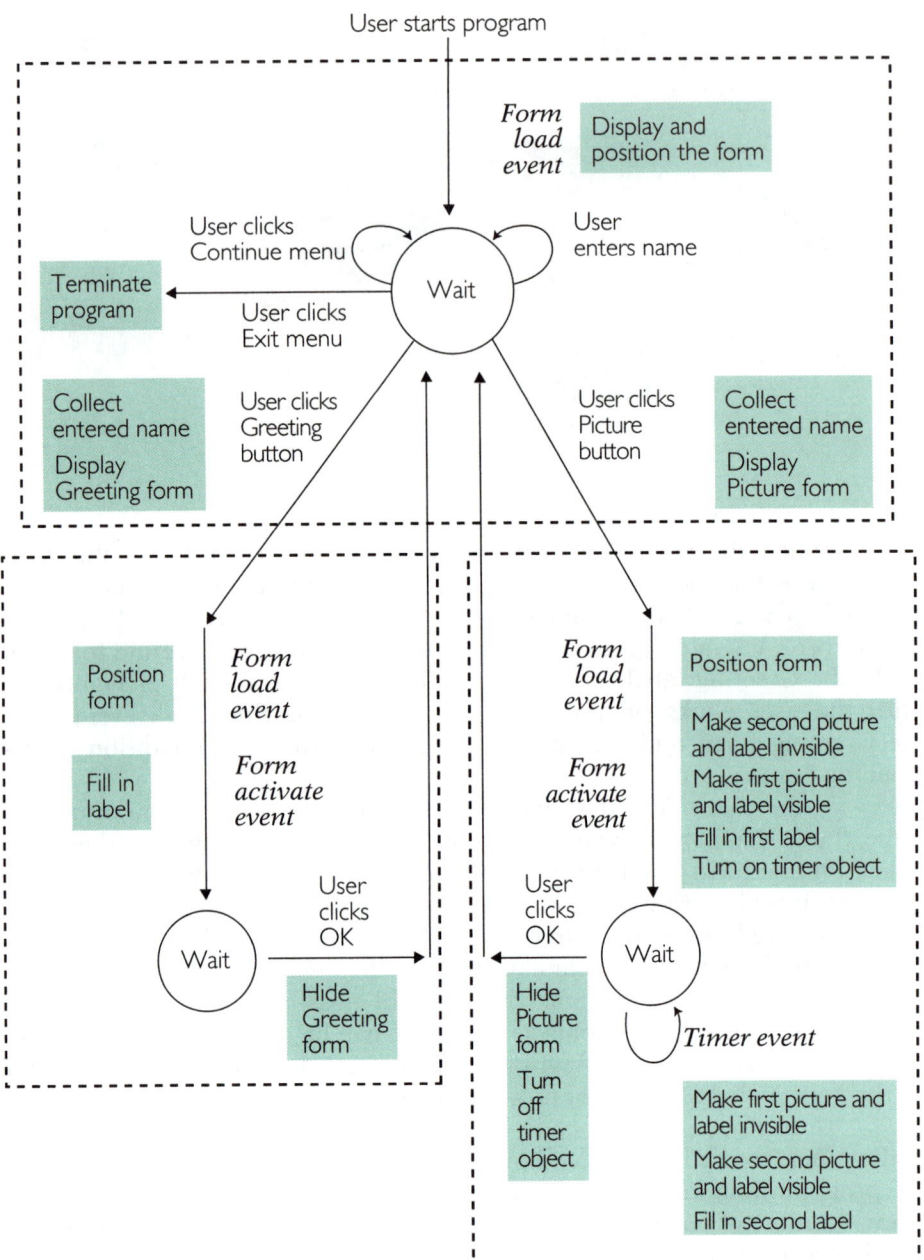

Figure 2.6 shows the Code window when it is displaying one of the event procedures associated with this button. The title bar denotes that the button is indeed on the *lab1b* form. The Object box at the top of the Code window gives the name of the object, and the Procedure box (abbreviated Proc) gives the event (here's the object-event pair idea). In Figure 2.6, the code responds to the cmdOK1B_Click event. When the program is running and the cmdOK1B button on form *lab1b* is clicked, the instructions shown in this window execute.

The first program statement in the cmdOK1B_Click event procedure is a standard procedure heading

```
Sub cmdOK1B_Click
```

Words with special meaning in a programming language are called **reserved words** or **keywords**. In Visual Basic, reserved words are color highlighted in blue (the default color, which can be changed by choosing Environment under the Visual Basic Option menu). **Sub** is a reserved word indicating the beginning of a procedure. (This is a historical holdover from earlier versions of BASIC, in which procedures were called "subroutines.") The program statement

```
End Sub
```

marks the end of a procedure. All the rest of the code for a procedure, called the **procedure body**, goes between the heading and the End Sub statement.

Program statements must conform to strict **syntax**, that is, rules about which words and combinations of symbols are allowable. One rule is that anything on a line that follows a single quote mark is ignored by Visual Basic. Hence the single quote mark can be used to denote a **comment**, a remark intended to be read only by people trying to understand the code, not by the computer. Comments are also color highlighted in Visual Basic (the default color is green) for easier recognition. In Figure 2.6, the phrase "Leaving this screen" is not a Visual Basic programming statement; it is a comment explaining the statement that comes before it on the same line. As a programmer, you may think that your code is crystal clear, but it won't be to someone else (and it won't be to you after several months!), so it is important to get into the habit of commenting your code. Comments should be written while you write the code, when everything is fresh in your mind.

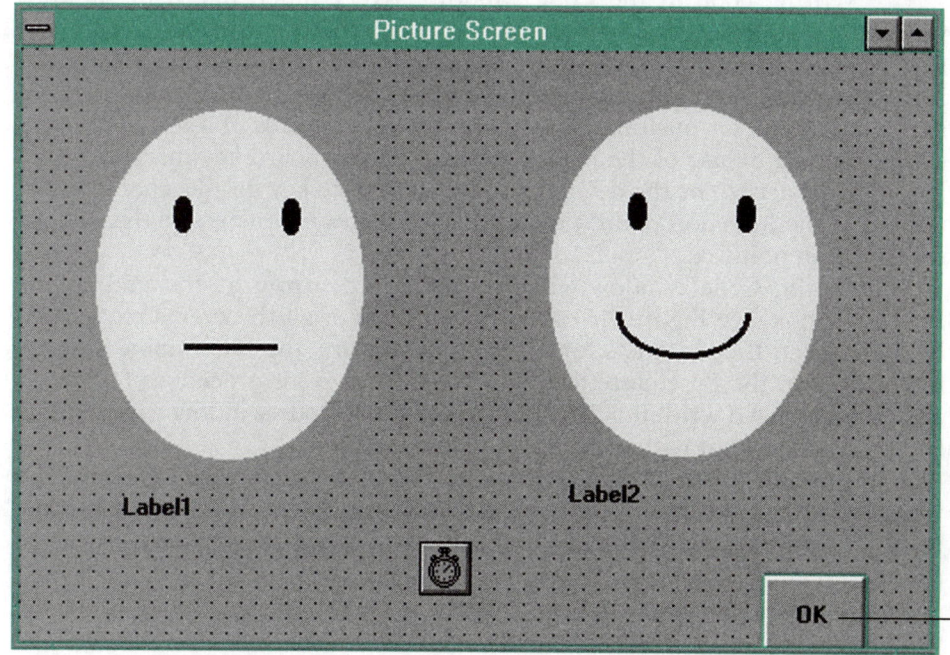

Figure 2.5
Form *lab1b* from the *lab1* project

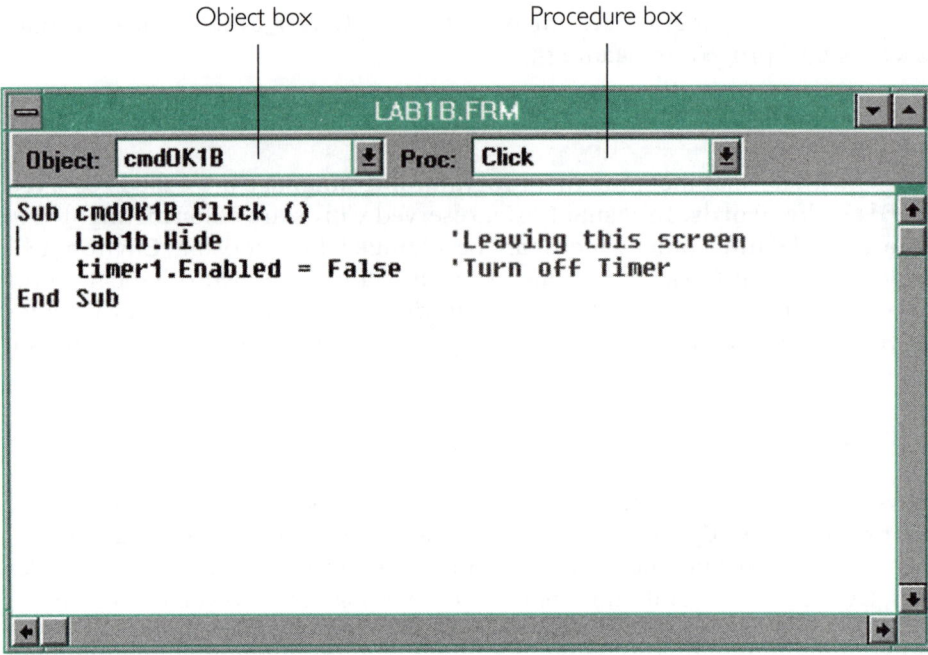

Figure 2.6
Example of the Code window

The details of the code won't mean much right now, but you can get a general idea of what happens. Looking at the first statement in the procedure, you can see that "leaving this screen" is accomplished by hiding the form, that is, making it no longer visible. This reveals the first form, which, as it happens, was underneath this form all the time. The second statement disables or "turns off" the timer by setting its Enabled property to False. If and when this form appears again through another click of the appropriate button on the opening form, the timer will be restarted to control the little animation sequence.

Writing code in the Code window is very much like using a word processor. The mouse cursor within the Code window assumes the I-beam shape used in many windows text-processing programs; the blinking cursor is the text insertion point. Clicking the mouse anchors the text insertion point at the mouse cursor position. As you are typing, mistakes of a few characters can be deleted by use of the backspace key (the keyboard key marked with a left-pointing arrow) or the delete key. The backspace key deletes characters to the left of the insertion point; the delete key deletes characters to the right of the insertion point.

In the Code window, clicking the down arrow at the end of the Procedure box (see Figure 2.6) drops down a list of all the events recognized by that object. If code exists for an event procedure, the event name appears in boldface in the Procedure drop-down list. Any event procedure for which code has not been written will be displayed in the Code window as a heading and an End Sub, but with an empty body, as in Figure 2.7.

Initially, all the event procedures for an object are empty. But even when the program is completed, most events won't have any associated code. It would be a very busy object indeed that in a single program would want to react to every event it is capable of recognizing.

Clicking the down arrow at the end of the Object box in the Code window drops down a list of the other control objects on the form and the form itself. To see the code for other objects on the form or for the form itself, select from this list.

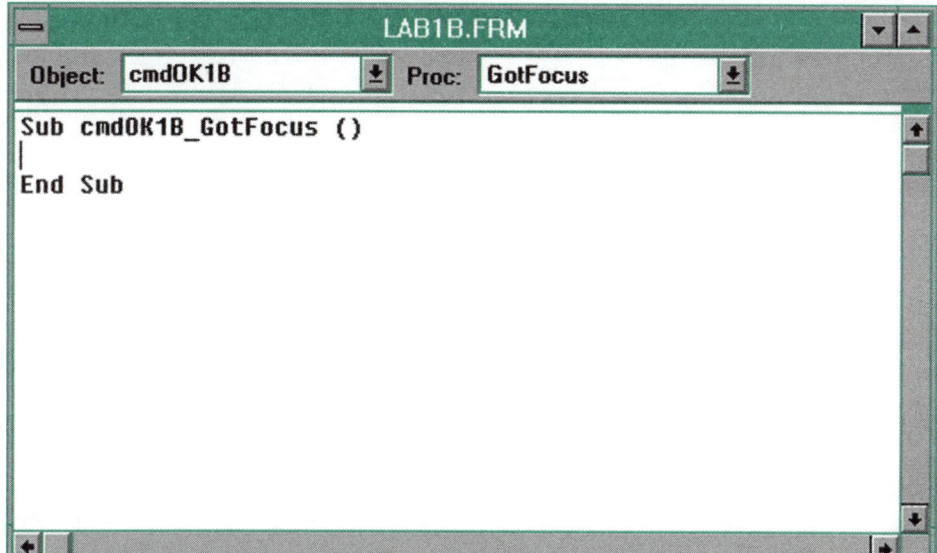

Figure 2.7
Empty event procedure

Thus you select the object-event pairs by scrolling through both the Object box and the Procedure box lists in the Code window. There are some shortcuts to locate those object-event pairs for which code exists. When the Code window is active, the View menu allows you to move to the next nonempty procedure for that form by choosing Next Procedure; you can go backward through the nonempty procedures by choosing Previous Procedure. You can also use the PageUp and PageDown keys on the keyboard to move from one nonempty procedure to another. Again when the Code window is active, the hot key F2 brings up a View Procedures window that lets you see the names of all the nonempty procedures in the project and select the one for which you want to see the code.

In addition to event procedures, a Visual Basic program can include general procedures. A **general procedure** is code that is not associated with a particular event, so that the user cannot directly cause that code to be executed. However, an event procedure (or another general procedure) can invoke (call) a general procedure and cause it to be executed.

Table 2.1 summarizes terms introduced in this section.

TERM	MEANING	WHEN IT OCCURS
Event	An action recognized by an object	The user, a program statement, or a system activity triggers the event
Event procedure	Code that responds to an event on an object	Executes when that event is recognized by that object
General procedure	Code not associated with a particular event	Executes when called by a program statement

Table 2.1
Events and procedures—definitions

Name: _____   Date Due: _____

LEARNING OBJECTIVES

- Using the Visual Basic Code window
- Editing program code

1. ____ Bring up the *lab1.mak* project in Visual Basic; use the Project window to view *lab1.frm*.

   ____ Bring up the Properties window for the form. Note that there are settings for Width, Height, Left, and Top.

2. ____ To bring up the Code window for *lab1.frm*, go to the Project window and do one of the following:

   OPTIONS
   - View *lab1.frm* and then double-click on the form.
   - View *lab1.frm* and then pull down the View menu and select Code.
   - View *lab1.frm* and then use the hot key F7.
   - Highlight *lab1.frm*, select View Code, drop down the Object list, and select Form.

3. ____ What's the object now shown in the Object box?

   ____ What's the event now shown in the Procedure box? Any object recognizes a number of events, but the Code window for an object always opens to an event for which code has been written, if such an event exists.

4. ____ The Load event for a form occurs when the form is first loaded into memory as the program begins to execute before it is displayed on screen for the user to see. Judging by the comments in the Form_Load procedure, what does this procedure do?

Starting up the Code window

____ Drag the form window to the upper left corner of the screen.

____ Run the program; where does the form appear on the screen when the program executes?

____ Go back to design mode and look at the Form_Load procedure again.

____ Turn the last two lines of the procedure body into comments by placing a single quote at the beginning of the line. When you do this, what change do you see in the Code window?

____ Now run the program again. Where does the form appear on the screen when the program executes?

____ When the form is loaded, the Form_Load procedure code is executed; as the statements in the (original) procedure body are executed, they set the form's properties of Width and Height, Left and Top. Those properties were also set at design time in the Properties window. Which setting takes precedence, that is, determines how the form looks when the program is run?

Navigating through the Code window

____ Go back to design mode, bring up the Code window, and make the last two lines of the Form_Load procedure back into program code by removing the single quote.

5. ____ Use the drop-down Object list to see the other objects on this form. Select cmdGreeting, which is the "Click here for greeting" button on the form. What's the event for which you are seeing the code?

6. The first line of code in the body of this procedure uses a Call statement. **Call** is another reserved word used within a procedure to invoke a different procedure. The word following "Call" is the name of the procedure being invoked.

   ____ What is the name of this procedure?

7. The procedure *getname* is a general procedure. It is not tied to any particular event that might occur on this form because it is in fact invoked by either of two events, cmdGreeting_Click or cmdPicture_Click. This procedure is a form-level general procedure on the form ***lab1.frm***.

   ____ To find the code for a form-level general procedure, use the drop-down Object list in the Code window to select "general," which is always the first item in the list. Then use the Procedures drop-down list to select the procedure.

   The purpose of the *getname* procedure is to collect the text the user entered in the text box on the opening form, presumably the user's first name, and store it somewhere so that the rest of the program can use it. The *getname* procedure stores the user's name in a "variable" called *yourname*. For now, just think of *yourname* as a box—actually a location in the computer's memory—into which the user's first name is placed.

   ____ Make the existing single statement in the procedure body a comment.

   ____ The Code window works just like a word processor, so you can easily edit program code. Add a new statement in the procedure body (before the End Sub) that reads exactly as follows.

   | **Editing code** |

   ```
   yourname = "King Kong"
   ```

   ____ Now run the program; be sure to enter your name in the text box. What happens and why?

   ____ Back in design mode, restore the *getname* procedure to its original form.

8. ____ View the code for the ***lab1a*** form. As for the first form, the Code window opens by default on the Load procedure. Scroll through the Procedure drop-down list.

Events for which code has been written are shown in boldface. For what other form event has code been written?

The difference between the Load event and the Activate event for a form is this. The Load event occurs when the form is loaded into the computer's memory, and that occurs when the program begins to execute. The Activate event occurs every time a form becomes the active window. Form *lab1a* could become the active window numerous times if the user repeatedly clicked on the appropriate command button on form *lab1*.

____ Look at the code for the Activate event by selecting the event in the Procedure list. When this procedure executes, it sets the Caption property of the label on form *lab1a*, overriding whatever the Caption property was set to in design mode.

____ Run the program, type in a name, and then click the "Click for greeting" button. With the program still in run mode, return to the opening form (by pressing the OK button), enter a different name, and then click the same button. What happens?

____ How does the Form_Activate code for form *lab1a* make use of the variable *yourname*?

9. ____ Information about the value of yourname must be shared among multiple forms in this program. The value for yourname is obtained in a general procedure that is part of the opening form. That value is used in an event procedure for the lab1a form (and also in an event procedure for the lab1b form). In order for multiple forms to understand what yourname is, yourname is described (more formally, this description is called a "variable declaration") in a separate module, or code module. A code module is listed separately in the Project window.

____ To get to the code module, do one of the following:

OPTIONS
- Go to the Project window and select **lab1.bas**, and then View Code. (Note that the choice of View Form is disabled once you select **lab1.bas** because there is no form!)
- Click on Window on the menu bar and select Procedures; then select **lab1.bas** and press the Enter key or click on OK.
- Use the shortcut key F2 to bring up the View Procedures window, then select **lab1.bas** and press the Enter key or click on OK.

The word following "As" in the declaration for a variable tells the type of data the variable will hold, which could be various kinds of numbers or, as in this case, a sequence of characters.

____ What is the word Visual Basic uses to describe a sequence of characters?

10. ____ Go back to the opening form, **lab1**, and look at the Code window.

____ Find the code for mnuExit_Click (object mnuExit—one of the pull-down menu choices on the form—and event Click).

____ What is the single keyword in the body of this procedure?

This is what terminates execution of the application program.

____ Now exit the Code window and view form **lab1.frm**.

11. ____ Use the Visual Basic Toolbox to put a new command button on the form. What caption appears by default for this button?

You are going to write code for this button so that the user can exit the application program by clicking the button rather than by using the File menu and selecting Exit.

____ Bring up the Properties window for this button and change the caption for the button to something appropriate (delete what's currently in the Settings box and type something new).

____ Bring up the Code window for this button (double-clicking the button itself would be easiest). As the body of the Command1_Click procedure, insert the single keyword that will stop program execution. Run your program and try out your new button.

12. Exit Visual Basic, saving all changes.

> **QuickCheck 2.2**
>
> 1. True or false: Control objects all recognize the same set of events.
> 2. Every event procedure is associated with what pair of things?
> 3. What is a common event for which a command button is likely to have a nonempty event procedure?
> 4. True or false: The Code window shows only those event procedures for which code has already been written.
> 5. Why can the Visual Basic reserved words **Sub** and **End Sub** be thought of as "bookends"?

2.3 Big picture of event-driven programming

Figure 2.4 illustrates how the *lab1* program waits for user action and responds to various events. While the *lab1* program uses multiple forms, its wait-for-an-event-then-respond behavior is typical of even the simplest Visual Basic program. When a Visual Basic program begins running, some events automatically occur for the first form the user will see, called the **startup form**. These events include the Load event and the Activate event. If there is any code for these procedures, it will be executed at this time, so the Form_Load event procedure is often written to do things like position the form on the screen, as in the *lab1* project. After that, the program is still running, but nothing happens until some other event occurs.

Thus the big picture of all event-driven programming is given by Figure 2.8. After some start-up activities, the program enters a "wait loop," where it sits and cycles through a process that just repeatedly looks to see whether an event has taken place. Once an event takes place, if there is code to respond to that event, that code is executed. When execution of that code is complete, the program returns to its wait loop until the next event occurs. Eventually a termination event occurs that causes the program to stop.

The code to respond to certain events is built into Visual Basic. These are basic windows events like clicking on the maximize button in the title bar of a form window. For most events, however, the programmer must write the code.

The user, by his or her actions, decides which events will occur in what order. Event procedures will ordinarily do much of the work. Here's an exception: Code can occur in general procedures that are invoked by other procedures. It is possible to write a Visual Basic program in which, for example, the Form-Load procedure calls a general procedure, and the general procedure contains all the rest of the program code. In this case, starting the program is the only user-initiated event. However, this is an extreme case more in the spirit of traditional programming than in the spirit of a windows-based program that anticipates lots of user interaction.

Figure 2.8
Overall event-driven programming picture

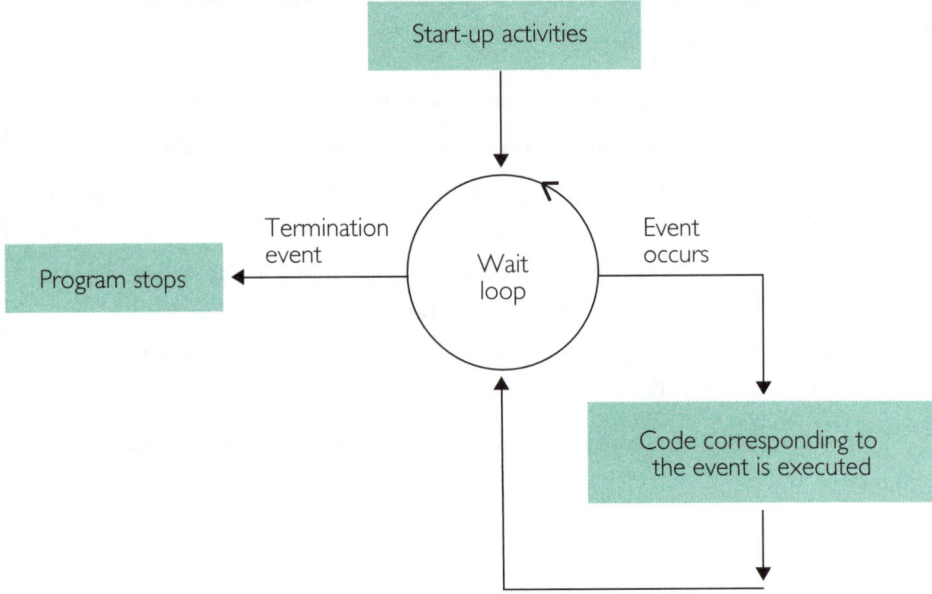

Figure 2.8 is a generic picture that tells how any event-driven program, including a Visual Basic program, executes. To write a specific Visual Basic application program, you must decide on the particular events and responses that will suit the application you are trying to build. These decisions are part of program design.

2.4 Modest program design

Program design is the process of deciding how the problem is to be solved. As noted in Figure 2.8, the design of a program consists of a series of representations of the program that begins close to the user requirements and ends close to program code. The design thus consists of one or many different views of the problem solution.

For a Visual Basic program, one of those views will almost certainly include the layout of the form or forms. This does not mean that you need to decide right away on the physical arrangement of control objects on a form; although such decisions are important, they can come somewhat later in the design process. But it does mean that you have to decide what the control objects are, and what the function of each is in the overall solution scheme. More particularly, what are the object-event pairs for which you want some action to take place, and what action do you want for each one?

Note that this consists of breaking up the problem solution into small pieces, primarily event procedures. Visual Basic code is not found all in one place, but in the many different Code windows that correspond to object-event pairs. This is one of the primary reasons why a Visual Basic program design must be approached differently than a traditional program design.

Because the Visual Basic programs you will be writing for a while will be small and relatively simple, you won't need many different views in your design. In fact, one view of the overall design will be sufficient at this point. An **Object Task Card (OTC)** is a simple yet effective design representation.

In an OTC design view, each form that will be in the program is represented as an index card. It is helpful to actually use index cards in this design process because in a program with multiple forms, like *lab1*, they can be arranged to show which form is visible at any time. Each form card will list the control objects to appear on that form. Those objects for which event procedures are to be written are called **active objects**. The card lists all active objects, the type of each object, the event to which each active object is to respond and the task to be done as the response (which indicates the code to be written for this event procedure). Some objects don't respond to any event but are merely there as static objects or as recipients of the actions of active objects. These are called **passive objects** and are listed on the card as well. No code needs to be written for these objects. For example, clicking a command button might cause some message to be written in a label. The button is an active object, and code must be written for its Click event; the label is a passive object and requires no code. Labels are usually passive objects; their primary purpose is to display information.

As an example, Figure 2.9 shows an OTC design for the startup form in the *lab1* project. Under Active Objects is listed each object-event pair for which some task is be carried out, and a description of the task. Note that the Exit menu pick that ends the program is included because, as you saw in Lab 2.2, there is code to carry out this task. The other menu pick (Continue) and the menu heading (File) are passive objects. Other passive objects are the label and the text box on the form.

Figure 2.9 also gives a description of the task to be done by the general procedure on the form, *getname*. Note that both command buttons on

Figure 2.9
OTC design for the startup form in the *lab1* project

OPENING FORM — LAB 1			
Active Objects	**Object Type**	**Event**	**Task**
Lab1	form	Load	Position and size the form.
mnuExit	menu item	Click	End the program.
cmdGreeting	command button	Click	Call the *getname* procedure. Bring up the greeting form.
cmdPicture	command button	Click	Call the *getname* procedure. Bring up the picture form.
Passive Objects			
lblPrompt	label		Display instructions for the user to enter a name.
txtName	text box		Place for the user to enter a name.
mnuFile	menu item		Pull-down menu.
mnuContinue	menu item		Empty menu pick.
General Procedures			
getname			Get the user name from the text box and store it in the variable *yourname*.

the form make use of the *getname* procedure. Indeed, *getname* is made a general form-level procedure so that its code is available to more than one object on the form.

It is important to note that this particular example is being developed backward! The program has already been written, and the OTC design is being "retrofitted" to what already exists (sort of like writing the outline to a paper after the paper has been written). That's why all the object names are already known. Also note that the behavior of this form as described in the OTC design agrees with the top part of Figure 2.4.

The design process is intended to be done first, as a guide to developing the program. While a design may not be necessary for a simple program, you should get in the habit of designing your programs. Ultimately, when programs become more complex, the result of trying to write them directly at the keyboard without prior planning is at worst a complete waste of time and at best a program that could no doubt be improved on (just like a long paper will suffer for lack of a coherent outline). Recall the statement in Chapter 1 that coding typically occupies only 15 to 20 percent of program development time. Analysis and design, the first two steps in the programming process, typically require 40 to 50 percent of the total development time (testing and debugging occupy the rest of the development time). If professional software developers feel the need to carefully design their programs ahead of time, it is because they have learned that jumping right into code is not the time-saver it may appear. If you want to save time in the long run, then learn from their example and set aside time to think through your program design before you plunge into writing it at the keyboard.

Name: _____   Date Due: _____

LEARNING OBJECTIVES

- Writing code to set a label caption
- Designing and writing a complete Visual Basic application program

1. ____ Open your *message.mak* project from Lab 1.3.

2. ____ Change the form caption to "My message".

   ____ Make the label caption blank (just delete the present caption).

3. ____ Bring up the Code window for the Command1_Click event. When the button is clicked, you want a message to appear in the label. The code for this event must therefore set the label's caption property. A similar task was done in the Form_Activate code for form *lab1a.frm*. A single statement of the form

   ```
   Label1.Caption = "your message here"
   ```

   will work.

   ____ Add the appropriate code. Your message should be a statement about your favorite food. Be sure to put your message within quotation marks.

Setting a label caption in code

4. Looking at your form, there is one more cosmetic change to make. What is it? (Hint: Does your program user know what to do?)

   ____ Make this change

   ____ Run your program to be sure it works. Save your files.

5. Now it's time to do a complete new application. This program will be a little entertainment about famous movie quotes. Each time the user clicks one of three buttons showing movie titles, a famous quote from that movie will be displayed in a single label on the form. Brief instructions to the user to explain what the program does and how to use it go in a second label on the form.

Designing a new application

   ____ Using the "card" shown on page 58, do an OTC design for this program. For object names, you can just use Command1, Command2, Label1, and so on. Assume that you are willing to accept the default size and position that Visual Basic uses for a new form, so you won't need any code for the Form_Load event.

MOVIE FORM

6. Now that you have a design for your program, the next step is to build the form.

____ Open a new project in Visual Basic. Before you do anything else, save the form as **movie.frm** and the project as **movie.mak** (use Save Project As...). Then save your work frequently as you proceed (use Save Project or the Toolbar button).

____ "Populate" the form with the necessary control objects as specified by your design. Arrange them in some reasonable way.

____ Apply cosmetic changes to your form, such as color schemes and captions (of the form, the buttons—which you may have to resize—and the labels). Use the following movies:

>Gone with the Wind
>Star Trek, The Motion Picture
>The Wizard of Oz

7. ____ How many event procedures do you need to write code for?

8. ____ Write the necessary code. The movie quotes are:

>Frankly, my dear, I don't give a damn.
>He's dead, Jim.
>Toto, I don't think we're in Kansas anymore.

9. ____ Test your program. Save your work. Exit Visual Basic.

QuickCheck 2.3

1. The first form the user sees in a Visual Basic application is called the _____.
2. OTC stands for _____.
3. What two categories of objects are described on an OTC card?
4. How do you make a label appear empty on the screen?
5. True or false: Setting the caption of a label in program code works only if there is no value for the label set at design time.

Review Questions

1. Objects such as command buttons and labels that appear on forms are called _____.
2. Properties of objects are set at design time using the _____ window.
3. What is the relationship between the properties of an object and the events it can recognize?
4. What is the difference between event-driven programming and imperative programming?
5. A section of code associated with an object-event pair is called an _____.
6. What is a procedure body?
7. What is syntax?
8. The standard procedure heading begins with the reserved word _____.
9. How do you write a comment in Visual Basic?
10. How can you use the Code window to find the event procedures for a given object?
11. If an event procedure has an empty body, what happens when the program executes and that event occurs?
12. If you want to view existing code for a project, what is the advantage to using the View Procedures window rather than scrolling through the Object and Procedure boxes in the Code window?
13. A section of code that is not associated with an event is called a _____.
14. What causes a general procedure to be executed?
15. The Project window gives you a choice of what two actions with respect to a form in a Visual Basic project?
16. Explain the difference between a Load event and an Activate event for a form.

17. Explain the statement: "Event-driven programs spend much of their execution time in a wait loop."
18. "Visual Basic code is not found all in one place." What are the implications of this statement in program design?
19. What is the difference between an active object and a passive object on an OTC card?
20. What decisions does the OTC design process force you to make about a form?

Exercises

Reading code
In Exercises 1–5, assume that a Visual Basic project exists with several forms; the startup form has one label named Label1, and one command button. What is the effect when each of the following Visual Basic statements is executed?

1. `Label1.Caption = "Here is the information you wanted"`
2. `Form2.Show`
3. `Label1.Visible = False`
4. `Label1.Top = 2800`
5. `Label1.Height = 1000`

Writing code
6. Write a Visual Basic statement to set the caption property of the Command1 button to read "ANSWER".
7. Write a statement that, when executed, puts "Sales Report" in the title bar of Form1.
8. Write two Visual Basic statements to position a form in the upper left corner of the screen.
9. Write a Visual Basic statement that, when executed, makes Form2 disappear.
10. Write a Visual Basic statement that sets the caption of the Command1 button to be the same as the caption of the Command2 button.

Exploring further
11. Using your *message.mak* project from Lab 2.3, add a second button that, when clicked, displays a second label with a message about your favorite drink.
12. Using your *movie.mak* project from Lab 2.3, add two more movies and their quotes.
13. Given the OTC design for a form on page 61, explain what you think the form will look like, how you think the user will interact with the program, and how the program will respond.
14. Do an OTC design for the *lab1a* form in the *lab1* project (you may need to look at the program to see everything that is going on).
15. Do an OTC design for the *lab1b* form in the *lab1* project (you may need to look at the program to see everything that is going on).

FORM 1			
Active Objects	**Object Type**	**Event**	**Task**
Form1	form	Load	Position and size the form.
Command1	command button	Click	Compute the average of two scores and write the result in Label2.
Command2	command button	Click	End the program.
Passive Objects			
Label1	label		Display instructions for the user to enter scores.
Label2	label		Display the average of two scores.
Text1	text box		Place for user to enter score 1.
Text2	text box		Place for user to enter score 2.

Projects

1. You have decided to create a program to help your nephew with geography. Design and write a program that displays various state names on buttons. When a button is clicked, the capital city of that state is displayed.

2. You want to do some market research on the effectiveness of advertising slogans. You plan to interview people in the local mall by naming five well-known slogans and taking down responses about the product or company that uses each slogan. After the interviews, people can see how well they did by running a Visual Basic program in which they click on buttons showing slogans and then see the corresponding company name. Design and write such a program. Include a button on the form that the user can click to end the program.

3. Design and write an automated astrological assistant that allows the user to click on a range of dates and see the name of the corresponding sign of the zodiac. For example, the sign for those born from July 23 through August 22 is Leo. (Consult the horoscope section of a newspaper for the rest of the information you need.)

4. To gain a master seaman license, you must memorize the international flag signals. You write an automated flashcard program to help you remember the flag signals for the five vowels a, e, i, o, u. The *flag.mak* project shows your form design, with five command buttons and the corresponding flag for each button contained in an image control (the same control used to hold the smiley-face pictures in the *lab1* program). Whenever a button is clicked, the corresponding flag should appear and the previously visible flag, if any, should disappear. Write and test the code for this program.

   (Hints: Use the Properties window to scroll through the properties for an image control. Find the property that affects whether the image control can be seen. For each button, write code that sets this property for the correct image control so that it can be seen, and for all the other image controls so that they cannot be seen. The code syntax is similar to how you set the label caption property, except that on the right side of the equal sign, the value you are setting should not be in quotes. The code for all five buttons is quite similar. Once you have written it for one button, you may want to copy and paste it, using the Edit menu, to the Code window for the other buttons and there edit the minor changes needed.)

5. You plan to write an automated reminder program for your boss that shows important dates. For each month, a click of a button brings up a list of holidays, birthdays, anniversaries, and so on. Design and write the software for two months. Instead of displaying the information in one or more labels on the same form, have each button open a pop-up window that displays the information for that month on multiple labels. Each pop-up window should have an OK command button that hides that window.

(Hints: A new form for a project can be created either by using the File pull-down menu and selecting New Form or by clicking on the New Form Toolbar button. Create the new form before you write code to show the form. Resize the new forms to be small windows. Consult Figure 2.6 for the code on how to hide a form.)

CHAPTER 3

User Interface; Project Management

KEY POINTS

- The user interface of a computer program has a large effect on how useful the program is, and it should be designed carefully.
- The Toolbox is the Visual Basic source for control objects to place on forms.
- The Text Box control allows the user to enter data as the program is executing.
- The Visual Basic MAK file keeps track of all the other files (FRM, BAS, and VBX) necessary in a project.
- Objects can be acted on by methods.
- Controls of a single type can be grouped into an array, which minimizes the amount of code to be written.

3.1 What is the user interface?

An interface, according to the dictionary, is "a point at which independent systems interact." A **user interface** is the point at which the user (of something) interacts with that thing. The user interface for your automobile is the dashboard, steering wheel, and gas and brake pedals. This is where you interact with your automobile, giving it directions (turn left, slow down, and so on) and receiving information from it (current speed, oil pressure, and so on). The user interface for a bank machine is the control panel that allows you to enter your PIN number, the type of transaction you want, and so on, and the screen that displays instructions or information. The user interface for a microwave oven is the control panel to set the time and power level, and an audio mechanism to signal completion.

The design of a user interface determines the usefulness of a product. If a system presents a user interface that is difficult to understand, the product will not be well received. (The overworked term "user-friendly" generally refers to the user interface.) VCRs have been the target of much humor for their often confusing and nonstandard user interfaces.

A standard user interface for all instances of one type of product allows a user familiar with one instance to easily pick up on how to use another instance. For example, it is standard in an automobile to have the brake pedal on the left and the gas pedal on the right. Most automobiles have the ignition switch somewhere on the steering column. Many have the headlamp and windshield wiper controls on a stalk on the steering column. The commonality of these user interfaces allows you, sitting in the driver's seat of an unfamiliar automobile, to quickly figure out how to run it.

In a safety-critical system, a standard user interface can be crucial. (You don't want to mistake the gas pedal for the brake!) A new air traffic control system is under development for the Federal Aviation Administration. The designers of the new system have been constrained to make the new user interface as similar as possible to the old one in order to reduce the chance of even momentary confusion on the part of an air traffic controller, which could have fatal consequences.

With respect to computer software, the user interface is what the user sees and interacts with when the program executes. If the user interface is confusing or awkward, the user will not be productive (or happy) running the program. One of the advantages of windows-based programs is a certain level of standardization or consistency in the user interface. The title bars all look alike, pull-down menus are accessed in the same way, and so on. This standardization helps the user to accommodate quickly to a new piece of software. In a Visual Basic application program, the windows look comes "for free." The rest of the user interface must be designed by the programmer.

3.2 Visual Basic Toolbox

The most obvious aspect of the user interface of a Visual Basic application program is the look of the various forms, which become the windows the user sees when the program executes. A form's appearance is determined by which control objects are on the form and how the properties of the form and control objects are set.

Control objects are placed on forms by using the Visual Basic Toolbox. Figure 3.1 shows the Toolbox for the Standard Edition of Visual Basic. The Professional Edition Toolbox has icons for all of these controls plus many others. (Figure 3.1 also appears in Appendix D for reference.) You've used the Toolbox to put command buttons and labels on forms. The steps are the same for placing any control on a form.

Thus, to place a control object on a form do either of the following:

OPTIONS

▶ Click on the Toolbox icon for that control, then move the cursor (which is now a crosshair) to the desired location on the form and click-and-drag to insert the object.
▶ Double-click on the Toolbox icon for that control to paste the object on the form, then drag the object to its desired location and resize it.

Each of the controls has one purpose for which it is most commonly used. You have already used command buttons and labels. The following brief summary of how these two controls are typically used should agree with your experiences to date:

Command button: This control is usually used to cause some action to take place when the user clicks on the button at run time, that is, when the program is running. The Click event procedure is the one most commonly programmed.

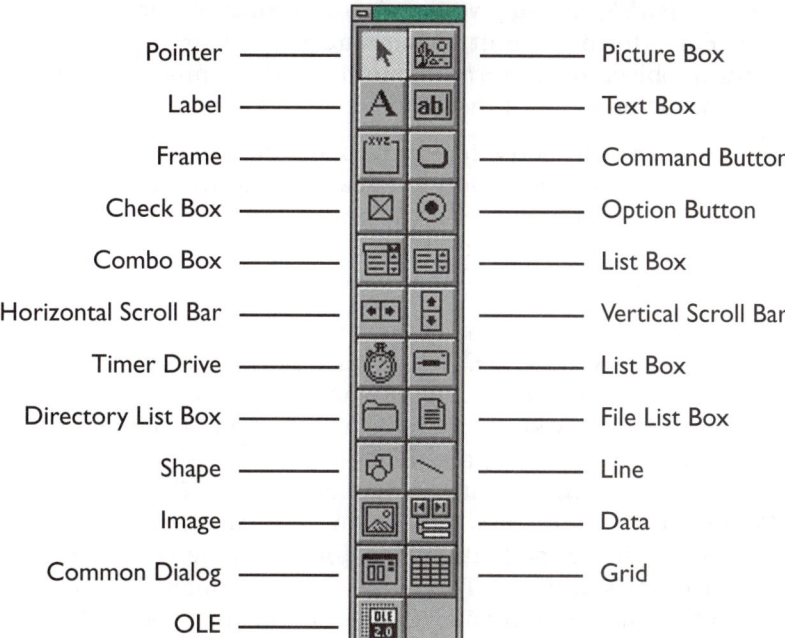

Figure 3.1
Visual Basic Toolbox

Label: This control is usually used to display text. The user cannot modify the text when the program executes. Labels are seldom active objects (in the terminology of OTC design), so although they recognize certain events, there are often no event procedures programmed for a label.

There is one icon on the Toolbox, the **Pointer**, that does not represent a control object. Clicking on the Pointer tool regains control of the cursor in order to select, move, or resize objects.

3.3 Common properties

Although each object has its own list of properties, there are some properties that apply to many objects, including command buttons, labels, many of the other controls, and the form object. You can find more information on these and other properties by using the Properties window. Highlighting a property in the Properties window and pressing F1 brings up the context-sensitive Help system with information about that property.

Left, Top: These give the position of a form relative to the screen or of a control object relative to the form on which it resides. The form's position is always given in twips. Setting the **ScaleMode property** on a form to a different unit of measure (inches or centimeters, for example) changes the units in which the position of a control object on that form is measured.

Height, Width: These give the size of a form or control object. For a form the unit of measure is the twip, and for a control object on a form the unit is determined by the ScaleMode property of the form.

Caption: This property applies to many objects that display text. For a form the caption appears in the title bar, for a button it is what appears on the button, and for a label it is the text displayed within the label. Captions can be any string of characters, including spaces.

Name: The name of an object is how that object is referred to in Visual Basic code. When an object is first created, Visual Basic gives it a default name that consists of the object type followed by an integer. The default names for forms in a given project are thus Form1, Form2, and so on, and for the command buttons on a given form, Command1, Command2, Command3, and so on. You can change these names by editing the Settings box for the Name property in the Properties window. The name GetTotal might be more indicative than Command3 of the action that takes place using a certain command button, and this more descriptive name would make the code for the button easier to understand. Names can be any string of letters, digits, and underscore characters up to 40 characters in length, but must begin with a letter. (Spaces are not allowed in a name.)

When there are many types of objects on a form, it may be useful to include a prefix in the object name that indicates the type of object it is. A common three-letter prefix convention uses cmd- for names of command buttons, as in cmdGetTotal. Under this convention, names for forms begin with frm-, for labels with lbl-, for text boxes with txt-, and so on. Names of control objects on the opening form of the lab1 project follow this plan, as shown on the OTC of Figure 2.9. This naming convention for objects clarifies the type of object being referred to in program code. It also groups like objects alphabetically in the Properties window Object box and in the Code window Object box.

If you decide to change the name of an object, try to do it before you write any code. If the event procedure Command3_Click is empty, that is, you haven't written any code for the body of the procedure, and you change the button name from Command3 to cmdGetTotal, Visual Basic automatically changes the event procedure name to cmdGetTotal_Click, and you can then write the code. However, if you have already written code for the Command3_Click procedure and you then rename the button, your code won't be made the body of the cmdGetTotal_Click procedure. Instead, that (new) event procedure will be empty, and your Command3_Click procedure will be whisked into the "general" section of the form's code as a general procedure. From there, however, it can be cut and pasted back into the proper place by using the Edit menu (see Section 3.8 for a discussion of the Edit menu).

The Caption property is, by default, set to the same value as the default Name, but *the name and the caption are two quite different things.* The caption is what you see on the object, while the name is how the program code identifies that object. Be sure that you understand this distinction; in particular, changing an object's Name property in the Properties window has no effect on the object's appearance.

FontName, FontSize, FontBold, FontItalic, FontUnderline: These properties apply to any object that displays text. The settings control the typeface used, the point size of the typeface, and whether the text is to appear boldface, italic, or underlined.

Enabled: This is a property that toggles between true and false. When the Enabled property is false, the object cannot respond to any events. As with menu items, text that is displayed on a control that is not enabled will appear dimmed when the program is executing.

Visible: This property, which also toggles between true and false, determines whether an object can be seen when the program is executing. The **lab1** program manipulates Visible properties to show and hide the smiley faces and their accompanying labels.

Most properties can be set in the Properties window at design time, and can also be reset by program code when the program executes at run time. In the **lab1** project, the Left, Top, Height, and Width properties were reset in the Load event procedure for each form. A few properties are run time only.

In order to refer to an object's property within Visual Basic code, you use the object name (name, not caption), followed by a dot, followed by the property name. Thus

```
Label1.Height
```

NOTATIONAL NOTE FOR VISUAL BASIC CODE

A **property** of some particular object is denoted by

ObjectName.PropertyName

Example: `Command1.Width`

An **event** recognized by some particular object is denoted by

ObjectName_EventName

Example: `Command1_Click`

The first notation (with the dot) relates to Figure 2.1 on page 33; the second notation (with the underscore) relates to Figure 2.3 on page 41.

(pronounced "label one dot height") refers to the Height property of the Label1 object on the current form and

```
Form2.Caption
```

refers to the Caption property of Form2.

3.4 Text box

In the *lab1* project, the user enters his or her first name in a **Text Box** control. The text box icon in the Toolbox is shown here.
On the form, a text box looks like a rectangular area in which text can appear. However, the text in a text box is not the result of its Caption property. A text box has no Caption property. Instead, it has a property called **Text**. The new name is to emphasize the difference between the text that appears in a text box and the text that appears as the caption of a control object when a program is running—namely, the user can edit the text in a text box while the program is executing. The user can never directly change any object's caption by retyping it (although the user may be able to cause code to execute that changes the caption).

The value of a text box's Text property can be set at design time or within program code at run time. Thus a text box can be used simply to display information. However, unless the text box has its Enabled property set to False, the user can edit this text. This means that the information being displayed is not protected or "stable." To merely display information, a label is a better choice than a text box.

The more usual function of a text box is to serve as a place for the user to enter data as the program is executing. That data is then available to the program. How does the program capture what the user enters? When the user types in a text box, that string of characters becomes the value of the text box's Text property. This value can be assigned to a variable, which can then be used in the rest of the program. Recall that in the *getname* procedure of *lab1*, the single line of code is

```
yourname = text1.Text 'set yourname to value entered in text box
```

and *yourname* is then used to display the user's name in the labels on the *lab1a* and *lab1b* forms.

If a text box is to serve as a place to collect data from the user, there should be a **prompt** to the user about the kind of data being requested. The prompt is an instruction to the user about entering data in the text box. One could set the Text property of the text box at design time to contain the prompt, but then the user would destroy the prompt by typing over it and be unable to refer to it as a check that he or she has entered the right kind of data. Instead, there should be a label control near the text box whose caption contains the prompt. The Text property should be set at design time as the empty string, so that nothing shows in the text box when the user first sees it. Alternatively, the Text property could be set with a default input value, which the user could either accept or edit.

The text box control has the usual properties of size, position, and all the properties dealing with the appearance of the fonts. It also has unique properties, some of which are described in Table 3.1.

Table 3.1 Additional properties of the text box control

PROPERTY	POSSIBLE VALUES	DEFAULT VALUE	PURPOSE
MultiLine	True or False	False	When False, only one line of text can be entered; when True, multiple lines can be entered.
ScrollBars	0–3	0	Controls whether horizontal and/or vertical scroll bars appear on the text box. 0 = no scroll bars 1 = horizontal scroll bars 2 = vertical scroll bars 3 = both
MaxLength	Non-negative integer	0	Controls the maximum number of characters the user can enter; 0 = no maximum set.

The text box control can recognize a number of events. If the text box is being used to collect user input, then two particular events are the most likely ones to be programmed. The **Change event** occurs whenever the value of the Text property changes. This would occur as soon as the user types a character in the text box (or deletes a character already there). If your program is using the value of the text box in some obvious way, such as displaying it as part of a message somewhere on the form, you may want a change in the text box to be reflected at once as a change in the message. If so, you would put the code to assemble the message within the Change event procedure for the text box.

The form may contain a number of text boxes; the user progresses from box to box filling in information like name, street address, and so on (reminiscent of paper forms). One way for the user to get from one text box to another is to press the Tab key. When this is done, the cursor moves to the new text box, ready for data entry. The new text box experiences a **GotFocus event** at that point, while the old text box experiences a **LostFocus event**. The LostFocus event therefore signifies that the user has completed entering data into the old text box and that that piece of data is ready for processing; code to process that piece would be put in the LostFocus event procedure for the old text box.

Name: _____   Date Due: _____

LEARNING OBJECTIVES

- Exploring Label properties
- Setting properties in code
- Exploring Text Box properties

LAB 3.1

1. ____ Start a new project in Visual Basic.

   ____ Put your name in the title bar of the form.

   ____ Change the background color of the form.

   ____ Save the file in the appropriate directory with the name *lab3-1.frm.* Save the project as *lab3-1.mak.* Save your work often as you proceed.

2. ____ Put one command button somewhere near the bottom of the form.

   ____ Change the caption of the button to "Change Display". (If the button isn't big enough to show all of the caption, resize the button.)

3. ____ Put three labels somewhere near the top of the form. Make each label initially 600 twips wide and 1000 twips high.

   ____ Change the Names of the labels to Display1, Display2, and Display3, respectively. (Note that the Captions do not change.)

4. What is the value of the AutoSize property of Display1?

   ____ Change the caption of Display1 to "This is a very long caption that does not fit within the label." What happens?

5. ____ Change the caption of Display2 to "This is another very long caption that does not fit within the label." Note that the WordWrap property is False.

Exploring Label properties

____ Change the AutoSize property to True. What happens?

6. ____ Change the caption of Display3 to "This is another very long caption that does not fit within the label."

____ Change the WordWrap property to True.

____ Now change the AutoSize property to True. What happens?

Explain how the AutoSize and WordWrap properties work.

7. ____ Delete labels Display1 and Display2. (Select each and press the Delete key.)

What is the current font name and font size for Display3?

____ Change to a different font name.

8. ____ Drop down the list of font sizes for Display3 and note another font size that is available for this new font name. Instead of changing the font size in the Properties window, however, you'll use the command button and write code to change the font size. (So an event on one object is being used to change a property of another object.)

___ Bring up the Code window for the Command1_Click procedure. To assign a new value for a property within code, use the following kind of statement:

ObjectName.PropertyName = new value of property

___ Write the code to change the font size for Display3.

___ Run the program, and click the button.

What happened?

Setting properties in code

When you return to design mode, note that the type size has returned to the previous setting. A change in a property that is made by code at run time lasts only while the program is executing; it does not permanently affect the setting in the Properties window.

9. What label property affects whether you can see through the label to the form beneath? Do not change the value of this property in the Properties window, but note the numeric code that represents the "see-through" configuration.

___ Add one more line of code to the button click event procedure so that when the button is clicked, the user sees through the label. (Give the new value of the property by its numeric code.) Run your program. Terminate execution.

10. Do some experimenting, then explain what each of the following label properties affects:

Alignment

BorderStyle

ForeColor

11. ____ Put a single text box on the form of height 500, width 2500.

What are the current dimensions of the *form*?

____ Now set the ScaleMode property of the form to inches.

What are the current dimensions of the *form*?

What are the current dimensions of the *text box*?

Explain what has happened.

Exploring Text Box properties

12. What are the values of the following properties of the Text Box? (Compare with Table 3.1.)

MultiLine:

ScrollBars:

MaxLength:

____ Change the Text property setting to blank.

____ Change the ScrollBars property to 1 (horizontal). Note that nothing happens. When MultiLine is set to False, changing the ScrollBars property has no effect.

____ Change the ScrollBars property back to 0.

13. ____ Run the program and try to enter a long line of text that extends past the boundaries. What happens?

14. ____ Run the program and try to enter two lines of text by pressing the Enter key at the end of the first line. What happens?

____ Now set the MultiLine property to true and repeat this experiment. What happens?

____ Make the Text Box taller and repeat this experiment. What happens now?

15. ____ Set the ScrollBars property to add a horizontal scrollbar to the text box.

____ Run the program and type in one long line of text. How can you use the scrollbar after you stop typing?

16. ____ Set the MaxLength property to 10.

____ Run the program and try to type in a text string that is longer than 10 characters. What happens?

Describe when this feature might be useful. (Hint: Suppose this text box is for the user to enter a Social Security number.)

17. ____ Set the MultiLine property back to False, and set the MaxLength property back to 0.

____ In the command button Click event code, put a statement that sets the Enabled property of the text box to false.

____ Run the program; enter some text, and then click the button. What is the effect? Can you still enter text?

18. ____ Set the PasswordChar property to *. (Setting this property has no effect when MultiLine is True.)

____ Run the program and enter text. What happens?

Explain when this feature might be useful. (Hint: Consider the name of the property you just set.)

19. ____ Save your work, then exit Visual Basic.

> **QuickCheck 3.1**
>
> 1. Describe the user interface for a vending machine.
> 2. What is the most common use for a label control?
> 3. To let the user type in data, what sort of control can be used?
> 4. What is a prompt?
> 5. What is the effect of the AutoSize property for a label?

3.5 Project management

The term "project management" usually refers to supervision of the entire process of software development, including budgeting, time management, personnel issues, and so on. However, Visual Basic uses the term "project" to refer to a Visual Basic application, in particular, the collection of files making up an application. This section discusses how to manage these files.

A file is a unit of electronic storage for related items of information. A file may contain a document generated by a word processor, a spreadsheet generated by a spreadsheet program, a computer program, data to be used by a computer program, and so on. One of the functions that Windows provides through its File Manager is the capacity to administer files: copy them, move them, delete them. (See Appendix B for an overview of the File Manager.)

Visual Basic also does its own file management for the files associated with a Visual Basic project. Files are identified by a filename followed by a dot followed by a three-letter **file extension**. The file extension identifies the type of file. The file extension for a Visual Basic form file is FRM, and there is a separate FRM file for each form. When you first save your project, Visual Basic will suggest a filename for each form, but it isn't a very meaningful name; use your own file name (*movie.frm*, *lab3-1.frm*, etc.) instead.

A form file contains all the information about the layout of the form, its control objects, their properties, and any event procedures written for that form or any of its control objects. The form file also contains any form-level general procedures. Recall that event procedures are not the only kind of code. A general procedure is code that is not associated with a particular event. If only a single form, or the objects on that form, need to use that code, it can be written in the Code window for the "general" section of that form (like the *getname* procedure in **lab1**). Anything in the general section of a form is also saved in the form file. In other words, a form file contains everything necessary to reconstruct the form and all its code.

General procedures may be needed by more than one form. Such procedures are written in one or more **modules**, which are separate from any form. Modules also contain descriptions of variables that are used in more than one form (like *yourname* in **lab1**). A module is stored in a file with the extension BAS, and a BAS file contains all the code for that module. Again, supply a meaningful filename when you first save a module file.

The Project window for a Visual Basic application will therefore list at least one FRM file and possibly one or more BAS files. However, in scrolling through the Project window, you may have noticed files with VBX extensions and wondered what they are. In addition to the controls that are already available in the Visual Basic Toolbox, specialized controls can be purchased from vendors. These are called **custom controls** and are stored in files with the extension VBX. The Standard Edition of Visual Basic comes with three custom controls (CMDIALOG.VBX, GRID.VBX, and MSOLE2.VBX), and the Professional Edition provides many more. A Visual Basic application that makes use of any of these controls needs access to the appropriate file. The three custom controls mentioned above are, by default, loaded with any project and hence are listed in the Project window for any application.[1]

Visual Basic also maintains a separate file for each project with the extension MAK, as in *lab3-1.mak* (again, choose a good filename the first time you save your work). The MAK file (not listed in the Project window, but named in the Project window title bar) is the "master file" for a project. It stores information on what other files are part of the project. It is an ordinary text file, and can be seen or edited with any text editor software. The MAK file contains the names of all FRM files for the project, all BAS files for the project, and all VBX files for the project.

An existing Visual Basic project is opened by selecting the MAK file for that project, which contains the information on what other files for that project need to be available to the Visual Basic environment. If one of these files is missing, Visual Basic will give an error message. This list of files is the one displayed in the Project window when the project is opened.

The MAK file also contains additional information, such as which form should be the startup form (the first form listed in the MAK file is considered to be the startup form) and the initial position and size of the Project window when the Visual Basic environment opens.

Figure 3.2 shows the MAK file for the *lab1* project. Because this project doesn't use the custom controls, the three lines that reference those files could be deleted from the MAK file.

Figure 3.2
LAB1.MAK file

```
LAB1.FRM
C:\WINDOWS\SYSTEM\CMDIALOG.VBX
C:\WINDOWS\SYSTEM\GRID.VBX
C:\WINDOWS\SYSTEM\MSOLE2.VBX
LAB1.BAS
LAB1A.FRM
LAB1B.FRM
ProjWinSize=77,384,252,122
ProjWinShow=2
IconForm="Form1"
Title="LAB1"
ExeName="LAB1.EXE"
```

It is helpful to keep all FRM and BAS files connected with a project, as well as the MAK file, in the same directory. Then to identify a file, the MAK file needs only the file name, not the entire path name (directory information). If the MAK file for a project contains path names for files, and the project files are copied using the Windows File Manager to some other directory, the MAK file has to be edited to reflect the new file locations. If the files are saved from within Visual Basic to some new location, then the MAK file must be saved last so that it contains the correct file locations.

---

[1] A little file in the Visual Basic directory called AUTOLOAD.MAK contains the names of the three custom control files. This text file can be edited to delete any of these names. For any new projects created after this change, the control corresponding to the deleted file name will not be loaded when the project is opened. A missing control can be added to a project if needed by choosing Add File under the File menu.

To sum up, in order to successfully open a project in the Visual Basic environment, the MAK file and all the files—FRM files, BAS files, and VBX files—named in the MAK file must be present. Of course, the Visual Basic software itself must be present as well.

However, to merely *execute* a Visual Basic application program, the Visual Basic software is not required. Usually all that is required is an EXE file (executable file) for the project, plus one additional file called VBRUN300.DLL. In order to create an EXE file for a project, load the project into Visual Basic and choose Make EXE File... from the Visual Basic File menu. This creates a file with the filename you choose and the EXE extension. The file VBRUN300.DLL is normally found in the C:\WINDOWS\SYSTEM directory. If you copy this file and your EXE file to a disk and then load them onto another machine (putting the VBRUN300.DLL into C:\WINDOWS\SYSTEM or wherever Windows is on that machine), then the Visual Basic application will run on that machine with no Visual Basic software required. All that is required is to use the File Manager to find the EXE file and then double-click on that file name, just as you ran **lab1.exe** without first going into the Visual Basic environment. For projects that use custom controls, you may need to provide additional files.

Although the Visual Basic system manages files to the extent it keeps track of what it needs, this has nothing to do with the security of those files. You need to take the same precautions with Visual Basic files as with any other computer files.

Rule number one is to save your files frequently as you work, in this case, as you develop your Visual Basic application. Then in the event of a power surge, a system crash, or some other calamity that befalls your machine while you are working, you will lose only what you have done since you last saved the files.

Rule number two is similar. Make backup copies of your files on a second set of diskettes. Don't rely on one set of diskettes (or on your machine's hard drive or network server) to preserve your only copy.

3.6 Printing a project

As a Visual Basic project increases in complexity, especially as event procedures get created and are attached to various objects, it gets more difficult to remember where things are. Even Visual Basic pros have a hard time keeping track of all of the pieces of code. It is nice to be able to see the whole project at once in written form. Choosing Print under the Visual Basic File menu brings up the dialog box shown in Figure 3.3.

You may choose either Current (if you want a printout only for the current form or module) or All (if you want information on all forms and modules.) You may choose one or more of the following:

Form—for a graphical "picture" of the form design

Form Text—for a text description of form properties and object properties that have been modified from their default values, plus size and location of control objects on the form

Code—for the code for any event procedures or general procedures that exist for the form

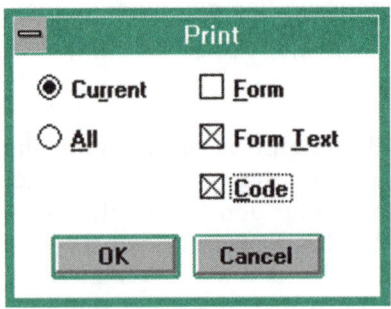

Figure 3.3
Visual Basic Print dialog box

Thus, choosing All, Form Text, and Code gives you a hard-copy (printed) output of all objects, properties, and code. You can therefore see all the code at once, and could reconstruct each form and all the code if, despite your precautions, all the electronic files should ever be damaged.

Printing from the Print dialog box gives you a printed record of all the program design components, but it doesn't give you a dynamic view of what the program looks like during execution. It would be nice to be able to capture an image of the form when the program is running. Visual Basic provides a way to do this. The command

```
Form1.PrintForm
```

will cause the image of Form1 to be printed (assuming, of course, that your machine is connected to a printer). Such a statement could be included in the Form1_Click procedure code, and the effect would be to capture an image of the form every time you click the mouse on the form during program execution. For somewhat technical reasons, it is best to have the AutoRedraw property of the form set to True at design time if you plan to print the form in this fashion.

3.7 Methods

Code you write for an event procedure causes some action to take place when that event is recognized by an object. However, objects themselves can be the recipients of actions that take place on them. Visual Basic supplies a limited number of built-in actions, called **methods**, that act on objects. Each object type can be acted on by its own list of methods as illustrated in Figure 3.4, a by-now familiar sort of picture.

PrintForm, discussed in the previous section, is a method that acts on Form objects. **Hide** and **Show** are also methods that act on forms. (Aside: There may be a bit of confusion about the Hide and Show methods, which apply only to forms. The Hide method, as one might guess, removes the form from view. Invoking the Hide method is equivalent to setting the Visible property of the form to False. The Show method is equivalent to setting the Visible property of the form to True. So you can either use the Hide and Show methods or set the Visible property to control the appearance and disappearance of Form objects. However, the Hide and Show methods cannot act on control objects. The appearance and disappearance of control objects must be managed by manipulating the Visible property.)

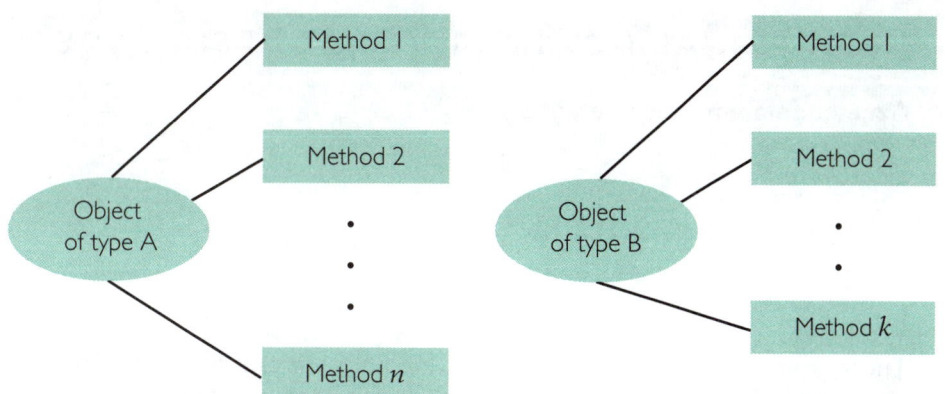

Figure 3.4
Each type of object has its own set of methods.

The only code needed for a method is one statement to invoke the method. Then Visual Basic automatically carries out the action defined for that method on the target object. A method is invoked on an object by a statement of the form object name, followed by a dot, followed by the method name. Thus

`Form1.Hide`

invokes the Hide method on the object Form1. This statement appears to follow the notational rules—the syntax—for referring to an object property, yet if you look in the Properties window for the Form object, you will not find a Hide property.

You now know that there are three things associated with each object type: its properties, the events it recognizes, and the methods that can act on it (see Figure 3.5). The Visual Basic Help screen for any object type has links to these three lists, so you can see exactly what applies to each object type.

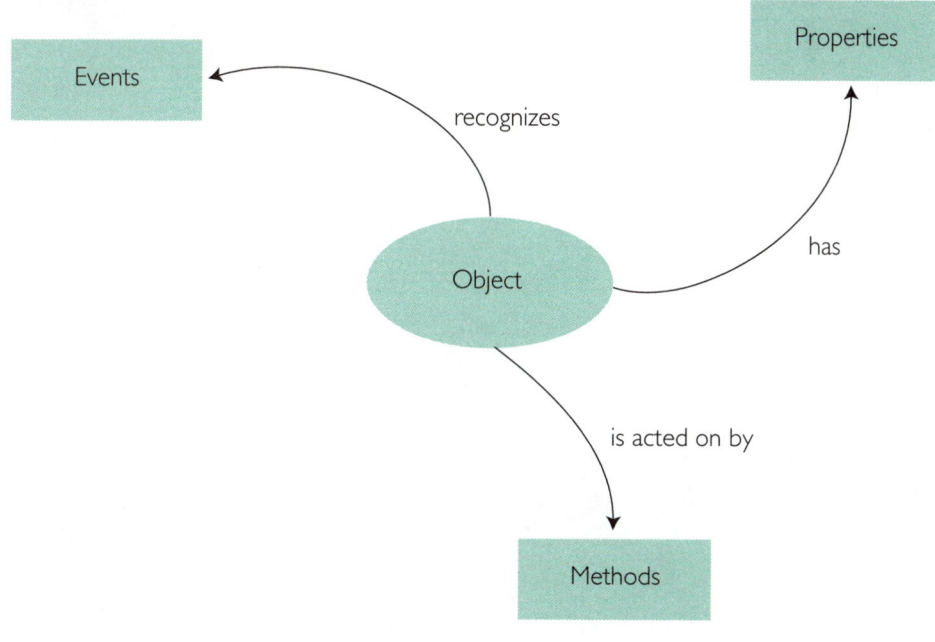

Figure 3.5
The three facets of an object type

> **NOTATIONAL NOTE FOR VISUAL BASIC CODE**
>
> A method statement is written as
>
> *ObjectName.Method*
>
> This looks exactly like the way to name an object property:
>
> *ObjectName.PropertyName*
>
> There are three ways to tell them apart. Methods are usually verbs (denoting action), like Hide and Show, while properties are usually descriptions, like Visible or Caption. Also, a method is invoked by simply using the method statement. Thus
>
> ```
> Form1.Hide
> ```
>
> is a complete statement as it stands. An object property is only part of a statement, perhaps a statement that assigns a new value to the property:
>
> ```
> Form1.Left = 1200
> ```
>
> Finally, a method name is color highlighted in Visual Basic (the default color is blue), while a property name is not.

Name: _____   Date Due: _____

LAB 3.2

LEARNING OBJECTIVES

- Understanding a MAK file
- Printing a project
- Tracing through an entire program
- Using the PrintForm method

1. ____ Open Notepad (usually found in the Windows Accessories Group). Notepad is a very simple text editor.

   ____ Under the File menu, choose Open.

   ____ In the dialog box, under "List Files of Type:", ask to see all files.

   ____ Look for the file **lab1.mak** and open it. You should see a file that looks like Figure 3.2

2. Edit this file as follows:

   ____ Delete the three lines that refer to the custom controls. (Again, the **lab1** project does not make use of these controls, so these files do not need to be part of the project.)

   ____ Cut the line that says LAB1B.FRM by first selecting (highlighting by dragging over it) that line, then selecting Cut from the Edit menu. In any standard Windows program, "cutting" a selected item places that item in a temporary storage area called the **Clipboard**.

   ____ Move the cursor to the beginning of the first line.

   ____ Click to anchor the insertion point and hit Enter to create a blank line at the top of the file.

   ____ Put the insertion point at the top of the file and select Paste from the Edit menu. This "pastes" the contents of the clipboard into the file at the insertion point. The first line of your file should now say LAB1B.FRM.

   ____ Use Save As... from the File menu to save the file with the name **mixup.mak**.

   ____ Exit Notepad.

3. ____ In the Visual Basic environment, open the project **mixup.mak**. **Mixup.mak** is an alternate MAK file for the **lab1** project. What files are listed in the Project window?

> **Editing a MAK file in a text editor**

What is different about the Toolbox, and why?

____ Run the program; what happens and why?

Editing a MAK file in Visual Basic

4. The sort of editing you did on the MAK file in Notepad can be accomplished within the Visual Basic environment as well. To see this, you'll reverse some of those effects.

____ From the Visual Basic File menu, choose Add File... and look for the file GRID.VBX (look in C:\WINDOWS\SYSTEM).

____ Add this file. What happened to the Toolbox? What changed in the Project window?

____ From the Visual Basic Options menu, choose Project.

____ Using Start Up Form, change the setting so that **lab1** is again the startup form.

____ Run the program again to see that it behaves normally.

Printing the Lab1 project

5. Be sure you have a printer on line before you proceed with the rest of this lab.

____ Using Print from the Visual Basic File menu, print the Form Text and Code for all the forms and modules. (The result should be about 9 pages.)

Note in this **listing** (hard copy) of the project that for each form, the properties of all objects are given first, followed by code for the various (nonempty) procedures. What is the total number of (nonempty) procedures for the **lab1** project? (Remember that each procedure begins with **Sub** and closes with **End Sub**.)

With all of the code in hand, the final (promise!) work with the *lab1* project is to completely **trace** the code. Tracing program code is a pencil-and-paper exercise of simulating a running program to see exactly what code statement gets executed when, and what takes place as each statement executes. While the Visual Basic debugger gives the ability to do this on line, it is still helpful to study a listing and follow where each current statement is to be found.

6. When a Visual Basic project is executed, several things happen to the startup form (which is determined by the MAK file):

   First, a Show method is applied to the form. The Show method for a form not only makes the form visible but also initiates the following two events.

   A Load event takes place for the form if the form is not yet loaded into memory.

   An Activate event also takes place, which "gives the focus" to the form (makes it the active window).

   Thus the form gets loaded into memory, becomes visible, and becomes the active form.

   ____ Look either in your listing or in the Visual Basic Code window at the Load event procedure for form *lab1*, the startup form. When the Load event for this form takes place, the code in this procedure is executed. It sizes and positions the form on the screen, making use of the properties of a special **Screen** object that refers to the actual computer monitor screen.

   Tracing the lab1 project

   Now suppose the user has entered a name in the text box and has clicked on the cmdGreeting button. The code for the cmdGreeting_Click event on form *lab1* executes.

   ____ Find this code in your listing or the Visual Basic Code window. The first statement calls the *getname* procedure. What is the next line of code that will be executed?

When this statement executes, the string of characters the user entered in the text box is stored in the variable *yourname*. What is the next line of code that will be executed?

This statement applies the Show method to form **lab1a.** This in turn causes a Load event for form **lab1a.**

7. ___ Look at the code for the Load event on form **lab1a.** This code sizes and positions the new form right on top of the old form, so when this new form becomes visible, the first form seems to disappear. After the new form becomes visible, the Activate event takes place, and the Activate event procedure for form **lab1a** is executed.

   ___ Look at the code for the Activate event. This code modifies the caption of the label to include the greeting message. The variable *yourname* is part of the greeting, and since *yourname* contains the user's first name (or whatever the user typed in the text box), that is what will be displayed as part of the greeting message within the label caption.

   Now suppose the user clicks the cmdOK1A button on form **lab1a.** What statement is executed?

   Applying the Hide method to the **lab1a** form makes it disappear and reveals the original form that was beneath it the entire time.

8. ___ In Visual Basic, run the **lab1** program, enter a name, and click the button for the greeting.

   ___ Once the greeting screen appears, and while you are still in run mode, drag the window for that screen. What happens?

   Go back to design mode.

9. ____ Look either in your listing or in the Visual Basic Code window. Suppose the user clicks on the cmdPicture button on form **lab1**. What are the next three lines of code that are executed?

   1.

   2.

   3.

10. ____ After the Show method is applied to form **lab1b**, what two events happen next?

11. ____ Look in your listing or in the Code window at the code for the Form_Load procedure for form **lab1b**. What is the effect of this code?

12. ____ Look at the code for the Form_Activate procedure for form **lab1b**. These Visual Basic statements make sure that when that form becomes the active form, the second image and its label are not visible and the first image and its label are visible, along with a new caption for the first label that incorporates the text stored in *yourname*. It also "enables" (turns on) the Timer1 object.

    ____ Look in your listing or in the Visual Basic Properties window at the properties for the Timer1 object. The property called **Interval** determines how long, in milliseconds, after the timer is enabled until a Timer event takes place. (The Timer event is the only event a timer control object can recognize.)

    ____ In the Visual Basic Code window, modify the Form_Activate event code for form **lab1b** to read

    ```
    timer1.Enabled = False
    ```

    Now the timer is not turned on when this form appears.

    ____ Run the program and click the button for pictures. What happens?

____ Back in design mode, change the Form_Activate code back to enable the timer.

13. ____ Look at the code for the Timer1_Timer event. What will happen when a Timer event occurs?

Suppose the first two lines of this code are not there. In the Visual Basic Code window for the Timer1_Timer event procedure, instead of removing the first two lines, place a single quote before each line. This turns each line into a comment, which will be ignored.

____ Run the program, again going to the picture form. What happens and why?

____ Back in design mode, restore the Timer1_Timer code to its original form.

Using the PrintForm method

14. ____ Write a Form_Click procedure for form *lab1* that applies the PrintForm method to the form.

____ Run the program, enter a name, and click on the form. You should get a run-time image of the form from your printer, including the user input in the text box. (Because this is a graphic image, it may take a while to print.)

____ Exit Visual Basic; do not save any changes.

> **QuickCheck 3.2**
>
> 1. The file that manages all other files in a Visual Basic project has a file extension of _____.
> 2. What are files with a VBX extension?
> 3. True or false: To print the run-time image of an executing Visual Basic program, choose Print from the File menu.
> 4. An action that acts on an object is called a _____.
> 5. What does it mean to trace program code?

3.8 Editing code

Minor typing errors on a line of code in the Code window can be corrected by using the backspace or delete keys. To correct bigger mistakes and to do some other editing tasks, you will use the services of the Visual Basic Edit menu (Figure 3.6).

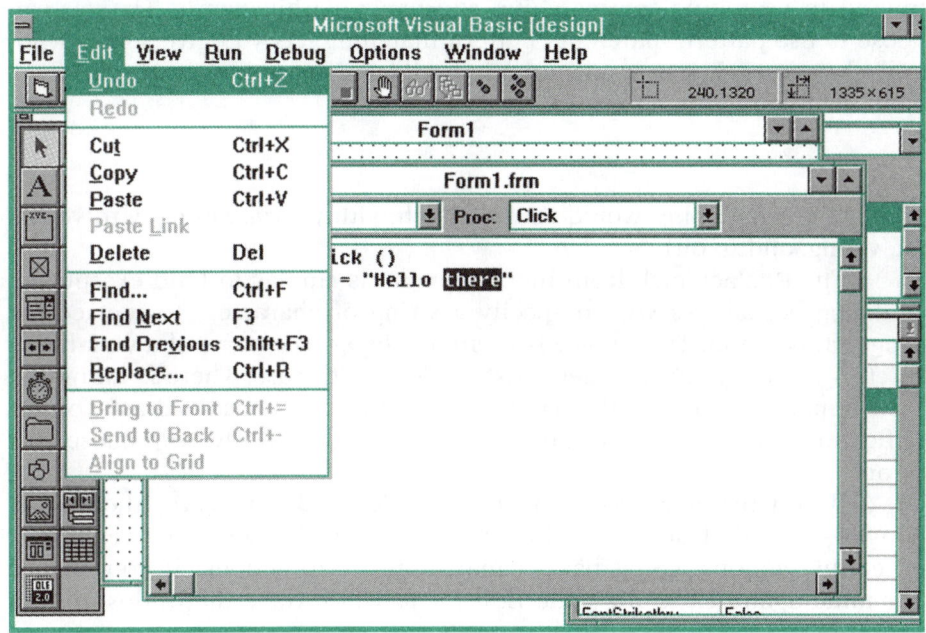

Figure 3.6
Visual Basic Edit menu

Many of the options in the Edit menu are enabled only when a section of text has been selected. To select text, click and drag over the portion you want to select; the selection will be highlighted (as is the word "there" in Figure 3.6). Selected text can be deleted by choosing Delete or Cut from the Edit menu (or by pressing the delete key on the keyboard). Selected text can be *moved* by choosing Cut from the Edit menu, which moves the selected text to the Clipboard, clicking the insertion point somewhere within the code (perhaps in a different Code window), and then choosing Paste from the Edit menu, which inserts the text from the Clipboard at the insertion point. Selected text can be *copied* by choosing Copy from the Edit menu, which copies the selected text to the Clipboard, clicking the insertion point somewhere within the code, and then choosing Paste from the Edit menu. If part of the code from one procedure will work in another procedure, don't retype it; copy and paste it.

Visual Basic code is usually written one programming statement per line. Lines cannot exceed 255 characters, and no statement can be split across two lines. To "navigate" within a line of code, use the keyboard arrow keys to move one character right or left. The End key will move the cursor to the end of the current line of code, and the Home key will move it to the beginning of the current line. Keyboard arrow keys will also let you move up or down one line of code at a time. For faster vertical progress through a long section of code, the PageUp and PageDown keys will work. Ctrl-End (holding down the Ctrl key and pressing the End key) will move the cursor to the end of the procedure; Ctrl-Home will move the cursor to the beginning of the procedure. Of course the Code window scroll bars will also let you scroll through the code both horizontally and vertically.

Other choices from the Code menu (Find and FindNext) allow you to search your code for a particular string of characters. This is useful, for example, to find all occurrences of a particular variable or object. Choosing Find or FindNext brings up the dialog box shown in Figure 3.7. Here you can enter the string you are looking for and specify whether you want the search confined to the current procedure, the current module (form), or all the code in the project. You can ask for a match with whole words only, as opposed to searching for matching substrings within words. Or you can choose to use pattern matching. Pattern matching lets you give some "wildcard" characters. For example, an * is a wildcard for any character or characters, so a search for

```
you*
```

using pattern matching would find a match with *yourname* (or with youth, you, young, and so on).

The Replace pick from the Edit menu is similar to Find except that the dialog box allows you to specify a string of characters to replace the string that is found. This choice is useful to change the name of a variable or object. Naturally, such changes must be done with care. There is an option in the Replace dialog box that causes Visual Basic to pause and ask you for verification for each replacement; it's a good idea to always choose this option.

If you regret changes you have made—and you regret them early enough—all is not lost. The Undo pick from the Edit menu will reverse your last editing actions, going back a maximum of 20 actions. If you change your mind again, Redo from the Edit menu will reverse the Undos up to a maximum of 20 actions.

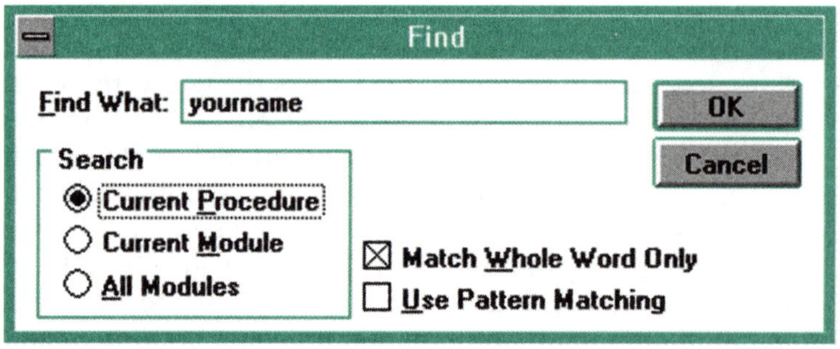

Figure 3.7
Find dialog box

3.9 Control arrays

We are all familiar with computer-generated form letters. The body of the letter is essentially the same for the hundreds or thousands of recipients. Each letter is "personalized" with an individual name and address. What's the advantage to form letters? They only need to be written once and then personalized for each recipient.

Sometimes in a Visual Basic application it is useful to have a number of instances of the same type of control on one form, each instance having event procedures that are essentially alike except for a reference to the specific control object. The event procedures are like form letters; they are written once and then "personalized." The easiest way to handle this situation is to use a collection of control objects called a **control array**.

All the elements in a control array must be the same type of object, say, all command buttons or all labels. To create a control array of buttons, for example, create the first button. The default name is Command1. Then create a second button and change its name property to Command1 also. This will bring up a dialog box that notes that you have chosen a duplicate name and asks whether you want to create a control array. If you choose Yes, then the names of the buttons become Command1(0) and Command1(1). (The same effect is achieved by copying and pasting the Command1 button.) Subsequent buttons created with the name Command1 become Command1(2), Command1(3), and so on. The buttons all share the same name but are numbered from 0 to 3 (or more). The number (0, 1, 2, 3, and so on) that identifies each specific control is called the **array index** of the control.

For a control array, one event procedure per event is written for the entire array. In the case of the array of buttons, for example, there is only one Click event procedure and its heading looks like

```
Sub Command1_Click (Index As Integer)
```

The new part of the procedure heading occurs in parentheses after the event procedure name. The notation "Index As Integer" says that when one of the command buttons in the array is clicked, the array index of that button—which will be an integer quantity—is passed to the procedure and is available for use within the procedure body. This is how the procedure body gets "personalized" for each button. For example, within the Command1_Click procedure the following line of code could appear:

```
Label1.Caption = "This is button number" & Index
```

which would print

> This is button number 0

or

> This is button number 1

and so on, depending on the button clicked.

In summary, control arrays are groups of similar control objects that share common event procedures, but within the procedure bodies, the array index of each particular control is available to "personalize" the code. You'll see a specific example in the next lab.

THOUGHTS ON PROGRAMMING

User Interface Design

The user interface is a significant factor in making a computer program useful and well accepted. The layout of the forms and the placement and other properties of the various controls affect what the user sees when a Visual Basic program runs. Making decisions about what objects are needed and what their properties should be is an important part of the user interface design process. It can even involve aesthetic qualities like the most restful color to use for the background of the form, or the most pleasing proportions for a button. Alignment of like objects or a uniform size for like objects can make the form look more "restful" and less "obtrusive" as the user works.

However, the user interface involves all the program-user interactions. This includes how the program asks for input data from the user, how the user requests actions to be taken by the program, and how the program displays the results. Does the program make clear what kind of data it is asking for? Is there an easy mechanism for the user to enter the requested data?

You have seen one Visual Basic mechanism for entering data, namely the text box control. If a text box is used as a data-gathering mechanism, is there a nearby prompt that clearly explains what the user is to enter? One mechanism for the user to request actions within the program is the command button. If command buttons are used, are their captions self-explanatory? When a command button is clicked, is the effect what the user might be led to expect from the caption? How does the program display its results? If results are written somewhere on the form, are they clearly labeled so the user knows what he or she is seeing? If the results are printed to paper (an option you'll later see how to do), are they organized in a manner that is clear and easy to read?

Does the program disable controls and/or menu choices that do not apply to the current situation so that the user cannot make inappropriate choices? If the user makes an appropriate choice on an enabled control but then decides that it is not what he or she really wants to do, is there an escape mechanism? Does the program trap inappropriate data values (for example, a value like 4.37 for the current date), give an appropriate error message, and allow the user a chance to recover?

Considerations of user interface design in the general sense discussed here require a large part of the total time spent designing and planning a program. Several principles should guide the programmer as the user interface is designed:

1. The user interface should be *internally consistent*. For example, if there are multiple forms, each with a button that does the same task, then these buttons should be located in the same position on each form and should have the same caption.

2. The user interface should be *transparent*. In other words, the user should not be aware of the user interface itself but only of the task the program is supposed to perform. The user interface is there to assist in the smooth and efficient operation of that task, not to intrude itself between the user and the task. A user interface that obscures relevant options or suggests options irrelevant to the task, or even one that is merely gaudy, is calling attention to itself rather than letting the user "see through" to the task he or she wants to do.

    The GUI (graphical user interface) concept lends itself to user interfaces that are potentially transparent because the user can interact with the program visually by dragging objects, clicking on icons, and so on. However, it is certainly possible to design bad GUIs!

3. The user interface should be *protective*. If you as the user select some drastic action to be performed, a good user interface will double-check and allow you an escape valve. For example, if you choose an action within a program that will cause a file to be deleted, the user interface should confirm that you do indeed want to delete the file, and allow you to change your mind, perhaps by selecting a "cancel" option.

A complex software package often uses a *flexible* user interface that can be changed as the user wishes. A novice user may want the maximum help displayed via toolbars with buttons, whereas an expert user may prefer to access functions through keystrokes and will sacrifice the toolbar for added screen "real estate." Conversely, a novice user may not want to see a toolbar for options he or she does not need or does not yet know how to use, whereas a more advanced user may be ready to use that functionality and want the toolbar to be present.

Name: _____   Date Due: _____

LAB 3.3

LEARNING OBJECTIVES

- Using control arrays
- Designing and writing an application with text boxes
- Arranging a more complex form

Using control arrays

1. ____ To illustrate how control arrays work, do another version of the movie program from Lab 2.3. It's easier to start from scratch than to modify your existing program. From the user interface perspective, this program will be identical to the previous version; it is simply implemented differently. The idea is still to have the user click on one of three command buttons and see an appropriate quote, but this time the three buttons will be organized as a control array. Instead of a single label to display the quote, there will be three labels, also in a control array. The buttons will manage which label is displayed.

   ____ Open a new Visual Basic project and save the files as ***newmovie.frm*** and ***newmovie.mak***.

   ____ Put a label on the form with user instructions (you could copy and paste this from your previous program).

   ____ Create an array of three command buttons.

   ____ Scroll through the Object box of the Properties window and note that these buttons are listed as Command1(0), Command1(1), and Command1(2). Each button has its own Properties window. Look at the index property for each button and confirm that the index value matches the value in parentheses.

   ____ Change the captions to show the three movie titles (Gone with the Wind; Star Trek, The Motion Picture; and The Wizard of Oz).

   ____ Create an array of three labels. Scrolling through the Object box in the Properties window, how are these three labels identified?

   ____ Change the captions of the labels to the appropriate quotes ("Frankly, my dear, I don't give a damn", "He's dead, Jim", and "Toto, I don't think we're in Kansas anymore"). *Be sure* that the index number of the label for a quote and the index number of the command button for that quote's movie agree.)

___ For each label in the array, set its Visible property to False.

___ Stack all the labels on top of one another on the form.

2. Now you need to add appropriate code. Is there a Code window for the Click event for each button? Explain.

When one of the three buttons is clicked, it is identified by its index. The result of the click event should be to display the label with the same index. What is the single statement needed to do this? (Hint: You have set each label's Visible property to False in its Properties window.)

Where should this statement go?

___ Add the appropriate code and test your program thoroughly (click the buttons several times). What is the problem?

3. ___ Add appropriate code for the command button LostFocus event so that when another button is clicked (and thus the previous button recognizes a LostFocus event), the previous button's label disappears.

___ Run your program again, testing it thoroughly.

___ Save your work.

Designing an application with text boxes

4. The new application is a rather simple one. The user will enter his or her first name and last name in two separate text boxes, then click on buttons to see the name displayed in a label in one of two ways:

> first last
> last, first

___ Do an OTC design using the "card" shown here. Don't forget user prompts.

NAMER FORM

5. ____ Open a new project in Visual Basic. Save the files as *namer.frm* and *namer.mak*.

   ____ Build your form with the necessary control objects. Set the properties as appropriate. (Hint: As you switch the focus from one control to another of the same type, the property selected in the Properties window remains the same. So it is easier to put all the objects of one type on the form at once, then cycle through them and change, say, all their captions, then all their alignments, and so on, rather than to set all the properties of each individual object as you put it on the form.)

6. The code for the two command buttons is similar. You want to change the value of what object and what property?

   You have already written some code that changes the value of a property. The general form of such a statement is

   ObjectName.PropertyName = new value of property

7. ____ In this case, the new value of the property is not just a string of characters (within quotes) that you supply. What two items do you need to use in order to make the new value of the property?

To make one long string of characters out of shorter strings, you use the **concatenation operator**, symbolized by &. Thus

```
"good" & "bye"
```

would be displayed as

```
"goodbye"
```

8. ____ Write the necessary code. Use the concatenation operator and the two items from your answer to number 7 above. Spaces and/or punctuation have to be provided by strings in quotes.

9. ____ Test your program.

   ____ Save your work.

Arranging a more complex form

10. Here's the beginning of an application program that will act like a simple four-function calculator (add, subtract, multiply, and divide numbers). The form will be built now, and the code to complete the application will be added later. The OTC design below was guided by looking at a real calculator, although almost any real calculator does much more than our simple calculator program will do.

CALCULATOR FORM – LAB3

Active Objects	Object Type	Event	Task
Ten buttons	array of command buttons	Click	Act as the numeric keypad; adds a digit to the displayed number.
Enter	command button	Click	Store the currently displayed number.
Add	command button	Click	Add the the currently displayed number to the stored number
Subtract	command button	Click	Subtract the currently displayed number from the stored number.
Multiply	command button	Click	Multiply the currently displayed number by the stored number.
Divide	command button	Click	Divide the currently displayed number into the stored number
Clear	command button	Click	Clear the display
Passive Objects			
lblReadout	label		Display the number being entered. Display the result.
lbl Text	label		Display the word "Results" over the readout label.

11. ____ Open a new Visual Basic project for the calculator application. Save the files as **calc.frm** and **calc.mak,** and be sure to save your work often as you proceed.

    ____ Color the form, and put the words Marie's Calculator (use your own name) in the form's title bar.

    ____ The numeric keypad requires ten buttons, one for each of the digits 0, 1, 2, 3, 4, 5, 6, 7, 8, 9. The purpose of each button is the same—to contribute its digit toward building up the current number being entered. Because all ten buttons do essentially the same thing, they can be made into a control array. Do this.

    ____ It is convenient that these index values are also the digits needed. Put a caption on each button that matches its index value.

12. ____ Add six buttons, with appropriate captions, for the four arithmetic operations, the Clear button, and the Enter button. Use the notation * for multiplication and the notation / for division.

    ____ Also give each button a name that indicates its purpose.

13. ____ Put a blank label named lblReadout on the form in which to display the results, and put another label named lblText with the word "Results" in some nice typestyle so the user will know what the blank label is for.

14. ____ Do a final check to be sure your form presents a useful and attractive user interface. Save your work. Exit Visual Basic.

QuickCheck 3.3

1. Describe how to copy a section of code from one procedure to another.
2. True or false: In the Code window, long Visual Basic statements wrap around to another line.
3. What identifies each separate member of a control array?
4. Array indices begin with what number?
5. The symbol _____ represents string concatenation.

Review Questions

1. Can the user change the text in a label? If so, how? Can the program change the text in a label? If so, how?
2. To give the size and position properties of a control object in a unit other than a twip requires changing the ScaleMode property of what object?
3. Explain the difference between the caption of an object and the name of an object.
4. If you are going to change the name of an object, why should you do that before you write code for the object?
5. For a label control, describe when you might set the Enabled property to False as opposed to setting the Visible property to False.
6. True or false: Code that changes the setting of a control object property must be written in an event procedure for that object.
7. Explain the difference in use between a label and a text box, both of which can display text.
8. A text box on a form will often have a label nearby; why?
9. When would a general procedure be written in a code module as opposed to the general section of a form?
10. Explain the purpose of a Visual Basic MAK file for a project.
11. What is the purpose of a Visual Basic EXE file?
12. Explain the difference between a property, an event, and a method.
13. Name two form methods.
14. True or false: Files can be added to or deleted from a project from within the Visual Basic environment.
15. To reverse the effect of an editing change in code, pick _____ from the Edit menu.
16. What is the main advantage of using a control array?
17. What is the definition of the user interface of a computer program?
18. Give two aspects of a Visual Basic program's user interface in addition to the appearance of the form and controls.
19. Name three guiding principles in designing a program's user interface.
20. What is a transparent user interface?

Exercises

Reading code

In Exercises 1–5, assume that a form named Form1 contains a single text box named Text1, a single label named Label1, and an array of two command buttons named Command1(0) and Command1(1).

What is the effect when each of the following Visual Basic statements is executed?

1. `Label1.Caption = Text1.Text`
2. `Text1.Text = "Now is the time for " & Label1.Caption`
3. `Form1.Visible = False`

The following is the click event procedure for the command button array.

```
Sub Command1_Click (index As Integer)
    Label1.Caption = index
End Sub
```

4. What happens when Command1(0) is clicked?
5. What happens when Command1(1) is clicked?

Writing code

6. Write a Visual Basic statement that will cause a run-time image of Form2 to be printed.
7. Write a statement to change the size of the type in text box Text1 to 12 point.
8. Write a statement to change the size of the type in text box Text2 to the point size the user enters in text box Text1.
9. Write the code for the click event of a button that copies the text in Text1 into Text2 and then disables Text1.
10. Write a Visual Basic statement to change the caption of Label3 to the concatenation, with a single space in between, of the strings that are the current captions of Label1 and Label2.

Exploring Further

11. Start a new Visual Basic project and put a text box on the form. Note the shape of the mouse cursor as it moves across the form. The mouse cursor shape changes to an I beam over the text box, which suggests its text-editing function. What happens to the mouse cursor when the text box is not enabled? Which setting of which form property changes the shape of the mouse cursor to a "permanent" hourglass? Why would it be a poor idea to do this?
12. Start a new Visual Basic project, and resize the form window by dragging on the border. Note the shape of the mouse cursor on the form border. Experiment with the BorderStyle property of a form and explain what the various settings do. Note how the mouse cursor is affected.

13. Experiment or consult on-line Help to determine the effects of each of the following form properties:

    ```
    ControlBox    MaxButton    MinButton    WindowState
    ```

14. Critique the user interface of a familiar product or device as to its ease of use. Decide whether it can be classified as a GUI.

15. Modify your program *namer* from Lab 3.3 to collect the user's middle initial and write the name in one of the two following forms, where M is the middle initial.

    ```
    first M. last     or     last, first M.
    ```

    Read on-line Help on the TabIndex property, and fix your program so that the user can tab in a logical order from one text box to another.

Projects

1. To try out effects for an advertising campaign, the user should be able to enter a company name and then click on different command buttons to see the name displayed in various fonts, sizes, and attributes of bold and italic. Design and write such a program. Provide the user with at least four different display options.

2. Design and write a program in which, as the user enters his or her name letter by letter in one text box, the name is displayed in reverse order in another text box. (Hint: The expression Right$(Text1.Text, 1) represents the rightmost single character currently in the text of Text1.)

3. Your company manufactures personalized fortune cookie messages. You want a program that allows the user to enter three descriptive words or phrases about himself or herself (example: tall, smart, beautiful, male, bungee-jumper, and so on) and, at the click of a button, displays a fortune cookie message that incorporates those three words or phrases in some meaningful way. Design and write this program.

4. Open the file colors.mak. Arrange the following controls on the form in a pleasing way. Set the properties as instructed, although to improve appearance you may wish to change other properties as well.

    Label (Label1) with the caption "Choose a color, then click the Color It! button."

    Array of four option buttons (Option1(0), Option1(1), Option1(2), Option1(3)) with captions Red (index 0), Yellow (index 1), Green (index 2), Blue (index 3). To find the icon in the Toolbox for the option button, consult Figure 3.1.

    Command button (Command1) with the caption "Color It!"

    Label (Label2) with the caption "Enter your first name:".

    Text box (Text1) with the text property set to blank, to hold the name.

Command button (Command2) with the caption "Click here to see your name in lights."

Label (Label3) with a blank caption; this will display the name.

Timer (Timer1) with its Interval property set to 500 and its Enabled property set to False.

(All necessary code for this program is hidden away in the general section of the form; once you have created the user interface according to the above instructions, the code will "magically" go to the correct places and you can run the program.)

5. Your local grocery store is equipping its carts with an electronic screen display to allow shoppers to find items within the store more easily. The opening screen is a display of command buttons with alphabetical ranges, for example: K–N. The shopper who wants to locate items beginning with K through N, for example, clicks on this button, which brings up a screen containing information like

   Ketchup, Aisle 8.

   Design and write this program. To create a new form, either use the File pull-down menu and select New Form or click on the New Form Toolbar button. Create a new form before you write code to show the form. Provide a button on each form to get back to the opening screen.

Data Storage; Input and Output

CHAPTER 4

KEY POINTS

- Devising algorithms is a key part of low-level design.
- The fundamental algorithmic constructs are I/O, data manipulation, assignment, conditional processing, and looping.
- The Print method can be applied to a Picture Box control for output.
- Visual Basic allows you to single-step through a program one line of code at a time.
- A variable's data type dictates how the content of that variable is stored in memory.
- Setting Option Explicit means that all variables must be declared.
- The input box provides an input mechanism alternative to the text box.
- Program documentation is an important and ongoing part of program development.

4.1 Building the pieces

The OTC design representation requires starting with the task that the program as a whole is to solve and breaking it up into smaller tasks (subtasks). This is the essence of **high-level design**, the early part of the design continuum (see Figure 1.9). High-level design concerns division of labor, not the details of program code, or even how the various subtasks will be accomplished. The emphasis is on *what* is to be done, not *how* to do it. (The OTC approach is a bit more detailed than some high-level design representations because subtasks are assigned to appropriate objects or general procedures, but how to do the subtasks is still not stated.)

Eventually one must proceed to **low-level design** and consider each of the subtasks and the necessary steps to accomplish them. This is still part of the program design process. Once these steps have been formulated in detail, they must be translated into Visual Basic code. This is the **program implementation** phase. If the low-level design has been properly done, there should be an almost seamless transition between the final low-level design and program implementation.

As an example of low-level design, Figure 4.1 describes the steps in a simple programming task, a rather trivial problem of adding two numbers. This may be a subtask that is part of a Visual Basic program; if so, it might be assigned to a command button click event. However, forget about Visual Basic for the moment. The instructions shown in Figure 4.1 are not written in Visual Basic or any other programming language, for that matter. They are simply English statements that convey the steps to carry out in order to solve a problem. The idea of each step is clear, although not the details of exactly how it would be done within the computer.

A sequence of well-defined steps to carry out a task is called an **algorithm**. An English-language representation of an algorithm is called **pseudocode** (as opposed to the code of some programming language). Devising an algorithm to perform the subtask at hand is fundamental to low-level design. It is often helpful to design the algorithm "on paper," using a pseudocode representation, and think it through carefully to be sure it does the job.

Figure 4.1
Pseudocode algorithm for adding two numbers

Collect the value for *Number 1*

Collect the value for *Number 2*

Assign to *Sum* the value of the quantity
(*Number 1* + *Number 2*)

Display the resulting value of *Sum*

In the algorithm of Figure 4.1, there are three distinct activities going on. First, some data is collected; second, that data is processed to produce a new result; third, the new result is displayed. This pattern is typical. Computer programming in the most general sense involves collecting data, processing that data in some way that converts it from "raw data" into useful information with respect to the task at hand, and making that resulting information available to the user.

Recall that the computer stores everything—data values and program instructions—using sequences of 0s and 1s. This is called **binary representation** ("binary" because of the two available symbols, 0 and 1). When the program executes, the binary instructions tell the computer how to transform the binary sequences representing data values into new sequences representing results. At the front end, an encoding scheme is used to find the appropriate binary form for each data value to be stored. At the back end, the encoding rules are reversed in order to decode the binary results into a form that humans can understand. Figure 4.2 illustrates the general process.

There must be mechanisms within the program to collect the data values. Perhaps the user is asked to supply data while the program is executing (as in the ***lab1*** program where the user is asked to enter a first name). Another possibility is that the data is supplied by an external data file that exists independently of the program. Similarly there must be mechanisms to display results, either on a computer screen or on hard copy from a printer; the results could also be stored in an external file for later use. The data values supplied to the program are collectively called **input**. The results from the program are called **output**.

Every language has its own ways to handle the tasks of collecting data and displaying results. In other words, each language has its own ways to manage **I/O** (**Input/Output**). Because of its GUI and its event-driven nature, Visual Basic has a much greater variety of I/O mechanisms than more traditional procedural languages. For example, in Visual Basic a text box can collect user input. A label's caption property displays text, and the caption property can be set within program code; therefore this is a mechanism for displaying output.

Program instructions to process data values also vary from one programming language to another. At the least, a language is expected to provide instructions that will perform simple data manipulation tasks like adding two

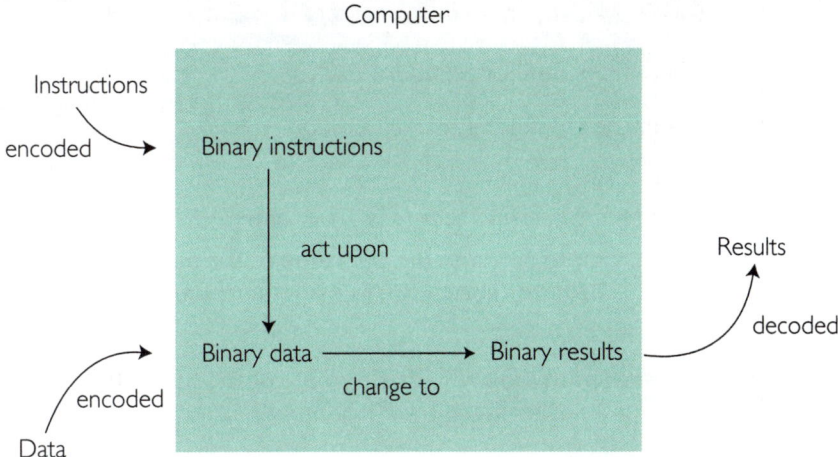

Figure 4.2
What happens when a program executes

numbers together. The resulting sum must be stored somewhere in the computer's memory in order to be displayed later as output. The sum can be thought of as occupying a location in memory; to store the result, a program instruction sets the correct value of the binary sequence at that location. Such an instruction is said to be *assigning* a value to that memory location, so you will need to see what an **assignment statement** looks like in Visual Basic, as well as how to do basic data manipulations (like addition) in Visual Basic.

Figure 4.3 shows the algorithm of Figure 4.1 again, this time with the input, process, and output segments marked. The four steps of the algorithm are to be carried out in turn, beginning with step 1. This is an example of **sequential** processing.

Input   ⎡Collect the value for *Number 1*
        ⎣Collect the value for *Number 2*

Process Assign to *Sum* the value of the quantity *(Number 1 + Number 2)*

Output   Display the resulting value of *Sum*

Figure 4.3
Pseudocode algorithm for adding two numbers showing input, process, output

To do more interesting things, algorithms need the capability for nonsequential processing, which does not proceed step by step from top to bottom. One nonsequential form is **conditional** processing. In conditional processing, some condition is evaluated that is either true or false at the moment; if the condition is true, one thing is done next, and if it is false, another thing is done next. Figure 4.4 shows a pseudocode algorithm the telephone company might use in computing your monthly long-distance bill. In this algorithm, the symbol * stands for multiplication. If it is true that you are a preferred customer (Preferred Customer Status is true), then your monthly bill is computed at 75 percent of the Standard Rate. Otherwise, your monthly bill is computed at the Standard Rate. This is an example of conditional processing.

Figure 4.4 Pseudocode conditional algorithm for computing telephone bill

Input
- Collect the value for *Minutes Used*
- Collect the value for *Standard Rate*
- Collect the value for *Preferred Customer Status*

Process
- If *Preferred Customer Status* is True then
  - Assign to *Monthly Bill* the value of the quantity *Minutes Used* * (0.75) * *Standard Rate*
- otherwise
  - Assign to *Monthly Bill* the value of the quantity *Minutes Used* * *Standard Rate*

Output Display the resulting value of *Monthly Bill*

Another variation on sequential processing is to use a **looping** mechanism, which does some group of instructions, possibly multiple times. Some true-false condition determines how many times the instructions within the loop are executed. Figure 4.5 shows a pseudocode algorithm to compute the total number of sales of some item at a chain of stores. The number of items sold at the first store is the first entry in the total. After that, the repetitive process of "collect a number and add it to the running total" continues as long as there are more stores left to report.

Figure 4.5 Pseudocode looping algorithm to compute total sales

Input Collect the value for *Number Sold* (for first store)

Process Assign to *Total* the value of *Number Sold*

While there are more stores do steps (a) and (b)

Loop
- Input (a) Collect the value for *Number Sold* (for next store)
- Process (b) Assign to *Total* the quantity (previous value of *Total*) + *Number Sold*

Output Display the value of *Total*

Sequential processing, conditional processing, and looping can be mixed and matched in various ways. In the algorithm of Figure 4.5, the two statements within the loop are executed sequentially. They are straightforward statements, but there could be a conditional statement within a loop. Or a loop within a loop. Or a loop as one of the choices within a conditional statement. And so on. In this way, more complex algorithms can be constructed. What is perhaps surprising is that these building blocks of sequential processing, conditional processing, and looping are the only processing patterns required to construct any algorithm, no matter how complex, from programs that process IRS returns to those that guide the Space Shuttle to those that do your word processing.

(In a high-level view of event-driven programming, the idea of looping is illustrated in Figure 2.8, both in the wait loop, which is executed until an event occurs, and in the "looping back" to the wait loop state after event code is executed. You can imagine conditional processing occurring in the user's head, where the decision is made to click this or that command button, for example, and cause this or that event to take place. So these ideas of conditional processing and looping also occur, in a way, at the overall program level as well as at the subtask level.)

When you write computer code, sequential processing is what you get unless you force conditional processing or looping. You will need to learn about Visual Basic statements for conditional processing and looping.

Of course, you've already written several complete Visual Basic programs, and you did that before you were introduced to low-level design, I/O, conditional processing, and so on. The programs you've written, however, have accomplished their tasks by doing only one thing: setting the property of an object. Setting a property is done by a Visual Basic statement of the form

ObjectName.PropertyName = new value of property (a)

as in

```
Label1.Caption="Here's what you entered:" & Text1.Text
```

The problem is, you can't do much with a programming "vocabulary" of the single statement form (a). In fact, (a) itself is a special form of a more general Visual Basic statement.

As hinted above, some time will be devoted to increasing your vocabulary, that is, learning other legitimate Visual Basic statement forms. This will allow you to move from the design of an algorithm to its implementation.

Learning a new programming statement involves learning both the *syntax* and the *semantics* of the statement. **Syntax** refers to what combinations of which symbols are legitimate (recognized by the language). **Semantics** refers to what those combinations of symbols mean. As an example, the string of symbols

fish whale the the wrote

violates the rules of syntax for an English language sentence. The string of symbols

the fish wrote the whale

is a syntactically correct sentence, with adjectives, nouns, and verbs all in acceptable positional relationships within the sentence. The semantics of the sentence are obscure, however; what does it mean? The sentence

the fish ate the whale

is both syntactically correct and semantically clear, if surprising.

Syntax and semantics apply not only to programming statements themselves but to all aspects of the programming language, including smaller pieces from which statements may be built. In a statement of type (a), for example, the left side

ObjectName.PropertyName

is a syntactically correct form, and semantically means a reference to an object's property.

So for the next few chapters the task is to learn the Visual Basic syntax and semantics for:

I/O
Data manipulation
Assignment
Conditional processing
Looping

It's time to move beyond tinkering with the appearance of forms and control objects, and tackle more significant programming!

4.2 Identifiers

Although data items must be stored in binary form at various locations in memory, the Visual Basic programmer does not need to worry about where data are stored. Each item of data can be given a name and referred to by name within the program. Visual Basic takes care of keeping track of the memory address where that item is stored.

In Figures 4.3 to 4.5, names in italics like *Number 1* and *Total* are symbolic names representing quantities that these algorithms deal with. The values of these quantities are not known until the algorithms are used. Such quantities are called **variables**. Visual Basic has rules for naming variables, and they are the same rules as those for naming objects. In fact, the same rules hold for naming procedures. A name is also called an **identifier**. The Visual Basic syntax for an identifier, whether it be an object identifier, a variable identifier, or a procedure identifier, is given by the following rule:

> An identifier is a string of up to 40 characters that begins with a letter; uses letters, digits, and underscore characters; is not a Visual Basic reserved word.

Note that some of the names used in Figures 4.3 to 4.5 include spaces, which are not allowed in Visual Basic identifiers. Hence to translate these pseudocode algorithms into Visual Basic code, it is necessary to change these names to make them legal identifiers. For example, *Number Sold* could be written as *NumberSold* or *Number_Sold*.

Although there are quite a few reserved words that must be avoided in naming variables or other program parts, they are words that you are unlikely to choose. Why would you want to name a variable **Sub** or **End**, for example? Should you inadvertently choose a reserved word as a variable name, Visual Basic will issue a warning message. Variable names should be chosen to be as meaningful as possible in the context of the task at hand. Since you have up to 40 characters, don't hesitate to use *New_Interest_Rate* as a variable identifier rather than *X2*. Identifiers are **case insensitive**, meaning that *New_Interest_Rate* and *new_interest_rate* are considered by Visual Basic to be the same.

Variable names represent memory locations where actual values will be stored when the program executes. It is important to distinguish between the *name* of the variable (which represents the memory address) and the *value* of the variable (which is the content stored at that address). Figure 4.6 illustrates; of course, the value 347 would actually be stored in binary form.

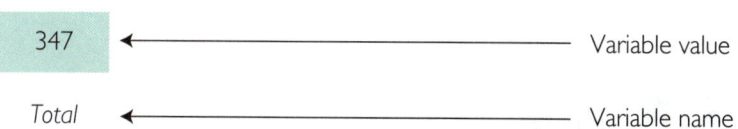

Figure 4.6
The difference between a variable's name and its value

4.3 Assignment statement

The **assignment statement** gives a value to a quantity. In Visual Basic the assignment statement has a very simple syntax:

destination = expression

where "destination" is either

VariableName

or

ObjectName.PropertyName

The semantics of this statement is that the expression on the right side of the equal sign is evaluated, and its value is then assigned to the variable or the property on the left. Statements such as:

```
yourname = Text1.Text
Total = 347
overtime_rate = 1.5*Rate
Label1.Caption = "Sales for Last Quarter"
Label1.Caption = Label2.Caption
```

all have the proper form. The first statement is the body of the *getname* procedure from **lab1.** The next statement assigns the value 347 to the variable with the name *Total*. This statement produces the condition shown in Figure 4.6. In the third statement, the expression on the right side is more complex; the current value of the variable *Rate* is multiplied by 1.5 and the resulting value is stored in *overtime_rate*. Statements 4 and 5 assign values to the Caption property of the Label1 object. In statement 4, the fixed string of characters shown within the quote marks is assigned; in statement 5, whatever text string is the current value of the Label2 caption becomes the Label1 caption.

The meaning of an assignment statement such as

```
Total = 347
```

is reinforced if it is read as "Total gets 347" (meaning Total is getting the new value 347) rather than "Total equals 347." This emphasizes that the equal sign means assignment, not equality. For example, the statement

```
X = X + 1
```

is nonsense if thought of as an equation, but it is a perfectly good assignment statement, assigning to the variable X a value 1 greater than its current value.

Now you know why statements to set a property value are a special form of a more general statement. They are forms of the assignment statement.

4.4 Print method

The **Print method** can be applied to several types of objects. As the name suggests, applying the Print method to an object causes something to be printed on or in the object. The **Picture Box** control is one of the objects to which the Print method applies. The picture box, for which the Toolbox icon is shown here, appears on a form as a rectangular area. This area can be used to display printed output.

As an example, the statement

```
Picture1.Print "This is a message"
```

will print the string of characters within quotes in the picture box Picture1. The statement

```
Picture1.Print Total
```

will print the current value of the variable *Total* in the picture box. These are examples of the more general syntax

```
Picture1.Print expression list
```

which will print in the picture box the current values of the expressions in the list.

As a way to display output, applying the Print method to a picture box is an alternative to writing the output in a label caption. The advantage to the Print method approach is that output can be formatted in various ways. As one illustration, the two statements

```
Picture1.Print "First line"
Picture1.Print "Second line"
```

produce two lines of output in the picture box Picture1. The two statements

```
Label1.Caption = "First line"
Label1.Caption = "Second line"
```

result in only "Second line" appearing in the label caption because the second statement resets the caption. While it can be done, it is cumbersome to force two lines of output in a label caption.

Name: _____ Date Due: _____

LEARNING OBJECTIVES

- Working with the assignment statement
- Exploring conditional and loop statements
- Using the single-stepping feature of Visual Basic

LAB 4.1

1. ____ Open the project *prac.mak.* The large rectangular area on the form is a picture box.

   ____ Go into run mode and click the Practice Assignment button. What values are printed in the picture box?

   ____ Go back to design mode and look at the Click event code for this button. Explain how each of the printed values was obtained.

2. ____ Add two statements at the end of this procedure that will cause the sum of the current values of *a* and *b* to be printed in the picture box. What do you expect will be printed?

   Working with the assignment statement

   ____ Run your program, using the Practice Assignment button. Did you get the result you expected?

   ____ Delete the two statements you just added.

   ____ Write a single statement that will have the same effect. What is that statement? (Try it to be sure it works.)

3. ____ Look at the Click event code for the "Try out conditional" button and decide what you expect will happen when this code executes.

____ Run the program, clicking this button. What happens?

Exploring the conditional statement

____ Change the assignment statement within the code to set the value of *a* to 2.

____ Rerun the program. What happens now? Why?

Using single stepping

4. ____ The Visual Basic environment provides a number of aids for debugging code. Among them is the ability to have your program execute line by line (statement by statement) so you can see exactly what is happening when. This process is called **single stepping**.

In order to activate the single-stepping feature:

____ Go into run mode but don't click any of the three command buttons on the form.

____ From run mode, go into break mode by doing any of the following:

OPTIONS
- Choose Break from the Run menu.
- Press Ctrl-Break (hold down the Ctrl key and press the Break key).
- Click the Break button on the Toolbar, which is [ ] .

Note that the title bar of the main Visual Basic window now reflects that you are in break mode. Also, the Debug window (which opens every time a program is executed but is usually covered by the form window) has been made the active window and has moved to the foreground. For now, just ignore the Debug window.

____ Click on the Form window to make it the active window.

5. ____ To activate single stepping, do one of the following:

OPTIONS
- Choose Single Step from the Debug menu.
- Press the hot key F8.
- Click the Single Step button on the Toolbar (the one with a single footprint)

Single stepping through code

6. ____ Click the "Try out conditional" button. You now see the Code window displaying the Click event code for this button. The statement that is about to be executed is highlighted. What is this statement?

____ Press F8 or click the Single Step button again. This executes one statement and advances the highlighting to the next statement to be executed, which is the conditional statement.

____ Do another single step. What program statement HAS BEEN SKIPPED and why?

____ If necessary, move the Code window aside so that you can see the picture box on the form. Watch the picture box as you do the next single step. What happens?

____ Do two more single steps; what are the last two statements executed in this procedure?

From break mode, it is possible to go back to either run mode or design mode by clicking the appropriate Toolbar button or making the right menu choice.

____ Go back to design mode.

7. ____ Examine the code for the "Try out looping" button and decide what you expect will happen when this code executes.

Trying out the loop statement

____ Run the program, clicking this button. What happens?

8. ____ Go into break mode and single-step your way through the Click procedure for the looping button. Keep track of the value of the variable *a* as you go along; notice that its value gets changed by an assignment statement within the loop. How many times does the code within the loop get executed?

9. ____ Go back to design mode.

   ____ Change the assignment statement at the beginning of the looping button Click code so that *a* gets set to the value 5.

   ____ Run the program, using the "Try out looping" button. What happens and why?

10. ____ Go back to design mode.

    ____ Change the assignment statement at the beginning of the looping code so that *a* gets set to the value 6.

    ____ Run the program; what happens and why?

    ____ Single-step through this procedure now. Notice how the statements within the loop are not executed at all.

11. ____ Go back to design mode.

    ____ Change the assignment statement at the beginning of the looping code so that *a* again gets set to the value 2.

    ____ Change the statement

    a = a + 1

    within the loop to a comment.

    ____ Run the program again, clicking the looping button. What happens and why?

You have just fallen victim to an **infinite loop**. Obviously infinite loops are something to try to avoid as you are writing code. Here you effectively removed the assignment statement that changed the value of a. Before the loop statement, a has the value 2, so the condition $a \leq 5$ is true and the statement within the loop is executed. Because of your modification, the value of a is never changed within the loop, so the condition $a \leq 5$ remains true forever, and the statement within the loop is executed forever (or at least until Visual Basic recognizes an error condition, displays an error message, and halts your program execution).

12. ____ Exit this program; you do not need to save changes.

> **QuickCheck 4.1**
> 1. Why is Section 4.1 called "Building the pieces"?
> 2. What is pseudocode?
> 3. What do a programming language's I/O mechanisms accomplish?
> 4. *destination = expression*
>   is the syntax for the _____ statement.
> 5. Explain how an infinite loop can occur.

4.5 Declarations

Part of the program design process involves determining what quantities the program needs to deal with. In other words, what are the variables your program will need to use to store values? We noted that it is important to give a variable a meaningful identifier, but even before that, you have to know that you need this variable at all.

Within a Visual Basic program, a variable *Temperature* can be introduced (the technical term is *declared*) by the following statement form:

```
Dim Temperature As Integer
```

Dim is a reserved word indicating that this is a declaration statement. *Temperature* is the variable identifier. **As Integer** says that the type of data to be stored in this variable is integer data (numbers of the form –17, 283, and so on, as opposed to numbers with a decimal point like 45.72 or character strings like "Washington").

The Dim statement in general has the form

```
Dim VariableName As data type
```

Declaring a variable by using the Dim statement accomplishes three things:

1. It acknowledges that your program will need to store some quantity, the purpose of which should be reflected in the variable identifier chosen.
2. It describes the type of data to be stored.
3. It requests Visual Basic to set aside one or more memory locations to store this data and allow the program henceforth to refer to those locations by the variable identifier.

Visual Basic supports the data types shown in Table 4.1. These basically fall into two categories, data types to store numbers (Integer, Long, Single, Double, Currency) and data types to store strings of characters (String * n and String), plus one oddball data type (Variant).

Table 4.1
Visual Basic data types

TYPE NAME	DESCRIPTION	COMMENTS
Integer	Nondecimal value between −32,768 and 32,767	For storing "small" integers. Values are stored exactly.
Long	Nondecimal values between −2,147,483,648 and 2,147,483,647	For storing "big" integers. Values are stored exactly.
Single	Decimal values between (approximately) −3.4E38 and 3.4E38	E means exponent of 10, so $24E3 = 24 * 10^3 = 24{,}000$ For storing decimal numbers. Values are stored approximately.
Double	Decimal values between (approximately) −1.8E308 and 1.8E308	For storing huge decimal numbers. Values are stored approximately.
Currency	15 digits to the left of decimal point, 4 digits to right	Values are stored exactly.
String * n	Strings of characters of fixed length n	Example: "Nathan" is a string of 6 characters.
String	Strings of characters of varying length up to (approximately) 65,500 characters	Example: "Nathan is a good student" is a string of 24 characters (spaces count).
Variant	A "chameleon" data type that stores whatever you want to put there	Maximum flexibility but potentially confusing. See discussion below.

Why are there so many different data types? Because numbers without decimal points, numbers with decimal points, and strings of characters are all differently encoded into binary form for storage in memory. Visual Basic has to know the type of data to be stored in a particular memory location to know how to do the encoding and decoding.

How do you decide which data type to use in a declaration? You are declaring a variable, which means that you want to store some quantity. First decide whether that quantity is a number or a string of characters. A quantity that consists entirely of letters of the alphabet (like a customer's name) is certainly a string of characters. However, a quantity that contains digits can be treated as a string of characters if no computations will be done with the digits (as in a telephone number or a Social Security number). A string quantity whose length can vary should be declared as type String, as in

```
Dim CustomerName As String
```

A string quantity whose length is a known fixed value should be declared as type String * n, where n is the length of the string. A declaration for a variable to hold Social Security numbers, for example, could be

```
Dim SocialSecurity As String * 9
```

because all Social Security numbers are 9 digits long.

If your quantity is numeric rather than string, then decide whether it contains a decimal point or not. For example, the number of a certain item in stock at your local bike store will be a whole number (no decimal point), so a variable to contain this data could be declared by

```
Dim NumberInStock As Integer
```

Attempting to store a value outside the range of –32,768 to 32,767 in a variable of type Integer results in an **overflow error**. To store a large integer use type Long. For example, a variable to represent the number of registered voters in a city could be declared by

```
Dim NumberOfVoters As Long
```

Your county property tax rate is probably a decimal number, so a variable to contain this data could have the declaration

```
Dim TaxRate As Single
```

To store a very large decimal number, use type Double, as in

```
Dim LightYearsDistance As Double
```

An integer quantity like 3 can be written with a decimal point as 3.0; integers can therefore be stored in variables of type Single or type Double. But more memory space is required to store these data types, and more time to do computations with them. Think of the four data types

> Integer
> Long
> Single
> Double

as increasing in the requirements they make upon the computer, and pick the "lowest level" of data type that can accommodate your expected range of data values. You want a data type that is "not too big, not too small, but just right."

It is customary to group all variable declarations at the beginning of a procedure. Multiple declarations can be put in the same Dim statement, so it is legitimate to write

```
Dim Value1 As Integer, Value2 As Integer
Dim PayRate As Single, Title As String
```

Of the two remaining data types in Table 4.1, Currency will be discussed briefly in the next chapter, and Variant should not be used. Here's why. The Variant data type accommodates itself to whatever value is assigned to it. Suppose that X is declared as a variable of type Variant. If you write a statement to assign an integer value to X, then X stores that value as an integer, using the smaller integer type (Integer as opposed to Long) if possible. If you write a statement to assign a decimal value to X, then X stores that value using the smaller decimal type (Single as opposed to Double) for that value if possible. If you write a statement to assign a string value to X, then X stores that value as a string. This certainly relieves the programmer of the responsibility of thinking ahead of time about what kind of data X will represent. And this is exactly where the potential for confusion lies. During the course of a single Visual Basic procedure, the following three assignment statements could occur:

```
X = 3
    .
    .
    .
X = 13.7
    .
    .
    .
X = "Your stock portfolio has decreased by 4.9%"
```

Exactly what is the role that X is playing in this procedure? Because of the ability to "abuse" Variant type variables in this way, you should avoid them.

Visual Basic provides several other ways to declare variables besides the Dim statement (see Appendix G). These are more obscure than the Dim statement in that the reader of the resulting code has to be more knowledgeable to determine what type has been chosen. In fact, Visual Basic doesn't require you to declare variables at all! Suppose that in the middle of a procedure, you suddenly decide to use a variable called *Speed* and assign it the value 24.8. *Speed* was not declared as a variable, but when Visual Basic gets to the statement

```
Speed = 24.8
```

it recognizes that you need a new variable, conjures up a variable of type Variant named *Speed*, and stores 24.8 in that variable as type Single, the simplest type to accommodate the number you have assigned. The variable *Speed* now has all the potential for confusing use that any type Variant variable has.

Worse, the ability to create new variables "on the fly" allows the following situation to take place. You have a type Integer variable named *Quantity* and type Single variables named *Price* and *TotalCost*. Your intention is to compute the value of *TotalCost* by using the following assignment statement (remember that * stands for multiplication):

```
TotalCost = Quantity * Price
```

If the current value of *Quantity* is 25 and the current value of *Price* is 9.95, then *TotalCost* should receive the value 25 * 9.95 = 248.75. However, you make a typing error and instead write the statement

```
TotalCost = Qantity * Price
```

Visual Basic sees *Qantity*, which has not been declared as a variable, thinks you want a new variable, and helpfully creates one for you. Because you are using this supposed new variable in the context of a numeric computation, Visual Basic initializes the value of *Qantity* to 0. The expression on the right side of the assignment statement therefore has the value 0 * 9.95, which results in a value of 0 being assigned to *TotalCost*. If *TotalCost* is immediately displayed as output, this erroneous value may be obvious, but if *TotalCost* is used in further computations, the error can spread to contaminate other values your program is trying to compute. In other words, your program produces garbage results!

There is a way to make Visual Basic require that all variables be declared before use. In any project, go to the declarations part of the general section of the form and type "Option Explicit". This means that all variables must be explicitly declared. A better alternative is to pull down the Visual Basic Options menu, choose Environment, and make sure that the setting for

Require Variable Declaration

is "Yes," as shown in Figure 4.7. This will automatically insert Option Explicit in all future projects, although it has no effect on a project created before the switch was set.

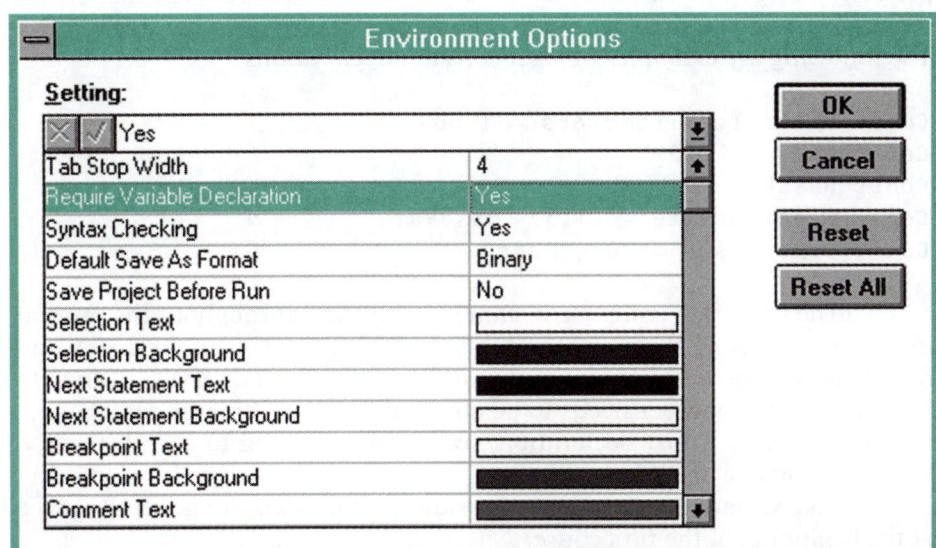

Figure 4.7
Setting the Visual Basic environment to require variable declarations

Under Option Explicit, attempted execution of the statement

```
TotalCost = Qantity * Price
```

dumps you into design mode looking at the Code window where the statement occurs. The offending identifier *Qantity* is highlighted and an error message says "Variable not defined".

Always operate in Visual Basic with the Require Variable Declaration switch set to "yes." Being forced to declare all variables in your program accomplishes two things:

1. It protects you from typographical error consequences like the one described.
2. It requires you to think through the quantities and their data types that your program will use; this sort of advance planning reduces errors and makes your program development go more smoothly.

Of course, if you later find that you need another variable, you simply add its declaration statement.

4.6 Constants

Variables are quantities whose values are unknown ahead of program execution or whose values can change during execution. Other quantities are fixed values that you do not want the program to be able to change. For example, you may write a program in which miles are converted to kilometers. The conversion factor is a constant value (1.609) that your program needs to use but should not change. You can declare such values as **constants**.

Identifiers for constants follow the usual rule. The form of the declaration statement is:

`Const` *ConstantName* = *expression*

The expression can be a numeric constant (1.609), an arithmetic expression using numeric constants or previously declared constants, or a string constant expressed within quotation marks, also called a **literal string**. The following are examples of legal constant declarations:

```
Const Miles_To_Kilometers = 1.609
Const Pi = 3.14159
Const BaseRate = 8.40
Const OvertimeRate = (1.5) * BaseRate
Const Supervisor = "Big Boss"
```

The benefit of using a constant like *BaseRate* throughout the program instead of just using the number 8.40 is twofold. First, because of a meaningful identifier, the code is easier to understand. Second, if the value that *BaseRate* represents ever needs to be changed, the programmer can change it in one place (the Const declaration), rather than having to search the code for every instance of 8.40.

Like variable declarations, constant declarations are generally placed at the beginning of the procedure.

4.7 *Val* and *Str$* functions

Suppose someone asks you to write your street address, which you give as

23 W. Main Street

The "23" here is being used as a character string, not a number. No one is going to add this 23 to some other number or multiply it by some other number. However, if your boss asks you how many hours you worked last week in order to compute your wages, and you respond

23

the 23 here is being used as a number. It will be multiplied by your pay rate to compute your total pay.

The *string* "23" is not the same as the *number* 23. (Remember that character strings and numbers are stored differently in computer memory.) This is an important distinction. A numeric expression cannot be assigned to a variable of string data type. A string expression cannot be assigned to a variable of numeric data type.

Visual Basic does, however, provide a way to take the *string* "23" and turn it into the *number* 23, and also a way to do the reverse. These type transformations are done by using functions.

A **function** in Visual Basic is code that can be **invoked** (caused to be executed) within a procedure. The function code does some computation or performs some action and, when completed, returns one value to the procedure that invoked it. That value is contained in the function name. In other words, the function name is like a variable in that it can have a value; the value of the function is set by executing the function code. A function invocation consists of the name of the function, together with any other pieces of information, called **arguments,** that the function needs to know in order to do its job.

A Visual Basic programmer can write functions of his or her own within a program, but Visual Basic also provides a number of useful built-in functions. The code for such functions is supplied by Visual Basic and is never seen within the program that uses the function. The two functions needed to convert from string to number and vice versa are the *Val* function and the *Str$* function.

The *Val* function takes a single argument that is a string representation of a number and returns the value of that string as a number. Thus

```
Val("23")
```

is an invocation of the *Val* function where the argument is the literal string "23" and the value returned is the *number* 23. A function invocation, like a variable name, is always part of a Visual Basic statement. It is a syntax error to simply write the function on a line by itself, as it is written here. This is like having a variable name sitting on a line by itself; neither is a legitimate Visual Basic statement.

The following two statements, however, are legal Visual Basic code:

```
Dim Quantity As Integer
Quantity = Val("23")
```

In the second statement, the *Val* function is used as the right side of an assignment statement. The result of the *Val* function acting on the string "23" is the number 23, and that number is then assigned to a variable of numeric data type. Numerical computations could also be done on this number, so that the statements

```
Dim Quantity2 As Integer
Quantity2 = Val("23") * 2
```

are legal and would assign the integer 46 to *Quantity2*.

The *Val* function actually extracts a number from the first part of a string. For example,

```
Val("23 W. Main Street")
```

returns the integer value 23. *Val* proceeds from left to right in the string and stops at the first character that cannot be part of a numeric representation; the rest of the string is ignored. Blanks are disregarded. If a string begins with a character that is not part of a numeric representation, *Val* returns the value 0. Further examples of the *Val* function are:

FUNCTION	VALUE RETURNED
`Val("-24.63 Fahrenheit")`	–24.63
`Val("2 7 9")`	279 (blanks are ignored)
`Val("4,572")`	4 (commas are not a legitimate part of a numeric representation)
`Val("Test_Score")`	0 (first character is T)
`Val(Test_Score)`	93 if Test_Score is a string variable whose value is the string "93"

The *Str$* function takes a single argument that is a numeric expression and returns a string. The value of

`Str$(23)`

is the string " 23". (Note that there is one extra space in front of the string for the sign of the number. For a plus sign, this is left blank; that is, the plus sign is implied. *Str$*(–23) would result in the string "–23".) This expression could be assigned to a variable of string type.

The two functions *Val* and *Str$* act as a two-way street connecting the world of string data and numeric data (Figure 4.8).

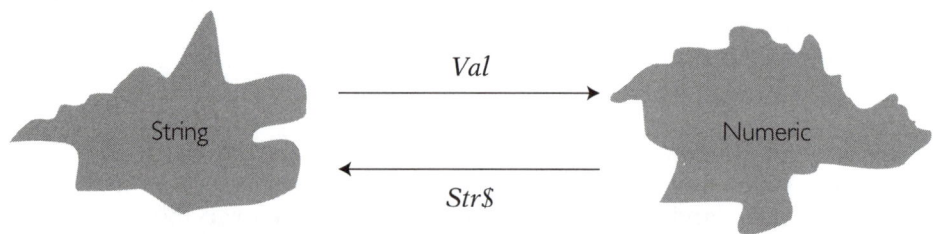

Figure 4.8
The *Val* and *Str$* functions perform conversions

These conversions are necessary more often than one might think because the value obtained from the Text property of a text box is strictly a string. So is the value of the Caption property of a label.[1] Suppose, for example, that some data is to be obtained from a text box; it will be string data. It is to be processed in some way, and the result written out, as string data, in a label (or another text box). If the original string data needs only string manipulations, that is, if strings are only going to be rearranged, concatenated, or displayed somewhere else, then there is no need for conversion, and the bottom path in Figure 4.9 can be used. However, if the original string data represent numeric values on which numeric computations must be done, then the data must be converted to numeric form, the computations done, and the results converted back to string form for output display (the left, top, and right paths in Figure 4.9).

---

[1] The Text property and the Caption property in fact contain values of type Variant, but it is cleaner to treat them as string type and insist on using the Val and Str$ functions.

4.7 VAL AND STR$ FUNCTIONS • 127

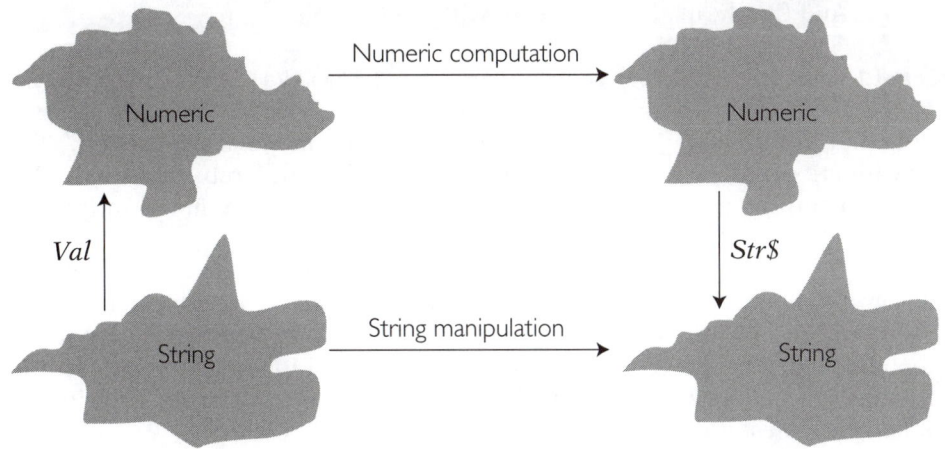

Figure 4.9
Data manipulation paths for string input and output

Here's a rather lengthy example using a text box and a label together with four intermediate variables, which illustrate the four "corners" in Figure 4.9.

```
Dim Original_String As String
Dim Final_String As String
Dim Number_Entered As Integer
Dim Twice_The_Number As Integer

'Collect the input and convert numerical string to a number
Original_String = Text1.Text
Number_Entered = Val(Original_String)

'That number is doubled
Twice_The_Number = Number_Entered * 2

'Result converted back to a string
Final_String = Str$(Twice_The_Number)

'Write the output
Label1.Caption = "Twice your value is " & Final_String
```

An alternative is to use only two intermediate variables:

```
Dim Number_Entered As Integer
Dim Twice_The_Number As Integer

'Collect input in numerical form
Number_Entered = Val(Text1.Text)

'Double the number
Twice_The_Number = Number_Entered * 2

'Write the output as a string
Label1.Caption = "Twice your value is " & Str$(Twice_The_Number)
```

And finally, in a concise form with no variables:

```
Label1.Caption = "Twice your value is " & Str$(Val(Text1.Text)*2)
```

Note that in this single assignment statement, the functions are "nested." The *Str$* function has as its single argument twice the value returned by the *Val* function acting on *its* single argument, which is the value entered in the text box.

Don't imagine from this little example that if you are sufficiently clever, you'll never need to use any variables! This is decidedly not true. Furthermore, minimizing the number of variables in your code is not the goal; instead, you should be trying to write code that is correct, of course, but also easy to understand. Perhaps the middle example presented, with its use of two variables, is easiest to understand.

4.8 Implementing an algorithm

The task at hand is to obtain two decimal numbers from the user, add them, and display the sum. As a high-level design, you decide to use two text boxes to collect the user data and a label to display the results. The computations will be done by a command button. The OTC design in Figure 4.10 also incorporates the necessary user prompts. Figure 4.11 shows a possible form layout that follows this design.

Figure 4.10 OTC design for addition task

ADDER FORM			
Active Objects	**Object Type**	**Event**	**Task**
cmdAdd	command button	Click	Adds the numbers entered in two text boxes, displays result in lblAnswer.
Passive Objects			
Label1	label		General instructions to user.
Label2	label		Prompt for first number.
txtNumber1	text box		Place for user to enter first number.
Label3	label		Prompt for second number.
txtNumber2	text box		Place for user to enter second number.
lblAnswer	label		Displays the sum of the two numbers.

The command button is to add the two numbers and display the result. Figure 4.1 at the beginning of this chapter contains a pseudocode algorithm for doing just this task. Figure 4.12 shows the pseudocode again, together with the corresponding Visual Basic code for the command button,

4.8 IMPLEMENTING AN ALGORITHM • 129

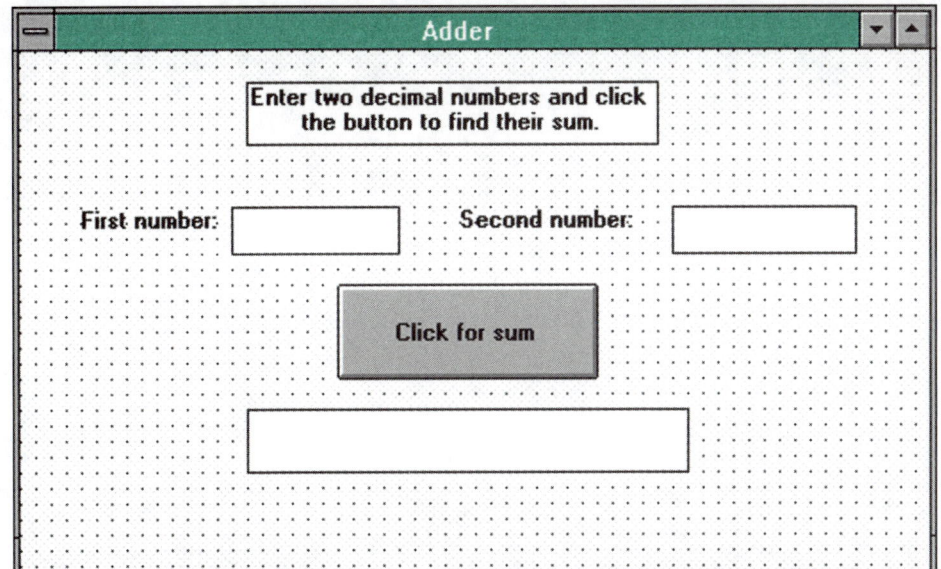

Figure 4.11
Form layout for the adder program

which implements this algorithm. Three numeric variables are needed to store the two numbers and the sum; these are declared as type Single because they are decimal numbers. The symbols ↪ and ↵ denote the continuation of a long statement that in Visual Basic code must be written in one line.

Although this is a very simple application, it has now gone through a high-level design (OTC), a low-level design (pseudocode algorithm), and an implementation (Visual Basic code). More complex high-level designs, with more than one active object, require multiple algorithm designs and implementations.

Figure 4.12
Implementing the addition algorithm

```
Sub cmdAdd_Click ()
'Collects two decimal
'numbers, computes and
'displays their sum

Dim Number1 As Single
Dim Number2 As Single
Dim Sum As Single
```

Algorithm	Implementation
Collect the value for *Number 1*	`Number1 = Val(txtNumber1)`
Collect the value for *Number 2*	`Number2 = Val(txtNumber2)`
Assign to Sum the value of the quantity (*Number 1 + Number 2*)	`Sum = Number1 + Number2`

Display the resulting value of *Sum*	`lblAnswer.Caption = "The ↵`
	`↪ sum is " & Str$(Sum) ↵`
	`End Sub`

(a) Algorithm (b) Implementation

Name: _____   Date Due: _____

LAB 4.2

LEARNING OBJECTIVES

- Developing a low-level design
- Coding a simple computation

1. ____ Run the **adder.mak** program to see that it behaves as anticipated. Examine the form and the code for the command button, and compare with Figures 4.11 and 4.12.

2. ____ Open a new Visual Basic project.

   ____ Save the files as **birth.frm** and **birth.mak**.

   ____ Put "Greeting Card" in the form's title bar.

   ____ Color the form background.

3. ____ The idea of this program is for the user to enter his or her name and year of birth (not his or her age). Clicking on a command button (with the caption "Happy Birthday") will cause the message

   > Happy Birthday, xxx
   > Your age this year is yyy

   to be printed in a picture box on the form, where xxx is the user's name and yyy is the user's age in years this year. The click event procedure for this button contains all the code for the project.

   ____ Complete the high-level design for this program using the OTC "card" here. The command button is the only active object.

BIRTH FORM			
Active Objects	**Object Type**	**Event**	**Task**
cmdBirthday	command button	Click	Compose and print message.
Passive Objects			

____ Put the necessary controls on your form.

____ Set the Tab Index property of the two text boxes to 0 (user's name) and 1 (user's year of birth).

Developing a low-level design

4. ____ The phrase "Compose and print message" used in the high-level design simply says that the command button is to carry out the main job of the program, but gives no details on how that is to be done. The low-level design worries about such details. An algorithm must be devised for the task assigned to the command button. A pseudocode outline of the algorithm follows the input-process-output pattern.

____ Fill in the blanks to complete this algorithm:

Collect _____

Collect _____

Compute _____

Print output in the picture box.

5. ____ This pseudocode leaves some questions that need to be addressed before the Visual Basic code can be written. Exactly how is the user's age computed? What variables should the procedure use to store the quantities relevant to the task?

Although the data and results the procedure must manage are determined by the task, the number of variables needed depends on how wordy or concise you wish to be in writing your code (just as the last example in Section 4.7 could be written using four, two, or no variables). For this task, it is a reasonable option to use three variables.

____ Think about the task at hand in terms of three variables, and then fill in the following table:

NUMBER	VARIABLE IDENTIFIER	WHAT IT REPRESENTS	DATA TYPE
1			
2			
3			

In your Visual Basic project (specifically, in the command button's click event procedure):

___ Declare the current year as a constant.

___ Declare the three variables. Include a comment for each variable telling what it represents.

___ Write the code to collect the input.

6. ___ Write below (in English) what must be done to compute the user's age this year, and thus fill in more details of the algorithm:

Coding a simple computation

___ Now add the appropriate statement to your code.

7. ___ Printing the output in the picture box can be done by applying the Print method. The Print method prints anything, regardless of its data type, so you don't have to worry about converting numbers to strings.

___ Add the necessary statements to finish the project (use two Print method statements to get the two lines of output).

___ Add comments to explain what your code does.

___ Run your program to be sure it works properly.

___ Save your work

8. ___ Look in the Visual Basic Help system for the function *Ucase$*, and explain what it does.

9. ___ Modify your program so that the message that is printed on the form gives the user's name in capital letters, regardless of how it was typed in the text box.

10. (Extra credit)

   ____ Add an Image control to your form. The icon is 🖼 .

   ____ Set its Visible property to False.

   ____ Use the Paintbrush program (found in the Windows Accessories group) to make a small picture of a lighted candle.

   ____ In Paintbrush, use the cutout tool to select the item, and Copy it (Edit menu) to the Clipboard.

   ____ In Visual Basic, select the Image control and highlight its Picture property in the Properties window.

   ____ Paste (Edit menu) the picture from the Clipboard into the Image control.

   ____ Add code to your command button to display the image control when the button is clicked.

11. ____ Run your program to be sure it works properly.

   ____ Save it.

> **QuickCheck 4.2**
>
> 1. The Visual Basic reserved word Dim is used with what kind of statement?
> 2. The difference between a variable of type Integer and one of type Long is _____.
> 3. Where are variable declarations for a procedure usually found?
> 4. A string constant must always be written within _____.
> 5. What is the result of
>   Val("76 trombones")

4.9 Input box

The options at this point for collecting input data and displaying output are:

> For collecting input, enter text in a text box.
>
> For displaying output, write in the caption of a label (or the text of a text box) or use the Print method to print to a picture box.

Another Visual Basic input mechanism is the **input box**. An input box is a form of dialog box. This means that it can pop up as a window in the middle of an executing program with a request for user input. Figure 4.13 shows a typical input box.

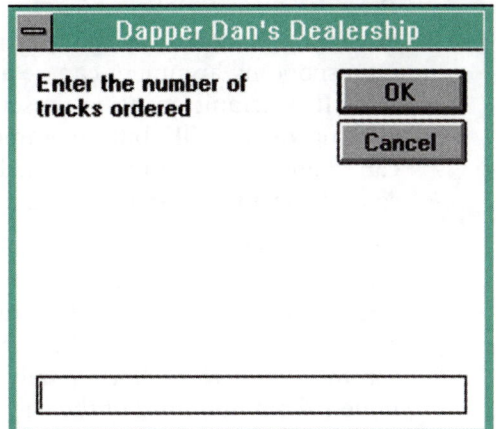

Figure 4.13
An input box

Notice that the input box comes equipped with the windows fundamentals of a title bar and a control-menu box. It also contains some message that prompts the user for input, a text box at the bottom to accept text input from the user (Figure 4.13 shows the insertion bar already positioned here for the user to begin typing), and OK and Cancel buttons.

The purpose of the input box is to capture as a string quantity the text the user enters, which is restricted to a single line. Clicking on the OK button or pressing the Enter key captures whatever text is currently in the text box; clicking the Cancel button (or pressing the Esc key) captures an "empty string" (no characters). The input box thus takes over the job previously done by using a label (for the prompt) and a text box (for the input), all in a self-contained little window.

How do you get an input box into a program? Use another Visual Basic built-in function named *InputBox$*. This handy function, when invoked, causes an input box to pop up and collects the text string that the user enters in the text box. This string is the one value that the function *InputBox$* returns; after this function has executed, the "variable" that is the function name *InputBox$* has the value that is the string of characters the user typed. This value can be assigned to a regular string variable that has been declared within the program.

The *InputBox$* function can have up to five arguments. The syntax for the *InputBox$* function is:

`InputBox$` *(prompt, title, default, left, top)*

where the words in parentheses will be replaced by function arguments when the function is invoked. They have the following interpretation:

> *Prompt:* Specifies the message that appears in the input box to prompt the user for what to enter. The corresponding argument can be a literal string (up to 255 characters allowed) or the name of a string variable whose content is the prompt message. This is the only required argument.
>
> *Title (optional):* Specifies the string that appears in the title bar of the input box. The corresponding argument can be a literal string or a string variable. If it is omitted, the title bar of the input box is blank.
>
> *Default (optional):* Specifies the string that appears in the text box if you want to give the user a suggested input string. The corresponding argument can be a literal string or a string variable. If a default string is present, the user can accept it by clicking on the OK button immediately; otherwise, the user can change it by typing over it. If a default string is not present, the text box is initially blank, as in Figure 4.13.
>
> *Left, top (optional):* The distance in twips from the left and top of the screen, respectively, where the input box appears. The left and top arguments must either both be present or both be absent. If absent, the position of the input box is chosen by default to be horizontally centered and vertically positioned about one-third of the way down the screen.

Consider the following section of code, which might be part of a command button click procedure:

```
Dim TruckOrders As String
Dim Banner As String
Banner = "Dapper Dan's Dealership"
TruckOrders = InputBox$("Enter the number of trucks
    ordered", Banner)
```

The input box shown in Figure 4.13 appears when the last statement above is executed. In this invocation of the *InputBox$* function, the prompt is specified by a literal string, the title is specified by a string variable, and the three remaining arguments are omitted.

If an optional argument is skipped, the appropriate number of commas must appear. Thus

```
TruckOrders = InputBox$("Enter the number of trucks ↵
↳ ordered",,"25")
```

brings up an input box with the same prompt, nothing in the title bar, and a suggested value of 25 already in the text box, which the user can accept or change (Figure 4.14).

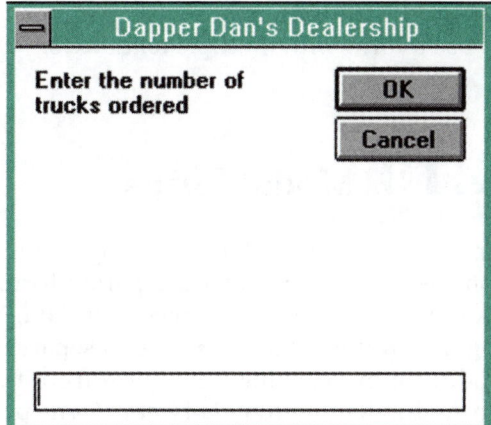

Figure 4.14
Input box with default value supplied

In either case, when the user clicks OK or presses the Enter key, the value of the string currently in the text box is assigned to the string variable *TruckOrders*, and this variable can then be used in the rest of the program. Because the function returns a string value, the variable on the left of the assignment statement must be a string type variable. This variable can subsequently be included as part of a string output, as in

```
Label1.Caption = "The number of trucks ordered is " & ↵
↳ TruckOrders
```

which would produce (assuming 25 is the value entered in the text box)

The number of trucks ordered is 25

But as a string variable, no arithmetic can be done on *TruckOrders*. For example, if the number of trucks ordered is supposed to be added to the number of cars ordered, then code such as

```
Dim NumberTrucks As Integer
NumberTrucks = Val(InputBox$("Enter the number of trucks ↵
↳ ordered",,"25"))
```

is needed. The situation with an input box thus parallels that with the ordinary text box, in which the data captured is string data, and if it is needed as numerical data, the services of the *Val* function must be used.

Although the left and top arguments of the *InputBox$* function can control the positioning of the input box on the screen, there is no way to control the size or proportions of the input box. These are set by Visual Basic. Another point of interest is that an input box is a **modal window**. This means that the user cannot make any other Visual Basic window active while the input box is open. This forces the user to have to deal with the input box and not to be able to ignore it or work around it.

You now have two input mechanisms, the input box and the text box. Which should be used when? The determining factor is probably the amount of data to be requested from the user. Recall that the input box pops up on the form, and no other window can become active while the input box is open. This is fine for one or two items of data, in which case you want to get the user's attention and make sure he or she provides this piece of data before going on. However, if there is a lot of data to be supplied, the user will grow annoyed with these continuing pop-ups and demands. It's better in that case to use a form with multiple text boxes.

4.10 Modal forms

Another alternative for collecting input from the user is to design a customized input box using a separate form. Suppose, for example, you would like the user to enter two pieces of data. You want the effect of a pop-up dialog box. Rather than pop up two separate input boxes, you can create a second form by selecting New Form from the File menu or clicking on the New Form Toolbar button. This new form pops up by having the Show method applied to it. On the form, you can use two separate prompts and two separate text boxes for collecting input data. Figure 4.15 shows such a form.

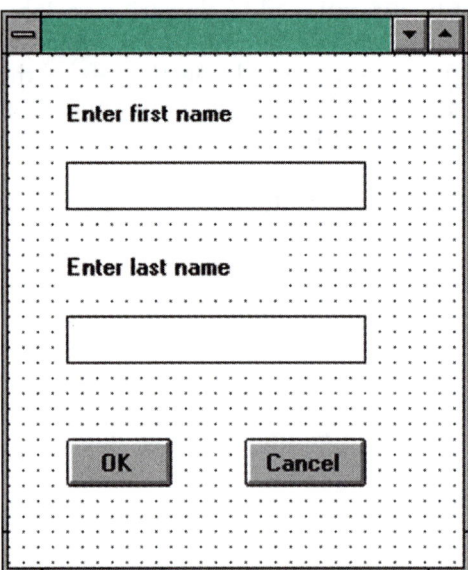

Figure 4.15
Separate form used as a specialized input box

The user clicks the OK button in Figure 4.15 when he or she is satisfied with the data entered in the text boxes. The code for this button hides this pop-up form; the data entered in the text boxes is available for the invoking form to use.

```
Sub cmdOK_Click ()
    Form2.Hide
End Sub
```

The user clicks the Cancel button to erase the data entered and start again. Code for the Cancel button sets the Text property of each of the text boxes to blank, but leaves this form for another try at data entry.

```
Sub cmdCancel_Click ()
    Text1.Text = ""
    Text2.Text = ""
End Sub
```

A form may be a modeless or modal window. Modeless is the default. To force this pop-up form to be modal, so that the user cannot make another window active and bypass the input process, use the statement

```
Form2.Show 1
```

The optional "1" forces Form2 to be modal.

THOUGHTS ON PROGRAMMING

Documentation

Program documentation is any material that allows a program to be more easily understood. Documentation is written for two audiences. **User documentation** helps the user of the program better understand how to run the program. **Technical documentation** helps a programmer understand how the program works. The programmer who needs to understand how the program works may be the same individual who wrote the program or someone else who is modifying the program or using part of the program's code in another program. Even when you are the program's author, you won't remember all the details of what you were thinking when you designed and wrote the program, and documentation is a record of your thought process. It will help either you or someone else who didn't write the original code to reconstruct that thought process later.

Both user documentation and technical documentation come in internal and external forms. **Internal documentation** is documentation that is part of the program. **External documentation** consists of manuals, notebooks, video tapes, and so on, that are distinct from the program.

Internal user documentation for a Visual Basic application program can take several forms. The user interface is part of the user documentation; the way objects are placed on a form or what their captions say, the prompts that appear for text boxes and input boxes, and so on, can give the user visual or textual cues on how to operate the program. A more direct form of user documentation is an on-line help system. (In the Visual Basic environment, you are a user of the Visual Basic software, and the Visual Basic on-line help system provides documentation on how to use that software effectively.)

External user documentation consists of user manuals or other materials supplied to the program user to enhance his or her understanding of how to use the program. This can include not only the nuts and bolts of what button to click, but also:

> Overall purpose of the program
> Expected data
> Expected form of the data
> Facilities provided to validate that the data have the expected form
> Expected form of the output that the program will provide
> Interpretation of the output
> Hardware and software requirements needed to run the program

The amount of external (and internal) user documentation varies depending on the program's complexity, its intended use, the level of expertise of the intended users, whether it is a commercial product (designed for sale) or an in-house program, and so on.

Internal technical documentation consists of items or techniques within the program code to make it more understandable to someone reading the code, as opposed to running the program. Here are some aspects of internal documentation:

> Meaningful identifiers for objects, variables, and procedures
> Liberal use of comments
> Good use of white space
> Good program structure

Visual Basic will operate with identifiers that are meaningless (*X, Z, T2*) or "cute" (*Dopey, Sneezy,* and *Grumpy*), but such identifiers will not make clear the purpose of your code. If a procedure computes the average grade for a test, then use the heading

```
Sub AverageGrade      not      Sub Mike
```

(In the demonstration program for Lab 4.1, ***prac.mak,*** less-than-terrific variable names like *a, b,* and *c* were used; names like this are OK for little bits of code that don't do much and that you are just constructing to try something out.)

Comments should provide an explanation of the code. This normally includes some sort of opening comment at the start of any procedure saying what the overall procedure accomplishes, how it makes use of data values available to it at the start, and what new values it produces. It is customary when declaring variables to put a comment beside each declaration explaining what purpose that variable serves within the program (even though the variable identifier should partially describe this).

Comments should also appear within the code to explain what is happening at various points. This aspect of commenting is rather an art. A comment on every line of code is not appropriate. For example, the following comment is trivial and distracting:

```
Days = Days + 1  'Increases the value of Days by 1
```

On the other hand, an entire procedure that has lines and lines of code without a single comment is not going to be understandable. Think of writing code as writing a paper or a news article. The comments are equivalent to the theme sentences of paragraphs; they describe what is going on in the upcoming section of code. Just as you break up a paper into meaningful topic paragraphs, so your code should be written in chunks, each of which does some cohesive little task and each of which has a comment describing that task and how it is accomplished.

The analogy of sections of code as paragraphs carries over into the idea of using white space. Paragraphs in English are identified by spacing and/or indentation. Spacing and indentation also help make code more readable. Here is one of the event procedures from the program used in Lab 4.1:

```
Sub cmdLoop_Click ()
'a is a variable

    a = 2

'Here is an example of a looping statement
    Do While a <= 5
        Picture1.Print "hello"
        a = a + 1
    Loop

End Sub
```

The following version is equivalent but much harder to read. There is no use of vertical white space to separate the code into sections, and there is no use of horizontal white space to indent the sections of code or indent the body of the while loop (those statements that get executed on each pass through the loop).

```
Sub cmdLoop_Click ()
'a is a variable
a = 2
'Here is an example of a looping statement
Do While a <= 5
Picture1.Print "hello"
a = a + 1
Loop
End Sub
```

The Visual Basic environment makes indentation easy. The Tab key indents a line, and each new line is automatically indented to the same depth as the previous line. Multiple lines can be indented as a group by selecting (highlighting) them and then using the Tab key. To move farther left to a previous level of indentation, just press the backspace key.

The last aspect of internal technical documentation is good program structure. Program structure includes an appropriate division of labor between the various procedures of the program. As the design for the task at hand is developed, for all but the most trivial of tasks there will be a number of subtasks. These are smaller jobs that work together to accomplish the whole. Breaking out these subtasks into individual procedures makes the overall design of the program clearer. Thus the way the program is organized into individual procedures and the way those procedures work together serve as part of the internal documentation. Visual Basic's object orientation encourages this separation into subtasks; each object (form or control) can have separate code—do a separate subtask—for each event it recognizes.

External technical documentation includes a complete description of the problem to be solved. It may include any or all of a high-level design representation, a description of the overall plan for the solution, a breakdown into subtasks, explanations of which subtask is done in which procedure, pseudocode descriptions of each procedure (from which the Visual Basic code was written), a listing of the code, who wrote the code, and how the data are transformed by the actions of each procedure. This information may be given by drawings or charts, as well as in text form. The external documentation also provides information on the results of testing the program, any errors that were found, how and when the program was changed to fix these errors, and who did the changes. All these materials make up the **technical reference manual**. This manual covers the entire life span of the program, from the original statement of the problem to the most recent change made. Keeping the documentation current is an ongoing and important task.

The following table summarizes the various types of documentation.

	USER	TECHNICAL
Internal	User interface On-line help	Identifiers Comments White space Program structure
External	User's manual	Technical reference manual

Name: _____   Date Due: _____

LAB 4.3

LEARNING OBJECTIVES

- Using the input box
- Using a second form
- Writing a complete Visual Basic application using:
    Custom colors
    A more complex algorithm
    The *Format$* function

1. ____ Open your **birth.mak** project from Lab 4.2.

   ____ Use Save File As... from the File menu to save the form file with the new name **birth2.frm**. Use Save Project As... from the File menu to save the project file with the new name **birth2.mak**.

2. ____ Change the program so that, instead of using two text boxes for input, it uses two input boxes. Use the default screen position for the input boxes. Once again, all the code should be associated with the click event on the command button.

   Using the input box

   ____ Remove the unused controls from the form.

   ____ Run the program to be sure it works properly.

   ____ Now run the program and click the command button repeatedly, giving various data values. Can you describe a potential problem? (Hint: This problem occurs sooner or later, depending on the size and shape of your picture box.)

   Consult Visual Basic Help for information on the **Cls method.** You want to apply this method to the picture box object. What is the syntax of the appropriate statement?

   ____ Put this statement early in your command button Click procedure. Run your program and click the button repeatedly, giving various data values, to be sure you have solved the problem.

   ____ Save your files.

Using a second form

3. Now for a third version of the birthday problem.

   ____ Open the **birth2.mak** project.

   ____ Save the files as **birth3.frm** and **birth3.mak.**

   ____ Rewrite the code so that input is obtained from a single customized input box that collects both the user's name and year of birth at once. Use a modal form. (Hint: If an object on Form1 needs to reference a property of an object on Form2, use the syntax *Form2!ObjectName.PropertyName.*)

   ____ Run the program to see that it works properly for a single user.

   ____ Run the program and click repeatedly, giving different data values. Describe two problems with the pop-up form the second time you see it.

   You take care of "housecleaning" tasks on the pop-up form by adding code to that form's **Activate event** procedure, which occurs whenever that form becomes the active window.

   ____ Set the text property of each of the text boxes to blank.

   ____ Apply the **SetFocus method** to the first text box, so that the insertion bar will be on that text box, ready for the user to enter data.

   ____ Test your program to see that it works successfully after these changes, and save your files.

Writing a new application

4. The next project is to allow customers to choose from three different carpet samples. This time, instead of using an OTC as a high-level design representation, more or less the same information is given in descriptive form.

   For each of the three samples, there is a label displaying the carpet color and also showing the name of this sample, another label giving the price PER SQUARE YARD of this sample, a label in which the final cost will appear, and a label for this label that says "Cost to you". So one carpet sample might look like the following; there will be three such samples on your form.

   14.95

   Topaz

   Cost to you

There are also two text boxes on the form for the user to enter the length and width of the room IN FEET, and a label for each text box with a prompt about the data to enter.

____ Open a new Visual Basic project.

____ Give an appropriate title to your form.

____ Arrange the control objects. You should have a total of 14 labels and two text boxes. (You can save time by copying and pasting some control objects, although you do not want a control array. Copying a control copies its properties as well, but none of its associated code.)

____ Make the cost labels and the text boxes blank.

____ Enter the prices as 1 or 2 digits, the decimal point, and 2 digits (like 14.95).

____ Save your work as **carpet.frm** and **carpet.mak.** Continue to save your work often as you add to it.

5. ____ Define some custom colors for your carpet samples; this will allow you to show some texture instead of just flat colors. Use the Help system to see how to do this.

Adding custom colors

6. The user will enter the room dimensions in the text box, and then click on the label for the desired sample.

____ Add one more label that gives these directions to the user.

7. All the code will occur in the Click event procedures for the three sample labels (here's one case where you write code for a label). The algorithm for such a procedure needs to be developed. A little thought produces the following pseudocode outline:

Developing the algorithm

> Get the data values for
>> price
>>
>> room length
>>
>> room width
>
> Compute the area (remember to change units; the symbol for division is /)
>
> Compute the cost
>
> Write the cost to the appropriate label

____ Identify the controls you will use to collect input data and those to which you will write the output. In order to improve the readability of your code, change the NAMES (not the captions) of these controls.

_____ Make a list of the variables the procedure needs, and state what data type each is. (Note: A user may give the width of the room as, for example, 14.5.)

_____ Pick one of the three samples to work with, and declare your variables.

_____ Try running your program to see that Visual Basic understands all your declarations.

8. _____ Write your procedure code for one sample, following the pseudocode outline. If you want to proceed slowly and carefully, you can add one instruction at a time along with an instruction to print to the Debug window the value you have just obtained or computed; use the syntax

`Debug.Print` *value*

Run your program after each new instruction is added, and look in the Debug window to be sure that the value printed is correct. When everything runs correctly, then delete these print instructions. (Hint: Remember that the label caption and the text box text are strings that must be converted to numbers to do arithmetic; then the numeric result must be converted back to a string to display in a label. Use the appropriate Visual Basic functions.)

Using the *format$* function

9. _____ Test your program for this one sample carpet. Try some room dimensions that are decimal data values like 14.5 and 19.6.

What's "wrong" with the output?

The Visual Basic *Format$* function can be used to control the appearance (format) of the output. For example, the expression

`Format$(cost, "currency")`

takes the numeric variable called *cost*, converts its value to a string, and formats that string with a $ sign and two digits after the decimal point, exactly as we usually see monetary values displayed. The literal string "currency", used as an argument to the *Format$* function, produces this effect. Other literal strings used in the *Format$* function have different effects.

____ Use the *Format$* function (instead of *Str$*) to display the output.

10. ____ Test your code thoroughly.

____ When you are sure it is working properly, copy and paste your code to the Click event procedures for the remaining two sample labels and make any necessary changes.

11. ____ Test everything again! Save your work.

> **QuickCheck 4.3**
> 1. The single required argument for the *InputBox$* function is _____.
> 2. An input box is a modal window, which means _____.
> 3. True or false: "White space" in Visual Basic code means leaving the form background color white.
> 4. What method erases text that has been printed in a picture box?
> 5. How is the *Format$* function an improvement over the *Str$* function?

Review Questions

1. Explain why high-level design is done before low-level design.
2. A sequence of well-defined steps to solve a task is called _____.
3. What are the three basic types of processing from which every algorithm can be constructed?
4. Explain the difference between syntax and semantics.
5. Give the Visual Basic syntax for identifiers.
6. Name three kinds of things in Visual Basic for which an identifier is required.
7. True or false: *Flowrate* and *FlowRate* would be considered two different identifiers in Visual Basic.
8. Explain the difference between a variable name and a variable value.
9. Assignment statements can be used to set the value of what two kinds of things?
10. Explain what "single-stepping" does.
11. Why are there multiple numeric data types?
12. Give the three things that are accomplished by a **Dim** variable declaration statement.
13. What does Option Explicit do? Give two reasons why Option Explicit should be used.
14. When a Visual Basic function is invoked, how many values does it return, and where are these values found?
15. In what sense are the *Val* and *Str$* functions opposites?
16. Explain when you might use input boxes as opposed to text boxes for collecting user input.
17. How can you create a customized input box?
18. What are the four types of documentation?
19. Name three forms of internal technical program documentation.
20. Explain why technical program documentation is important.

Exercises

Reading code

1. What will be printed in the picture box after the following code is executed?

   ```
   Dim A As Integer
   Dim B As Integer
   A = 13
   B = 2 * A
   A = A + 1
   Picture1.Print A + B
   ```

2. What will happen when the following statement is executed? (Assume *Answer* has been declared as a string type variable.)

   ```
   Answer = InputBox$("Tell me your favorite sport", ↵
   ↳ "Sports Trivia", "Soccer")
   ```

3. The caption of Label1 contains "42". What will be printed in the caption of Label2 by the following line of code?

   ```
   Label2.Caption = Str$(Val(Label1.Caption))
   ```

4. What will be printed in the label as a result of the following code if 82.40 is entered in the text box?

   ```
   Const Discount = 0.25
   Dim Price As Single
   Dim SalePrice As Single
   Price = Val(txtPrice.Text)
   SalePrice = Price - (Price * Discount)
   lblSalePrice.Caption = "The sale price is " & ↵
   ↳ Str$(SalePrice)
   ```

5. Read through the following code and then correct the error in the algorithm.

   ```
   Dim TuitionLastYear As Single
   Dim TuitionThisYear As Single
   Dim PercentIncrease As Single

   TuitionLastYear = Text1.Text
   TuitionThisYear = Text2.Text
   PercentIncrease = TuitionThisYear/TuitionLastYear
   Label1.Caption = "Percent increase in tuition is " & ↵
   ↳ Str$(PercentIncrease)
   ```

Writing code

6. Write a declaration statement to make *MyScore* a variable of type integer.

7. Write a statement that will print the value of the variable *BookTitle* in the picture box Picture1.

8. Write a declaration statement to give *TaxRate* the constant value 0.05.

9. Write two statements that will collect a string value for the user's name from an input box, and display the name in a label (Label1). Assume that all variables have been declared.

10. Write three statements that will collect a number from a text box (Text1), multiply that number by 14, and display the results in a label (Label1). Assume that all variables have been declared.

Exploring Further

11. Rewrite the *lab1* program so that it uses an input box to collect the user's name.

12. Rewrite the carpet program from Lab 4.3 so that each carpet sample uses input boxes to collect room dimensions.

13. The daily rotation of the earth on its axis is slowing at the rate of 1/1000 second every 100 years. Part of a program dealing with astronomy needs to compute the number of seconds lost after a given number of years. Write a detailed pseudocode description of the algorithm for this computation.

14. In the tax code for a certain state, a worker making less than $40,000 per year can deduct full medical expenses. Workers making $40,000 or more per year must reduce their medical deductions by 2 percent of the amount by which their income exceeds $40,000. Give a detailed pseudocode description of the algorithm for computing medical deductions; you can use a conditional structure like that shown in Figure 4.4.

15. A dieter wishes to compute the average number of calories consumed per day by entering data for each day and then clicking a button to see the average. Give a detailed pseudocode description of the algorithm for this task; you can use a looping structure like that shown in Figure 4.5.

Projects

For each of the following, do both a high-level design and a pseudocode outline of your algorithm or algorithms before you write the program.

1. An automobile's onboard computer tracks the average gas mileage, monitors the amount of fuel left in the tank, and displays the "range" (the expected distance the car can travel without refueling). Write a program that uses input data of gas mileage in miles per gallon and fuel in gallons and gives the expected range as output.

2. Unit pricing for grocery items is usually presented as some number of cents per ounce. Write a program that converts such a figure into dollars per pound. Use an input box to collect the data.

3. You want a program to help track daily gains or losses in the stock market. Changes in stock prices are typically reported in whole number and fractional form; that is, a stock may go up 1 1/8 (dollars) in value or fall 3/4 (dollars) in value. Write a program in which the user can enter the name of the stock, the number of shares owned, and the day's change in price (as a whole number, numerator, and denominator, that is, three

separate entries). The program should compute and display the dollar amount of gain or loss.

4. The formula for the weight of an object (in Newtons) is given by multiplying the mass of the object (in kilograms) by the acceleration of gravity (in meters per second^2). This is the formula known to all physics students as

   $F = ma$

   On earth, the acceleration due to gravity is 9.8 meters per second^2. On Jupiter, it is 84.98 ft per second^2 (note the units; 1 meter = 3.281 feet). Write a program that will compute the weight (in Newtons) of an object on Jupiter given its weight (in Newtons) on earth.

5. a. Write a program to manage a checkbook. The user should be able to enter the balance in the account, then click one button to enter the amount of a deposit and another button to enter the amount of a check. The output should be the new balance.

   b. Write a brief user's manual for your program. In particular, address how your program handles the case of a user who writes a check exceeding the current balance. (Your program probably does nothing special here, but whatever it does, you should tell the user about it. If you want to try something more sophisticated in your program, check the on-line Help system for information on the If-Then-Else statement.)

CHAPTER 5

Data Manipulation

KEY POINTS

- Decimal values are stored approximately; this can lead to round-off errors.
- Rules of operator precedence help determine how an arithmetic expression is evaluated.
- Arithmetic expressions are generally evaluated by converting everything to the most complex data type involved.
- When an arithmetic expression is assigned to a variable, its value is converted to the data type of that variable.
- Visual Basic supplies intrinsic functions for mathematical and financial calculations, date and time representation, and string manipulation.
- Analyzing user requirements and translating them into specifications is the starting point for software development.
- In order to create attractive text output, the Print method allows some control over spacing; the *Format$* function provides mechanisms for additional control over the appearance of text output.

5.1 More on decimal numbers

Chapter 4 introduced the data types supported by Visual Basic. The numeric data types Integer and Long are for storing smaller and larger nondecimal numbers, respectively. Single and Double are for storing smaller and larger decimal numbers, respectively.

When nondecimal numbers are translated into binary form for storage, the result is an exact representation of the original number. This means that after execution of the statements

```
Dim MyNumber As Integer, TwiceMyNumber As Integer
MyNumber = 275
TwiceMyNumber = MyNumber * 2
```

the memory location referred to by the name *MyNumber* contains the binary representation of the precise value 275, and the memory location referred to as *TwiceMyNumber* contains the binary representation of exactly 550, no more and no less.

However, the binary representation of a decimal number may be only an approximation. The reason is that the memory space allocated to store that decimal number can contain only a certain number of 0s and 1s, so there is a limit to the number of significant digits that can be stored. This is similar to your calculator. When you compute 1 divided by 3 on a calculator, the answer is displayed as something like 0.333333333. This is not the true value of 1/3, but an approximation to the true value up to 9 significant digits. Visual Basic variables of type Single store about 7 significant digits; variables of type Double store about 15. The number of significant digits desired might be one reason to do a computation using type Double rather than type Single data, even though the values are small enough to fall within the range of type Single.

As an example of the difficulties that can arise from limited significant digits, suppose only five significant digits can be stored. Then the values 324.15 and 4.2 can each be represented accurately. When these numbers are multiplied, their product is 1361.43. Given a limit of five significant digits, this result is stored as 1361.4, a value 0.03 off from the correct answer. If this answer is then used in another computation, and that result used in still another computation, and so on, the cumulative effect of such **round-off errors** can be significant.

Here's another surprising example of the limit on significant digits. Algebraically, the two quantities

$$(x - y) + z \quad \text{and} \quad (x + z) - y$$

produce identical results for any numeric values of x, y, and z. But if the values x and z differ greatly in magnitude, the computed results will not be identical. Consider the following code, where the notation 2E+20 means the number 2 followed by twenty 0s.

```
Dim x As Double
Dim y As Double
Dim z As Double

'note that large numbers can be entered using E-notation
x = 2E+20
y = 2E+20
z = 1.1
Picture1.Print (x - y) + z
Picture1.Print (x + z) - y
```

The first result is 1.1, which is the correct answer, but the second is 0. Why the difference?

The grade-school algorithm to add decimal values is to line up the decimal points and add the digits. The computer works with its binary representation in much the same way. If the two numbers being added are of vastly different sizes, as is the case with 2E20 + 1.1 ($x + z$ in this example), then after "lining up the decimal points," the total spread of digits may exceed the number of significant digits that can be stored. The least significant digits (the 1.1 in this case) are lost.

If your program is handling financial transactions for the First National Bank of East Waupaukeneta, you can't afford round-off errors. The Visual Basic Currency data type stores decimal values with up to 4 decimal places by first multiplying such values by 10,000 (which moves the decimal point 4 digits to the right) and storing the result as a 19-digit integer. Integer representation and integer arithmetic are exact; they avoid round-off errors. At the end, the decimal point is inserted again. The range of values for type Currency is between −922337203685477.5808 and 922337203685477.5808.

5.2 Arithmetic expressions

You have already done some simple computations in Visual Basic. Table 5.1 summarizes the available arithmetic operations. In addition to the standard operations of addition, subtraction, multiplication, division, and taking the negative of a number, Visual Basic supplies three others.

Table 5.1
Arithmetic operations

OPERATION	SYMBOL	EXAMPLE EXPRESSION IN VISUAL BASIC	RESULT
Addition	+	2.0 + 1.4	3.4
Subtraction	−	7 - 4	3
Multiplication	*	4.1 * 2	8.2
Division	/	3.1 / 6.2	0.5
Negation	−	−12	−12
Exponentiation	^	4 ^ 2	16
Integer quotient	\	17 \ 8	2
Integer remainder	Mod	17 Mod 8	1

The operation of exponentiation means raising to a power. In Table 5.1,

```
4^2
```

stands for 4^2, so the value is 16. The exponent (power) need not be an integer, however. An expression like

```
3.56^1.4
```

is legitimate and results in a value of approximately 5.916.

The integer quotient and integer remainder operations work like the parts of long division. For example, long division of 17 by 8 looks like the following:

$$\begin{array}{r} 2 \\ 8\overline{\smash{)}17} \\ \underline{16} \\ 1 \end{array}$$

The quotient is 2 with a remainder of 1 (8 "goes into" 17 twice, with 1 "left over"). The Visual Basic integer quotient operation gives the quotient, and the Visual Basic Mod operation gives the remainder (look at the last two lines of Table 5.1). Be sure to note that ordinary division uses a slash symbol /, whereas integer quotient uses a backward slash \.

An arithmetic expression is any legitimate string of numeric constants (like 1.4 or −7), numeric variables (variables with a numeric data type), and arithmetic operation symbols. If *x* and *y* have been declared as type Integer and Double, respectively, and have already been given values, then

```
x + 3      (y/x) - 2.4      x = y^3      x = 23\10      y = 23/10
```

are all legitimate arithmetic expressions. "Legitimate" means following correct rules of syntax for an arithmetic expression; there is no need to go into details over these rules because you've used them since grade school. For example,

```
+ + x/3 ^
```

is not legitimate, and you would never write this anyway!

So far, expressions have appeared in two places. One is on the right side of an assignment statement:

destination = expression

Here the expression is first evaluated, then the resulting value is assigned to the variable or object property on the left side. Expressions can also be used with the Print method:

`Picture1.Print` *expression*

Here the expression is first evaluated; then the resulting value is printed in the picture box. In each of these two uses, the first thing that happens is the expression is evaluated. What are the rules Visual Basic uses to evaluate expressions?

In complex expressions, there must be a way of deciding which operations will be performed first. Just as in ordinary algebra, parentheses help make clear the order of evaluation, as quantities in parentheses are evaluated first. In case of nested parentheses, the evaluation is done from the innermost set of parentheses outward. Some parentheses can be omitted because of **precedence rules**, conventions about which operators take **precedence** (are performed first) over others. Table 5.2 shows the order of precedence of Visual Basic arithmetic operations from highest to lowest; an operation with a higher level of precedence is performed before an operation with a lower level of precedence. If there is a "tie," the operations are done left to right.

Table 5.2 Rules of precedence for operations

OPERATION
^
− (negation)
*, /
\
Mod
+, − (subtraction)

According to these rules of precedence,

```
1 + 3/4
```

is interpreted as 1 + (3/4) because / has a higher precedence than +. If you want to indicate that the addition is to be done first, then you must override the order of precedence by using parentheses:

```
(1 + 3)/4
```

The expression

```
2 * 3 ^ 2 Mod 5 + 12 - 5
```

is evaluated as follows:

`2 * 3 ^ 2 Mod 5 + 12 - 5`	Exponentiation is done first,
`((2 * (3 ^ 2)) Mod 5) + 12 - 5`	then multiplication, then Mod.
`((2 * 9) Mod 5) + 12 - 5`	
`(18 Mod 5) + 12 - 5`	
`3 + 12 - 5`	Addition and subtraction have
`(3 + 12) - 5`	the same order of precedence,
`15 - 5`	so are done left to right.
`10`	

Although rules of operator precedence allow the elimination of some parentheses, the object is to write an expression in the clearest possible manner. Even though

```
x/y * 4 and (x/y) * 4
```

give the same value, the second expression is clearer. Parentheses should always be used when there might be the slightest possibility of confusion for the human reader of the code.

Clarity in writing expressions is often a judgment call. Is it clearer to write the expression

```
(Temp2 - Temp1)/(time2 - time1)
```

or to declare two more variables named *TemperatureDifference* and *TimeDifference*, assign

```
TemperatureDifference = Temp2 - Temp1
TimeDifference = time2 - time1
```

and then use the expression

```
TemperatureDifference/TimeDifference
```

This decision should be based on maximum clarity in the code, not on the fact that one way requires a few more lines of typing than the other. Typing time is cheaper than confusion time!

When an arithmetic expression is evaluated, the component parts may have different numeric data types. Again, think of the types

>Integer
>
>Long
>
>Single
>
>Double

as representing in some sense increasing space or complexity required in the storage of values. As a general rule, when an arithmetic expression involves mixed data types, the result is converted to the most complex type involved. Thus if x is a variable of type Single with a value of 1.7, the result of evaluating the expression

`x + 3`

is a type Single value of 4.7. Because the internal representation of decimal and nondecimal numbers differs, the process of adding two decimal numbers differs from the process of adding two nondecimal numbers, and there's no way to handle a mixture. When the expression x + 3 is evaluated, the representation in memory of the integer value 3 is changed to the type Single representation of the decimal number 3.0, and the operation is carried out using two type Single decimal numbers. Similarly, if x is type Single and y is type Double, the result of evaluating

`x * y`

will be type Double.

Exceptions to this general rule are shown in Table 5.3.

Table 5.3 Exceptions to the rule of converting everything in an expression to the most complex type involved

> 1. When a type Long and a type Single are used in +, −, *, and /, the result will be type Double rather than type Single.
>
> 2. Exponentiation produces a result of type Double.
>
> 3. Division between two integers produces a result of type Single or (if outside of the range of type Single) Double, even if the division "comes out even." Thus the result of 12/4 is type Single, not type Integer.
>
> 4. The operations of integer quotient and integer remainder are intended to be performed on nondecimal values. Decimal values are first rounded to type Integer or Long before the operation is done; the result is type Integer or Long.

One final note about evaluating expressions is in order. When a variable is declared, Visual Basic initializes that variable to a default value. For numeric variables, the default value is 0. The program statements

```
Dim Total As Integer
Picture1.Print Total + 3
```

print the value 3 in the picture box because *Total* is initialized to 0 and has not subsequently been assigned any other value. To avoid confusion, however, it is still good programming practice to **initialize variables** with an assignment statement. The code

```
Dim Total As Integer
Total = 0
Picture1.Print Total + 3
```

leaves no doubt as to the value of *Total* going into the expression

```
Total + 3
```

Once an expression is evaluated, it can be assigned to a variable or its value can be printed. When the value is printed it is usually printed in the simplest form that can express the value. Thus

```
Picture1.Print 12/4
```

prints 3 in the picture box rather than 3.0 or 3.0E0, even though the expression 12/4 evaluates to a type Single value.

When an arithmetic expression is assigned to a variable, its value is converted to the data type of that variable. If a decimal value is assigned to a type Integer or type Long variable, it will be rounded. If a type Double value is assigned to a type Single variable, it will be rounded to the seven significant digits that can be stored in a type Single variable. If a type Single value is assigned to a type Double variable, extra (possibly nonzero) digits are added, but they are not significant digits.

5.3 String expressions

Compared to arithmetic expressions, string expressions are easy. The only operation that can be done on strings is **concatenation**, which means joining strings together. The symbol for the concatenation operation is &. You have already been using concatenation to display output in a label caption or print it in a picture box. As an example, the string expression

```
"Hob" & "goblin"
```

evaluates to "Hobgoblin". Similarly, if *FirstWord* and *SecondWord* have been declared variables of type String, then

```
FirstWord = "Hello"
SecondWord = " there"
Picture1.Print (FirstWord & SecondWord)
```

results in

      Hello there

being printed. Note that the space printed between "hello" and "there" occurs because it is part of *SecondWord*.

The **null string** is a string with no characters. To initialize the Text property of a text box, for example, one can do the following assignment:

```
Text1.Text = ""
```

Visual Basic initializes string variables to the null string.

A string expression can be assigned to a string variable, either a fixed-length string variable or a variable-length string variable. If a string expression is assigned to a variable-length string variable, that variable just takes on the string as its value (variable-length strings can be up to 65,500 characters long). If a string expression is assigned to a fixed-length string variable, one of the following two conditions can occur:

1. If the string expression results in a string that is shorter than the fixed length, the string is padded on the right with blank characters.

2. If the string expression results in a string that is longer than the fixed length, the string is truncated on the right.

Name: _____   Date Due: _____

LEARNING OBJECTIVES

- Exploring data types of expressions
- Trying out numeric and string assignments

LAB 5.1

1. ____ Open a new Visual Basic project.

   ____ Put a picture box on your form and set its height property to 5700 so it is big enough to see all of the output.

   ____ Declare the variables shown. The object of this lab is just to test bits of code, so the Form_Click procedure is a good place to put everything.

Variable	Type
x	Integer
y	Long
z	Single
w	Double
t	Single
a	String
b	String * 5

2. ____ Begin by exploring how Visual Basic stores numeric values. Visual Basic provides a function called *VarType* that can be used to determine the data type of any expression. The syntax is

   `VarType(expression)`

   The function returns a numeric value that is a code for the data type. Here's the code:

VARTYPE VALUE	DATA TYPE
2	Integer
3	Long
4	Single
5	Double
6	Currency
8	String

   Type the following lines of code exactly (except for the comments, which are for your information) and run your program.

```
Picture1.Print VarType(15)
Picture1.Print VarType(43756)
'The ! forces 'storage as type 'Single.
Picture1.Print VarType(15!)

'The # forces 'storage as type 'Double.
Picture1.Print VarType(15#)

Picture1.Print VarType("15")
Picture1.Print VarType("Mary")
```

Exploring expression data types

What values did you get? Look back at each line of code to see why that value was given.

____ Now try

```
Picture1.Print VarType(15.0)
```

What value did you get?

With no instructions to the contrary, how does Visual Basic store decimal values?

Look back at your code. The last line you typed has been changed to

```
Picture1.Print VarType(15#)
```

Does this confirm your previous answer?

Trying out numeric assignments

3. ____ Type the following lines of code and run the program.

```
x = 324 * 745
Picture1.Print x
```

What happens? Why? (Use your calculator.)

___ Change this to

```
y = 324 * 745
Picture1.Print y
```

What happens and why? (Remember that the expression is first evaluated, then assigned to a variable.)

___ Now try

```
y = 324 * 745.0
Picture1.Print y
```

Why is this successful?

Note that in this computation, 745.0 gets stored as type Double. In evaluating 324 times a type Double, 324 gets converted to type Double, so the product is type Double. When that value is assigned to a type Long variable, it gets rounded to a whole number value.

4. If x has the value 7 and z has the value 28.4, what do you expect to be the value of each of the following expressions?

```
x + 2 * z / 4
(x + 2) * z / 4
x Mod 2
x \ 2
x ^ 2 - 5
7 + 2.4E + 45
```

___ Write code to assign values to x and z and print the values of these expressions. Run your program and compare your answers with what you expected.

5. ___ Enter the following statements and run your program:

```
y = 7
z = 12!
Picture1.Print VarType(y^2)
Picture1.Print (12.6 Mod 4)
```

```
Picture1.Print VarType(y*z)
Picture1.Print VarType(8/2)
```

Each of these four Print statements illustrates one of the four exceptions to the general rule of expression evaluation.

____ Put numbers 1 to 4 beside the Print statements to show which illustrates which.

6. ____ Try the following code in your program. What happens and why?

```
w = 12432.789
x = w
Picture1.Print x
```

Trying out string assignments

7. ____ Try the following code. What gets printed and why?

```
a = "Mississippi"
b = a
Picture1.Print b
Picture1.Print a & b
Picture1.Print a & Str$(x)
```

8. ____ What happens with this line of code and why?

```
x = a
```

9. ____ Here's a harder question. Run the following code and write the two answers you get.

```
x = 12
w = 624.5
t = x / w
Picture1.Print t + w
Picture1.Print (x/w) + w
```

Now explain why the two answers differ.

> **QuickCheck 5.1**
>
> 1. Large nondecimal numeric values should be stored in variables of type _____.
> 2. Decimal values requiring more than seven significant digits should be stored using type _____.
> 3. The value of the expression 3 ^ 2 * 4 is _____.
> 4. The value of the expression 14 \ 3 is _____.
> 5. What happens when a decimal value is assigned to a variable of type Integer?

5.4 Intrinsic functions

You have already used some of the functions provided by Visual Basic as built-in, or **intrinsic,** functions. These include the *Val, Str$, InputBox$,* and *VarType* functions. In this section you will look at other common functions, although not all the intrinsic functions that Visual Basic provides. No one memorizes all the details of all the functions. You should simply skim through this section so you know the kinds of functions that are available. Then when you need a particular function, you can return here to check on the details or look for further information in the on-line Visual Basic Help system.

Remember that a function is invoked by giving the function name together with any arguments (data needed by the function). The general form of a function invocation is therefore

> *FunctionName(argument list)*

The function executes its code, after which it returns a single value, which may be used just like any other variable in a program. The value can be printed, assigned to another variable, etc. Thus

> `Picture1.Print` *FunctionName(argument list)*

or

> *VariableName = FunctionName(argument list)*

are legitimate statement forms. The Visual Basic statement

`Picture1.Print VarType(15)`

is an example of the first form, and

`TruckOrders = InputBox$("Enter the number of trucks ordered", ,"25")`

is an example of the second form.

Functions can usually be categorized by the type of task they perform. Table 5.4 lists functions that are mathematical in nature.

Table 5.4 Visual Basic mathematical functions

	FUNCTION NAME	ARGUMENT	RETURNED DATA TYPE	DESCRIPTION	EXAMPLE
1	Abs	Any numeric expression	Same as argument	Absolute value	Abs(-17) returns 17
2	Sgn	Any numeric expression	1 if arg > 0, 0 if arg = 0, −1 if arg < 0	Indicates sign of argument	Sgn(-17) returns −1
3	Sqr	Numeric expression with value ≥ 0	Single or Double	Square root	Sqr(16) returns 4
4	Sin	Numeric expression representing radians	Single or Double between −1 and 1	Sine of an angle	Sin(3.141593/2) returns .9999999999999 [sin(π/2) = 1]
5	Exp	Numeric expression with value < 709	Single or Double	e to a power	Exp(1) returns 2.718282 [$e^1 = e$]
6	Log	Numeric expression with value > 0	Single or Double	Natural logarithm	Log(2.718282) returns 1.000000063106 [ln e = 1]
7	Rnd		0 ≤ Single < 1	Random-number generator	Rnd returns .7055475

Function 1, *Abs*, computes the absolute value of a number, which is its magnitude regardless of its sign. Function 2, *Sgn*, indicates the sign of the number. Function 3 takes the square root of a nonnegative number. Function 4 is the sine function, one of several trigonometric functions that Visual Basic provides. Functions 5 and 6 are the exponential function and its inverse, the logarithmic function. If functions 4 to 6 don't mean anything to you, don't worry; you don't have to use them in the rest of this book. The remark "Single or Double" for Returned Data Type for functions 3 to 6 means that the data type of the value returned depends on the data type of the argument. If the argument is type Integer, Single, or Currency, the returned value is type Single; if the argument is type Long or Double, the result is type Double. This reflects the fact that there is no point in carrying out computations to 15 significant digits when the data on which those computations are based are only good to 7 significant digits.

In Table 5.4, the examples use very simple arguments, but a numeric expression (also called an arithmetic expression) can be fairly complicated, as seen in Section 5.2. The following illustrates a more complex expression used as an argument to the *Abs* function.

```
Dim x As Double
Dim y As Double
Dim z As Double
x = 24.1
y = 14.2
z = Abs(-((x * Sqr(y)) Mod 12) ^ 3)
Picture1.Print z
```

The result that gets printed is 343. (You could try this on your calculator to see why this is the correct answer.)

In Table 5.4, no argument is given for the *Rnd* function. There is an optional argument, but to understand it, you need to understand in more detail what the *Rnd* function does. The *Rnd* function returns one decimal number that is greater than or equal to 0 but less than 1. The first time the *Rnd* function is invoked as a program executes, the value returned is determined by Visual Basic. As the program continues to run, every time the *Rnd* function is invoked, the value returned depends on the previous value returned. Rerunning the program starts the sequence again. However, the first value returned is always the same (0.7055475). Because each subsequent value depends on the previous one, the entire sequence of numbers generated within any run of the program will always be the same from one run to the next. The values generated in one run look as if they are random, but since they repeat each time, they are not really random but **pseudorandom**. The reason to have pseudorandom rather than truly random numbers is to allow for program testing and debugging. It is hard to pinpoint problems when the numbers being used are not repeatable. Once the program is working properly, the Visual Basic **Randomize statement** (which consists of just the single word "Randomize") is used at the beginning of the program. This sets the "seed" for the *Rnd* function, which generates a truly random value for the first value (and hence for the sequence as a whole). The seed is based on the Visual Basic *Timer* function, which returns the number of elapsed seconds since midnight according to the system clock. This value will change from one run of the program to the next.

If an argument is given to the *Rnd* function, it has the following effect:

Argument value > 0:   Generates next random number in the sequence; this is the same effect as using *Rnd* with no argument.

Argument value = 0:   Generates the number most recently generated.

Argument value < 0:   Generates the same number every time; its value depends upon the argument value.

The ability to generate random numbers is useful in programs that use statistical data sampling or simulate games of chance.

Table 5.5 gives three Visual Basic intrinsic financial functions. The *Pmt* function has to do with an annuity. An **annuity** is a series of cash payments made regularly at a fixed interest rate. The annuity could be a loan, in which you borrow some amount of money at a fixed interest rate and make

Table 5.5 Visual Basic financial functions

FUNCTION NAME	ARGUMENTS	DESCRIPTION
1 Pmt	rate = interest rate per nper = number of periods pv = present value fv = future value due = when in period payments are due	Payment per period
2 Ipmt	rate = interest rate per period per = payment period nper = number of periods pv = present value fv = future value due = when in period payments are due	Amount of payment that is interest
3 SLN	cost = initial cost salvage = final value life = length of useful life	Depreciation for a single period using straight-line method

payments on the loan each month. Or the annuity could be an investment, in which you save a fixed amount each month that is invested at a constant rate. The arguments follow.

rate: the interest rate per payment period that you are being charged for your loan or that your investment is earning

nper: total number of payment periods during the life of the loan or investment

pv: the present value for a loan is the amount borrowed; the present value for an investment is 0

fv: the future value for a loan is 0 (assuming you are going to pay it all off); the future value for an investment is the total value after the last payment

due: 0 if the payment is due at the end of the payment period, 1 if the payment is due at the beginning of the payment period

The *Ipmt* function (2 in Table 5.5) also pertains to an annuity. It returns the amount of each payment that is attributable to interest. The one additional argument is the payment period for which you want this value.

The *SLN* function (3 in Table 5.5) performs straight-line depreciation of an asset using its initial cost, its salvage value at the end of its useful life, and the length of its useful life. Straight-line depreciation is one of the ways businesses can compute depreciation on equipment for tax purposes. Like some of the mathematical functions, this function may not mean much to you and will not be used further in this book.

As programming languages go, Visual Basic provides some nice functions to handle date and time. Table 5.6 shows only a few of the many options available.

Table 5.6 Some of Visual Basic's date and time functions

	FUNCTION NAME	ARGUMENT	RETURNED DATA TYPE	DESCRIPTION	EXAMPLE
1	Now		Variant	Current date and time	Now returns something like 7/18/96 5:40:22 PM but result can be formatted many ways
2	Date$		String * 10	Current date in mm-dd-yyyy format	Date$ returns 07-18-1996
3	Day	Date expression	Integer between 1 and 31	Day of the month	Day(Date$) returns 18
4	Time$		String * 8	Current time in hh:mm:ss format	Time$ returns 17:40:22
5	Hour	Time expression	Integer between 0 and 23	Hour of the day	Hour(Time$) returns 17

In addition to the *Day* function (3 in Table 5.6) there are *Month* and *Year* functions; in addition to the *Hour* function (5 in Table 5.6) there are *Minute* and *Second* functions. There is also a *Weekday* function that returns an integer between 1 (Sunday) and 7 (Saturday) for the day of the week.

The last group of functions to be considered are string-based functions. They make it possible to pick a string apart and look at individual sections or even individual characters. Thanks to functions like the ones shown in Table 5.7, Visual Basic is very good at string manipulations.

It's worth saying again that, despite the number of tables in this section, not all Visual Basic's intrinsic functions have been covered and neither have all the intricate variations on some of the functions discussed. For detailed information, be prepared to consult the Help system. And if you think there ought to be a function to do some particular thing because it sounds so convenient, there may indeed be such a function, so search Help under any likely names or topics.

FUNCTION NAME	ARGUMENT	RETURNED DATA TYPE	DESCRIPTION	EXAMPLE
1 UCase$	String expression	String	Changes to all uppercase	UCase$("Jose") returns "JOSE"
2 LCase$	String expression	String	Changes to all lowercase	LCase$("Hot Dog") returns "hot dog"
3 Len	String expression	Long	Length of string	Len("abcdefg") returns 7
4 Left$	String expression, n	String	Leftmost n characters in string	Left$("ice cream", 3) returns "ice"
5 Right$	String expression, n	String	Rightmost n characters in string	Right$("island", 4) returns "land"
6 Mid$	String expression, k,n	String	n characters in string from position k on	Mid$("Klingon", 4,3) returns "ngo"
7 LTrim$	String expression	String	Strips leading blanks	LTrim$(" Hi") returns "Hi"
8 RTrim$	String expression	String	Strips trailing blanks	RTrim$("Hi ") returns "Hi"
9 InStr	String expression 1, string expression 2	Long	Position of string 2 in string 1; 0 if not found	InStr("abcde", "d") returns 4
10 Space$	Number n in range of type Long	String	String of n blanks	Space$(5) returns " "

Table 5.7

Some of the Visual Basic string functions

Name: _____ Date Due: _____

LEARNING OBJECTIVES

- Using arithmetic expressions to complete the calculator project
- Doing a more complex low-level design
- Using general procedures
- Splitting the Code window

LAB 5.2

1. ____ Using the Windows File Manager, locate and run the file *mycalc.exe*.

   In Lab 3.3, you designed a calculator screen that may look something like the one shown here. There are three important observations about how to operate the calculator. First, only nonnegative integer values can be used because there is no way to enter a negative sign or a decimal point. Second, as the user clicks the buttons on the keypad, the number is displayed as the caption of a label. Third, this calculator (as do some commercial calculators) uses **RPN, Reverse Polish Notation**. This means that the arithmetic symbol for the operation to be done is typed AFTER the numbers instead of between the numbers. Thus you select

   2 [ENTER] 3 *   rather than   2 * 3

   RPN is easier for the program to handle because both numbers are available by the time the operation is encountered.

   ____ Try a few computations on this calculator.

   With the work done on data manipulation in this chapter, you will be able to write the code for your own calculator program, and it will work the same way.

2. ____ Open your *calc.mak* project. Be sure that all of the following are present:

   An array of command buttons, indexed 0 to 9, that are the numeric keypad.

   Four arithmetic operation buttons, an Enter button and a Clear button, all with names (as well as captions) that clearly indicate their purpose.

   A label that displays the string "Result".

   A label named lblReadout acting as a little window in which the result will appear.

Completing the calculator project

3. ____ Put the following code in the Form_Load procedure to set the position of the form when the program is executed. (If you have changed the name of the form, then change the code accordingly.)

```
'Center form horizontally.
Form1.Left = (Screen.Width - Width) / 2
'Center form vertically.
Form1.Top = (Screen.Height - Height) / 2
```

4. What one Visual Basic statement will set the caption of the readout label to the null string?

____ Insert this statement so that the readout caption is initialized to the null string when the program begins to execute.

5. Each calculator computation requires two numbers, the first number entered and the second. This means the program needs two numeric variables, which have to be declared. If the variables are declared within a command button procedure, such as the addition button's click procedure, then only that procedure knows about these variables. The subtraction button, for example, would not be able to use these variables.

____ Declare two variables named *number* and *old_number* of type Integer in the **general section** of the form. Variables declared or procedures written in the general section of a form are accessible from anywhere within the form.

Doing a more complex low-level design

6. The high-level design of the calculator project is complete. The subtasks have been determined and assigned to appropriate objects, the form has been designed, and the important (form-level) variables have been determined. Now it is time to do the low-level design in the form of devising the algorithms for each of the various subtasks. This project is a bit more complex than those you have done so far because there are more subtasks, hence more algorithms to be developed.

Using general procedures

The two numbers involved in each computation will be taken from the lblReadout caption, and the final answer will be displayed in the lblReadout caption. Hence the left-top-right situation in Figure 4.9 applies: the data is type string representing numbers, numeric computations need to be done, and the output will be type string. A bit of thought reveals that the type conversions (the left and right of Figure 4.9) must be done in all four arithmetic operations. Rather than write the same code four times, two procedures called *get_number* and *put_answer* will handle the details of the type conversions. They will be **general procedures**, placed in the general section of the form and from there accessible anywhere within the form. (Note that this is a design modification because the original OTC calculator design in Lab 3.3 did not mention general procedures. It is perfectly acceptable, indeed even necessary, to add further details to the program design as you go along.)

____ Enter the following code in the general section of the form. Just begin typing below the variable declarations; as soon as you complete the first line, you get a new Code window for this procedure.

```
Sub get_number (number)
'This procedure takes the string of digits
'now in the lblReadout label, makes it a
'number, and assigns it to the variable number

    number = Val(lblReadout.Caption)
End Sub
```

What part of Figure 4.9 does this procedure accomplish?

7. ____ Here is the outline for the second procedure. Fill in the missing line and make this another general procedure.

```
Sub put_answer (number)
'This procedure takes number and writes it
'as a string in the lblReadout label

    put one line of code here
End Sub
```

8. All the buttons for the numeric keypad are in a control array, so it is only necessary to write the code once.

____ Go to the Click event Code window for the array. Notice that "index As Integer" appears in parentheses as part of the procedure heading. This means that each button's index number is known to the procedure. To check this, put the statement

```
Debug.Print index
```

in the procedure and run the program. Click on various keypad buttons and check the Debug window. What happens?

What is the relation between *index* and a keypad button caption?

____ Now erase this line of code and replace it with

```
lblReadout.Caption = lblReadout.Caption &
    LTrim$(Str$(index))
```

Explain what this statement does; you may want to run the program to see what happens. (Hint: The string in lblReadout's caption is built up by concatenation one digit at a time as keypad buttons are pressed. Look back at Table 5.7, and also remember that *Str$* leaves a space for the sign of a number.)

9. When the user is done with the first number in the calculation, the Enter button is pressed. This sets things up to receive the second number. Below is the code for the Enter button click procedure.

____ Add this code; explain what the second and third lines of code do and why they are here (the explanation for the first line is given).

```
Call get_number(number)      'Invokes the get_number
                             'procedure to take the
                             'current string in
                             'lblReadout.Caption and
                             'put it into the numeric
                             'value number.
old_number = number

lblReadout.Caption = ""
```

10. After the user puts in all the digits for the second number, he or she clicks on an operation button. Below is an algorithm in pseudocode for the addition click event procedure.

    Give *number* the value of the current string in the readout label
    Add this new number to the old number, resulting in a new value of *number*
    Display the result in the readout label

    ____ Translate each line of pseudocode above to a Visual Basic statement and add this code to your program.

    ____ Try your program with an addition calculation. If it does not work properly, examine your code carefully to find out where the problem is.

11. ____ Write a pseudocode description for the subtraction click event procedure.

    ____ Write the code for the subtraction click event procedure.

    ____ Run your program with a subtraction calculation.

12. Sometimes it is convenient to copy and paste code from one procedure to another, and then modify the copy as needed. The copy-and-paste operation would be easier if you could see both sections of code at the same time. In order to do this, you can **split the Code window.** To do this:

    Splitting the Code window

    ____ Go to the Code window for the addition click event procedure.

    ____ Put the cursor on the dark line just above the vertical scroll bar of the Code window. The cursor shape will change to a horizontal bar with a double-headed vertical arrow through it.

    ____ Drag the cursor down; this also drags the **split bar** of the Code window and divides the Code window into two horizontal panes. You can toggle the focus back and forth between the two panes by clicking the cursor or by pressing F6. Each pane can hold a different procedure from the same form.

    ____ Put the multiplication click event procedure in the second Code window pane.

    ____ Copy and paste the addition code into the multiplication pane.

___ "Unsplit" the Code window by dragging the split bar back up to the top of the Code window.

___ Modify the multiplication code.

13. ___ Write the code for division.

___ Run the program and try multiplication and division, using small numbers.

14. ___ Write the one statement for the click procedure for the Clear button, which allows the user to start over and do another calculation if desired.

15. ___ Now try your calculator on the computation

250 * 723

What happens and why? (Hint: Think about the error message you got.)

___ To solve this problem, change your variable declarations to type Long.

___ Test your program by doing this computation again.

16. ___ Now run your program on the computation 12/5. What is the result? Why?

___ If this computation caused a problem, fix your code.

___ Test your program thoroughly.

> **QuickCheck 5.2**
> 1. Data values needed by a function are given to the function by means of _____.
> 2. What is the value of the Visual Basic expression `Sqr(36)`?
> 3. In order to generate truly random numbers in a program, what statement should be used at the beginning of the program?
> 4. What is the value of the Visual Basic expression `Mid$("hockey-stick", 7, 5)`?
> 5. To see code from two procedures on the same form at the same time, you can _____.

5.5 More on the Print method

So far you have printed to a picture box or to the Debug window. The general syntax for the Print method is

    ObjectName.`Print`   *expression list*   *trailing punctuation*

The object name can be a form name, the name of a picture box, Debug, or Printer, which results, respectively, in printing output directly on a form, in a picture box, in the Debug window, or on the printer. These four are the only object types that support the Print method. The object name in the Print method is optional in some cases; if it is omitted in an event procedure, printing is done on the current form.

    No attention has been paid so far to the niceties of spacing or formatting with the Print method, which is partially controlled by the punctuation within the expression list and the trailing punctuation. None of the fine points of printed output spacing apply to the Debug object because the Debug window is just intended for a quick look at what's happening, not for any finished product that the user will see. Printing directly on a form somewhat distorts the usual purpose of a form as a container for other objects, although printing on a form can be used for quick and dirty output that won't appear in the finished program, much as the Debug window is used. Printing where the appearance of the output is a concern is usually done either to a picture box on the form or to the printer for hard copy output.

    The items in the expression list of the Print method can be object properties, string literals, variables, arithmetic expressions, or even function invocations. Without further instructions, string literals are printed exactly as is. Numeric values are printed with a leading space for the sign (a negative sign occupies this space if the number is negative, and for zero or positive numbers there is just a blank). Numeric values also have a trailing blank after the number. Decimal values that would require many digits to print in decimal form will be printed in exponential form. However, it is possible to impose many different formatting options for both string and numeric data by using the powerful *Format$* function discussed later in this section.

THOUGHTS ON PROGRAMMING

Requirements Analysis and Problem Specification

The very first step in creating a computer program is deciding what is wanted. Assume there is a "client" who has come to you and asked that a program be written. (The client could be you or your instructor or someone else.) The client has certain requirements that he or she wants satisfied by this program. **Requirements analysis** is the term used for determining and understanding these requirements. Requirements analysis is an important part of the programming process. The time and effort devoted to this task pays dividends many times over. Careful requirements analysis prevents wasted efforts in developing software that is not what the client wants. Even if the client is you yourself, requirements analysis is still important in order to clarify your task before you begin, although it may be a less formal process than it would be for a different client.

As an analogy, imagine that you are building a house for someone. You would not dream of starting on the building without first discussing what the requirements of the buyer are. Although a computer program is certainly easier to change than a physical structure, there is still time and money involved in changing things after the fact. Why take this chance when a little effort up front can prevent a false start?

No doubt the client has some problem that he or she wants the computer program to solve. A first step in requirements analysis is to explore the details of this problem in order to determine whether it is feasible or even possible to solve it by using a computer program. Perhaps the effort involved in developing a computerized solution is not worthwhile, given the scale of the problem. Assuming that a computerized solution should be pursued, the exact nature of the problem needs to be nailed down.

What is the task to be done? What are the input data available to carry out this task? What is the desired output or result? That's the bare bones of the matter, but there are other issues to explore. Are there any special or exceptional situations that may arise in the context of this task, and if so, how should they be handled? Are there special requirements (due to government regulations, standard industry practice, company policy, and so on) about how the task must be solved? Are there related tasks that ought to be done at the same time? Do input data already exist in electronic form? If so, what is the size of the data file? What is the format of the data stored in the file? What is the desired format of the output?

All these issues might be termed **functional requirements,** because they are concerned with the functionality of the program to be written, that is, the job to be done. If a program fails to meet its functional requirements, it is basically giving "wrong answers" to the problem it is supposed to solve. But in addition to functional requirements, there are also **performance requirements** that are concerned with how the program acts while it is doing its job. What should the user interface look like? How long should the program take to produce its results? What is the amount of computer memory needed for the program to run? How easy is it for the typical user to run the program?

The client may have only a general idea of what he or she wants done. It is part of the software development process to work with the client to elicit the total requirements for the program, much as the builder works with the home buyer. A variety of techniques exist for talking through requirements, involving the client, the software developer (who is often at this stage called a **systems analyst**), and perhaps a representative of the eventual program users. Continuing involvement of the client, the developer, and the user throughout the software development process is more likely to produce a product that will satisfy the needs of the client.

The result of the requirements analysis process is a complete understanding of the functional and performance requirements. This is usually captured in a written document that will become part of the total documentation package of the program. The requirements are usually stated in the language of the client, not the language of the software developer. These requirements often have to undergo a translation process into a tighter and more technical form that can be turned over to the software designers. This process is called **problem specification**. The result is another piece of the documentation package. The specification document will be referred to often during program design, implementation, and testing to be sure that the program being developed meets the specifications.

This process of requirements analysis and problem specification seems unnecessary in light of the programs you have so far written. These programs, however, have been very small. The larger the project, the more care must be taken in all the steps of its development, beginning with requirements analysis and problem specification.

If the items in the expression list are separated by semicolons, then they are printed as if concatenated; that is, no intervening spaces are inserted. Thus

```
Picture1.Print "good"; "bye"
```

results in

>goodbye

in the picture box. The statement

```
Picture1.Print "number is"; 4; "gallons"
```

results in

>number is 4 gallons

because of the space in front of the 4 for the sign, and the trailing space after the 4. That spacing is fixed by the kind of data being printed, not by any spaces between the list entries. The separating semicolon can be omitted, as in

```
Picture1.Print "number is" 4 "gallons"
```

which gives the same output. This is equivalent to separating list elements with semicolons; in fact, semicolons are automatically inserted by Visual Basic. Finally, the same effect can be obtained by using the string concatenation operator, as has been done up until now:

```
Picture1.Print "number is" & " 4 " & "gallons"
```

Here, however, the 4 is treated as a string character and the spacing must be supplied as part of the code. So, to sum up, separating items in the expression list by semicolons (or spaces) results in concatenation.

The items in the expression list can also be separated by commas. To understand the effect of the comma separator, think of "print zones" that are each 14 characters wide. With the comma separator, the first list element is printed left justified within the first print zone (starting in column 1); the second element is printed left justified within the second print zone (starting in column 15), and so on. Elements that are longer than 14 characters are printed in their entirety, with succeeding list elements bumped into zones farther to the right. The zone idea can be useful to print tabular output, in which you want things lined up in columns. Further control of horizontal spacing can be obtained by using the two functions *Tab* and *Spc* (see Lab 5.3).

Any discussion of the spacing of characters using the Print method will be affected by the type font used. In fixed (**monospace**) fonts, each character takes exactly the same amount of space. In **proportional spaced** fonts, not all characters take the same amount of space. "Fat" letters like "m" and "w" take a lot of space; "skinny" letters like "l" and "i" take very little. Hence it is more difficult to precisely align text using a proportional spaced font. The font for a picture box can be set either in the Properties window at design time or in code at run time.

The FontName, FontBold, FontItalic, and FontSize properties all apply to the Printer object as well, but can be set only in code. The fonts available on the printer can be found by doing a test run that uses the two properties FontCount and Fonts of the Printer object. The following code prints a sheet of paper with a listing of all the available printer fonts, with each font name displayed in that font.

```
Sub Form_Click ()
   Dim index As Integer

      'index enumerates all available fonts
      For index = 0 To Printer.FontCount - 1

      'set printer font to choice index
      Printer.FontName = Printer.Fonts(index)

      'print the font name
      Printer.Print Printer.FontName
      Next index

   'print the page
   Printer.EndDoc
End Sub
```

If, for example, your printer supports the font named Century Gothic and you decide you would like your printed output displayed in that font, then use the Visual Basic statement

```
Printer.FontName = "Century Gothic"
```

somewhere in a procedure in order to set the printer font.

The expression list used with the Print method can be empty; this has the effect of printing a blank line. No trailing punctuation at the end of the expression list results in a carriage return; that is, the next output is printed on a new line. A trailing semicolon means that the next output will be concatenated with the current output, and a comma means that the next output will be printed in the next zone on the same line.

The exact location where printing is to take place can be controlled by specifying the coordinates at which to begin printing. CurrentX and CurrentY are properties of form, picture box, or printer objects. The pair (CurrentX, CurrentY) represents the coordinates of the print head (where the next printed output will start) relative to the upper left corner of the object. The measurement is in twips or whatever the scale mode of the object is. The initial (CurrentX, CurrentY) is (0, 0); this is why printed output to a picture box has always begun in the upper left corner. The CurrentX and CurrentY properties cannot be set in the Properties window, but can be set at run time. Thus if the ScaleMode property of the picture box is set to twips (the default unit), then

```
Picture1.CurrentX = 600
Picture1.CurrentY = 1000
Picture1.Print "Hello"
```

results in placing the top of the "H" in "Hello" 600 twips right of and 1000 twips below the upper left corner of the picture box.

The ScaleWidth and ScaleHeight properties of a form, picture box, or printer give the internal width and height of the object in the current units of measurement. These are the dimensions of the area available for printing. The ScaleHeight property is different from the Height property, which gives the external dimensions of the object, including borders, title bars, and so on. Similarly, ScaleWidth is different from Width. ScaleWidth and ScaleHeight can be used to set values for CurrentX and CurrentY relative to the area available for printing. Thus

```
Picture1.CurrentX = Picture1.ScaleWidth/2
Picture1.CurrentY = Picture1.ScaleHeight/2
Picture1.Print "*"
```

prints the * in the center of the display area of the picture box.

Table 5.8 summarizes some of the mechanisms available with the Print method to control spacing.

Table 5.8 Mechanisms to control print spacing

MECHANISM	RESULT
Semicolon between expression list elements	Concatenation
Space between expression list elements	Concatenation
Comma between expression list elements	Zone printing
Empty expression list	Blank line
No trailing punctuation	Carriage return
Trailing semicolon	Next print concatenated
Trailing comma	Next print in next zone
Tab function	Moved to specified column
Spc function	Specified blank characters inserted
(CurrentX, CurrentY)	Print head position specified

The Visual Basic *Format$* function provides a great deal of flexibility in the way individual items are printed. The *Format$* function returns a string value. The general syntax is:

`Format$` (*expression, formatting string*)

The choices for the formatting string depend on whether the expression has a numeric data type or a string data type or represents a date/time. Visual Basic provides a number of intrinsic formatting strings. For example, if the expression is a numeric data type, two intrinsic formatting strings are "currency" and "percent". One of the intrinsic formatting strings for string data is >, which forces uppercase output. So

```
Picture1.Print Format$("the answer is ", ">")
    Format$(0.034, "percent")
Picture1.Print Format$(42.537, "currency")
```

results in

> THE ANSWER IS 3.40 %
> $42.54

User-constructed formatting strings can be built. Here are examples for date/time data:

```
Picture1.Print Format$(Now, "mmm d")
Picture1.Print Format$(Now, "mmmm, yyyy")
```

results in

> Mar 21
> March, 1996

Visual Basic documentation uses eight pages to describe formatting strings, so this discussion has barely scratched the surface! As usual, consult on-line Help for details.

For printing to the Printer object two special methods apply. The **NewPage method** is a request to end the current page and put the next printed output on a new page; this also resets CurrentX and CurrentY to (0, 0). (You automatically get a new page when the program runs, so don't use this method at the beginning of your program or you'll just generate an extra blank page.) The **EndDoc method** initiates printing on the page; until this method is applied to the printer, information to be printed is stored in memory.

Name: _____ Date Due: _____

LAB 5.3

LEARNING OBJECTIVES

- Working with string data
- Exploring features of the Print method

1. ____ Open a new Visual Basic project. You'll just be testing bits and pieces of code, so you can work in the Code window for Form_Click, and print directly on the form, using the syntax

   `Form1.Print` *expression list*

   What is the Visual Basic statement to print each of the following values on the form? (Hint: You'll need some of the Visual Basic string functions from Table 5.7.)

   Working with string data

   Last three letters of "barbecue"

   Length of the string "barbecue"

   Position of the "r" in "barbecue"

   ____ Try your code to see that it works.

2. ____ Declare a string variable *x*.

   ____ Assign the value "A quick brown fox" to *x*.

   ____ Write Visual Basic statements to print each of the following values on the form:

   The word "quick"

Position of the first "o" in the string

____ Try your code to see that it works.

3. ____ Can you find a Visual Basic statement (or statements) that will print the position of the second "o" in the string "A quick brown fox"? (This is fairly difficult; you may need to add two numbers.)

____ Try your statement to see that it works.

____ Open a new Visual Basic project. You don't need to save the current one.

4. ____ Your business does a lot of mail advertising to its customers. Information kept about a customer includes the mailing address, the last line of which is stored in the following format:

city name, ss nnnnn   (a)

where ss represents the two-letter state abbreviation and nnnnn represents the five-digit Zip code. For example

Anytown, IN 46243

is in the form of (a). You want a program that, starting with an address like (a), will return just the ZIP code, so that mail can be targeted to certain areas.

Customer information would usually be kept in a file, but since you don't yet know how to work with files, just have the user enter an address of form (a) in a text box. When the user clicks on a button, the Zip code is displayed in a label.

____ Write a Visual Basic program that does this task. (Don't forget labels to tell the user what input is expected and what the output is. Also include comments in your code to make it more readable.)

5. ____ Add a second button that, when clicked, displays the city name in a label. (Why is this a harder task than the Zip code problem?)

6. ____ Save your files as *zip.frm* and *zip.mak*.

> **Exploring the Print method**

7. ____ Open a new Visual Basic project.

   ____ Put a wide picture box on the form.

   ____ In the Form_Click procedure, put the following statement:

   `Picture1.Print "123456789012345678901234567890123456 7890"`

   This will provide a "ruler" for output spacing.

   ____ Experiment with printing some characters. Is the default text font for a picture box proportional spaced or monospaced?

   ____ Change the font to Courier, which is a monospaced font.

   ____ Read the on-line Visual Basic Help on the *Tab* function and the *Spc* function.

   ____ Experiment with the Print method using *Tab* and *Spc*.

   ____ Does the *Spc* function work exactly as described in Help? Explain.

8. Make sure your computer is connected to a printer or to a network with printer availability.

_____ Write code for a button that will cause the following output to be printed on a sheet of paper.

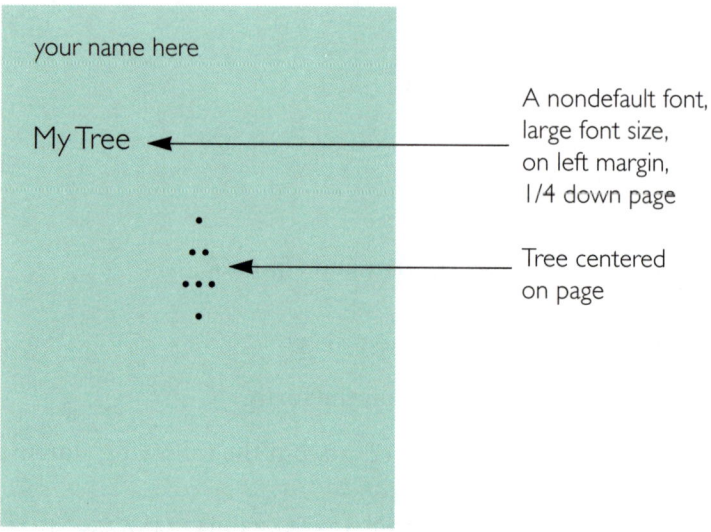

QuickCheck 5.3

1. Why is requirements analysis the first step in creating a computer program?
2. To print using print zones, separate items in the print expression list by _____.
3. To print a blank line on the printer, use the statement _____.
4. What Visual Basic statement causes the printer to actually print?
5. What would you expect as the output from the following statement?
   `Picture1.Print Format$(Now, "mm/yy")`

Review Questions

1. What is the source of round-off error in computations with decimal numbers?
2. The advantage of using data type Currency for financial transactions is _____.
3. According to the rules of operator precedence, which operation would be performed first, / or ^ ?
4. The value of the expression 8/4 * 2 is _____.
5. To override the order of precedence of operators, use _____.
6. A computation involving type Integer and type Single will be done using type _____ arithmetic.
7. True or false: Assigning a type Single value to a type Double variable doubles the number of significant digits.
8. True or False: If x is a variable of type Integer, the following assignment statement is legitimate because the string represents a number:

   `x = "42"`

9. Visual Basic initializes numeric variables to _____.
10. Visual Basic initializes string variables to _____.
11. What is the only string operation?
12. What happens when a string of 25 characters is assigned to a variable of type String *10?
13. What does the *VarType* function do?
14. Explain why the *Rnd* function is said to return pseudorandom numbers.
15. True or false: Intrinsic string processing functions do not always return string values.
16. What is involved in the process of requirements analysis?
17. Explain the difference between requirements analysis and problem specification.
18. Explain the difference between functional and performance requirements.

19. Name the two properties that can be used to set the exact location of printed output.

20. The appearance of individual items of output can be controlled by using the versatile _____ function.

Exercises

Reading Code

1. What is the value of the following expression?

   ```
   (23 \ 7) ^ 2 * 3 - 14 Mod 6
   ```

2. What is the value of the following expression?

   ```
   Abs(Sgn(-5)) ^ 15
   ```

3. What result would be returned by the following function?

   ```
   Mid$("Visual Basic", 2, 3)
   ```

4. What will be printed in the picture box as a result of the following code?

   ```
   Dim x As Integer
   Dim y As Long
   x = 14
   y = x + 3.4 - 2 * x
   Picture1.Print y
   ```

5. Describe the result of executing the following:

   ```
   Const MARK = "!"
   Picture1.CurrentX = Picture1.ScaleWidth / 2
   Picture1.CurrentY = Picture1.ScaleHeight * .95
   Picture1.Print MARK
   ```

Writing Code

6. Write an expression to find the square root of the product of the two numeric variables *OneNumber* and *TwoNumber*.

7. Suppose that *phone* is a string variable that holds a telephone number in the form

   1-808-555-9334

   Write a statement that prints the area code in Picture1.

8. Controls on a certain form are used as follows: lblPrice displays the price of a particular item and txtQuantity collects how many of that item the user is buying. Assume that sales tax has been stored as a percent (for example, 5.5 means 5.5 percent sales tax) in a constant called TAXRATE. Write code to compute the total cost to the user and display it in the label lblCost.

9. Assume that the value of π, which is approximately 3.14159, has been

stored in a constant called PI. Write code that will collect a value for the radius of a sphere from an input box and display the volume of the sphere in a label. (The formula is $V = (4/3)\pi r^3$)

10. The user will enter a name as

    first last

    in text box txtFirstLast. Write the code to display the name as

    last, first

    in text box txtLastFirst. In other words, Emily Bronte would become Bronte, Emily.

Exploring Further

11. Modify your calculator program so that the user can enter negative numbers. (You will need a second button with a minus sign as the caption, this one for entering negative numbers rather than subtracting.)

12. Modify your calculator program so that the user can enter decimal numbers.

13. Modify your calculator program so that it will take the square root of a number entered. If you did Exercise 11 and the user tries to take the square root of a negative number, your program will fail with an "illegal function call" message. At the moment, you can't do anything about this.

14. You plan to take out a loan of $1000 for one year at an annual interest rate of 8 percent. Your payments are to be made monthly, at the end of each month. You want to use the *Pmt* function to determine the amount you will owe each month. What are the values of the five arguments to this function?

15. Write the *Format$* function invocation to display today's date in the form

    Friday July 21, 1995

Projects

1. In 12-meter yacht racing, such as for the America's Cup, a formula is used to determine if a boat's rating R qualifies it as a 12-meter craft ($R = 12$). An approximation to this formula is given by

$$R = \frac{L + 2*D + \sqrt{S} - F}{2.37}$$

where L is the "rated length" of the boat (close to the length along the water line), D is the difference between the "skin girth" (the girth of the boat along the hull) and the "chain girth" (the girth of the boat as measured by a taut rope), S is the sail area, and F is the average freeboard (height of the deck above water). L, D, and F are measured in meters, S in square meters. Write a program to collect the necessary data, and compute and display R.

2. Write a "kaleidoscope" program. Set up a control array of 9 labels arranged in a 3×3 square, each with an empty caption and each a different color. When the user presses down on a command button, a random pattern of at most three of the labels appears. Releasing the button causes them to disappear. (Hints: Read what the Help file says about the *Rnd* function to learn how to generate a random integer between 0 and 8. Also read about the MouseDown and MouseUp events.)

3. You run a small sporting goods store. When a customer makes a purchase, you want to generate a personalized receipt. You want a program that allows you to fill out a computerized "form" to enter the necessary data. Clicking a button prints a hard-copy receipt with this same information nicely formatted, as in

   a. Write a set of functional requirements for such a program. Include

   > **Biff's Sports**
   > *where everyone's a good sport*
   >
   > ---
   >
   > Date: Feb 12, 1999
   > Sold To: Babe Ruth
   >   21 Yankee Stadium
   >   New York, NY 10023
   > Sport: **Baseball**
   > Item: bat
   > Cost: $17.35

   any assumptions or limitations (for example, you may want to assume that each customer buys only one item). Can you think of any performance requirements?

   b. Design and write the program.

4. You are taking over as the manager of a chain of health food stores. You have plans to upgrade your advertising budget and to do some store renovations. For each store, your plan is to spend 7 percent of the average of the last three months' income on advertising and to spend 4 percent of that average on renovations. Write a program that collects the income for each of the last three months in three text boxes and gives the user a choice of two command buttons, one to compute advertising costs and one to compute renovation costs. If the user chooses advertising, the average of the last three months' income is displayed in a label, and the advertising costs are displayed in another label. If the user chooses renovations, the average and the renovation costs are displayed. Because both command buttons need to compute the average of the three text box values and display the result, write a general form-level procedure to do this subtask. (Hint: The procedure is invoked with the statement

Call *ProcedureName*. You want the average to be displayed with a dollar sign, but "currency" may not be your best choice of formatting string.)

5. In your company, computer users are given three-letter passwords, using uppercase letters only. For protection, these are issued to users in an encoded format known as a shift cipher, or a Caesar cipher (so called because Julius Caesar used it to transmit military information). A number *n* between 1 and 25 is chosen as the amount of shift, and each letter in the password is encoded as the letter that occurs *n* places farther along in the alphabet, with the last *n* letters shifted in a cycle to the first *n* letters. For example, if *n* = 2, then AMP would be encoded as COR. Write a program based on a shift of 2 that allows the user to enter a three-letter password and obtain the encoded form or to enter a three-letter encoded password and obtain the original password. Assume that Y and Z are never valid password letters. (Hint: Read on-line Help about the *Asc* and *Chr$* functions.)

CHAPTER 6

Procedures

KEY POINTS

- The rules of scope for procedures, variables, and controls determine where they can be recognized and used.
- Information is passed into and out of a general procedure or a function by the use of arguments and parameters.
- A user-defined function can be written to compute a single value.
- "Top-down design" is a way to overcome complexity as you plan your program.

6.1 Introduction

In high-level program design, the objective is to break the overall task down into subtasks. This "modular" approach to program design is a tool that makes the complexity of the total task manageable; the programmer can focus on one thing at a time. Procedures go hand-in-hand with subtasks. Each procedure should be responsible for carrying out one subtask. Procedures can be added to the program one at a time and tested as they are added. When an error occurs, it is easy to pinpoint where the problem lies. When a change in the program is needed, it is easy to see which procedure needs to be changed.

Once you have decided that you need a procedure to do a certain subtask, you then must decide where to put that procedure. Procedures within a Visual Basic program can exist at several different "levels." Procedures use variables, and variables can be declared at several different levels, so you must also decide where to declare variables. These decisions will be based both on the role the procedure or variable is to play and the *rules of scope* of Visual Basic. Procedures, like functions, may need information passed to them by way of arguments. Finally, you may decide that a subtask could best be accomplished by writing your own function.

This chapter discusses the Visual Basic rules of scope, how procedures receive (and give back) information, and how to write your own Visual Basic functions.

6.2 What is scope?

Visual Basic statements can be written to

        invoke procedures.
        assign values to variables.
        assign values to object properties.

When a statement is executed that invokes a procedure or assigns a value to a variable or to an object property, the procedure name, variable name, or object name must be "known" or "recognized" by the part of the code containing that statement. **Scope** in a programming language has to do with where things are known or recognized. As an analogy, your name or face may have a scope consisting of your home town, a sports figure may have national scope, and the President of the United States has international scope.

Scope is controlled by rules within the language. Visual Basic has rules for the scope of procedures, variables, and objects. Because of the way a Visual Basic program is composed of many little pieces, an understanding of scope is particularly important.

6.3 Scope of procedures

You know that there are several types of procedures. **Event procedures** are associated with particular object_event pairs on a particular form. Thus the Command1_Click procedure is invoked when the Command1 button on a particular form is clicked. **General procedures** are not associated with particular objects or events. The *get_number* and *put_answer* procedures in the calculator were general procedures. General procedures may be applicable only to a particular form, in which case they are written in the general section of the form. They may also be used by more than one form in a project, in which case they are placed in a separate code module, which is a .BAS file. Figure 6.1 shows the three locations where procedures may be found in a Visual Basic project.

The scope of a procedure determines where that procedure is known, that is, where a statement invoking that procedure can be used. A statement to invoke a procedure has the following syntax:

`Call` *ProcedureName(argument list)*

You used a statement like this in your calculator program:

`Call put_answer(number)`

Call is a reserved word in Visual Basic indicating that a procedure is being invoked. The procedure name follows the standard rule for Visual Basic identifiers (a string of up to 40 characters that consists of letters, digits, and underscores; begins with a letter; and is not a reserved word). The argument list for a procedure serves the same purpose as the argument list for a function; that is, it passes along any pieces of information the procedure needs to know in order to carry out its work. If there are no arguments, the parentheses are omitted and the syntax is

`Call` *ProcedureName*

The important thing to note is the use of the procedure name to invoke the procedure. If the calling statement is not within the scope of the procedure, then the procedure name is not recognized. When the program is executed, the calling statement will result in a pop-up window with an error message "Sub or Function not defined" (see Figure 6.2, where the procedure name *ProfitMargin* is unrecognized). This is Visual Basic's way of saying, "I don't understand this procedure name you are trying to call."

Figure 6.1
The three locations for procedures

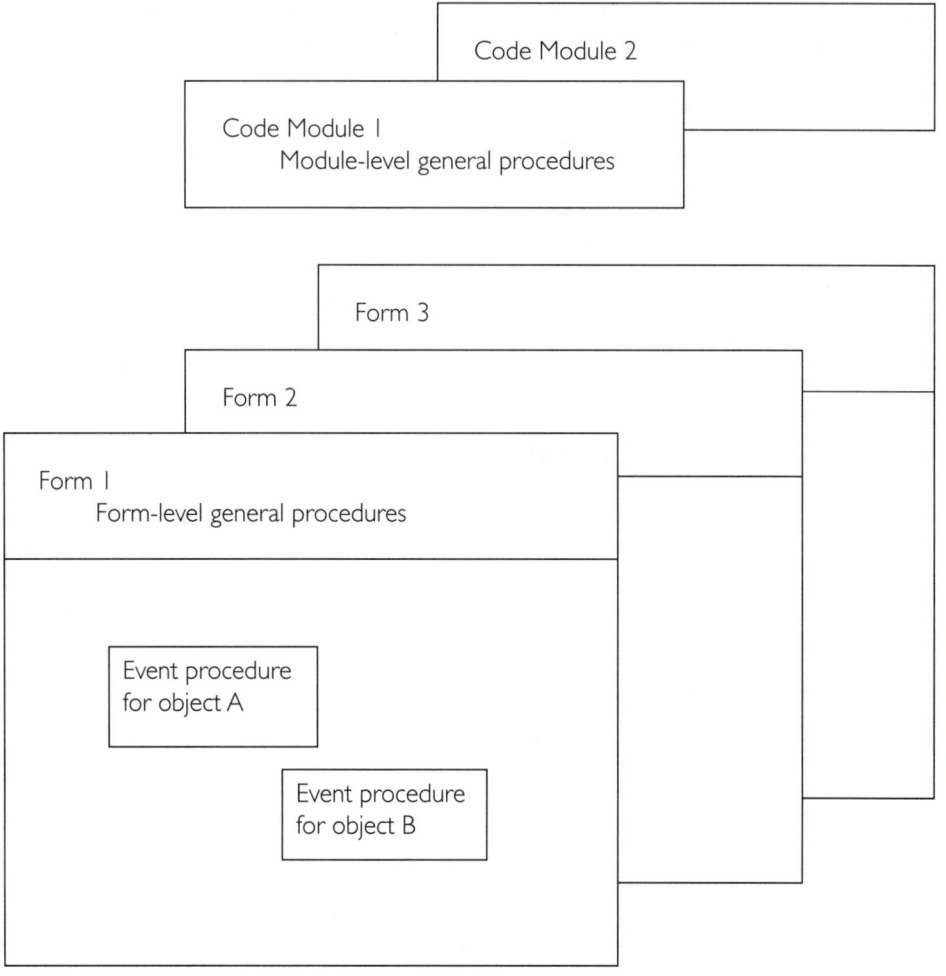

The rules of scope for procedures are:

The scope of an event procedure is throughout the form on which its object resides.

The scope of a general procedure in the general section of a form is throughout the form.

The scope of a general procedure in a code module is throughout the project.[1]

How does scope impact your program design? Suppose you have several objects on one form with event procedures that need some common code. You have two choices: you can repeat that code in several places, that is, in each of the event procedures, or you can put it in a general procedure in the general section of the form, where the scope rules say it can be invoked from any event procedure for any object on the form. Repeating the code in several places is not that difficult because you can copy and paste it, rather than retyping it. However, suppose that code is later changed. Then you will have to find all the copies of that code and make the change in every copy. This is fraught with peril, as you are very apt to overlook one of

---

[1]There is an exception. A general procedure in a code module that is declared Private—by putting the reserved word **Private** before "Sub"—is known only throughout that module.

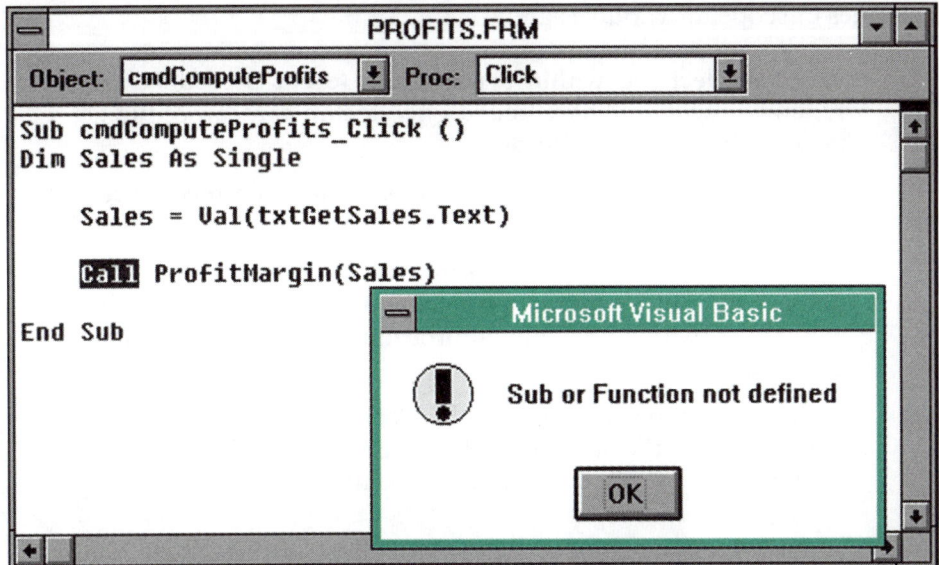

Figure 6.2
Error message for unrecognized procedure

the changes, and your code is then incorrect. A very important rule of thumb in programming is to have only one copy of code to do any one task. (Recall the *get_number* and *put_answer* procedures for the calculator were put in the general section of the form because they were used by all the arithmetic operation buttons.)

Similarly, if your project has multiple forms and you want to be able to do a common task from each of them, then the code for that task should go in a procedure in a code module, where, according to the rules of scope, it can be invoked from every form.

During high-level program design, your job is to determine the various tasks that need to be done in order to solve the problem as a whole. At the same time you are also making decisions about the forms and control objects to be used, and you can see whether there are multiple objects or multiple forms that all need to perform some common task or whether each task is associated with only a single object. Once these decisions are made, the rules of scope will determine where to put the procedures that carry out each task.

6.4 Scope of variables and control objects

Like the scope of a procedure, which determines where the procedure name is recognized, the scope of a variable determines where the variable name is recognized. A variable's scope depends on where it was declared, and also the keyword used in its declaration. Variables can be declared in several places:

> Within a procedure (an event procedure, a general procedure in the general section of a form, or a general procedure in a code module)
>
> In the declarations section of a form
>
> In the declarations section of a module

The rules of scope for variables are:

>Variables declared within a procedure (event procedure or general procedure) have scope only within that procedure; they are **local** to the procedure.

>Variables declared in the declarations section of a form have scope throughout that form.

>Variables declared with the "Dim" keyword in the declarations section of a module have scope throughout that module, that is, within any general procedures found within that code module.

>Variables can be declared in the declarations section of a module using the keyword **Global** instead of "Dim"; such variables have scope throughout the entire project.

Constants follow exactly the same rules of scope as variables. To make a constant known throughout the entire project, add the keyword "Global" in front of (not instead of) the keyword "Const". Global constants, like global variables, can be declared only in code modules.

There is one other wrinkle that applies to variables that are local to a procedure. Such variables, according to the rules, have scope only within that procedure. Outside that procedure, their names are not recognized. Indeed, the memory space to store a local variable, which is what the variable name represents, is ordinarily allocated when the procedure is invoked and then released (thus becoming available for other uses) when the procedure is exited. When the procedure is invoked again, new space for local variables is set aside and re-initialized. However, using the keyword **Static** instead of the word "Dim" in a variable declaration inside a procedure results in the memory location for that local variable being retained from one invocation of the procedure to the next. When the procedure is invoked for a second time, the value of the static local variable is the same as its value was when the previous invocation terminated. Putting Static in front of "Sub" in the code for a procedure has the same effect as declaring all local variables within that procedure using "Static". The rules of scope, however, are unchanged; local variables still are not recognized outside the procedure.

Figure 6.3 illustrates possible declarations. In (a), the variable *Amount* is local to the Command1_Click event procedure, and no reference to *Amount* can be made outside this procedure. In (b), both *ThisOne* and *Accum* are local to the form-level general procedure *Counter*. If *Counter* is invoked multiple times, *Accum* retains its value from the previous invocation because it was declared using "Static", whereas *ThisOne* is re-initialized to zero on each new invocation. In (c), *NextName* is declared in the declarations section of Form1, not within a procedure; *NextName* can be referenced anywhere on Form1, including within any event procedures for objects on Form1. The declarations in (d) are made in a code module. *TAX* is a global constant and *Company* is a global variable; their names are recognized anywhere in the entire project. *Total*, because it was declared using "Dim" instead of "Global", is recognized only within general procedures in Module1.

Because local variable names are unknown outside of the procedure in which they are declared, a variable local to procedure A (named, say, *NextItem*) could have the same name as a variable local to procedure B.

Figure 6.3
Sample declarations

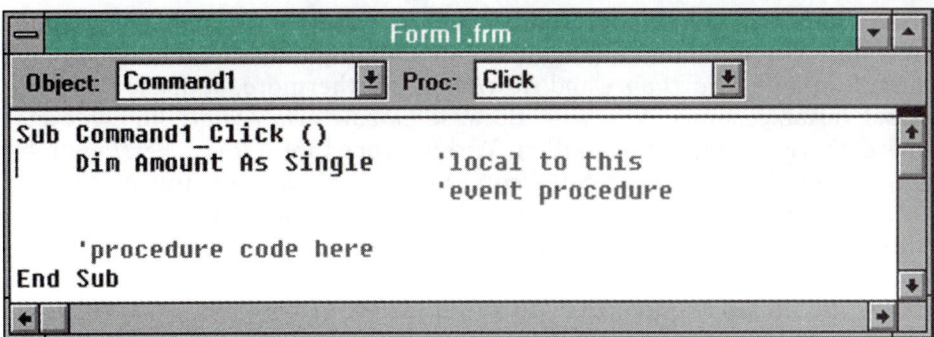

(a)

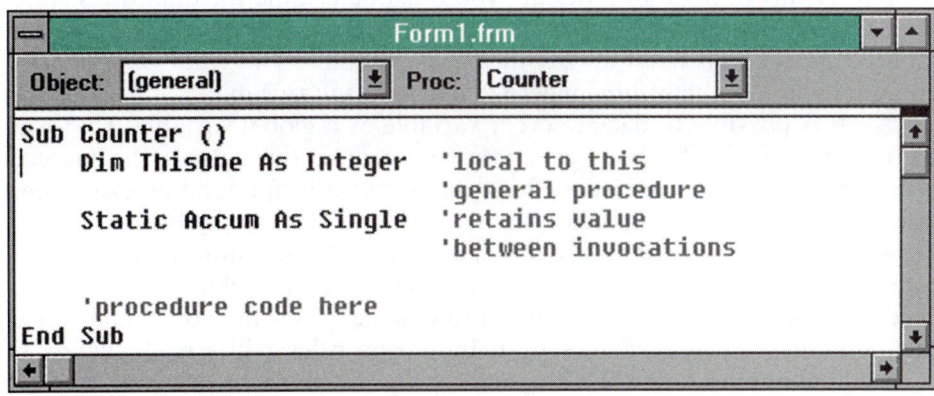

(b)

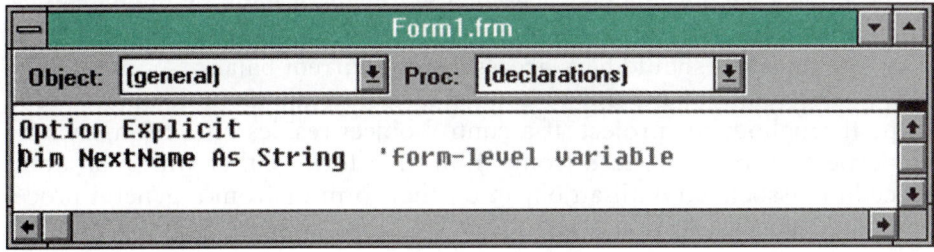

(c)

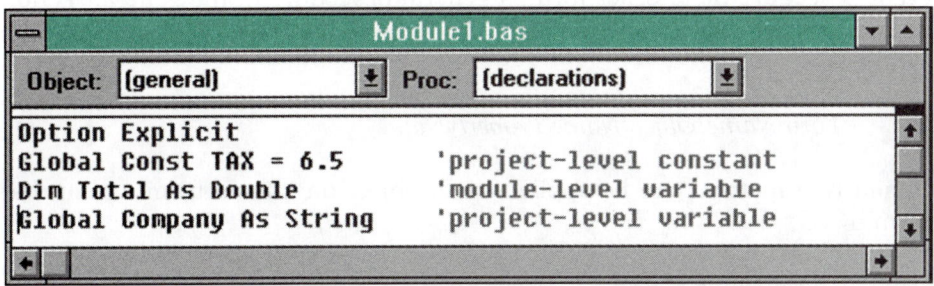

(d)

Visual Basic will not be confused because only the local variables in the one procedure currently being executed are recognized. It is as if there are two variables named $NextItem_A$ and $NextItem_B$. Furthermore, suppose there is a global variable named *NextItem*. Because global variables are known everywhere, there is a potential conflict. Within procedure A, does *NextItem* refer to the global *NextItem* or to $NextItem_A$? Visual Basic resolves this problem by always giving the local variable precedence; that is, a reference to *NextItem* within procedure A will always mean the local variable $NextItem_A$. While Visual Basic will not be confused, human beings reading code with duplicate names are apt to be confused. In the interests of code clarity you should avoid this situation if you are writing the entire program yourself. However, if many people are working on a large project, they are all free to use whatever local variable names they choose in their own procedures without having to confer with everyone else about duplicate names.

As part of high-level design, you must determine the quantities (variables) your program needs to use, and whether multiple procedures or multiple forms will need access to these variables. The rules of scope for variables will then determine where to declare each variable.

It is possible to declare every variable as a global variable. That way their names would be known in every procedure throughout the project. This appears to have the virtue of simplicity, but it is not good programming practice. Procedures have the capability to change variable values, and inadvertent changes to variables are a major source of programming errors. The rules of scope are intended to limit, as much as possible, a procedure's access to variables it is not supposed to change. The time you spend thinking about protecting variables by using scope rules will pay dividends in reduced debugging time. The larger the project, the more this is true. So if only one procedure needs to use a certain variable, make that variable local to that procedure. If only the procedures on one form need to use a variable, declare that variable in the general section of that form. Declare variables in a code module by using "Global" only if they are needed by multiple forms in the project. As an analogy, everyone who calls a bank-by-phone service should have access to the current rates of deposit (this is "global" information), but only you should have access to your current balance.

The scope of control objects is easiest of all. Control objects have scope throughout the project. If a control object resides on a form, then its properties can be referenced from within that form (either within an event procedure associated with an object on that form or from a general procedure in the general section of that form) by

ObjectName.PropertyName

To reference the object's properties from somewhere outside that form (an event procedure on another form, a general procedure in the general section of another form, or a code module), the form name must be given first. The syntax is

FormName!ObjectName.PropertyName

Similarly, a method can be applied to an object on a form from within that form by

ObjectName.Method

and from outside that form by

> *FormName!ObjectName.MethodName*

For example, if there is a Command1 button on Form1 and a Command1 button on Form 2, then the following could be the body of the Command1_Click procedure for the Command1 button on Form1:

```
Form2.Show
Form2!Command1.Caption = "changed by button on Form1"
Form2!Command1.Move 0
```

These statements do the following three things, respectively:

> Apply the Show method to Form2, and make Form2 the active window (after loading it if it is not already loaded).
>
> Change the caption on a button on Form2.
>
> Apply the Move method to a button on Form2, which moves the button so that its Left property is zero.

Thus property changes and methods are applied to a control object on a second form from a control object on the first form.

Table 6.1 summarizes the rules of scope for Visual Basic.

Table 6.1 Visual Basic scope rules

ITEM	SCOPE
Procedure	
Event procedure	Throughout the form
Form-level general procedure	Throughout the form
Module-level general procedure	Throughout the project
Variables and constants	
Declared in a procedure	Within the procedure
Declared in form declarations section	Throughout the form
Declared in module declarations section with Dim or Const	Throughout the module
Declared in module declarations section with Global	Throughout the project
Control objects	
Any kind of control object	Throughout the project

Name: _____   Date Due: _____

LEARNING OBJECTIVES

- Exploring the scope of procedures
- Exploring the scope of variables

LAB 6.1

1. ____ Open a new Visual Basic project.

   ____ Set the AutoRedraw property for the form to True.

   ____ Put two command buttons on the form.

   ____ Write a click event procedure for each button. When Command1 is clicked, the message "Form1-Command1 click event" should be printed on the form. When Command2 is clicked, the message "Form1-Command2 click event" should be printed on the form.

   ____ Test this to see that it works as expected.

2. These two event procedures are associated with particular objects on a form. As such, they should be accessible throughout the form.

   ____ Add one statement to the Command1_Click procedure that invokes the Command2_Click procedure. (You invoke this procedure by using the reserved word "Call" and the procedure name.)

   ____ Now run your program and click the Command1 button. What happens and why?

   ____ Delete this one statement and replace it with a statement that invokes the Command1_Click procedure.

   ____ Now run your program and click the Command1 button. What happens and why?

   ____ Delete this one statement.

3. ____ Go to the general section of the form and write a procedure called *Test*. Procedure *Test* should contain two statements that invoke the Command1_Click procedure and the Command2_Click procedure.

Exploring the scope of procedures

____ Put a third button on your form and give it the caption "run test". Its click procedure should contain a single statement that invokes the *Test* procedure.

____ Run your program and click the run test button. What happens and why?

4. ____ Go to the general section of the form and write a second procedure called *Test2*. This procedure should print "Test2" on the form.

____ Now add a third statement to procedure *Test* that invokes procedure *Test2*.

____ Run your program and click the run test button. What happens and why?

5. ____ To create a second form, do one of the following:

OPTIONS
- Click on File on the menu bar and select New Form.
- Click on the New Form toolbar button.
- Use the access keys: Alt-F (for File) followed by F (for new Form).

____ Put a command button on this form. When clicked, this button should print "Form2-Command1 click event" on the new form.

____ Add a button with the caption "Go to Form2" on your Form1; the click event for this button should invoke the Show method on Form2.

____ Run your program to see that the new button on the new form works.

6. ____ In the click event code for the command button on Form2, add code to invoke the *Test* procedure from Form1. What happens when you run your program and click this button? Why does this happen?

7. ____ In the click event code for the command button on Form2, add code to invoke the Command2_Click procedure from Form1.

____ Run your program. What happens now?

8. ____ Write a general procedure for Form2 called *Joker*. *Joker* should print "Joker" on Form2.

____ Put a second button on Form2 with the caption "run Joker" that invokes *Joker*.

____ Test this.

____ Now add a statement to the *Joker* procedure to invoke the *Test* procedure from Form1. What happens when you run your program and click the run Joker button?

Can the *Joker* procedure invoke the Command2_Click procedure from Form1?

9. ____ To create a code module, do one of the following:

OPTIONS
- Click on File on the menu bar and select New Module.
- Click on the New Module toolbar button.
- Use the access keys: Alt-F (for File) followed by M (for new Module).

____ In this module, write a procedure called *King*. When invoked, the *King* procedure prints "King" on Form1.

____ Add a button on Form1 to invoke the *King* procedure; test this button.

____ Now add code to procedure *King* to invoke the *Test* procedure from Form1. What happens when you run the *King* procedure?

Can you invoke the *King* procedure from the *Joker* procedure?

10. ____ Write a second procedure in the code module called *Queen*; can you invoke it from within the *King* procedure?

11. ____ To summarize the scope rules for procedures, fill in the following table using "yes" or "no" for each case.

↓ Can invoke→	Event procedure on same form	General procedure on same form	Event procedure on another form	General procedure on another form	General procedure in code module
Event procedure					
General procedure on a form					
General procedure in a code module					

Exploring the scope of variables

12. ____ Add the following two statements to the Command2_Click procedure on Form1.

```
x = 2
Form1.Print x
```

____ Declare *x* as an integer in the Command1_Click procedure on Form1. What happens when you run the program and click on Command2? Why?

____ Delete this declaration and declare *x* as an integer in the general procedure *Test* on Form1.

____ Run the program and try Command2 again. What happens and why?

____ Delete this declaration and declare *x* (using "Dim") as an integer in the declarations section of the code module. Now what happens when you run the program? Why?

____ Change this declaration to a Global declaration and run the program. Now what happens and why?

13. ____ In the Command1_Click procedure, declare *A* as an integer.

____ Add the following two lines of code:

```
A = A + 1
Form1.Print "A = " A
```

____ Run your program, clicking the Command1 button several times.

____ Now add "Static" to your declaration of *A* and repeat. Explain what happens in each case.

Exit Visual Basic; you do not need to save your work.

> **QuickCheck 6.1**
> 1. What is the reserved word that signals a procedure invocation?
> 2. What is the reserved word that is used at the beginning of code for a procedure?
> 3. The declaration for a variable *HighValue* of type Single that is to be known throughout a multiform project would be written as _____.
> 4. Where would the declaration of question 3 be written?
> 5. How would program code within Form2 refer to the Caption property of a command button called cmdTester on Form1?

6.5 Argument passing

A procedure with one or more arguments is invoked by a statement of the form

```
Call ProcedureName(argument list)
```

The argument list in the Call statement has a counterpart called the **parameter list** in the code for the procedure. The procedure code consists of a block of statements of the form

```
Sub ProcedureName (parameter list)
    'statements in the body of the
    'called procedure go here
End Sub
```

Within the body of the procedure, the parameters serve as "placeholders" for the arguments. They take on the values of the arguments when the procedure is invoked. The argument list and the corresponding parameter list are the means for communication between the *calling* procedure, where the Call statement is, and the *called* procedure. Information needed by the *called* procedure is passed into that procedure by way of the argument and parameter lists, and information computed within the *called* procedure and needed by the *calling* procedure is passed back out through these lists.

As an example, suppose there are two buttons on a form. When these buttons are clicked, one collects input consisting of two quiz grades from a set of two text boxes and one collects input consisting of two test grades from another set of two text boxes. In each case, the average of the two grades is computed and written as the caption of a single output label on the form. Figure 6.4 shows a possible form layout.

Because the averaging-and-output-writing task is common to both buttons, a general procedure called *DoAverage* can do this task. Then both the button click event procedures can call the general procedure. Obviously *DoAverage* needs to know the two numbers to be averaged, so these will be passed as arguments from the calling procedures. In addition, a third argument will pass information to *DoAverage* indicating whether the scores

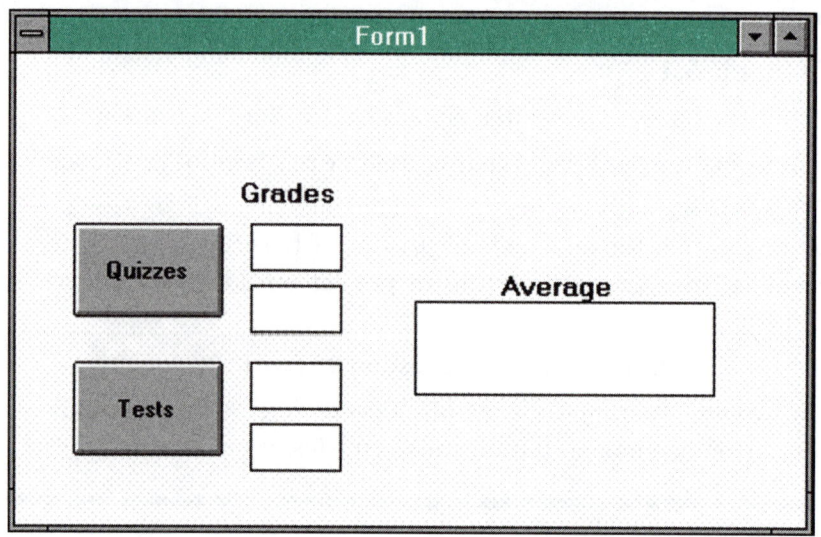

Figure 6.4
Possible form layout for the grade averaging program

are for quizzes or for tests, so that *DoAverage* can include this in the output. Here's how the code for the quizzes button might look:

```
Sub Quiz_Click ()
    Dim quiz1 As Integer
    Dim quiz2 As Integer
    Dim whichtype As String

    whichtype = "quiz"

    'get the input
    quiz1 = Val(txtQuiz1.Text)
    quiz2 = Val(txtQuiz2.Text)

    'find the average
    Call DoAverage(quiz1, quiz2, whichtype)

End Sub
```

The local variables *quiz1* and *quiz2* get the scores from text boxes (notice the use of the *Val* function). The local string variable *whichtype* identifies these as quiz scores. Three arguments (*quiz1, quiz2, whichtype*) are passed to *DoAverage* in the Call statement. The code for the Test_Click procedure is similar, with appropriate changes for tests instead of quizzes.

The code for the *DoAverage* procedure might look like the following:

```
Sub DoAverage (x As Integer, y As Integer, which As String)

    Dim Average As Single

    'compute average
    Average = (x + y) / 2
    lblOutput.Caption = which & " average " & Str$(Average)

End Sub
```

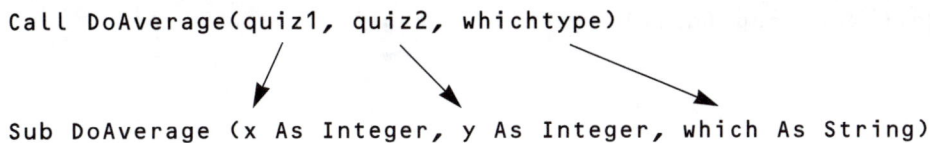

Figure 6.5
Argument passing between Quiz_Click and *DoAverage*

The *DoAverage* procedure has three parameters, *x*, *y*, and *which*. The arguments and the parameters match up by their positions in their respective lists. When *DoAverage* is called by Quiz_Click, the matchup works as shown in Figure 6.5. When the Call statement is executed, each parameter takes on the value passed to it by its counterpart argument. If the grades for the first quiz and the second quiz are 50 and 70, then after these values are entered in the text boxes and the quizzes button is clicked, the values 50, 70, and "quiz" are passed to the parameters *x*, *y*, and *which*, respectively. According to the code for *DoAverage*, $(x + y)/2$ is computed and stored in the local variable *Average*, and

    quiz average 60

gets written to the output label caption. (The parameter *which* supplies the word "quiz" in this output.)

A parameter list consists of a list of identifiers and their data types. The parameters act like variables in that they take on values used within the body of the procedure, but they are not declared as variables. Parameters are sometimes called "dummy variables." An argument and its corresponding parameter must have the same data type. However, as illustrated in this example, they do not have to have the same names. The *DoAverage* procedure is written as a generic recipe for what to do with two integer values and a string value. The calling procedure supplies the actual values when it invokes the procedure. When procedure Test_Click calls *DoAverage*, the matchup between arguments and parameters is illustrated in Figure 6.6 and *DoAverage* can work just as well with the values supplied by these new arguments. The fact that names in the parameter list of a general procedure can be generic and do not have to be the same as the arguments is what allows general procedures to be called from multiple places.

Suppose the general procedure was to compute the average but the Quiz_Click and Test_Click procedures were to print the result. Then the general procedure would still compute the average, but instead of printing it out, it would pass that value back to the calling procedure through another parameter. Each calling procedure would have a local variable for its average that would correspond with that parameter. Each local variable, incidentally, could be called *Average* because local variable names in different procedures—being local—can't be confused with one another. The parameter can be called *Average* as well. Because *DoAverage* does not print the message, there is no need for the *which* parameter (or the *whichtype* argument).

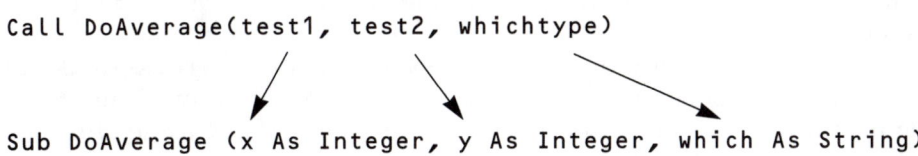

Figure 6.6
Argument passing between Test_Click and *DoAverage*

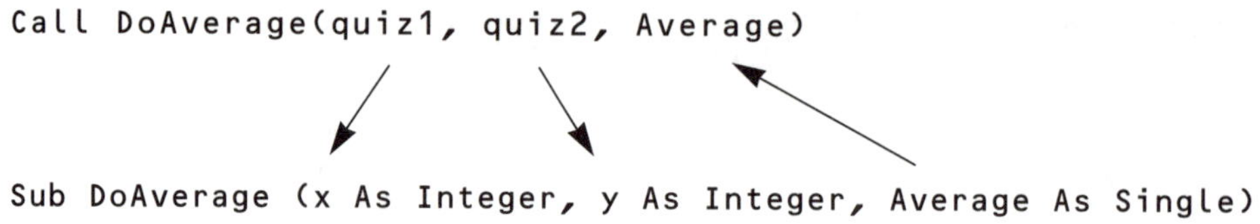

Figure 6.7
Argument passing between Quiz_Click and *DoAverage* where Quiz_Click prints the average

```
Call DoAverage(quiz1, quiz2, Average)



Sub DoAverage (x As Integer, y As Integer, Average As Single)
```

Figure 6.7 shows the matchup between Quiz_Click and *DoAverage* in this case. Notice that this time the third arrow goes from the parameter to the argument instead of from the argument to the parameter. That's because the information flow here is from the general procedure, where the value of *Average* is computed, back to the event procedure.

A matchup of arguments and parameters is technically called an **interface** between the calling procedure and the called procedure. Interfaces are where procedures "speak to" one another. Care must be taken that the argument and parameter lists have the same number of items, that corresponding items have the same data type, and that corresponding items represent the same things on both halves of the interface.

An argument is ordinarily **passed by reference**. What this means is that the corresponding parameter in the called procedure becomes another (temporary) name for the memory location where the value of the argument is stored. If the parameter is assigned a new value in the body of the procedure, the content of the memory location is changed. When the procedure is exited, the value of the corresponding argument back in the calling procedure has also been changed. You want this to happen when the called procedure is computing some new value that the calling procedure needs to know. The information flow is from the called procedure back to the calling procedure, as is the case with *Average* above.

But suppose the information flow is into the called procedure, that is, the called procedure needs to know something but should not change it, as is the case with *quiz1* and *quiz2*? Recall the statement in Section 6.4 about inadvertent changes to variables being a major source of programming errors. To prevent a procedure from changing an argument it needs for information only and has no business changing, the argument can be **passed by value** instead of by reference. What this means is that the corresponding parameter in the called procedure is allocated a temporary memory location that contains the value of the argument. The called procedure can see and use the value, but should it happen to make any changes to the value, the changes are made in this temporary location, not in the location of the real argument. After the called procedure is exited, the temporary location effectively disappears and the argument (in its original location) still has its original value.

As an analogy to explain the difference between passing by reference and passing by value, suppose that someone wants you to proofread a paper written with a word processor. He or she gives you the original electronic file for the paper and you edit it. Any changes you make are made to the original paper. This is the idea of passing by reference. Now suppose he or she gives you a copy of the file. You can see the document and you can make changes, but the changes do not affect the original file. This is the idea of passing by value.

In order to pass an argument by value, use the keyword **ByVal** before the corresponding parameter. Thus an improvement on Figure 6.7 is the interface shown in Figure 6.8, where the values of *quiz1* and *quiz2* are protected from modification by procedure *DoAverage*.

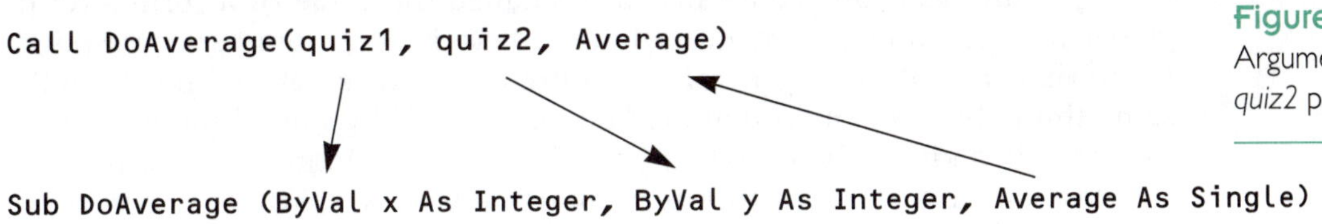

```
Call DoAverage(quiz1, quiz2, Average)



Sub DoAverage (ByVal x As Integer, ByVal y As Integer, Average As Single)
```

Figure 6.8
Arguments *quiz1* and *quiz2* passed by value

An argument passed by reference must be a variable because the corresponding parameter has to have access to the argument's memory location. An argument passed by value can be an expression of the appropriate data type as well as a variable, even though an expression does not name a memory location. The corresponding parameter stores the value of the expression in its own temporary location. An argument passed by value can even be an object property.

Event procedures are more limited than general procedures in the parameters they can have. For example, the click event procedure for a command button that is not part of a control array has no parameters. The Code window automatically provides a "shell" for the click event procedure that looks like the following:

```
Sub Command1_Click ()

End Sub
```

The parameter list is empty, and any attempt to add parameters results in an error message when the program tries to execute. If the button is part of a control array, then Index is its only formal parameter. The shell provided by the Code window looks like

```
Sub Command1_Click (Index As Integer)

End Sub
```

and no additional parameters can be added.

Event procedures cannot have arbitrary parameters, the way general procedures can, because of the dual way event procedures can be activated. A general procedure is executed only in response to a Call statement. You can use a Call statement to activate an event procedure, as in

```
Call Command1_Click
```

However, it is more often the case that an event procedure executes because the user generates the event, in the above case by clicking the Command1 command button. Suppose you were somehow able to put a parameter like "x As Integer" in the parameter list for a button click event procedure and that the click event is generated by the user. There would be no source for an argument to associate with this parameter. To solve this problem, the only parameters allowed for event procedures are those for which values can be determined in case the user generates the event. The Index of the button in a control array, for example, has a value associated with the button itself, whether the user clicks the button or whether another procedure calls the click event procedure.

If an event procedure needs to change the value of a form-level or global variable, it can do so even though there is no parameter corresponding to that variable. Any general procedure can, and sometimes must, do the same thing. Such changes that are "unannounced" by way of the parameter list are called **side effects**. While side effects are sometimes necessary, care should be taken to avoid **unintentional side effects**, where a procedure inadvertently changes the value of a form-level or global variable. The warning given early in this chapter about using rules of scope to protect access to variables was about this very point. Here's how such a thing can happen. Suppose there is a form-level variable called *Size*, and another variable local to some procedure called *Site*. Within this procedure, the programmer intends to set the value of *Site* by the statement

```
Site = 4
```

but makes a typographical error and instead types

```
Size = 4
```

There will be no error message because *Size*, like *Site*, is a declared variable. The unintentional side effect has been to change the value of the form-level variable.

Two things can be done to help protect against unintentional side effects. The first is to use some naming convention for nonlocal variables that makes it unlikely that they will be mistyped into local variable names. For example, all form-level variables could begin with *Form_*, as in *Form_Size*, and all global variables could begin with *Glo_*. The second is to note all intentional side effects in a procedure's opening comment, as in

```
'this procedure changes global variable Rate
```

Then any assignment statement changing the value of something that has not been so noted, is not a parameter name, and is not a local variable is suspect.

Name: _____   Date Due: _____

LEARNING OBJECTIVES

- Working with parameter passing
- Using the CONSTANT.TXT file

LAB 6.2

1. ____ Open the Visual Basic project **ave.mak**. This project computes the average of two quiz grades or two test grades using a general procedure *DoAverage*, as described in the first part of Section 6.5.

   ____ Run this program, and then examine the code for the two buttons and the general procedure.

2. ____ Now change this program so that the buttons, rather than the general procedure, write the average. The interface should look like Figure 6.8.

   > **Changing parameters in *ave.mak***

   ____ Test your revised program to be sure it works

   ____ Save the project as ***ave1.frm*** and ***ave1.mak***.

3. ____ Open the Visual Basic project ***jail.mak***. This file contains two general form-level procedures. The purpose of these procedures is to draw horizontal and vertical lines on the form by applying the **Line method** to the form. In order to draw a line, the Line method requires a pair of coordinates for the start of the line and a pair of coordinates for the end of the line. The coordinates (x, y) measure the distance horizontally and vertically from the top left corner of the form, like the Left and Top properties of control objects on the form.

   > **New project— numerical parameters**

   ____ Look at the *HORIZONTAL* procedure code. How does this procedure determine the starting coordinates for the line in order to give them to the Line method?

   How does it determine the coordinates for the end of the line?

Look at the VERTICAL procedure code. How does it determine the starting coordinates for the line?

How does it determine the ending coordinates for the line?

4. ____ Write one statement invoking the HORIZONTAL procedure that would cause a line to be drawn on the form that starts at (500, 1000) and is 800 units long.

____ Put a command button on the form with this statement in its click event code.
____ Run the program and try this button.
____ Delete the button.

5. ____ Put three command buttons on the form with captions "Box", "Table", and "Jail", respectively. Each button is to draw an appropriate figure in a reasonable place on the form by making use of the horizontal and vertical line-drawing capabilities provided by the general procedures. The figure on page 219 shows what the form might look like after all three buttons have been clicked.

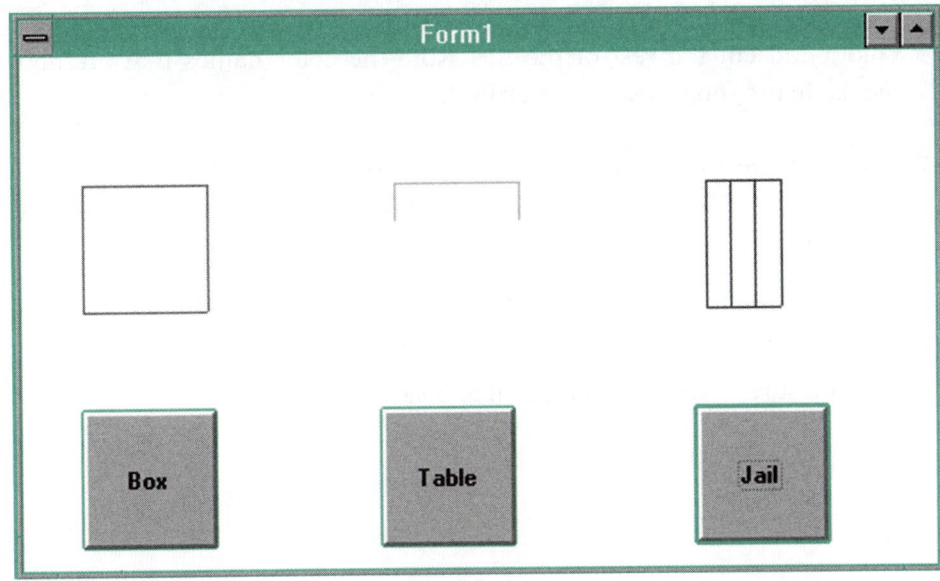

___ Write the necessary code. Be sure to add comments. Suggestion: Test the program frequently as you write the code. Then if something goes wrong, it is easy to pinpoint the difficulty.

6. ___ You may have noticed when setting the BackColor property of a form that the color choices are written in an encoded fashion, like &HFF00&, rather than by the color name, like "green." In setting a color property from within code, it would be nice to be able to use something simple like the word "green" instead of a number you can't possibly remember! Making the following constant declaration

> Global Const GREEN = &HFF00&

allows use of the color name throughout the project. Visual Basic provides a file called CONSTANT.TXT that contains many Global Const declarations for setting certain system values.

Using the CONSTANT.TXT file

___ Create a code module for the *jail* project and name it *jail.bas.*

___ In this module, choose Load Text from the File menu and select the file CONSTANT.TXT in the Visual Basic subdirectory (in the dialog box, choose either Replace or Merge).

_____ This is a big file; find the section that defines global constants for colors and cut the rest of the file. Note the color names that are now available for you to use in the project.

7. Setting the form's ForeColor property determines the color of graphical objects like lines that will appear on the form (as opposed to the BackColor property, which determines the background color).

_____ The box is to be drawn with red lines, the table is to be green, and the jail is to be blue. Modify the code as necessary.

_____ Be sure to test your program and save your work.

> **QuickCheck 6.2**
>
> 1. When a procedure is invoked, its parameters receive values from the corresponding _____ in the Call statement.
> 2. Does the data type declaration go in the argument list or the parameter list?
> 3. A called procedure is to compute a value and pass it back to the calling procedure; the actual parameter should be passed by _____.
> 4. True or false: Any global variable can be an argument to an event procedure.
> 5. Why must the CONSTANT.TXT file be loaded into a code module instead of into a form?

6.6 User-defined functions

You have used some of Visual Basic's intrinsic functions. It is also possible to write your own functions, called **user-defined functions**. Writing a function is something like writing a procedure. Each is a section of self-contained code that can be invoked from elsewhere, and each can have a parameter list. Functions are found at the form level or the module level and have the same scope rules as procedures. There are some differences, however, between functions and procedures.

The following section of code is for a simple function that doubles the value of any integer passed to it.

```
Function Twice (ByVal x As Integer) As Integer
     Twice = 2 * x
End Function
```

Code for a function begins with the reserved word **Function** rather than "Sub," and closes with **End Function** rather than "End Sub." The function name can be any legitimate identifier. The purpose of a function is to compute and return a single value, and that value is returned through the function name. Since no other quantities are to be changed within the function, all arguments can be passed by value. (Remember that the "ByVal" keyword before the parameter *x* in the section of code indicates that any changes to *x* within the function will have no effect on the corresponding argument.) The function name is a dummy variable, something that can carry a value but is not declared as a variable; however, the data type of the values the function can take on must be specified. That's done by using

As *datatype*

at the end of the function header. In the example, the final "As Integer" in the first line specifies that the function name *Twice* will be assigned integer values.

Because the function name returns the computed value, there must be an assignment statement within the body of the function code that gives that value to the function name. In this simple example, that assignment is the only line of code within the body of the function.

A function invocation consists of the function name together with arguments that match the function's parameters. This invocation is used as part of a program statement. It is not a stand-alone statement, as is a procedure invocation. For this example, the function could be invoked within a command button click procedure:

```
Sub Command1_Click ()
   Dim x As Integer
   x = 3
   Picture1.Print Twice(x)
End Sub
```

Clicking Command1 results in printing 6 in the picture box. Notice that the function invocation, Twice(x), is used within the statement applying the *Print* method to the picture box. The function is invoked, computes the value, returns it, and the result is printed, all in one statement.

So when should you use a function and when a procedure? You can use a function whenever there is a single value to be computed. You could, however, use a procedure to do the same thing. Here's a "procedurized" version of the same example.

```
Sub Twice (ByVal x As Integer, Twox As Integer)
   Twox = 2 * x
End Sub

Sub Command1_Click ()
   Dim x As Integer
   Dim Two_Times_x As Integer
   x = 3
   Call Twice(x, Two_Times_x)
   Picture1.Print Two_Times_x
End Sub
```

Here two names were needed—one for the procedure (*Twice*) and one for the argument (*Two_Times_x*)—instead of just one for the function name. An extra variable declaration was required. Also, an extra line of code was used to call the procedure. The procedure computed the value and returned it to the argument; then the argument was used with the Print method.

The function seems to be a cleaner approach when one computed value is required. A procedure must be used if several values are to be computed. Also, a function should concentrate on its one task. Within the body of a function it would seldom be appropriate to show another form, print a value, or call some procedure. If these are tasks to be done, let a procedure do them, not a function.

THOUGHTS ON PROGRAMMING

Top-Down Design

The next step in program development after requirements analysis and problem specification is **program design**. You have an understanding of the job to be done; now you must begin to plan how to do it.

The accepted philosophy in developing a program is to do a top-down design. To understand what this means, suppose that your assignment is to design and build a completely new automobile. There are thousands of parts in an automobile, so viewed as whole, this is a staggering task. However, you know that you can approach the job by viewing the car as the sum of components that work together—engine, transmission, brake system, and so on. You can decide on the components you need and how they will work together. After that you can turn your attention to each of the components and break them down into subcomponents that work together. You refine your level of detail at each step, until finally you reach the lowest level, where the individual pieces should be simple enough to design in their entirety without difficulty.

This process of **top-down design,** or **stepwise refinement,** is a way to manage the complexity of any large undertaking—designing an automobile, writing a book, developing software. The overall task is broken down into subtasks, each subtask into smaller tasks, and so on. Figure 6.9 illustrates the process. The more of this sort of planning you do ahead of time, the easier it is to build the car, write the book, code the software.

Visual Basic, by its very nature, encourages top down design to some extent. Objects on forms, with their associated event procedures, represent a breakdown of the overall task. OTC designs for forms utilize the top-down approach. In such a design not only are the subtasks identified, but certain control objects that will carry out some of these subtasks, for the most part through event

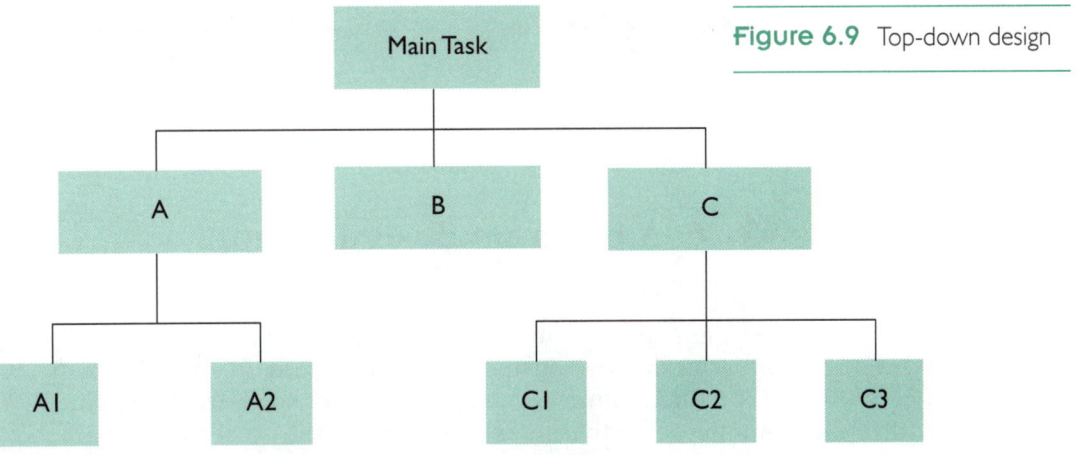

Figure 6.9 Top-down design

procedures, are also decided on. In the calculator project, for example, there were command buttons to enter the digits, to do the arithmetic operations, to clear the results window, and so on. Each button had code for a click event procedure. This divided the overall job of "writing a calculator" into subtasks.

Not every subtask will be associated with a control object. Some will be carried out by general procedures or by user-defined functions. Keeping in mind the scope of procedures, part of the planning involves where to place these general procedures (in forms or in code modules). In the calculator project, general form-level procedures *get_number* and *put_answer* were used because the tasks they carried out were needed by multiple control objects on the single form.

Although one motivation for a general procedure is to avoid duplication of code in multiple event procedures, there are other reasons why a subtask might be assigned to a general procedure rather than an event procedure. One reason is to keep the code for an event procedure as clean as possible; if the event procedure is to accomplish several subtasks, then these subtasks may be shunted off to general procedures to rid the event procedure of coding details. Suppose, for example, an event procedure is assigned to do task A in Figure 6.9. The code for the event procedure might consist of little more than arranging the communication between the two subtasks A1 and A2, which are carried out in general procedures. Subtasks of collecting input or displaying output are often relegated to procedures.

For another reason why a general procedure might be written, suppose some subtask is one that seems inherently useful, and might be something that other programs could utilize. Writing the code as a general procedure in a separate module makes it much more "portable" for use in other programs at another time.

6.7 A program design example

Auntie's Cash and Gas is a gas station and convenience store operation. It sells gas, drinks, and sandwiches. Auntie asks you to write a cash register program for her business. You hold some discussions with Auntie to carry out the requirements analysis phase of software development. You learn that Auntie wants the clerks who will run the program to be able to:

> enter the quantity of each item sold and have a running total for the customer maintained.

As part of program design, it is necessary to do more than identify the event procedures, general procedures, and functions that will be used to perform subtasks. How these subtasks interact must be considered, and the flow of data throughout the project planned. Decisions must be made on what quantities the program will work with, which variables will represent which data items, and where and how those variables should be declared, again with an eye to the rules of scope for variables. What, if anything, will be represented by global variables, what by module variables, what by form-level variables, and what by local variables? What should the interfaces look like between calling and called procedures or functions?

To identify all the subtasks and sub-subtasks; decide on control objects; assign tasks to event procedures, general procedures, and functions; make decisions about variables and interfaces; and so on, may require several passes through the design process, each time adding more detail. Referring to Figure 1.9, this is simply spiraling down from the requirements level closer to the code level, adding more detail in the process. Yet all the decisions mentioned here can be made without having to worry—yet—about the details of low-level code within each of the procedures or functions. In other words, this is still high-level design, not low-level (algorithm) design.

Again, the importance of advance planning—program design—cannot be overstressed, especially as projects grow larger and more complex. While it is tempting in an easy-to-use environment like Visual Basic to just sit at the keyboard and create objects on the fly, that is somewhat akin (in the earlier analogy) to deciding in the middle of the automobile production line, "Hmm, I guess I need a carburetor somewhere in here." The quality of software, like the quality of automobiles, is not enhanced by a haphazard approach.

ring up the sale and have the correct change computed.

issue the periodic reports on sales tax that are required by the state.

It turns out that each drink Auntie sells costs the same amount ($0.75) and each sandwich costs the same amount ($1.95). Gas is $1.189 per gallon. The sales tax rate is 4.15 percent, but no sales tax is charged on gas because that is already built into the pump price. Auntie has a performance requirement that the cash register program be so easy to operate that it is difficult for a clerk to ring up the wrong item.

Figure 6.10
First pass at the top-down design for Auntie's Cash and Gas

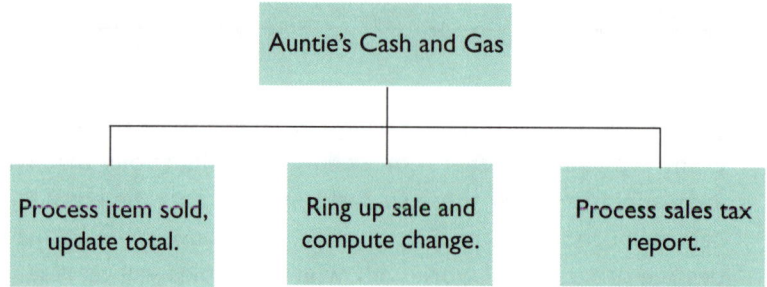

It is quite easy at this point to do a first cut at the top-down design (Figure 6.10). As a start at refining the design, you make the following notes about the subtasks that need to be done:

For each item sold, must compute the cost for that item.

Drink and sandwich items require sales tax computation.

Drink and sandwich items require updating of the running sales tax total.

Each item sold must update the running total.

When the sale is rung up, change from cash collected should be computed.

A written report on total sales tax collected must be available on demand.

A second pass at the design, incorporating these ideas, is shown in Figure 6.11.

Figure 6.11
More detailed design, Auntie's Cash and Gas

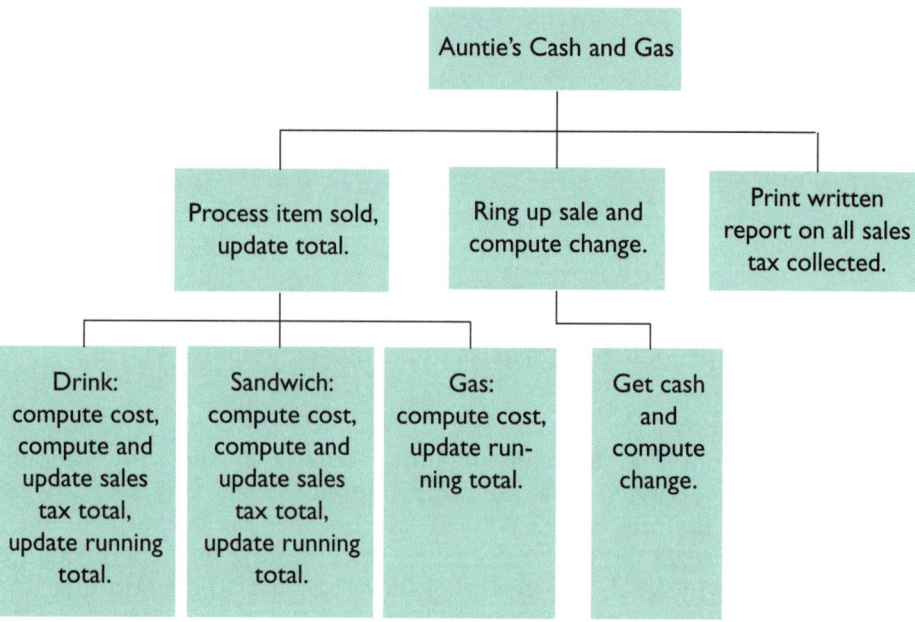

You identify the following minimum set of quantities your program will have to manage, although you may need to add others as you develop the code.

Item prices (fixed)
Number of each item ordered
Item costs for this sale
Sales tax for drinks and sandwiches
Running total for this sale
Cash received from customer
Change due to customer
Running total of sales tax for the duration of the program

You begin to plan where the responsibility for each subtask will lie (event procedures, form-level general procedures or functions, module-level general procedures or functions) and where each quantity will "reside" (as an object property or as a local, form-level, or module-level quantity).

On the basis of these plans, you do a preliminary screen design and show it to Auntie, explaining how you envision the program will work. Your screen design is shown in Figure 6.12. The quantity of an item is entered next to the icon for that item; then the item icon is clicked. Items can be processed in any order, and additional quantities of an item can be ordered. The running total as each item is processed is displayed in the Total area; the Ring Up Sale button collects information on the cash paid by the customer, displays that, and displays the change. The Clear button clears all output in preparation for another sale. The Sales Tax Report button generates a nicely formatted page with the name of Auntie's business and the total sales tax collected while the program was running. The Exit button ends the program.

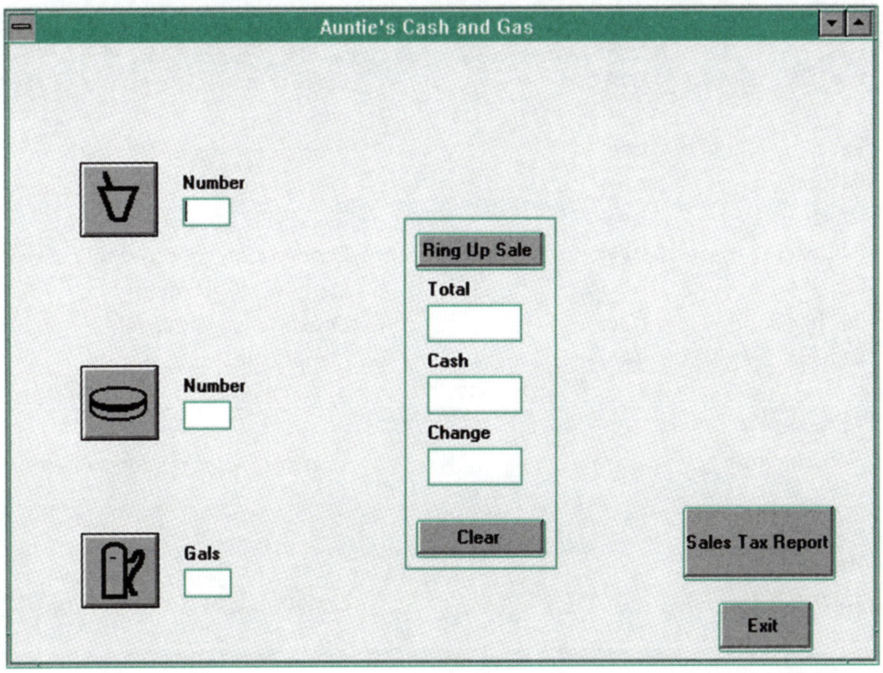

Figure 6.12
Screen design, Auntie's Cash and Gas

Design details of task responsibilities are shown in the OTC design of Figure 6.13. In Standard Visual Basic, command buttons cannot support icon graphics, so the icons for the items to purchase are in image controls disguised to look like buttons. This is why the OTC design has three active image control objects. The OTC design also reflects your decision to put the tasks of computing the sales tax for an item and updating the sales tax total as a form-level function and a form-level procedure, respectively, since both drinks and sandwiches generate sales tax.

The high-level design of this program is complete. The next task is to develop the low-level designs (algorithms) for each of the active objects shown in the OTC, as well as the function and the general procedure.

Figure 6.13
OTC design for Auntie's Cash and Gas

CASH AND GAS FORM			
Active Objects	**Object Type**	**Event**	**Task**
imgDrink	image control	Click	Process drink item.
imgSandwich	image control	Click	Process sandwich item.
imgGas	image control	Click	Process gas item.
cmdRingSale	command button	Click	Get cash (use an input box) and compute change.
cmdClear	command button	Click	Clear display for next sale.
cmdReport	command button	Click	Print sales tax report.
cmdExit	command button	Click	End program.
Passive Objects			
txtDrinkOrder	text box		Collect number of drinks this order.
Label1	label		Prompt for drink order textbox.
txtSandwichOrder	text box		Collect number of sandwiches this order.
Label2	label		Prompt for sandwich order textbox.
txtGasOrder	text box		Collect number of gallons of gas this order.
Label3	label		Prompt for gas order textbox.
lblTotal	label		Display running total this sale.
Label4	label		Identify lblTotal display.
lblCash	label		Display cash collected this sale.
Label5	label		Identify lblCash display.
lblChange	label		Display change this sale.
Label6	label		Identify lblChange display.
Function			
TaxCompute			Compute sales tax for an item.
General Procedure			
Totaler			Update sales tax total.

Name: _____ Date Due: _____

LEARNING OBJECTIVE

- Writing a Visual Basic application using image controls, a frame control, a function, and a procedure

1. ____ Open a new Visual Basic project. As you might expect, your assignment in this lab is to write the program for Auntie's Cash and Gas, using the screen design and the OTC design as guides.

   ____ Save your files as *cash.frm* and *cash.mak*.

   ____ Create three image controls on the form and give them appropriate names. The Toolbox icon for an image control is shown here.

   ____ To load the icons into the image controls, experiment with the **Picture property** for the image control object. The icons are in the bit-mapped picture files *drink.bmp, sand.bmp, gas.bmp*. The click event is available for an image control, but it does not have the three-dimensional effect of pushing a button. (You'll see in Chapter 9 how to create this effect.)

2. The "box" shown in Figure 6.12 around the Ring Up Sale button, the Clear button, and the intermediate labels is a **Frame** control object.

   ____ Put a frame on your form by double clicking on its Toolbox icon.

   ____ Now put the necessary controls inside the frame. Objects within a frame maintain their relative position, so you can move them as a group simply by dragging the frame.

3. ____ Finish the rest of the form layout as shown in Figure 6.12 with the naming conventions of Figure 6.13. (Save your work often.)

4. ____ Declare the important program variables, using the list from Section 6.7 as a guide. Think carefully about where to declare each variable; remember the rules of scope.

   ____ Add a comment for each constant and variable declaration describing what is being stored.

5. ____ Write a pseudocode description of the algorithm for processing a drink item, that is, the imgDrink_Click procedure. For this first pass at a section of low-level design, you can (temporarily) skip the details of argument passing.

6. ____ Decide on the interface details and implement the function to compute the sales tax for an item.

7. ____ Decide on the interface details and implement the procedure to update the running total of the sales tax.

8. ____ Now implement your design for the imgDrink_Click procedure from step 5. Be sure to use comments to document your code.

____ Test your program so far.

9. ____ Finish the rest of the code for Auntie's Cash and Gas. Include comments.

____ Test your program thoroughly. You will need an on-line printer to test the sales tax report feature of this program.

QuickCheck 6.3

1. Why can all arguments to a user-defined function be passed by value?
2. What is the purpose of the data type descriptor at the end of a user-defined function header?
3. What one statement must appear in the body of a user-defined function?
4. Explain how procedures and functions go hand in hand with top-down design.
5. In what way is a Frame control object useful?

Review Questions

1. What is the difference between an event procedure and a general procedure?
2. Name the three locations for procedure code. Describe the scope of each.
3. What happens when a statement that is not within the scope of some procedure tries to invoke that procedure?
4. If some task is common to two or more control objects on a single form, where should the code be written?
5. What is a local variable, and what is its scope?
6. What is a global variable, and what is its scope?
7. Can there be variables that are neither local nor global? Explain.
8. A local variable will not retain its value from one invocation of a procedure to the next unless the keyword _____ is used in the variable declaration.
9. Why not declare all variables in a project to be global variables?
10. What is the scope of a control object on Form2 of a project?
11. True or false: The argument list is found in the code for a procedure.
12. True or false: An argument can have a different name than that of its corresponding parameter.
13. Give the three ways in which the argument list and the parameter list must match.
14. Information that is needed by a procedure but should not be changed by that procedure should be passed _____ instead of _____. How can this be accomplished?
15. What is an unintentional side effect?
16. What is the purpose of a function?
17. Explain the difference between how a function is invoked and how a procedure is invoked.
18. What is top-down design?

19. Give three reasons for using general procedures.
20. Does the OTC design approach capture everything that must be done at the high-level design stage? If not, what is missing?

Exercises

Reading code

1. What is the effect of the following procedure?

    ```
    Sub Whoozit (a As String, b As String)
        Picture1.Print a & b
    End Sub
    ```

2. What will be the result when the following code is executed?

    ```
    Call McDonald("pig")
    Picture1.Print "Ee-I Ee-I Oh"

    Sub McDonald (animal As String)
        Picture1.Print "And on his farm he had a " & animal
    End sub
    ```

3. What will be returned by the following function if it is given an argument value of 5?

    ```
    Function mystery (n As Integer) As Single
    Const factor = 2
        mystery = factor ^ n - 4
    End Function
    ```

4. What is wrong with the following code for a function that is supposed to triple the value of its argument?

    ```
    Function triple (n As Integer)
        triple = 3 * n
    End Function
    ```

5. Below is a procedure invocation and the code for the procedure. What is the problem?

    ```
    Dim wins As Integer
    Dim losses As Integer
    Dim ratio As Single
        wins = 12
        losses = 5
        Call stats(losses, wins, ratio)

    Sub stats (ByVal x As Integer, ByVal y As Integer, ratio As Single)
    'computes the ratio of wins to losses

        ratio = x / y
        Picture1.Print ratio
    End Sub
    ```

Writing code

6. Below is the header for a function. Write a statement to invoke this function with the argument *number,* and print the value in Picture1.

```
Function DoIt (n as integer) As String
```

7. Below is the header for a procedure. Write a statement that invokes this procedure with arguments "stuff" and 14.

```
Sub winger (hype as string, count as Integer)
```

8. Write a function that takes an integer value between 1 and 26 and returns the corresponding letter of the alphabet.

9. Write a function that takes a decimal value representing a temperature in degrees Fahrenheit and returns a value representing that temperature in degrees Celsius.

10. Write a procedure that takes three integer parameters; the first two parameters represent a number of hours and a number of minutes, respectively. The procedure finds the total number of minutes, prints this value in a picture box, and returns the value to the invoking procedure through the third parameter.

Exploring Further

11. Modify Auntie's Cash and Gas so that instead of entering the number of drinks ordered and clicking the image control once, the user clicks the image control once for each drink, and the number ordered, as well as the running total, is automatically updated. Do the same with the sandwich and gasoline orders. (If you keep the text boxes on the form, you may want to turn off the blinking cursor since the user will no longer be entering data; make the Tab Stop property False.)

12. Modify your ***birth2.mak*** project from Lab 4.3 so that the greeting and the picture appear on a second form. Use a general procedure to display the output. Add two command buttons to the second form, one to exit the program and one to process another birthday greeting.

13. Create a Visual Basic project with three buttons on the form that have the captions "small print", "medium print", and "big print", respectively. Put a fairly large label on the form with a blank caption. In the Properties window for the label, choose a FontName for which there are multiple font sizes; write down three such sizes (small, medium, and large). Write the code for a general procedure that will write "This is the message" in the label caption. Clicking on any of the three buttons should invoke the general procedure and pass an appropriate font size as a parameter. The general procedure will set the font size property of the label before it prints the message.

14. Platypus Software sales have soared in the past three months. Write a Visual Basic project that collects three months' worth of sales and uses the Horizontal procedure (from **jail.mak**) to draw a bar graph of the sales on the form (assume the sales are relatively small so everything fits on the form).

15. a. Functions or procedures can be called from within other functions or procedures. A Visual Basic form has a text box, a label, and a command button. Here is the code for the button's click event along with code for two functions and two procedures. (By the way, this is just for illustration; a set of invocations this deep might well be considered rather confusing code.) By reading this code, what do you think will be printed in the label caption if the user enters the number 3 in the text box?

```
Sub Command1_Click ()
Dim number As Integer
number = Val(text1.Text)
Label1.Caption = One(number)
End Sub

Function One (ByVal x As Integer) As Integer
    Call Two(x)
    One = 2 * x
End Function

Sub Two (x As Integer)
    x = 2 * Three(x)
End Sub

Function Three (ByVal x As Integer) As Integer
    Call Four(x)
    Three = 2 * x
End Function

Sub Four (x As Integer)
    x = 2 * x
End Sub
```

b. Create a Visual Basic program that uses this code and run the program to confirm your answer to part (a).

c. Read the Help system on the topic "Calls command." Now run your program from part (b) and enter input in the text box, then go to break mode. Single-step through the program. As you enter each new function or procedure, check the growing list of active calls by clicking on the Calls toolbar icon, shown here. As each procedure or function is completed, check the active calls list and watch it shrink.

Projects

1. This is the same problem as Project 1 in Chapter 5. This time, use a separate procedure to collect the data, a function to compute R, and another procedure to display the output. Thus if clicking a command button causes the computation to be done, the code for that button's Click event procedure will contain essentially just declarations, a procedure call, a function invocation, and another procedure call.

2. Different credit cards require different minimum monthly payments and have different annual percentage rates (APR) of interest on the

unpaid balance. Design and write a Visual Basic program that collects the name of the card, the balance due for the month, the minimum payment due for the month, and the APR. The program computes the carry-over charge to the next month if only the minimum payment is made. Use a procedure to collect the input, a function to compute the carry-over charge, and a procedure to display the output. Be sure to pay attention to internal documentation—comments, good use of white space, meaningful identifiers, and so on.

3. Design and write a Visual Basic program for a hotel registration system. The program collects a guest's name and address and the assigned room number, which is a three-digit integer. It then prints an information sheet for the guest with the guest's name, room number, and the coded form of the room number that is stamped on the key. The code used by the hotel is to reverse the digits of the room number, so if the guest's room number is 123, then the key reads 321. Use a procedure to collect the input, a function to compute the room number code, and a procedure to print the information sheet.

4. A race car is being clocked on a 2.5-mile track. The stopwatch time is entered for each lap. A lap count is updated, and the average speeds in miles per hour for the last lap and for all the laps so far are displayed. Design and write a Visual Basic program to do this task. Design your program in top-down fashion, making use of procedures and/or functions. Begin with a design chart similar to Figure 6.10 or Figure 6.11, then do an OTC design. Finally, create the program.

5. a. Design and write a Visual Basic program to help a farmer plan the crops for next year. The input consists of the length and width of the farm in miles. There are three command buttons, one for corn, one for soybeans, and one for alfalfa. The farmer can enter the expected income per acre for each crop, and the percent of the total acreage to be planted in that crop. (There are 1760 yards in a mile, and 4840 square yards in an acre.) Clicking the button displays the expected income for that crop, as well as the remaining acreage available for other crops. Design your code in top-down fashion, making use of procedures and/or functions.

b. Now suppose the farmer acquires a second plot of land. Add a second form to your project that is similar to the first. Add a command button to each form to make the other form active. Revise your code to handle this situation; note particularly where you must move procedures or functions to minimize duplication.

CHAPTER 7

Conditional Processing

KEY POINTS

- Boolean expressions provide true-false condition testing.
- Visual Basic uses If-Then-Else and Select-Case statements for conditional processing.
- Option buttons and check boxes allow the user to select choices.
- Graphical representations can be used to capture various aspects of both high-level and low-level program design.
- The Visual Basic debugging facilities include tracing code, setting breakpoints, and setting watch expressions.

7.1 Viewpoint

Way back in Chapter 4, five fundamental constructs for building algorithms were identified. These were:

> I/O
> Data manipulation
> Assignment
> Conditional processing
> Looping

The options available at this point for collecting input include the input box and the text box. Output may appear as label captions or as printed text in a picture box or on a piece of paper. Graphical output by means of the Line method was used in Lab 6.2 (*jail.mak*). More input and output options will be encountered later.

Data manipulation was discussed in Chapter 5. Topics included numeric data types, how arithmetic and string expressions are evaluated, and the intrinsic functions Visual Basic provides for data manipulation.

The assignment statement is pretty simple. Just remember that the item to receive the new value is always on the left of the equal sign, and the expression representing the new value is on the right.

Nothing has been said yet about how to implement non-sequential processing, either conditional processing or looping. As discussed in Section 4.1, these processing alternatives change the line-by-line execution that takes place with sequential processing. The order of execution of statements is called the **flow of control**. Statements in a programming language that implement conditional processing or looping influence the flow of control and are called **control structures**. (Do not confuse this term, which refers to certain kinds of statements found within many programming languages, with "control objects," which refers to Visual Basic's Toolbox goodies.) Visual Basic control structures are discussed in this chapter and the next.

Because a Visual Basic program is event driven, the order in which subtasks are done (and procedures are executed) is determined in part by the user's interaction with the control objects on the form. For example, the clerk in Auntie's Cash and Gas determines when the Click event procedure for the drink image control is invoked—before, after, or in between sandwich and gas purchases. Once that procedure is invoked, however, it automatically invokes the function to compute the sales tax for an item. Hence the flow of control of a Visual Basic program *as a whole* is determined by:

What procedures the user initiates

What procedures or functions are invoked by other procedures

Now, however, the focus shifts down one level of detail. Assume that the overall planning and large-scale design has taken place; major tasks, subtasks of those tasks, sub-subtasks, and so on, have been identified and decisions have been made about control objects (and event procedures), form-level procedures, module-level procedures, functions, and the interfaces between them. It is time to write all the procedures and functions that accomplish the subtasks. The algorithms for the bodies of each procedure or function must be developed, and it is here that Visual Basic control structures enter in. Control structures influence the flow of control only within the procedure or function in which they occur.

7.2 Boolean expressions

Both conditional processing and looping depend on the ability to evaluate some true-false condition. A **Boolean expression** is any expression that evaluates to one of two values, true or false. Boolean expressions are the conditions that drive conditional processing and looping.

> Boolean expressions are named in honor of George Boole, a mid-nineteenth-century English mathematician and logician. Boole, the son of a poor shoemaker, dropped out of school in the third grade. Despite his lack of formal education, he taught himself mathematics and studied the works of the great Greek and Roman philosophers. Boole became convinced that logical thinking could be treated as a branch of mathematics, with computational rules. At the time, Boole's work was considered unimportant, as it appeared to have no real application. A century later, however, **Boolean algebra** became the cornerstone for the design of the electronic circuits from which computers are built, as well as the basis for Boolean expressions that direct the flow of control in many programming languages.

There are several forms of Boolean expressions. In the simplest case, Visual Basic provides two built-in constants, *True* and *False*. Obviously, *True* is considered true and *False* is considered false. Any arithmetic expression that evaluates to a nonzero value is considered true; any arithmetic expression that evaluates to zero is considered false. These forms of Boolean expressions are seldom used, however.

Generally, a Boolean expression involves **relational operators**. Relational operators are ways of comparing quantities. For example, "equals" is a relational operator, represented by an equal sign. The Boolean expression

```
(3 + 2) = (6 - 1)
```

evaluates to true because both sides of the equal sign represent the same quantity. If *Number* is an integer variable with current value equal to 7, then

```
Number + 6 = 2 * 5
```

evaluates to false. Note that these expressions are not complete Visual Basic statements, but must be used within statements. In particular, they are not stand-alone assignment statements because they do not have the correct syntax for assignment statements.

Table 7.1 shows the common relational operators.

Table 7.1 Common relational operators in Visual Basic

MATHEMATICAL SYMBOL	VISUAL BASIC SYMBOL	MEANING OF COMPARISON
=	=	Are two quantities equal?
≠	< >	Are two quantities unequal?
<	<	Is first quantity less than second?
≤	<=	Is first quantity less than or equal to second?
>	>	Is first quantity greater than second?
≥	>=	Is first quantity greater than or equal to second?

While "quantity" in Table 7.1 may be thought of as referring to a numeric item, relational operators can also be used to compare two string expressions. In this case, "less than" and "greater than" refer (almost) to the alphabetical ordering of the strings, that is, the order in which they appear in a dictionary, except that all uppercase letters are considered as coming before all lowercase letters. Thus

```
"bat" < "cat" and "bat" < "batty"
```

are true, but

```
"Bat" < "ant"
```

is also true (because of the uppercase "B"). Numbers cannot be directly compared with strings; this results in the same "type mismatch" error that arises from trying to assign a numeric value to a string variable, or vice versa. However, if *PaymentDue* is a numeric variable and *Balance* is a string variable, then the expression

```
PaymentDue < Val(Balance)
```

is legitimate and evaluates to either true or false. Likewise, the comparison

```
Str$(PaymentDue) <= Balance
```

can be done. (But remember that *Str$(PaymentDue)* includes a leading blank if *PaymentDue* is nonnegative.)

Control object properties can be tested in Boolean expressions. The following are legitimate Boolean expressions:

```
Label1.Caption = "OK"
Text1.MaxLength = 10
Image1.Visible = True
```

Notice that there are no quotes around "True" in the last expression; here "True" is the Visual Basic Boolean constant, not a literal string. As a matter of fact, since the Visible property of a control object is either true or false, this expression can be written as just

```
Image1.Visible
```

as in

```
If Image1.Visible Then ...
```

However, this requires a bit more thought on the part of the person reading the code, so the longer form (with the equals sign) is less confusing code.

The final form of Boolean expression arises by joining other Boolean expressions with **logical operators**. For example, the following expression joins two expressions with the And operator:

```
(X >= 0) And (X <= 7)
```

This expression is true whenever $X \geq 0$ is true and also $X \leq 7$ is true, which is whenever X is between 0 and 7, inclusive; otherwise it is false. The result of joining two Boolean expressions by the And operator is true exactly when both parts are true. Inequalities cannot be "chained together"; the expression

```
0 <= X <= 7       'ILLEGAL
```

while mathematically equivalent to the previous expression, is not a legitimate Boolean expression.

Table 7.2 describes the most common logical operators; an operator is **binary** if it joins two Boolean expressions and **unary** if it is applied to a single Boolean expression.

Table 7.2 Common logical operators in Visual Basic			
	VISUAL BASIC	**TYPE**	**MEANING**
	And	Binary	True if both parts are true.
	Or	Binary	True if at least one part is true.
	Not	Unary	Changes the truth value of a single expression.

7.3 If-Then-Else statement

The **If-Then-Else statement** is the usual way to implement a conditional statement in Visual Basic. Its syntax and semantics are very similar to the pseudocode version of a conditional statement that was used in Chapter 4. The syntax is

```
If Boolean expression Then
    statement block 1
Else
    statement block 2
End If
```

"If", "Then", "Else", and "End If" are Visual Basic reserved words, which appear in color in the Visual Basic Code window.

When such a statement is executed, the first thing that happens is the evaluation of the Boolean expression. If the expression evaluates to true, then the instructions in statement block 1 are executed and statement block 2 is skipped entirely. If the expression evaluates to false, then statement block 1 is skipped entirely and statement block 2 is executed. Under no circumstances are both statement blocks executed. After completion of the appropriate statement block, the flow of control passes to the next statement after the End If.

Here's a simple example. Suppose that X has been declared as an integer variable and has already been assigned a value by the time the following statement executes:

```
If X > 5 Then
    Picture1.Print "up"
Else
    Picture1.Print "down"
End If
```

If X has a value greater than 5, so that the Boolean condition "$X > 5$" is true, then "up" is printed in the picture box; otherwise "down" is printed. In this example, statement block 1 and statement block 2 are single statements, but they can consist of multiple statements. In

```
If (X <= 12) And (X + 1 < 7) Then
    X = X + 1
    Picture1.Print "bumped up X"
Else
    X = 2 * X
    Picture1.Print "doubled X"
End If
```

each statement block consists of two statements. Also, the Boolean condition is more complex, involving two Boolean expressions joined by And. If X has the value 4, for example, the first statement block is executed because $4 \leq 12$ and $4 + 1 < 7$. If X has the value 9, the second statement block is executed because, while $9 \leq 12$ is true, $9 + 1 < 7$ is false, so the And of the two Boolean expressions is false.

The statement blocks are indented (by using the Tab key when entering the code). Indenting is not a required part of the syntax of Visual Basic, but it makes the code easier to read because one can visually detect the various statement blocks. Compare the readability of the preceding code to the following, which is functionally equivalent:

```
If (X <= 12) And (X + 1 < 7) Then
X = X + 1
Picture1.Print "bumped up X"
Else
X = 2 * X
Picture1.Print "doubled X"
End If
```

Indenting is a well-accepted practice and part of internal documentation. The Visual Basic code editor, anticipating that you will indent code, starts each new line of code at the same tab stop as the previous line. To move left, press the Backspace key.

Now here's where things start to get interesting. Within the statement blocks of an If-Then-Else statement, any legitimate Visual Basic statement can occur, such as a call to some other procedure, another If-Then-Else statement (resulting in **nested If statements**), or a looping statement of the kind discussed in the next chapter. All algorithms can be constructed using only sequential, conditional, and looping flow of control because these statement forms can be combined in virtually limitless ways.

There are two variations on the If-Then-Else statement. In one of these something happens when a condition is true, but nothing happens when the condition is false. This is known as the **empty else** situation. In this variation, simply omit the Else part of the code. The syntax is

If *Boolean expression* Then
    statement block 1
End If

If the Boolean expression is true, statement block 1 is executed; if it is false, execution proceeds directly to the statement after the End If.

The following example of the empty else prints a notation whenever the integer X is a multiple of 5 (so that on division by 5 its remainder is zero); nothing is printed when X is not a multiple of 5.

```
If X Mod 5 = 0 Then
   Picture1.Print "Multiple of 5"
End If
```

The second variation on the If-Then-Else occurs when you want multiple choices of action instead of just two. The syntax is

If *Boolean expression 1* **Then**
  statement block 1
ElseIf *Boolean expression 2* **Then**
  statement block 2
ElseIf *Boolean expression 3* **Then**
  statement block 3
  .
  .
  .
ElseIf *Boolean expression k* **Then**
  statement block k
Else
  statement block k+1
End If

A little feature of the syntax should be mentioned here. "End If" is two words; if you happen to type this as "EndIf", Visual Basic recognizes what you want and automatically separates it into two words. Thus you can type it either way. "ElseIf" is a single word; if you happen to type "Else If", Visual Basic thinks you want an If statement as the first part of an Else statement block, and you get an error message because Visual Basic wants the If statement on the next line. Thus you must type "ElseIf" as a single word.

What is the semantics in the multiple choice variation? The first expression is evaluated; if true, statement block 1 is executed and everything else is skipped. If false, expression 2 is evaluated. If expression 2 is true, statement block 2 is executed and everything else is skipped. If false, it's on to expression 3. Each expression in turn is evaluated until one is found to be true, at which point the appropriate block is executed, and control then moves on to the statement after the End If. Note that more than one condition can be true, but it is the first true condition found that counts. If no expression is found to be true, the final Else block (statement block $k + 1$) is executed. The Else section, once again, is optional.

As an example of a multiway branch, the following code classifies an integer *X* by size:

```
If X = 0 Then
   Picture1.Print "zero"
ElseIf (X >= 1) And (X <= 10) Then
   Picture1.Print "small"
ElseIf (X >= 11) And (X <= 100) Then
   Picture1.Print "medium"
ElseIf (X > 100) Then
   Picture1.Print "big"
Else
   Picture1.Print "negative"
End If
```

The following table shows what is printed for various values of *X*:

X	Printed
0	zero
7	small
35	medium
223	big
−5	negative

This bit of code works exactly the same if the third condition,

`(X >= 11) And (X <= 100)`

is changed to

`(X >= 1) And (X <= 100)`

All values of X between 1 and 10 are still caught by the second condition, and "small" is printed. This, however, is certainly confusing code because it obscures the intent of the decision-making process.

7.4 Select-Case statement

The If-Then-Else statement and its variations use the evaluation of one or more true-false conditions (Boolean expressions) to guide the flow of control. Another Visual Basic statement allows conditional action to be based on the value of a more general expression. This time, look at an example first; *Temperature* is an integer variable in the following code:

```
Select Case Temperature
    Case 85 To 90
        Picture1.Print "hot"
    Case 70, 75, 78 To 80
        Picture1.Print "just right"
    Case Is <= 32
        Picture1.Print "freezing"
    Case Else
        Picture1.Print "no opinion"
End Select
```

The output for various values of *Temperature* is given in the following table. Even though the semantics of the Select-Case statement have not been explained, these results should not surprise you.

Temperature	Printed
85	hot
70, 75, or 78	just right
32	freezing
77	no opinion

The syntax of the general **Select-Case statement** is

```
Select Case test expression
    Case expression list 1
        statement block 1
    Case expression list 2
        statement block 2
        .
        .
        .
    Case expression list k
        statement block k
    Case Else
        statement block k+1
End Select
```

Here the test expression is any numeric or string expression. An expression list consists of items separated by commas. Each item in an expression list has one of three forms:

    Bounded form:
        expression 1 `To` *expression 2*   (Example: `85 To 90`)

    Single value form:
        expression   (Example: `75`)

    Single compare form:
        `Is` *relational-operator expression*   (Example: `Is <= 32`)

In the temperature example, the first expression list has a single item of bounded form; the second has three items, two of single-value form and one of bounded form; and the third has a single item of single-compare form.

    Suppose V denotes the value of the test expression. When V is compared with an item of bounded form, the result is true if V falls within the range described (for example, V is a numeric value that falls between 85 and 90, inclusive). When V is compared with an item of single-value form, the result is true if V equals the value of that single expression (for example, V equals 75). When V is compared with an item of single-compare form, the result is true if V is in the relation described with the given expression (for example, V is ≤ 32).

    The Select-Case statement works as follows: The value V of the initial expression is compared one by one with the all the items in expression list 1. If any of the results are true, then statement block 1 is executed, after which control then passes to the next statement following the End Select. If all the comparisons in the first expression list are false, then the next expression list is used. And so on. If all the comparisons in all the expression lists fail to produce a true value, the Else block is executed. In the example, the value 77 falls through all the way to the Else clause. The Else clause, by the way, is optional as it is in the If-Then-Else statement.

    As in the If-ElseIf form of the If statement, the first true condition in the Select-Case statement wins the race; even if later conditions are also true, they will never be tested.

    The Select-Case statement doesn't do anything that can't be done by an If statement, but it often does it in a clearer way. For instance, the example Select-Case statement could be replaced by the following code.

```
If (Temperature >= 85) And (Temperature <= 90) Then
    Picture1.Print "hot"
ElseIf (Temperature = 70) Or (Temperature = 75) Or ↵
↳ ((Temperature >= 78) And (Temperature <= 80)) Then
    Picture1.Print "just right"
ElseIf Temperature <= 32 Then
    Picture1.Print "freezing"
Else
    Picture1.Print "no opinion"
End If
```

Notice how parentheses are used to form the correct combinations in the long Boolean expression.

Of course, the statement blocks in the Select-Case statement can contain If statements or other Select-Case statements or looping statements or calls to procedures or . . . .

Name: _____   Date Due: _____

LAB 7.1

LEARNING OBJECTIVES

- Exploring relational and logical operators
- Trying out the If-Then-Else and Select-Case statements
- Writing a Visual Basic application using conditional processing

1. ____ Open a new Visual Basic project; put a command button and a picture box on the form.

   ____ In the Command1_Click procedure, declare X and Y to be integer variables and assign them values of 3 and 10, respectively.

   ____ Declare W to be a string variable, and assign it the value "Barney".

   ____ Include an If-Then-Else statement that prints "True" in the picture box if $X = 3$ and prints "False" otherwise.

   ____ Test your program to see that it behaves as expected.

2. ____ By changing the condition and rerunning the program each time, test the true-false value of each of the following Boolean expressions. Make sure you understand why each is true or false.

   Relational operators

   ```
   X <> Y
   ```

   ```
   X + 9 <= Y
   ```

   ```
   W <= "Big Bird"
   ```

   Logical operators

   ```
   (3 * X > Y) Or (Y < 17)
   ```

   ```
   (3 * X > Y) And (Y < 17)
   ```

                    Not (W > "cat")

                    X = "3"

    3. ____ Write a Boolean expression that is true when *X* is 3 and *Y* is not less than 12.

       ____ Enter this condition and run your program. What is the truth value?

If-Then-Else statement

    4. ____ Delete the previous code.

       ____ Still in the Click event procedure, make the following declarations:

```
Const PayRate = 10.00
Dim HoursWorked As Integer
Dim Pay As Single
```

       ____ Now fill in the following code to pay time and a half for hours worked over 40:

```
If _____ Then
   Pay = PayRate * 1.5 * (HoursWorked - 40) + PayRate * 40
   Picture1.Print "Pay = " _____
ElseIf _____ Then
   Pay = _____
   Picture1.Print "Pay = "; Pay
Else
   Picture1.Print "No hours this pay period"
   Picture1.Print "Pay = 0"
End If
```

       ____ Enter this code.

       ____ Run your program, assigning the following values to *HoursWorked*; record the value of *Pay* in each case. Check that your answers are correct.

50 _____
35 _____
0 _____

5. ____ Write a Select-Case statement to print "Odd" in the picture box if an integer variable *X* has the value 1, 3, 5, 7, or 9 and to print "Even" if *X* has the value 2, 4, 6, 8, or 10. Any other value of *X* results in printing "Too big".

> **Select-Case statement**

____ Enter this code, and try it to be sure it works correctly.

____ Exit this program; you do not need to save anything.

6. The next application is a Visual Basic program to simulate a slot machine. A suggested layout for the single form that is required appears here. Each of the little squares that holds a picture of a fruit is an image control (image controls were used in Lab 6.3). The image control on the left has been loaded with the picture file ***peach.bmp***, the middle image control uses the picture file ***banana.bmp***, and the right image control uses the picture file ***cherry.bmp***. (These picture files were created using

> **New application**

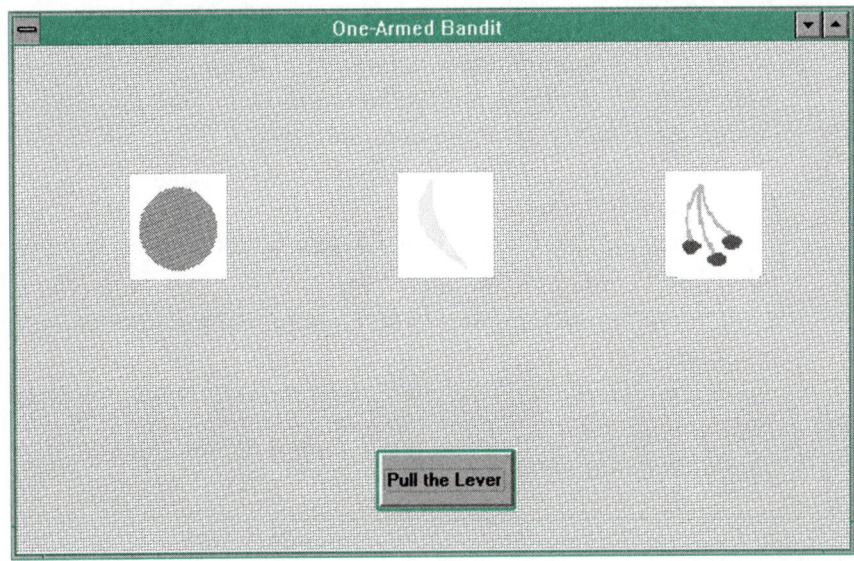

the Windows Paintbrush program.) However, there is more here than meets the eye. When the "Pull the Lever" button is clicked, each of the three positions on the form shows a random choice from among the three pictures. This is accomplished by having three image controls at each position, one with each picture, and managing which image controls are visible at any time.

____ Create the form for this project, using one command button and nine image controls, three for each position. The image controls will have no code associated with them, so use a control array of image controls; position them so that the image controls with indices 0, 1, and 2 are stacked together, so are those with indices 3, 4, and 5 and so are those with indices 6, 7, and 8. Save your files as **slot.frm** and **slot.mak**.

____ Load each group of three image controls with the three picture files. Make the image control with the lowest index in each stack hold the banana picture, that with the middle index in each stack the cherry, and that with the highest index in each stack the peach.

7. The code to make the slot machine work is contained in the command button's Click event procedure. Here's the plan. Use integer variables to represent each of the three stacks; every time the button is clicked, each variable is assigned a random value of 1, 2, or 3. The number represents which picture shows at that position. The declarations for the three variables are

```
Dim slot1 As Integer
Dim slot2 As Integer
Dim slot3 As Integer
```

A pseudocode outline of the algorithm is:

Randomize

Assign slot1 a random value between 1 and 3
Assign slot2 a random value between 1 and 3
Assign slot3 a random value between 1 and 3

If slot1 has the value 1 then
    show image1(0) (the banana) and hide the other two images
otherwise if slot1 has the value 2 then
    show image1(1) (the cherry) and hide the other two images
otherwise
    show image1(2) (the peach) and hide the other two images
Similar code for slot2
Similar code for slot3

____ Put the variable declarations in your code now.

8. ____ You may recall from Chapter 5 that the Visual Basic *Rnd* function returns a decimal number greater than or equal to 0 but less than 1. Consult the Help file on the *Rnd* function to see how to generate an integer value within some range. What is the formula to use?

____ Now write three assignment statements to assign a random integer between 1 and 3 to each of the slot variables. Remember to use the Randomize statement first so that the numbers are truly random.

____ Test your program so far by printing the values of *slot1*, *slot2*, and *slot3* on the form; run the program several times to see that you are getting random values. Keep the print statements in your code until after the next step.

9. ____ Now write the code to respond to the value assigned to *slot1*, using the preceding pseudocode outline. Remember that you can use a Visual Basic statement to change the value of a control object's properties. (Also remember to use comments throughout your code.)

____ Test your program; you should get various pictures in position 1, depending on the random values assigned to *slot1*. Check that your pictures agree with the numbers printed on the form.

____ When you are satisfied that your program is working properly, you can delete the print statements from your code.

10. ____ Complete the code for the other two slots. Test your program.

11. ____ Your slot machine is now working, but it isn't much fun because it doesn't notice when you "win," that is, when all three pictures agree. Add a label to your form that shows some congratulatory message.

____ Write the necessary code so that the label appears on any winning "pull of the lever" and then disappears on the next pull.

12. ____ Finally, add some code to the Form1_Load procedure so that the slot machine fills the screen when the program runs.

13. ____ Save your files.

14. This is such a fun program you may want to give it to your friends.

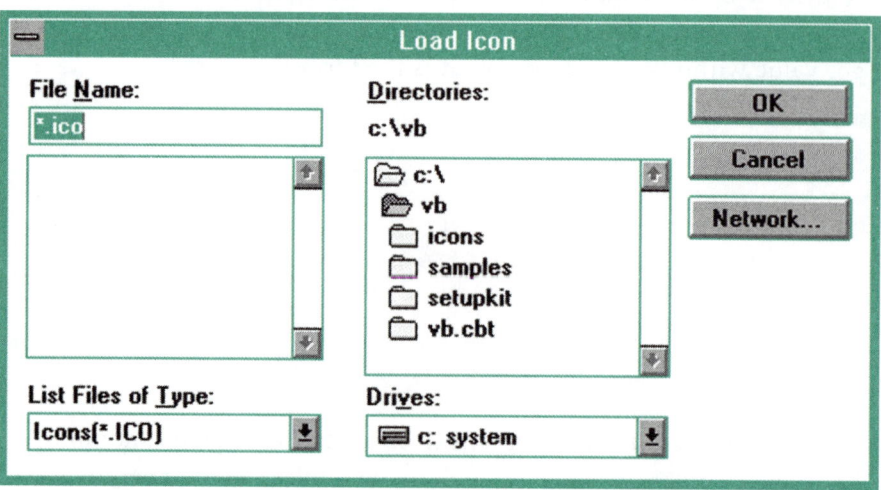

_____ From the File menu, choose Make.EXE File. In the dialog box that pops up, you will see a picture of the default Visual Basic icon for an application, shown here.

Instead of using the default icon, you will pick a different one.

_____ Cancel the Make.EXE File dialog box.

_____ In the Form1 Properties window, choose the Icons property. Click on the Properties window Settings box, which produces a dialog box similar to the one shown here. Visual Basic provides a number of icons stored by category in the C:\VB\icons subdirectory (or wherever your system has stored them).

_____ Open the *icons* subdirectory and then the *misc* subdirectory. Select bullseye.ico and click on OK or press Enter. (Available icons are described in Appendix B of the Visual Basic Programmer's Guide.)

_____ Now choose Make.EXE File from the File menu; the new icon will be displayed. Name the file ***slot.exe.*** You can distribute the resulting .EXE file (along with VBRUN300.DLL from C:\WINDOWS\SYSTEM) to anyone running Windows. To put the icon for this application on your desktop, you will need to use the Program Manager to create a New Program Item (ask your instructor for details).

QuickCheck 7.1

1. Flow of control in a program describes _____.
2. Write a Boolean expression to test whether an integer variable *Y* is between 5 and 10, inclusive.
3. Write a Boolean expression to test whether a string variable *Title* is either "King" or "Duke".
4. In the empty else form of the If-Then-Else statement, what happens when the Boolean expression evaluates to false?
5. True or false: A Select-Case statement can always be replaced by an If-Then-Else statement.

7.5 Control objects for making choices

Two more Visual Basic control objects provide the user with a way to make choices. These are the **option button** and the **check box**, both found on row 4 of the standard Toolbox. Their icons are:

Option button    Check box

Like command buttons and text boxes, the option button and the check box are features of windows-based programming that Visual Basic is supplying for you to use in your own applications. You'll recognize the option button icon as the one used throughout this book whenever you have a choice of actions in the Visual Basic environment.

Option buttons are typically used in groups of two or more, and check boxes are frequently used in groups. Figure 7.1 shows a group of option buttons, and Figure 7.2 shows a group of check boxes. The idea behind both option buttons and check boxes is to allow the user to make choices. The choices are described by the captions (which in Figures 7.1 and 7.2 have been left as the default values). The difference between the two controls is that the user can select only one option button at any one time from a group of mutually exclusive choices but can select multiple check boxes at any one time. In Figure 7.1, Option1 has been selected; this is shown by the black dot. If the user clicks on Option2, the black dot automatically moves from button 1 to button 2. Option buttons are sometimes called **radio buttons**, suggestive of the push buttons on a car radio, which can only be

Figure 7.1 Group of option buttons

Figure 7.2 Group of check boxes

pushed in (selected) one at a time. In Figure 7.2, Check2 and Check3 have both been selected; this is shown by the X in each of those boxes. Clicking a check box toggles the X on and off to select or deselect the choice. Once again, the important difference between the option button and the check box is that multiple check boxes, but only one option button, can be selected at once.

Both option buttons and check boxes have the usual properties of Left, Top, Height, Width, Caption, Name, and various font properties. Each also has a **Value property** that indicates the status of the control. The Value property of an option button can be set to True or False (selected or unselected). This property can be set in the Properties window at design time, by a Visual Basic statement executing at run time, or by the user clicking on an option button. When the Value property of any option button is set to True, the Value property for the other option buttons in the group is automatically set to False.

The Value property for a check box can be 0 (unchecked), 1 (checked), or 2 (shaded). Setting the Value property for a check box to 2 at design time or by code at run time results in the check box's being shaded gray. This can be used to indicate that the choice represented by that check box is inappropriate for the current conditions. However, a determined user can still select that check box at run time, changing its Value property to 1. Therefore setting the Value property to 2 is a suggestion that the user not make such a choice but is less binding than setting the Enabled property to False, which prevents the user from making that choice.

The Value property is what allows the code to recognize and react to the user's choice or choices. Both option buttons and check boxes respond to click events, and the response to a choice can be handled in the click event code for that control, as in

```
Sub Check1_Click ( )
   If Check1.Value = 1 Then
         Label1.Caption = "Check box 1 selected"
   Else
         Label1.Caption = ""
   End If
End Sub
```

Usually, it is some other procedure that wants to know the status of a group of option buttons or check boxes to respond accordingly. For example, some procedure reacts to a group of check boxes by code of the form

```
If (Check1.Value = 1) And (Check3.Value = 1) Then
         .
         .
         .
ElseIf (Check2.Value = 1) And (Check3.Value = 1) Then
         .
         .
         .
Else
         .
         .
         .
End If
```

As another example, suppose there is a command button whose purpose is to display a message in a label. Details of the message can be selected by choosing between two option buttons. Figure 7.3 shows what part of the form looks like. The click event procedure for the command button then contains code like

```
If Option1.Value = True Then
   Label1.Caption = "Welcome, credit card customer"
Else
   Label1.Caption = "Welcome, cash customer"
End If
```

Because option buttons and check boxes collect information on a user's choices, they serve as a form of input mechanism. In the option button example of Figure 7.3, the input can be obtained in a more laborious

Figure 7.3
Two option buttons with a command button

fashion by, say, having the command button invoke the *InputBox$* function with the prompt "Credit card customer or cash customer?" and assigning the string returned by the *InputBox$* function to some string variable called *Response*. The rest of the code would be similar to the previous version:

```
If Response = "credit card" Then
         Label1.Caption = "Welcome, credit card customer"
Else
         Label1.Caption = "Welcome, cash customer"
End If
```

Another control object from the Toolbox, the **Timer** control, functions as a little invisible stopwatch; its icon on the Toolbox is shown here.

A timer is never visible on a form, so it has no properties dealing with its size or appearance. In fact, it has very few properties. There is a Left property and a Top property but, since the timer is not seen, it doesn't matter where on the form you place it. The important properties are Enabled (True or False), which turns the timer on or off, and Interval, which sets the length of time (in milliseconds) between Timer events. The Timer event is the only event recognized by a timer control object; to have something happen every so often, put the code in the Timer event procedure. A timer was used in the **lab1** project to control the animation of the faces.

Name: _____ Date Due: _____

LEARNING OBJECTIVES

- Using option buttons and check boxes
- Using the Frame control
- Using a Timer control

1. ____ Open a new Visual Basic project.

   ____ Put one label and three option buttons on the form.

   ____ Choosing Option1 displays "1" in the label, choosing Option 2 displays "2", and choosing Option 3 displays "3". Write the code for each option click event, and then test your program.

   Using option buttons

2. ____ Add a second label and three check boxes. What is the Boolean expression that is true if and only if all three check boxes are checked?

   Using check boxes

   ____ If all three check boxes are checked, the second label reads "bingo"; otherwise it is blank. Write the code and test your program. Be sure it works regardless of the order in which the boxes are checked or unchecked.

3. Only one option button in a group can be selected at any time. Suppose you want a group of option buttons to allow a choice about something and then you want another group on the same form to allow a choice about something else. In this case, you need to use a **Frame** control. A Frame control was used in Lab 6.3 to group items so they could be moved together; that's one use for the Frame control.

   Frame control again

____ Put a frame around your option boxes and try to move them as a group. What goes wrong?

____ Read the Visual Basic Help section on frames. Even if the frame is an afterthought, you can still cut and paste existing controls into a frame. Try this with your option buttons, and then move the frame. What happens?

4. ____ The other use for the Frame control is to separate one group of option buttons from another. Add two more option buttons and run your program to see that they can be selected independently of the first group.

____ Exit Visual Basic; you do not need to save this project.

New application with a timer

5. ____ Write a digital clock program. Here's how it might look when it's running.

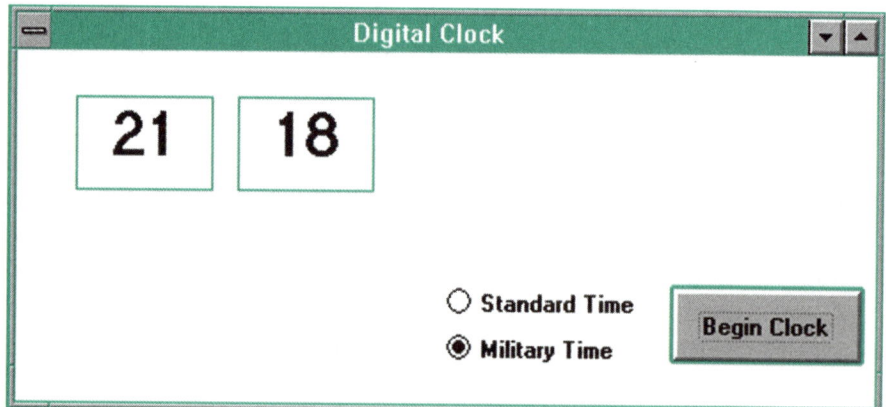

Use separate labels for hours and minutes. Once the clock is started, the time needs to be continually updated, so you need a Timer control; that's where you put the code to display the time. The Begin Clock button enables the timer; since you want the time display to come up quickly, make the timer's Interval property fairly short, say about 500. In order to find the values for hours and minutes, use the *Now* function along with *Format$*. (Consult the Help section on *Format$* to see which formatting string to use.) You should use a large font for the display. Note the two option buttons for standard (12-hour) and military (24-hour) time.

____ What's the best time of day to test your clock? Why?

____ Save your files as *clock.frm* and *clock.mak*.

QuickCheck 7.2

1. If the user should be able to select only one from several choices, what is the appropriate control object?
2. The user can reset the Value property of an option button at run time by _____ .
3. True or false: The Value property of a group of check boxes is coordinated so that when the Value property of one check box changes, so do the others.
4. What is controlled by the Interval property of a Timer control object?
5. Multiple groups of option buttons on a form can be achieved by using the _____ control object.

THOUGHTS ON PROGRAMMING

Design Representation

As discussed, **high-level program design** involves the identification of subtasks and decisions about information flow. In other words, it answers these questions:

> What control objects, procedures, and functions should be used, and where is the code to be located?
>
> What are the important variables and constants to use, and where are they to be declared?
>
> How will the various objects and code segments interact as the program executes?
>
> What are the details of the interfaces—the argument passing arrangements—for information to be exchanged among the various control objects and code segments?

Low-level program design is concerned with the individual procedures and functions. If the high-level design was properly done, then each procedure or function is intended to do a fairly small and specific subtask. Low-level design answers these questions for each subtask:

What algorithm (sequence of steps) will accomplish this subtask?

What flow of control is needed to support this algorithm?

Are any local variables required?

Are the services of any other procedure or function needed as part of the algorithm?

Once the low-level design is complete, the design process has successfully moved from requirements to "close to code" (see Figure 1.9). It should be a fairly easy step to translate the finished low-level design into code. In fact, software packages called **code generators** automatically produce code in a given language once the design has been specified.

In both high-level and low-level design, it is important to represent design decisions in a form that is helpful for the next stage. High-level design representation should aid low-level design. Low-level design representation should aid coding. And both are part of the total documentation package for the software.

The Object Task Card (OTC) design representation introduced in Chapter 2 captures some of the high-level design decisions. This might be called a "text-based" design representation, as it is done entirely with words.

Visual or graphical design representations can convey a lot of information at a glance. One such high-level design representation tool was introduced in Chapter 6. Figure 6.9, shown again as Figure 7.4, gives a graphical representa-

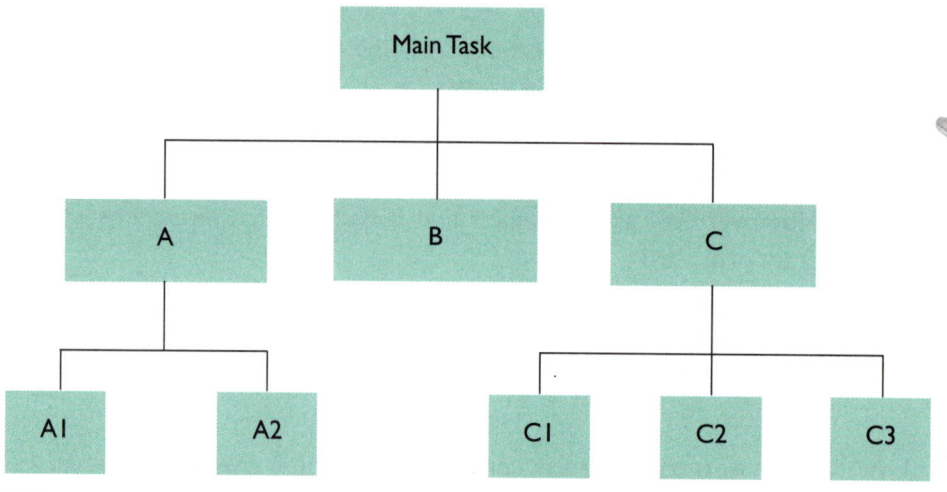

Figure 7.4
High-level design representation using a structure chart

tion of a top-down design that identifies subtasks, sub-subtasks, and so on. Such a figure is called a **structure chart.** There is some resemblance to an organization chart in a company; instead of departments that work for a particular vice-president, there are little jobs that work to perform a bigger job.

In Figure 7.4, assume that A1 represents a subtask to be done by a procedure called from within procedure A. Also assume that when A calls A1, there are three arguments in the interface. A passes information to A1 through arguments Q1 and Q2. A1 does some process using these quantities and finally returns a new value to A that is received by the third argument, Q3. Therefore Q1 and Q2 carry information into A1, and Q3 receives information from A1. (This is just the situation described in Figure 6.8.) The structure chart can be annotated, as in Figure 7.5, to show this information flow. If all such information flow is annotated, the structure chart becomes a **data flow diagram.** (It is sometimes the case that a quantity needed by a called procedure is also modified by that procedure and the new value returned to the calling procedure. Then the quantity carries information both in and out; this is denoted on the data flow diagram by a double-headed arrow.)

Structure charts and data flow diagrams provide useful visualizations of the decomposition of the overall problem. The boxes represent subtasks and

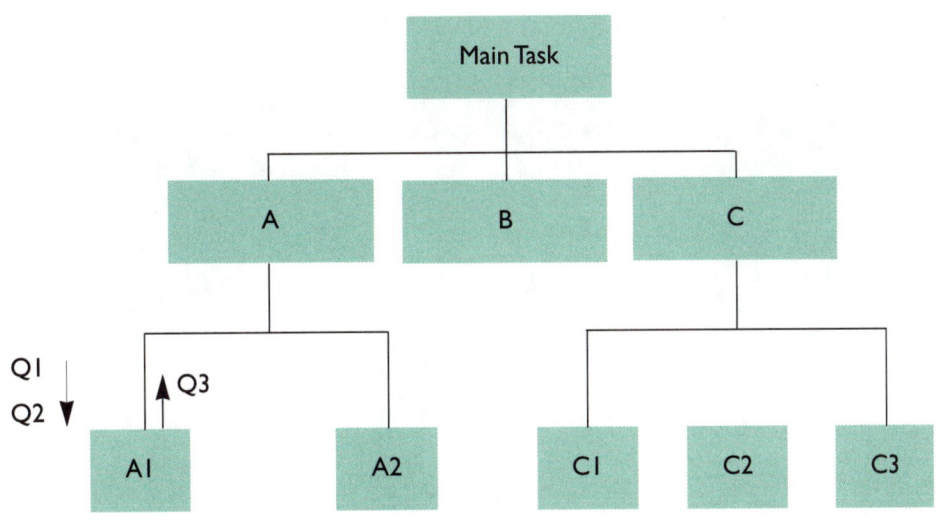

Figure 7.5
High-level design representation using a (partially completed) data flow diagram

the lines represent paths of communication via argument passing. These design representations convey ideas about task structure and relationships. Their major drawback is that they incorporate no sense of time or sequence. In event-driven programming, such as Visual Basic, it is important to visualize what the reactions are to various actions that the user can take or that the program code can initiate. The action-reaction view of a program can be captured in a different high-level design representation.

A **state transition diagram** identifies various states that the program may be in during the course of its execution. A **state** is a relatively static, "at rest" situation that occurs between significant events. For example, a form in a Visual Basic program that is waiting for the user to click on one of several command buttons constitutes one state for that program; nothing changes until some event (in this case, a user action) takes place. Graphically, a state transition diagram consists of circles and lines, similar to a structure chart or data flow diagram, but the circles represent states and the lines represent the transitions from one state to another that are caused by some event. Figure 7.6 shows the general idea of a state transition diagram. Here, State 1 is the initial state; according to the diagram, it is possible to return to this state by way of State 2 if the sequence Event 1 followed by Event 2 takes place. However, once Event 3 has taken place and the program moves into State 3, there is no way back. A state transition diagram, while capturing some of the dynamic aspects of a program's behavior, does not address task breakdown or division of labor within the program.

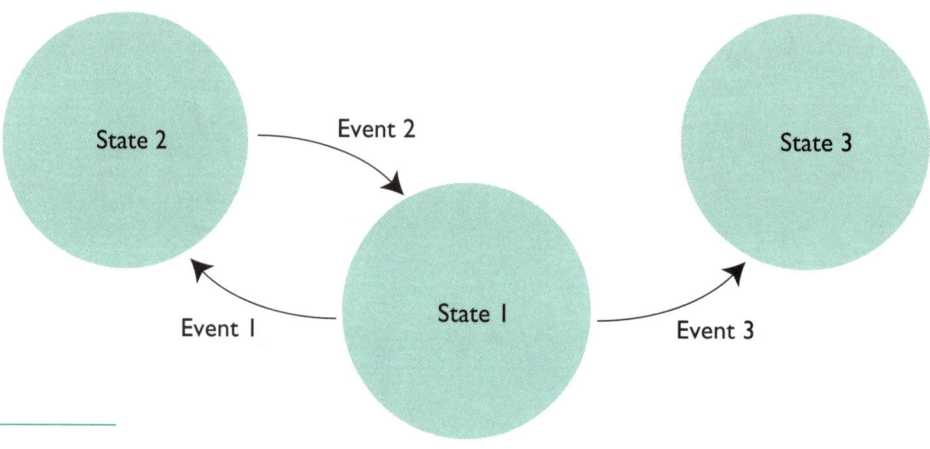

Figure 7.6

High-level design representation using a state transition diagram

Another high-level design representation borrows an idea from the movies. A **storyboard** is a series of sketches representing the scenes in a movie as the action progresses. For a Visual Basic program, a series of form designs is sketched out and arranged in various "scripts" or "scenarios" to represent the dynamic behavior desired in the program.

Structure charts, data flow diagrams, state transition diagrams, and storyboards are high-level design representations that convey different views of the program being designed, much as an architect's sketches of a home from the front, back, side, top, and so on, provide different views of the house being designed. Any or all of these graphical representations, as well as the textual OTC representation, may be useful in the design of any particular Visual Basic program.

What about low-level design representation? Pseudocode has been used to describe small sections of code such as the body of a procedure or function. The advantage of pseudocode is that it is but a short step to translate pseudocode into Visual Basic code. An alternative low-level design representation, called a **flowchart,** is graphical in nature. The idea behind the flowchart is to visually represent the flow-of-control options presented by sequential processing, conditional processing, and looping. The flowchart in Figure 7.7 illustrates a sequence of three statements, in which the middle one is a conditional (If-Then-Else) statement. Variations of the conditional statement can be incorporated into the flowchart; Figure 7.8a shows an If statement (empty else) and Figure 7.8b illustrates a Select-Case statement.

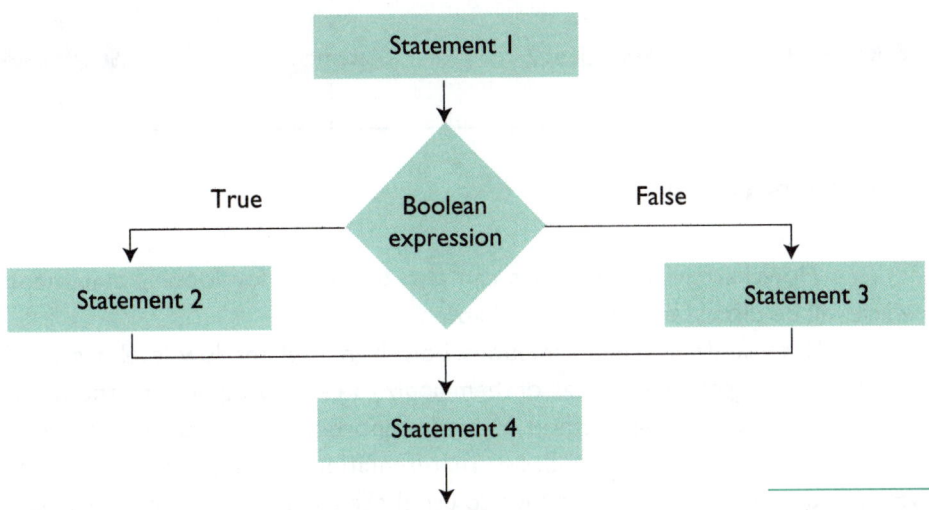

Figure 7.7
Flowchart with an If-Then-Else as the middle statement

Figure 7.8
Flowchart representation for other conditional statements

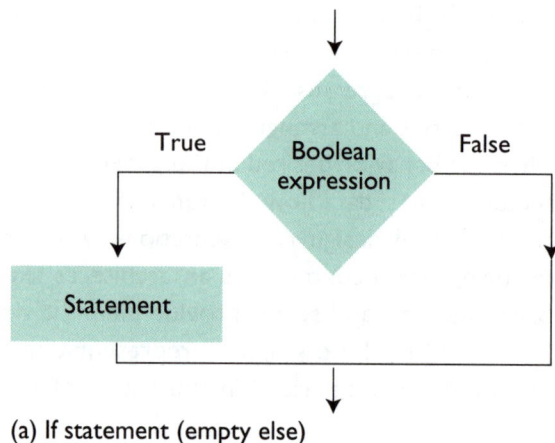

(a) If statement (empty else)

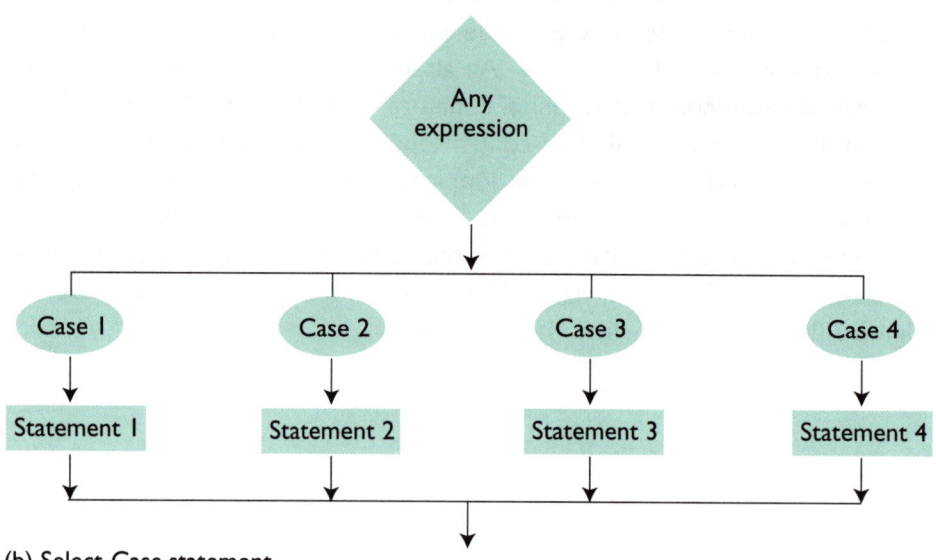

(b) Select-Case statement

Flowchart representations can also be drawn for looping statements, which will be discussed in the next chapter.

All these design representations, both high-level and low-level, are simply guidelines or suggestions. Not all of them apply to every program, and there is no one right representational method. What is important is for you to adopt, adapt, or develop your own tools for design representation that are expressive in conveying your design decisions and then to use those tools in a consistent manner.

7.6 Still another program design

A program is to be written to score participants in an international diving competition. Here are the scoring rules for a diving meet: There are seven judges. Each judge awards a score for a dive as any whole or half value between 0 and 10; for example, 8.5 is a valid score. The high and low scores from the seven scores are eliminated. The remaining five scores are added together. Then three-fifths of this total score is multiplied by the degree of difficulty of the dive. The result is the final score for that individual dive. The degree of difficulty of a dive is determined by the particular dive attempted and can run from 1.0 to 4.0 to the nearest tenth; for example, 3.2 is a valid degree of difficulty.

The program's requirements are fairly well determined. User input consists of:

- Diver's first and last name
- Description of the dive
- Degree of difficulty of the dive
- Seven scores from the judges

(The program should also provide a way to review a table of the kinds of dives and the degree of difficulty of each as a check that the right degree of difficulty has been entered for this dive.) The user can choose between a partial output screen, giving only the diver's name and the score, or a full output screen, giving:

- Diver's name
- Description of dive
- Degree of difficulty of dive
- Access to the table to review degree of difficulty (DoD)
- Score
- Maximum score and the country of the judge awarding that score
- Minimum score and the country of the judge awarding that score

If incomplete data have been entered when the user asks for a report, the user is not allowed to continue but must go back and finish the data entry.

A structure chart serves as a first cut at a high-level design view. Figure 7.9 identifies tasks and subtasks. Before deciding which of the tasks are to be done in event procedures, which in form-level functions, and so on, decisions must be made about which control objects (hence event procedures) are available. The program requirements indicate that multiple screens (forms) are involved. Instead of an OTC design of the various forms, the forms can be laid out as they might appear and then arranged for a storyboard walk through. Figure 7.10 shows a design for the initial screen. The plan is to have all the user input done by means of text boxes. This makes the "Get input data" subtask in Figure 7.9 easy; the input values are

Figure 7.9
Structure chart for the dive program

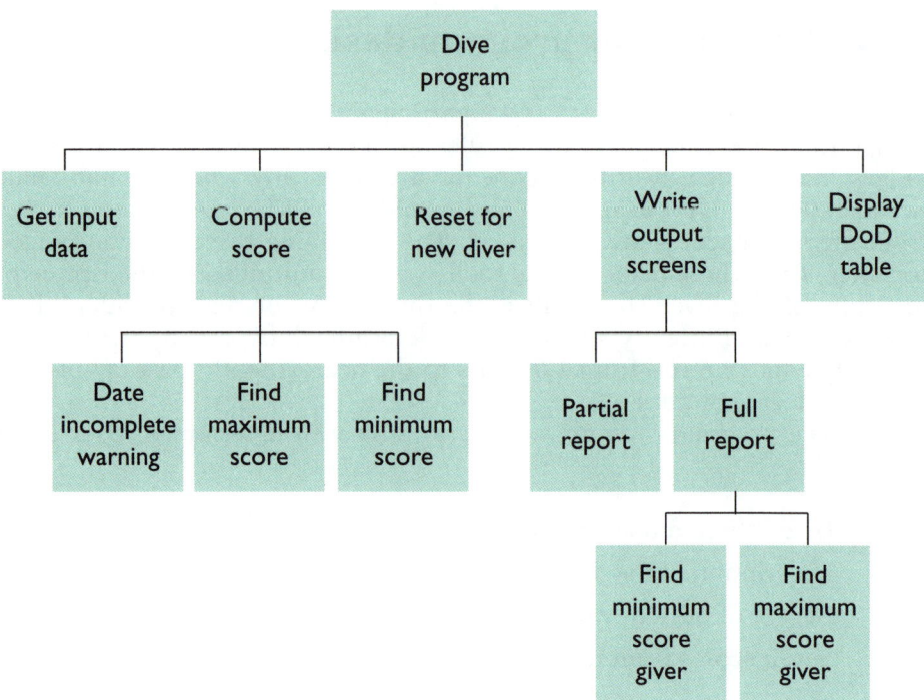

all found as the Text properties of various text boxes. The seven score text boxes all act alike, so they can form a control array, with a matching array of image controls containing the flags of the judging countries. (The flags are icon files found in the icon library of Visual Basic, usually located in the C:\VB\ICONS directory; icon file names end with .ICO.) From top to bottom, the flags represent the United States, the United Kingdom, Canada, Germany, Russia, France, and Japan. Unlike the cash register in Auntie's Cash and Gas, the icons here are only for identification and have no associated code.

If the user clicks the command button on this form to ask for the DoD (Degree of Difficulty) table, a separate small form is displayed containing text information. Figure 7.11 shows this new form with one sample entry.

Clearly most of the work is done when the user clicks on the Compute Score button. The seven judges' scores and the degree of difficulty of the dive are all required in the computation of the final score, so these data must be present, even if the diver's name and the description of the dive are missing. If the user asks to compute the score prematurely, before completing the essential data entry, a message form appears; Figure 7.12 shows the form design for this. This had better be a modal form (see Section 4.10) because the user should not be able to work around this problem but should be forced to finish the data entry.

Assuming the data entry is complete, a request for a partial report results in a form like that shown in Figure 7.13; a request for a full report results in something like Figure 7.14.

A dynamic design view of this program is presented in the state transition diagram shown in Figure 7.15. Here the various states are characterized to coincide with the display of various forms because the major events of this program—according to the storyboard design view—cause transitions to other forms.

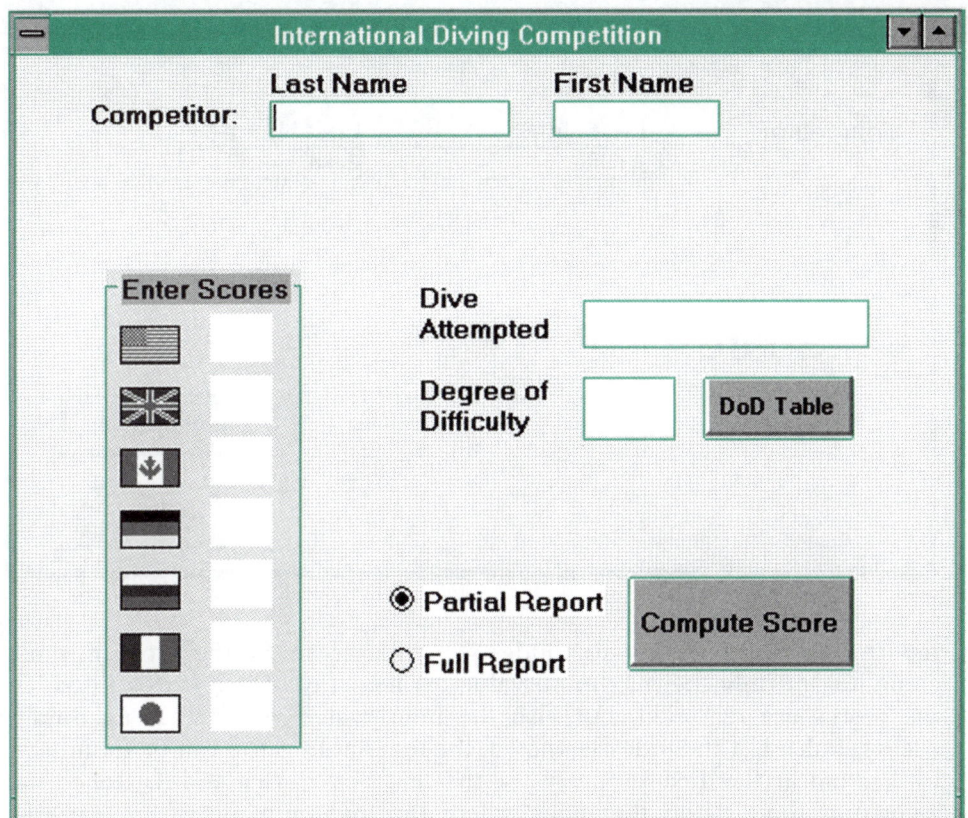

Figure 7.10
Opening form design for the dive program

Moving to low-level design, consider an algorithm for one of the subtasks identified in the structure chart, that of finding the maximum score. The classic algorithm for finding a maximum from among a list of things is to maintain a *CurrentMax* value, which represents the maximum value encountered so far in the list. The first item in the list is initially the current maximum. As each new element from the list is examined in turn, it is compared to the *CurrentMax* value; the *CurrentMax* value is adjusted if necessary. In the dive program, not only is the maximum score needed, but the full

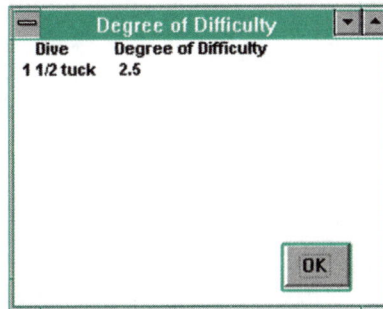

Figure 7.11
Design for reference form on degree of difficulty

Figure 7.12
Attention-getting form for incomplete data entry

Figure 7.13
Partial output report for the dive program

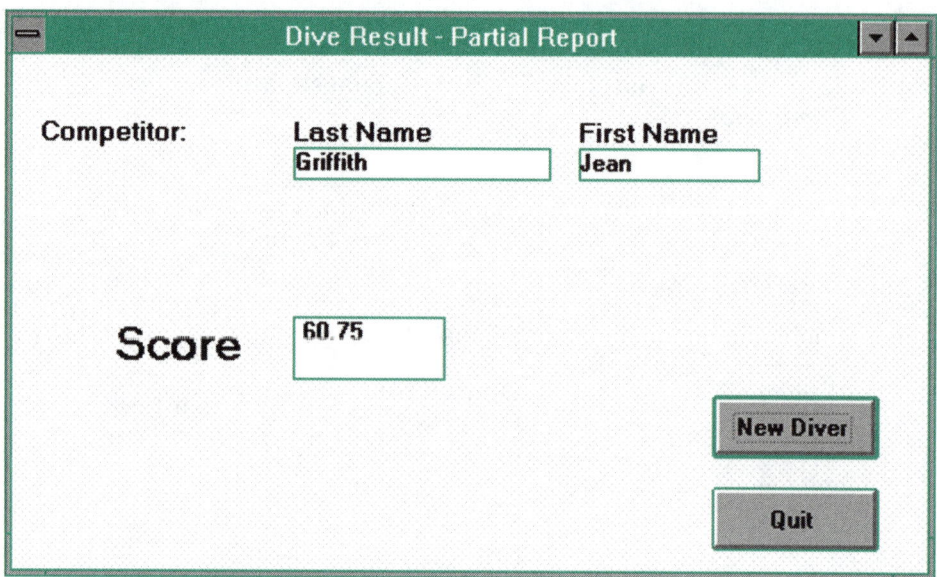

report also has to show which judge gave that score. So the program must compute not only the maximum value in the array of text boxes in which the scores are recorded, but also the index value where that maximum occurs. Indeed, if the index is known, the maximum value can be found just by looking at the Text property for the text box at that index. Hence the algorithm should find the index where the maximum occurs. A variable *MaxIndex* can store this information. The index values in a control array begin with index 0, so the seven text boxes that collect the scores have index values 0 through 6.

Figure 7.14
Full output report for the dive program

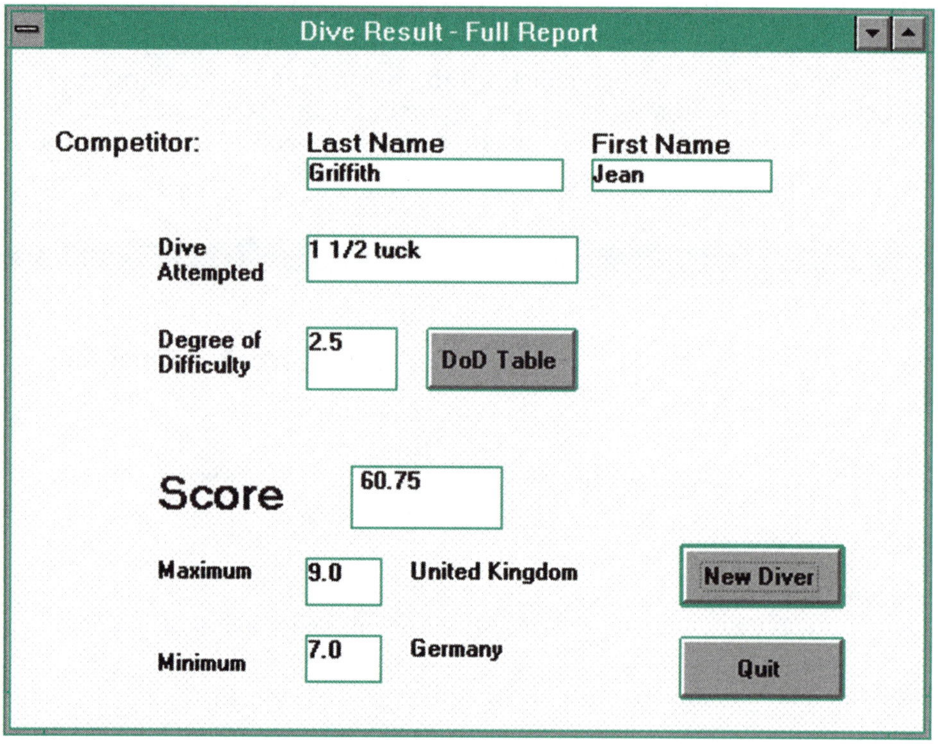

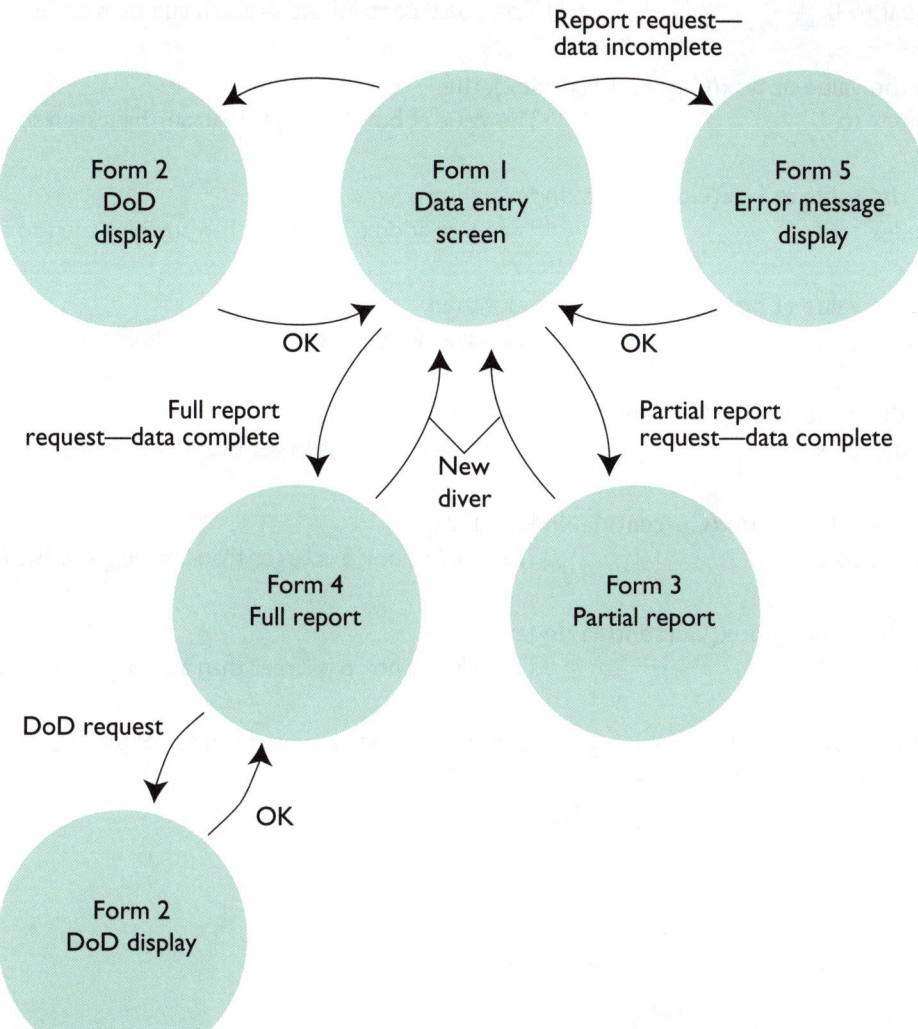

Figure 7.15
State transition diagram for the dive program

The Compute Score button on Form1 needs to know the value of *MaxIndex*, but this value is also needed to complete the display for the Full report option (Form 4). Consequently *MaxIndex* will be a global variable to ensure it is available for both these forms. To find *MaxIndex*, the first text box index is initially assigned as the *CurrentMaxIndex*, then *CurrentMaxIndex* is adjusted as each list item is examined. After all items in the list have been examined, the value of *CurrentMaxIndex* is the maximum index value. Figure 7.16 gives a pseudocode description of a FindMaxIndex algorithm to find the index in the text box array of scores where the maximum score occurs. The algorithm consists primarily of a succession of If-Then statements that test each new element in the list as a potential new maximum. Of course, the algorithm for finding the index for the minimum score is similar.

For the dive program, there are now several high-level design views and a low-level algorithm design for one key procedure. There is a good design plan at this point on which to build. While much remains to be done to create a functional Visual Basic program, this advance planning eases the transition to working code.

Set *CurrentMaxIndex* equal to 0   ' Text box 0 contains the largest value seen so far

If the value at box(1) > the value at box(CurrentMaxIndex), then
    change *CurrentMaxIndex* to 1   ' The value at box 1 is larger than anything seen so far

If the value at box(2) > the value at box(CurrentMaxIndex), then
    change *CurrentMaxIndex* to 2   ' The value at box 2 is larger than anything seen so far

If the value at box(3) > the value at box(CurrentMaxIndex), then
    change *CurrentMaxIndex* to 3   ' The value at box 3 is larger than anything seen so far

If the value at box(4) > the value at box(CurrentMaxIndex), then
    change *CurrentMaxIndex* to 4   ' The value at box 4 is larger than anything seen so far

If the value at box(5) > the value at box(CurrentMaxIndex), then
    change *CurrentMaxIndex* to 5   ' The value at box 5 is larger than anything seen so far

If the value at box(6) > the value at box(CurrentMaxIndex), then
    change *CurrentMaxIndex* to 6   ' The value at box 6 is larger than anything seen so far

Set *MaxIndex* equal to *CurrentMaxIndex*   ' CurrentMaxIndex is now the index of the largest value

Figure 7.16
Pseudocode for a FindMaxIndex procedure

7.7 Visual Basic debugger

Part of the integrated development environment that Visual Basic offers the programmer is a debugging facility to detect errors ("bugs") in the code. Now that the programs are becoming more complex, it's time to see how to use the debugging tools provided. (Did you think that you were the only one who wrote programs with errors? Everybody does; otherwise there would be no need for debugging facilities!)

Before looking at the debugger, it is helpful to classify the errors that a program can contain into three kinds. **Syntax errors** are those that violate the syntax rules of the programming language. Such errors are detected by Visual Basic. Some syntax errors can be detected by the code editor as soon as a line is completed (at least if the Syntax Checking switch under Options/Environment is left at its default value of Yes). For example, the attempted assignment

$x * 2 = x$

produces an immediate complaint as soon as you hit the Enter key because only a single variable, not an expression, can appear on the left side of an assignment statement.

The following code provokes an error message during run time that complains about the lack of an End If to finish off the If-Then-Else statement.

```
If x > 7 Then
    Picture1.Print "high"
Else
    Picture1.Print "low"
End Sub
```

Although this is a syntax error, it is not flagged right after entering the line

```
Picture1.Print "low"
```

because you may be going to add more code as part of the Else clause and then finish it up with the required End If. Visual Basic has to give you a chance to do that.

Error messages about syntax errors are relatively helpful in diagnosing the problem. By this time, you've no doubt seen a number of syntax error messages and been able to correct the difficulties.

Run-time errors are errors that occur when the program starts to execute a statement that attempts to perform some illegal operation. For example, the statement

```
Value = 12/x
```

produces a run-time error if x has the value zero when this statement executes, because division by zero is illegal. This is not a syntax error because the syntax is perfectly correct. It is an error for this particular execution attempt because of the current value of x. Visual Basic also provides error messages for run-time errors.

Logic errors occur when the solution algorithm is incorrect. Unlike syntax or run-time errors, there are no warnings or error messages from Visual Basic to signal that a logic error exists in the program. The program executes, displays output, and generally seems to be going quite well. However, closer examination reveals that something is wrong—one or more of the "answers" is incorrect, or the program responds to an event in some way other than it is supposed to. Here is where you have to be observant as you run your program. Are the answers what they should be for the given data? Have you tried other sets of data? Have you exercised all the possible user actions to make sure everything behaves properly? Just because a program runs successfully once does not guarantee that it is bug-free. You need to thoroughly test your program.

The first part of debugging a logic error, then, is recognizing that one exists. Next comes the task of tracking down where the error occurs in the code. Remember that you have no error messages from Visual Basic to help you pinpoint what is wrong. Perhaps you assigned the wrong value to a variable, or put the wrong condition in a Boolean expression, or invoked the wrong procedure (or the right procedure at the wrong time). Sometimes the source of the error is rather far away from the code where the consequences of the error ultimately become evident, so the process of locating and fixing logic errors involves a bit of detective work. Much of this detective work consists of holding your "magnifying glass" to the program while it runs; think of the Visual Basic debugger as your "magnifying glass."

274 • CHAPTER 7 • CONDITIONAL PROCESSING

To see what's going on inside a running program, you can suspend execution at any time and put the program into break mode. Any of the following actions will cause a program to go from run mode to break mode (you may remember doing this in Lab 4.1):

OPTIONS

- Choose Break from the Run menu.
- Press Ctrl-Break (hold down the Ctrl key and press the Break key).
- Click the Break button on the Toolbar.

Before going further, note what the options are to get a program out of break mode. To continue execution from the current point, do one of the following:

OPTIONS

- Choose Continue from the Run menu.
- Press F5.
- Click the Run button on the Toolbar.

To run the program again from the beginning, do one of the following:

OPTIONS

- Choose Restart from the Run menu.
- Press Shift-F5 (press F5 while holding down the Shift key).

And to go back to design mode from break mode, do one of the following:

OPTIONS

- Choose End from the Run menu.
- Click the Stop button on the Toolbar.

Once in break mode, you can single-step through your program by repeatedly doing one of the following:

OPTIONS

- Choose Single Step from the Debug menu.
- Press F8.
- Click the Single Step button on the Toolbar.

Each time you step, the program executes one line of code starting with the current procedure or function, which is displayed in the Code window. The line about to be executed is surrounded by a rectangle, and you can watch progress through the procedure just by following the rectangle. This process allows you to trace the flow of control of your program in detail; you see which branch of an If-Then-Else statement is executed, you follow every excursion to a function or another procedure and execute that function or procedure line by line, and so on. When an unexpected jump occurs and you end up in the wrong part of the code, you see exactly when that happens. A less detailed view of flow of control is obtained by procedure stepping. To procedure-step, do one of the following:

OPTIONS

- Choose Procedure Step from the Debug menu.
- Press Shift F8.
- Click the Procedure Step button on the Toolbar.

Each time you step, the current procedure is executed line by line, but execution of other procedures or functions invoked within the current procedure is done out of sight.

A still more detailed view of what's happening inside your program can be obtained by using the Debug window. The Debug window moves to the foreground when the program first enters break mode, but can get covered up as you step through the code. Choosing Debug from the Visual Basic Window menu makes it the active window again.

The Debug window has two parts. In the **immediate pane** you can ask to see the current value of a variable or a control object property, you can change a value and resume execution to see the effect, or you can try out a Visual Basic instruction to see what happens if it is executed at this point in the program. Figure 7.17 shows the immediate pane; the title bar indicates that you are looking at this window in the context of the *FindMaxIndex* procedure of DIVE.FRM, an implementation of the dive program. In fact, you were stepping through this procedure when you decided to check on the value of *CurrentMaxIndex*, so you printed that value in the Debug window. The rules of scope apply; if you attempt to print the value of *CurrentMaxIndex* outside of the *FindMaxIndex* procedure in which *CurrentMaxIndex* is a local variable, the variable name is not recognized.

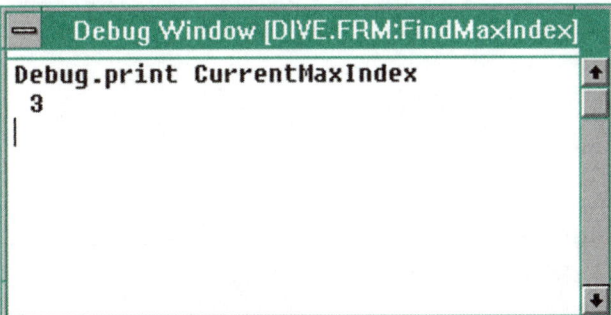

Figure 7.17
Example of the immediate pane of the Debug window

For both stepping through your program and viewing the Debug window, if you enter break mode when nothing is happening, that is, the program is waiting for some user action, then there is no procedural context. This means that the Code window doesn't appear when you step because nothing is executing; similarly, the Debug window displays the form name but no procedure or function name.

If you want to observe the value of a variable or expression as the program goes along, then you can set a **watch expression**. Figure 7.18 shows the dialog box that results from choosing Add Watch from the Debug menu. Here the debugger is asked to "watch" the expression *CurrentMaxIndex* in the context of the *FindMaxIndex* procedure in form DIVE.FRM. (Note the program can be made to automatically go into break mode from run mode when some watch expression becomes true or even changes its value.)

The next time you look at the Debug window, the second pane—the **watch pane**—is visible in addition to the immediate pane (Figure 7.19). Here the values of any watch expressions that have been set can be seen.

As an alternative to manually putting the program into break mode, or having Visual Basic do that automatically on the basis of conditions about watch expressions, you can insert a **breakpoint** in any line of code.

Figure 7.18
Use of the Add Watch dialog box

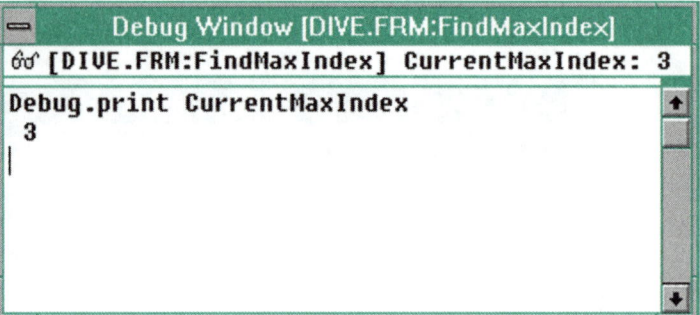

Figure 7.19
The Debug window showing both watch and immediate panes.

When the program executes, it goes into break mode just before executing such a line. To set a breakpoint in a line of code, set the cursor in that line of code in the Code window; then do one of the following:

OPTIONS
- Choose Toggle Breakpoint from the Debug menu.
- Press F9.
- Click the Breakpoint button on the toolbar.

The breakpoint line is highlighted in color in the Code window. When the executing program reaches the breakpoint line and goes into break mode, you can do the sorts of things already discussed: look at any watch expressions in the watch pane of the Debug window, work in the immediate pane of the Debug window, single-step from that point on, and so on.

Other choices from the Debug menu include:

Edit Watch: Allows you to edit, add, or delete watch expressions.

Calls: Lists all active procedures, that is, all procedures that have been invoked at this point but have not yet been completed.

This section has not explored all Visual Basic's debugging facilities, but it closes with a really neat one. While in break mode, you can put the cursor within a variable or highlight an expression in the Code window and then do one of the following:

OPTIONS
- Choose Instant Watch from the Debug menu.
- Press Shift F9.
- Click the Instant Watch button on the Toolbar (the little spectacles).

This brings up the Instant Watch dialog box (Figure 7.20), which shows you the current value of this expression or variable and allows you the option of adding it to your watch list.

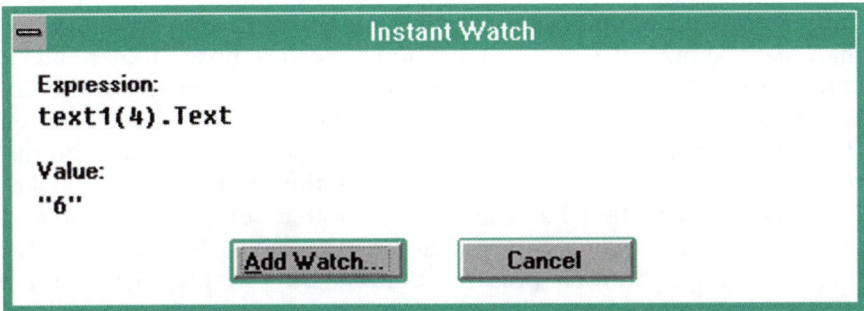

Figure 7.20
Instant Watch dialog box

Although Visual Basic provides you with several ways to examine the status of your program, its objects, and its quantities at any point in time, this alone does not make the debugging process successful. The debugger provides you with a set of tools. It is up to you to use them in some organized manner so that you gradually close in on the source of the error. Like the Help system, the Visual Basic debugger can be a great aid to your programming efforts, and facility with its use should be cultivated through practice.

7.8 Guiding the order of user actions

You already have some ways to guide the user's choice of actions in a running program. By setting the Value property to 2 in a check box, you suggest that it may be inappropriate for the user to make this choice. By setting the Value property of one option button to True at design time, you make it the easiest one for the user to pick. There are other ways you can channel the user's actions, or make it easier for the user to do one action as opposed to another.

In the dive program, the user has quite a number of text boxes to fill in. Data can be entered in any order simply by clicking on the various text boxes. This is helpful because, for example, the judges may not all have their scores ready at the same time. However, the program can be made to supply a default order. When the screen first appears, one of the text boxes can already have the focus, that is, be ready to accept input (shown by the blinking insertion bar appearing in that text box). The user does not need to move the cursor to enter text there. When finished with that text box, the user hits the Tab key and the focus automatically goes to another specified text box. This guides but does not enforce the sequence of user data entry. It also allows for movement from one data entry point to the next solely by keyboard commands, which for experienced typists are faster than pointing and clicking.

The **TabIndex property** directs the order in which control objects get the focus as the Tab key is pressed. Virtually every control has a TabIndex property. The TabIndex property is assigned automatically by Visual Basic in the order in which the control is created on the form, with higher TabIndex values assigned to newer controls. But this property can be changed in the Properties window. Once all your controls are on the form, you can reset the TabIndex property for each object to reflect the order in which you imagine the user is most likely to want to visit these controls. At a minimum, the user wants to visit text boxes for data entry and command buttons to choose certain actions. The user can simply tab from one control to the next; for example, you can set the tab index for a command button so that, as a default, it gets the focus *after* the text boxes that relate to data entry for the action that button performs. In the dive program the Compute Score button is normally visited after all the data items have been entered. (In fact, a warning message pops up if the user tries to compute the score before entering all essential data.) Just as the blinking insertion bar indicates the text box that has the focus, a dotted square around the caption indicates the command button that has the focus. In Figure 7.21, of the three command buttons present, Command2 has the focus. If the user presses the Enter key at this time, the effect is the same as clicking on Command2.

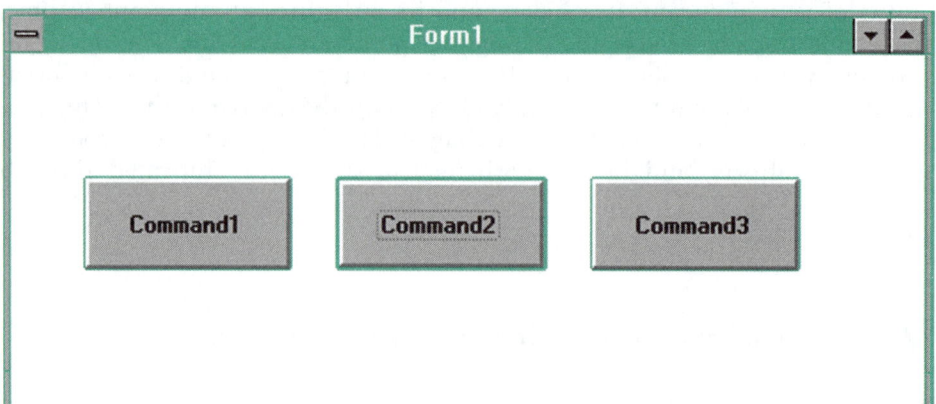

Figure 7.21
Command2 button has the focus

Although frames and labels have a TabIndex property, they cannot get the focus at run time (after all, the user isn't going to do anything with a frame or a label), so it doesn't matter what their TabIndex properties are set to. There may be other controls you wish to prevent from getting the focus during run time; this is accomplished by setting the **TabStop property** for those controls to False.

Two additional command button properties exist to make life easier for the user. One is the **Default property**. Setting the Default property of a button to True means that the click event for this button is activated when the user presses the Enter key. Only one button on a form can have a true Default value; the button appears on the form with a dark outline. There is a potential conflict here; what if Command1 has the focus but Command2 is the default button? This conflict is resolved by giving preference to the button with the focus; pressing the Enter key activates that button rather than the default button. The **Cancel property** of a command button has a similar effect, but allows the chosen button to be activated by pressing the Esc key. Only one button on the form can have a true Cancel property. The Default and Cancel properties work nicely together in a situation in which you expect the user to want to commit to some action (make that the default button) but you want to give an escape hatch for the user to back out (make that the cancel button).

The user's actions can be constrained by disabling certain controls at some point during program execution. Simply write a Visual Basic statement that sets the value of the **Enabled property** of the control object to False; then set it back to True by another statement when it is once again appropriate for that control to be available to the user.

At run time, executing a statement that applies the **SetFocus method** to an object gives that object the focus, provided both its Enabled and Visible properties are currently true. If either property is false, executing such a statement results in an error message of "Illegal function call". When the object receives the focus, it experiences a GotFocus event; it experiences a LostFocus event when the focus passes to some other object. In a text box, for example, the LostFocus event procedure is the place to verify that the data item entered meets a certain requirement before the user is allowed to proceed to another text box. If the requirement is not met, the text can be set to the null string and the SetFocus method applied, giving the user another chance to enter data in this same text box.

Name: _____ Date Due: _____

LAB 7.3

LEARNING OBJECTIVES

- Using the debugger
- Implementing the dive program

1. ____ You own a piece of property that is 120 feet long × 52 feet wide. The front of the property (one 52-feet edge) faces the highway, and the back side of the property is bounded by a stream (see figure).

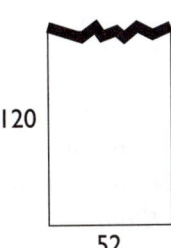

You want to fence in three sides of the property (no fence along the stream). Your options are to use redwood fencing along the front and chain link along the two sides or to use a picket fence along all three sides. You prefer the picket fence, so you will choose it if it is not more than $100 more than the redwood-chain link fence.

Suppose fence prices per foot are as follows:

    Redwood: $2.89   Link: $1.79   Picket: $2.47

Use your calculator to determine the following:

    Cost of redwood part _____

    Cost of chain link part _____

    Total cost of redwood-chain link (option 1) _____

    Cost of picket fence (option 2) _____

    Buy (circle one): redwood-chain link   picket

Now assume the following prices and redo your calculations:

    Redwood: $2.89   Link: $2.05   Picket: $2.47

    Cost of redwood part _____

    Cost of chain link part _____

    Total cost of redwood-chain link (option 1) _____

    Cost of picket fence (option 2) _____

    Buy (circle one): redwood-chain link   picket

2. ____ Open the Visual Basic project **fence.mak**. This application allows you to consider your two options for different fence prices.

   ____ Run this program for the first set of data you computed, and record the answers supplied by the program:

   Redwood: $2.89   Link: $1.79   Picket: $2.47

   Cost of redwood-chain link_____

   Cost of picket fence _____

   Buy (circle one): redwood-chain link   picket

Using the debugger

3. Use the Visual Basic debugger (trace execution, set breakpoints, watch variables, and so on) to find the errors in this program. Put a comment explaining anything you change. Be sure to test your program on the two cases you did by hand, as well as several other cases, to be sure it is working properly. Save these files as **fenceOK.frm** and **fenceOK.mak**.

Implementing the dive program

4. Implement the dive program in Visual Basic. Consider the following hints:

   a. Follow the design developed in Section 7.6.

   b. Let your program grow in small increments; test it after each new piece is added, and save your work often. Use file names **dive.mak**, **dive1.frm**, **dive2.frm**, and so on.

   c. Set the TabIndex property of the text boxes for input data in some reasonable way.

   d. To know whether the data entry is complete, maintain a variable *Datacount*. When any of the essential text boxes experiences a LostFocus event because the user has moved on to another text box, check to see if the text is null. If it's not, bump up the value of *Datacount* by 1. Then when the user asks to compute the score, test whether *Datacount* has reached a value big enough for all the essential data to have been entered.

   e. Translate the FindMaxIndex pseudocode into a general procedure with a single parameter representing the maximum index.

   f. Finding the index for the minimum score is similar to finding the index for the maximum score. Copy and paste the code and then make the necessary changes.

   ____ When your program is complete, test it thoroughly to be sure the code is correct and fix any errors you encounter. Save your work. Congratulations, this was a big job!

QuickCheck 7.3

1. What do the lines in structure charts and data flow diagrams represent?
2. What do the lines in state transition diagrams represent?
3. What is a breakpoint?
4. The two panes of the Debug window are _____ and _____.
5. The order of receiving the focus is determined by the control object's _____ property.

Review Questions

1. A Boolean expression can have one of two values, _____ or _____.
2. Which term best describes relational operators?
   Change values
   Compare quantities
   Select cases
   Nest conditions
3. The logical operator Or results in a false value only when _____.
4. An If-Then-Else statement is sometimes called a "branching statement"; explain why this is an appropriate name.
5. Which two types of statements select one path of action from multiple choices?
6. Explain what happens in a Select-Case statement if the test expression satisfies more than one expression list.
7. What is the major difference between option buttons and check boxes?
8. Explain why option buttons and check boxes "go with" conditional statements.
9. Why is the Value property of an option button Boolean whereas the Value property of a check box is numeric?
10. What control object allows code to be executed over and over at regular intervals?
11. Give three high-level graphical design representation techniques.
12. Give one low-level graphical design representation technique.
13. A manager allots 40 percent of the development time for a software project to design, and 10 percent to coding. Explain how he or she justifies this decision.
14. What aspect of program behavior do state transition diagrams and storyboard views provide that OTC designs and structure charts do not?

15. What are the three types of errors that can occur in a Visual Basic program?
16. For which of these error types is the Visual Basic debugger most helpful?
17. In order to follow the flow of control of your program, you use what feature or features of the Visual Basic debugger?
18. What is the watch pane of the Debug window for?
19. Why would you ever want to change the order of the TabIndex property of control objects?
20. What is the effect when the Default property of a command button is set to true?

Exercises

Reading code

1. What is the truth value of the following Boolean expression if *X* has the value 4.2?

    ```
    (X > 5.0) Or Not ((X - 1) > 4)
    ```

2. If *CriticalMass* has the value 5.72 and *Threshold* has the value 6.0 when the following statement is executed, what happens?

    ```
    If CriticalMass >= Threshold Then
        Call Stir
    End If
    ```

3. What is printed in the picture box when the following code is executed?

    ```
    Dim Score As Integer
    Dim Low As Integer
    Dim High As Integer
    Low = 15
    High = 20
    Score = 21
    Select Case Score
       Case Low To High, 22
          Picture1.Print "first case"
       Case Is > 15
          Picture1.Print "second case"
       Case Else
          Picture1.Print "third case"
    End Select
    ```

4. True or false: The following two statements produce the same output.

    ```
    If Not (a <= b) Then              If (a <= b) Then
        Picture1.Print "one"              Picture1.Print "two"
    Else                              Else
        Picture1.Print "two"              Picture1.Print "one"
    End If                            End If
    ```

5. True or false: The following two statements produce the same output. Explain your answer.

```
If (a < b) Or (c < > d) Then
    Picture1.Print "one"
Else
    Picture1.Print "two"
End If


If a < b Then
    If c < > d Then
        Picture1.Print "one"
    Else
        Picture1.Print "two"
    End If
End If
```

Writing code

6. Write a statement that squares the integer *X* if *X* has the value 7 and increases *X* by 2 otherwise.

7. Write a statement that squares the integer *X* if *X* has the value 7, increases *X* by 2 if *X* is between 10 and 15, and doubles *X* otherwise.

8. Write the following If statement as a Select-Case statement; *x* is type Integer.

```
If (x >= 4) And (x <= 6) Then
    Picture1.Print "one"
ElseIf x = 8 Then
    Picture1.Print "two"
End If
```

9. Write the following Select-Case statement as one of the variations of the If statement; *lotto* is type String.

```
Select Case lotto
    Case Is = Text1.Text
        Picture1.Print "one"
    Case "winner", "loser"
        Picture1.Print "two"
    Case Else
        Picture1.Print "three"
End Select
```

10. Rewrite the following code to something that is equivalent but easier to understand:

```
If (A >= B) And (B < C) Then
    Call One
ElseIf Not (A >= B) Or Not (B < C) Then
    Call Two
End If
```

Exploring Further

11. Write a calendar program that uses three check boxes and displays one or more of the following on the basis of which is checked:

    Current day of the week (Sunday, for example)

    Current month and date (November 15, for example)

    Current year (1996, for example)

    Use a picture box to display the output.

12. Write a calendar program that uses three option boxes and displays one of the following on the basis of which is selected:

    Current date in short form (12/02/96, for example)

    Current date with month first (December 2, 1996, for example)

    Current date with day first (2 December, 1996, for example)

    Make the short form the default choice. Use a picture box for output.

13. Modify the dive program from Lab 7.3 as follows: if the value entered for the degree of difficulty of a dive is not in the range between 1.0 and 4.0, then an error screen appears with an appropriate message. If the value entered for a score is not in the range between 0.0 and 10.0, then an error screen appears with an appropriate message.

14. Modify the calculator program from Chapter 5 so that it no longer uses RPN but the more usual **infix notation**. Thus instead of

    2 [ENTER] 3 *

    you do

    2 * 3

    Each operation symbol is keyed in between the two numbers. Instead of an Enter button, you need an = button.

15. If you did Project 5 in Chapter 5, modify your solution so that the amount of shift is part of the input and there are no restrictions on the letters used in the password. Letters at the end of the alphabet may have to be cycled around to the beginning of the alphabet. Again, password letters are all uppercase.

Projects

Do high-level and low-level designs for each of the following, and then implement your design. Test the resulting programs thoroughly.

1. This program collects a date from the user in month/date/year format and outputs the number of days remaining in that year. Be sure to account for leap year. Years evenly divisible by four, like 1996, are leap years, except for the century years. The only century years that are leap

years are those evenly divisible by 400, such as 1600, 2000, and so on. (*Hint:* Consult the Help section for *Format$*, which can act on a date expression.)

2. Modern software installation procedures often present the user with check boxes for submodules that can be installed or omitted at the user's discretion. Usually the amount of storage required to install each module is shown, and a running total of storage required is maintained as the user selects or deselects modules. Write a program to manage this task for five software modules. Module names and storage requirements are program constants.

3. Puddlejump Airlines has asked you for a program for its ticket agents to price tickets on their most popular flight, a round-trip connection between Wilbursville and Orvillesburg. The base round-trip rate is $140, but reservations made more than 30 days ahead get a 20 percent reduction. In addition, flights (either way) on Tuesday or Wednesday get a $15 discount, and flights (either way) on Saturday or Sunday cost an extra $20 surcharge. A stay of longer than 7 days earns a $30 reduction. The ticket price computed according to these rules is the fare for business class; first-class passengers pay a 15 percent surcharge on all tickets, and economy class passengers get a 10 percent reduction on all tickets. The program asks for the date of departure, the date of return, and the passenger class; the output is the ticket price with a summary of how the price was computed. (Hint: Consult the Help section for *Format$*, which can act on a date expression.)

4. You own a small auction house. When an item is put up for auction, sealed bids are accepted on that item. This program allows the user to enter up to five bids for a single item (amount bid and bidder's name) and then choose to see any or all of:

    The maximum bid and who submitted it

    The minimum bid and who submitted it

    The average of all bids submitted

5. A weekly payroll processing program collects input of:

    Employee name

    Address

    Social Security number

    The user chooses whether the employee is salaried or hourly. For a salaried worker, the program collects the annual salary. For an hourly worker, it collects the hours worked this week and the hourly pay rate. The output consists of a report showing name, address, and gross pay, plus any or all amounts withheld in the following categories, depending on what the user selects:

    Social Security

    Fringe benefits

    Federal taxes

    State taxes

Social Security is withheld at the rate of 6.2 percent of the first $62,700 of earnings for the year (assume that has not yet been exceeded) plus 1.45 percent of earnings for Medicare tax. Salaried employees have 4.75 percent of their earnings withheld for health insurance and 8.5 percent for retirement. Hourly employees have the same withholding rate for health insurance, but no withholding for retirement. Assume that Federal taxes are 28 percent of earnings after health insurance has been deducted and that State taxes are 6 percent of earnings after health insurance has been deducted. If all the above details are shown, then the total take-home pay is also displayed.

CHAPTER 8

Looping

KEY POINTS

- Looping in Visual Basic is done by one of the Do loop variations or by the For-Next statement.
- List box and combo box controls allow the user to make "discrete" selections.
- The scroll bar control allows the user to make "analog" selections.
- Prototyping a system brings the user into early design decisions.
- The sequential search algorithm compares the target value with each list value in turn until the target is found or the list is used up.
- A Forms collection acts like an array of forms.

8.1 Visual basic statements for looping

Chapter 7 discussed the statements that Visual Basic provides for conditional flow of control (If-Then-Else, Select-Case, and their variations). The final flow-of-control mechanism is looping, which allows a section of code to be executed multiple times. Visual Basic provides several statements to implement looping.

Before looking at the language elements that implement looping, note that the user can repeatedly generate a particular event, for example by clicking a command button several times in succession. If the user repeatedly generates the same event, then the code associated with that event is repeatedly executed; this is the essence of a loop, but it is controlled by the user rather than by the code.

Suppose you want to write a program that allows the user to keep track of a running total of positive numbers, often a useful task (to generate a retail store receipt, for example). Figure 8.1 shows a form designed to let the user enter a number in a text box and click a button to process that number. The user can do this as often as desired; the program maintains a running total in an output label. The Click event procedure for the Process Item command button contains all the program code (except for the trivial one line of code associated with the Exit_Click event). Figure 8.2 shows this code.

In Figure 8.1, the label caption that prompts the user for input reads "Item 1"; this is the caption value that is initially set in the Properties window for that control object. As the user runs the program and continues to process items, this caption changes to "Item 2", then "Item 3", and so forth. In the code of Figure 8.2, the variable i is used to accomplish this change (note how i gets incremented by 1 within this procedure). The procedure is executed once each time the user clicks the button, and it must remember

Figure 8.1
Form to maintain running total of numbers

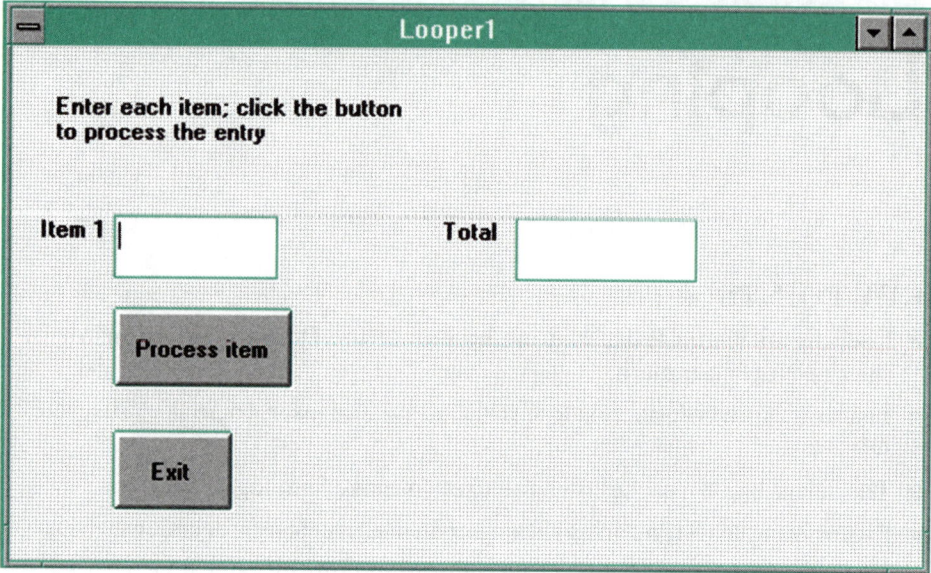

the value of *i* from the previous execution; this is why *i* is declared as a static variable. (Recall from Section 6.4 that a variable declared within a procedure using the keyword Static results in the variable's persisting and retaining its value from one invocation to the next.) Similarly, the value of *total* must be remembered from one execution to the next, so it is also a static variable. As noted in a comment, the code makes use of the fact that Visual Basic initializes numeric values to 0. Because the first instance of *total* has the value 0, the first item price can be added to it to start the running total. The values of *i* on successive executions are 0, 1, 2, 3 . . . , but the values 1, 2, 3, 4 . . . are displayed; the label caption displays the value of the expression *i* + 1 rather than *i*.

The code in Figure 8.2 adds the current item value to the running total and displays the result. The literal string "fixed" used with the *Format$*

Figure 8.2
Code for the Process Item command button

```
Sub cmdProcessItem_Click ()
Static i As Integer
Static total As Single
'Variables i and total are initialized to 0

    'add current value in txtItemprice to total
    total = total + Val(txtItemprice.Text)
    'write result in lblResult
    lblResult.Caption = Format$(total, "fixed")

    'go back for next item
    i = i + 1
    'update the prompt
    lblPrompt.Caption = "Item " & (i + 1)
    'blank out txtItemprice text box
    txtItemprice.Text = ""
    'give it the focus again
    txtItemprice.SetFocus

End Sub
```

function causes numbers to be displayed with at least one digit to the left and two digits to the right of the decimal point.

Once the running total has been updated and displayed, the code turns its attention to getting ready for the next item. As explained above, *i* gets incremented, but the text box for data entry also gets blanked out to get ready for the next entry. The final point to note about Figure 8.2 is the use of the SetFocus method on the data entry text box. Setting the TabIndex of this text box to 0 in the Properties window guarantees that the text box has the focus when the application executes, as shown by the blinking insertion bar that appears there. Once the user enters a value, the focus moves to another control object; the SetFocus method again gives the text box the focus in preparation for the user's next entry.

Now change the purpose of the command button in the previous example. Instead of processing a single item, which the user does over and over by repeatedly clicking the command button, the button initiates a loop to process multiple items. The user clicks the button only once. The responsibility for managing the loop has been moved from the user to the program. Figure 8.3 shows the new form.

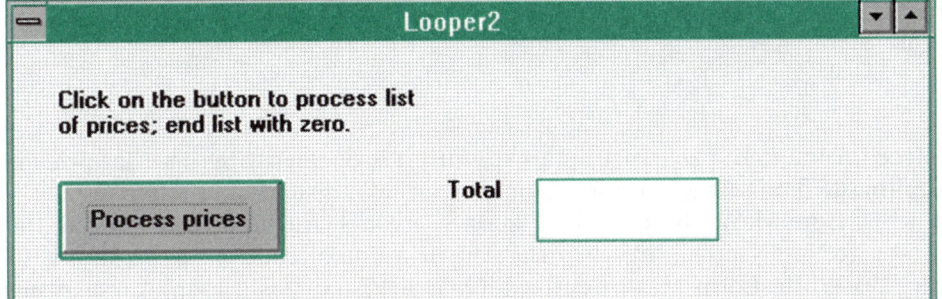

Figure 8.3
New form for running total

After clicking the button once, the user is repeatedly presented with an input box to collect the item prices. As indicated in the instructions on the form, the user signals the end of the item prices by entering a value of zero. Remember that the program is supposed to keep a running total of positive values, so that zero does not represent legitimate data, but instead signals the end of the legitimate data. Such a value is called a **sentinel value**. Figure 8.4 shows the code for the Process Prices command button, which again is the only significant code in the program.

In Figure 8.4, the variables *i* and *total* serve the same purpose as before; *i* is used to count through the items being entered, this time as part of the input box prompt, and *total* is the running total. Here these variables do not need to be declared as static variables because the button click procedure is executed only once. Also, *i* can be initialized to 1 (because the initialization statement is executed only once), so *i* can be used instead of *i* + 1 as part of the prompt. The variable *nextprice* serves as a temporary holding

Figure 8.4
Code for the Process Prices command button

```
Sub cmdProcessPrices_Click ()
Dim i As Integer
Dim total As Single
Dim nextprice As Single

    i = 1
    total = 0

    'get first price
    nextprice = Val(InputBox$("Price " & i, , , 1100, 3000))
    Do While nextprice <> 0
       'add price to total
       total = total + nextprice
       'write result in lblresult
       lblresult.Caption = Format$(total, "fixed")
       i = i + 1
       'get next price
       nextprice = Val(InputBox$("Price" & i, , , 1100, 3000))
    Loop

End Sub
```

place for the item price just obtained until it is decided whether that price is legitimate data or the sentinel value that signals the end of the data.

Here's how the code in Figure 8.4 works. An input box collects the first price and stores it in *nextprice*. The next line of code is the beginning of the **Do-While-Loop statement**, which is a Visual Basic looping construction. The block of statements to be repeated, called the **loop body**, is the section of code between the keywords "Do While" and "Loop". The loop body is indented to make it easier to see in the code—a common practice that you should follow.

At the top of the loop, the value of *nextprice* is tested to see whether it is 0. (Notice that a first value for *nextprice* has to be obtained before this point.) If the value of *nextprice* is not 0, the value is added to the running total, which is then displayed. Once again an input box collects the next value and stores it in *nextprice*. The process is then repeated; going back to the top of the loop, the value of *nextprice* is tested to see whether it is 0. If not, the value is added to the running total, the running total is displayed, and an input box collects the next value and stores it in *nextprice*; then it's back to the top of the loop to test the value of *nextprice* again. Whenever *nextprice* has the value 0 when the test is done at the top of the loop, the looping process stops and the procedure is exited; the value displayed at this point is the correct running total. As the name of the Do-While-Loop statement says, the loop continues *while* some condition is true (namely that *nextprice* does not have the value 0); when the condition becomes false (*nextprice* has the value 0), the loop terminates.

Visual Basic has several variations of looping statements, but in each case there must be a way to decide when to terminate the looping process and exit the loop. The variations all have to do with the protocols for testing the loop termination condition.

Flowcharts are a good way to illustrate four of the looping statements in Visual Basic. Figure 8.5a shows the flowchart for the Do-While-

8.1 VISUAL BASIC STATEMENTS FOR LOOPING • 293

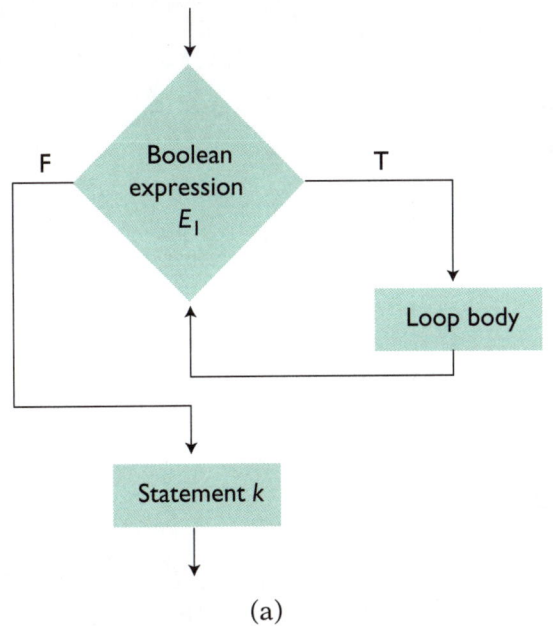

Figure 8.5
Do-While-Loop

```
Do While Boolean expression
    loop body
Loop
```

(a)   (b)

Loop statement, used in the previous example. A Boolean expression E_1 is evaluated at the top of the loop. If E_1 is true, the loop body is executed, then the expression E_1 is tested again. If it is still true, the loop body is executed again, then E_1 is tested again, and so on. This process continues as long as expression E_1 is true; the loop exit occurs when E_1 becomes false, and then execution proceeds to Statement k. Figure 8.5b shows the syntax of the Visual Basic Do-While-Loop statement that implements this flowchart.

Some statement or statements within the loop body must affect the Boolean expression; otherwise, if the expression is true at the top of the loop, it remains true forever, and the program executes the loop body forever. This condition, known as an **infinite loop**, was discussed in Lab 4.1. In the code of Figure 8.4, the Boolean expression is affected by the statement that reads the input box, assuming that the user eventually enters a value of 0. In this case, then, it is the user who ensures that the loop terminates. However, loop termination is not always under user control; should your program ever get into an infinite loop when you are running it, use the Ctrl-Break key combination to go into break mode.

As another example of the Do-While-Loop statement, the following section of code prints a list from "number 1" up to and including "number n", where n is some integer variable that has been assigned a value prior to execution of this code.

```
i = 1
Do While i <= n
    Picture1.Print " number" & Str$(i)
    i = i + 1
Loop
```

Here the loop body, which consists of two Visual Basic statements, is indented. The first statement in the loop body writes the output from this

Figure 8.6
Do-Until-Loop

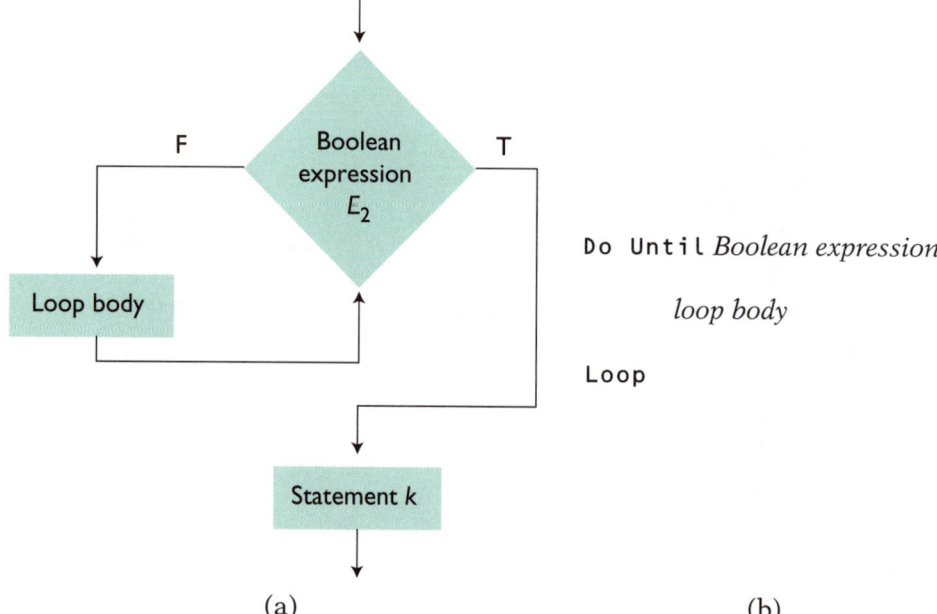

execution of the loop, and the second statement increases the value of *i*. It is because *i* increases at each pass through the loop that the loop condition

```
i <= n
```

eventually becomes false so that the loop terminates.

In Figure 8.6a there is another loop with the condition at the top, and in Figure 8.6b the Visual Basic **Do-Until-Loop statement** that implements it. This time the loop body is executed until the Boolean expression E_2 becomes true. This is the same as saying the loop body is executed while E_2 is false or, equivalently, while Not E_2 is true. Therefore any Do-Until-Loop can be converted to a Do-While-Loop (and vice versa) by negating the Boolean expression. Here is the code for the Do-Until-Loop version of the example for printing numbers in a picture box.

```
i = 1
Do Until i > n
   Picture1.Print " number" & Str$(i)
   i = i + 1
Loop
```

"Do until i > n" is the same as "do while i <= n".

In both the Do-While-Loop and the Do-Until-Loop, the Boolean expression is tested at the top of the loop. This means that the expression can fail the test, and the flow of control pass on to the next statement without ever executing the loop body at all. In both number-printing examples, this would happen if the value of *n* is nonpositive when the loop is first reached. In the Do-While-Loop, for instance, because *i* has just been set to the value 1, the expression

```
i <= n
```

is false right off the bat if *n* is nonpositive. The loop body is skipped entirely.

In two other forms of Visual Basic looping statements, the test for the Boolean expression that controls the loop is at the bottom of the loop. In Figure 8.7a, the loop body is executed once and then the Boolean expression

Figure 8.7
Do-Loop-While

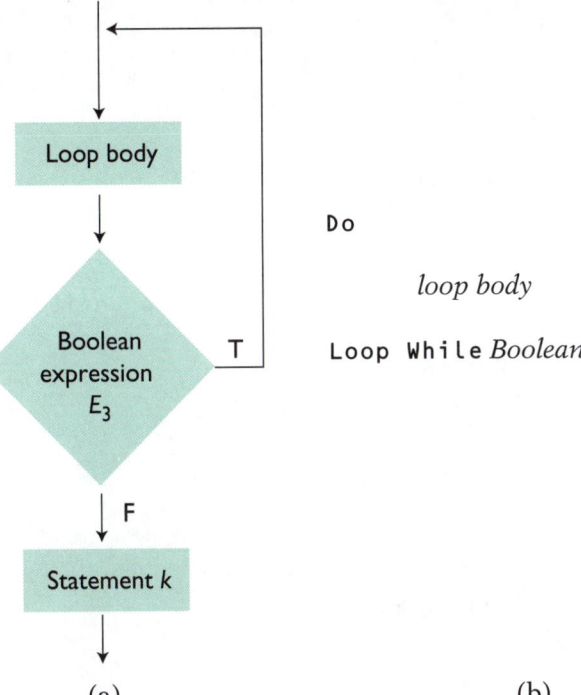

```
Do
    loop body
Loop While Boolean expression
```

(a) (b)

is tested; if the expression is true, the loop body is executed again and the expression is tested again; and so on. The loop terminates once the expression becomes false. This is implemented in the **Do-Loop-While statement** of Figure 8.7b. Here's the number printing example using a Do-Loop-While statement.

```
i = 1
Do
    Picture1.Print " number" & Str$(i)
    i = i + 1
Loop While i <= n
```

The difference between the Do-Loop-While (Figure 8.7) and the Do-While-Loop (Figure 8.5) is that in Figure 8.7, the loop body is executed at least once. Even if the Boolean condition fails when it is first examined, that test occurs only after one pass through the loop body. In the example, "number 1" is printed even if n has a nonpositive value. This makes the Do-While-Loop a slightly preferred statement; if there is any chance that you may not want to execute the loop at all, use a Do-While-Loop.

You can probably guess what the fourth construction is; it's the test-at-the-bottom equivalent of Figure 8.6. The **Do-Loop-Until** is shown in Figure 8.8. Here the loop body is executed before the first expression test; the loop terminates when the Boolean expression becomes true. Any Do-Loop-Until can be converted to a Do-Loop-While (and vice versa) by negating the Boolean expression. Here's the number-printing example using a Do-Loop-Until.

```
i = 1
Do
    Picture1.Print " number" & Str$(i)
    i = i + 1
Loop Until i > n
```

Figure 8.8
Do-Loop-Until

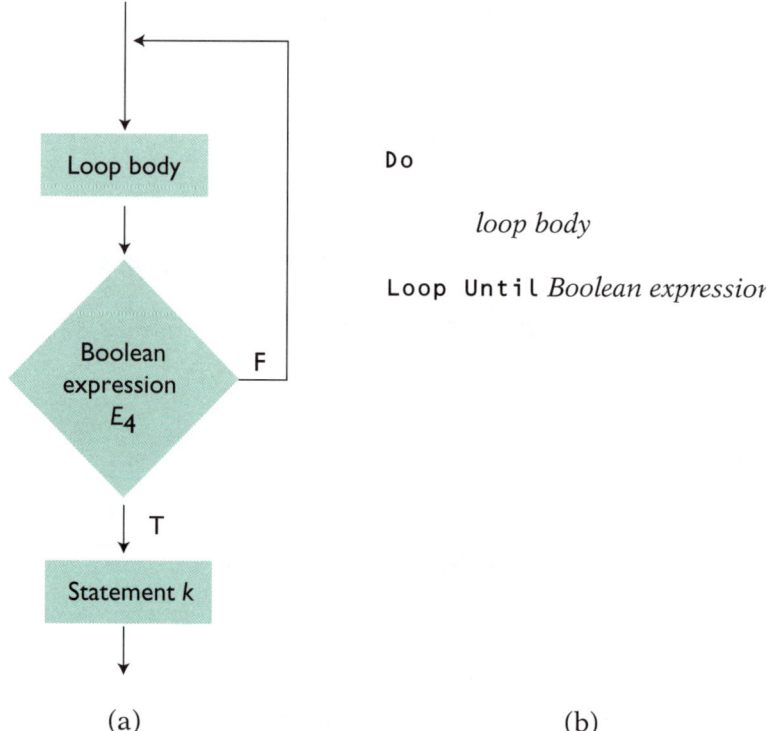

(a)   (b)

Again, the loop body in a Do-Loop-Until is always executed at least once, so if you don't want this to happen, use the Do-Until-Loop construction.

The Boolean expression used as the test condition in any of these looping statements can be a compound Boolean expression using And, Or, or Not logical operators. Figure 8.9 shows a modified version of the code to maintain a running total, where a constant *max* has been set in order to limit the number of items to process. A variable *count* keeps track of the number of items processed so far. The condition on the loop is now a compound condition; the loop continues provided the sentinel has not been found (*nextprice* <> 0, as before) and also provided the maximum number of values has not been exceeded (*count* <= *max*). If either of these conditions fails to hold, the loop is exited. Because there are multiple ways to exit the loop, the first statement after the loop is a conditional statement to determine exactly what caused the loop to terminate. If at this point the value of *nextprice* is not 0, then the maximum number of values was exceeded without a sentinel value ever having been seen; a message alerts the user to the situation.

These four looping statement types are relatively interchangeable, unless you need to allow the possibility for the loop body to be bypassed entirely. In that case, you must use one of the two test-at-the-top versions.

However, if a loop is to be executed a fixed number of times, then another Visual Basic statement called a **For-Next loop** can be used. A For-Next loop uses a numeric counter variable to count from some initial expression to some ending expression by fixed increments. Here's the number example implemented using a For-Next loop.

```
For i = 1 To n
    Picture1.Print " number" & Str$(i)
Next i
```

```
Sub cmdProcessPrices_Click ()
Const max = 10
Dim i As Integer
Dim count As Integer
Dim total As Single
Dim nextprice As Single

    i = 1
    total = 0
    'get first price
    nextprice = Val(InputBox$("Price " & i, , ,1100, 3000))
    count = 1
    Do While (nextprice <> 0) And (count <= max)
       'add price to total
       total = total + nextprice
       'write result in lblresult
       lblresult.Caption = Format$(total, "fixed")

       i = i + 1

       'get next price
       nextprice = Val(InputBox$("Price" & i, , , 1100, 3000))
       count = count + 1
    Loop
    If Not (nextprice = 0) Then
       Picture1.Print "Sorry, only " & max & " values allowed"
    End If
End Sub
```

Figure 8.9
Compound condition for loop termination

The variable *i* here serves both as the output value within the loop body and as the counter variable. The *i* is initially set to 1 and tested against the value of *n*. If *i* does not exceed *n*, the loop body is executed. At the Next statement, *i* is automatically incremented (increased by 1) and tested against *n* again; the loop terminates when *i* exceeds the value of *n*.

The general syntax for the For-Next statement follows.

For *counter variable* = *initial expression* **to** *final expression* **Step** *increment*

    loop body

Next *counter variable*

As in the example, the general For-Next statement works by setting the counter variable equal to the initial expression; if the counter variable does not exceed the final expression, the loop body is executed. At the Next line the value of "increment" is added to the counter variable, which is again tested against the final expression. The "Step increment" can be omitted, as in the example, in which case the increment is understood to be 1; that is, the counter variable is increased by 1 on each pass through the loop. When the counter variable has exceeded the final expression, the loop terminates. The increment can be negative, so that the counter variable counts down from the initial expression to the final expression. The increment can also be given by an expression.

Notice that in a For-Next loop, the controlling expression for loop termination, the counter variable, gets adjusted automatically on each pass through the loop whenever "Next" is encountered. In the Do statements, remember, you had to write code within the loop body to affect the Boolean expression. Indeed, if you write code within a For-Next loop body that changes the value of the counter variable, unexpected things can happen because you are disturbing the counting scheme.

You now have all the various Visual Basic control structures at hand. Furthermore, you can nest loops within loops, If statements within loops, loops within If statements, loops within If statements within loops, and so on. Much of the power of programming comes from this mix-and-match capability.

Nested For-Next loops are particularly useful. Figure 8.10a shows a section of code that prints a multiplication table in a picture box, shown in Figure 8.10b. The inner For-Next loop, with counter variable j, moves along one row of the multiplication table, and gives multiples of a fixed value of i. The outer loop, with counter variable i, changes more slowly; each value of i produces one complete row of the table.

Figure 8.10
Nested For-Next loops to print a multiplication table

```
Dim i As Integer
Dim j As Integer

For i = 1 To 10
    Picture1.Print i & "|";
    For j = 1 To 10
        Picture1.Print i * j;
    Next j
    Picture1.Print
Next i
```

(a)

```
1|1   2   3   4   5   6   7   8   9  10
2|2   4   6   8  10  12  14  16  18  20
3|3   6   9  12  15  18  21  24  27  30
4|4   8  12  16  20  24  28  32  36  40
5|5  10  15  20  25  30  35  40  45  50
6|6  12  18  24  30  36  42  48  54  60
7|7  14  21  28  35  42  49  56  63  70
8|8  16  24  32  40  48  56  64  72  80
9|9  18  27  36  45  54  63  72  81  90
10| 10  20  30  40  50  60  70  80  90 100
```

(b)

Loops are particularly prone to logic errors of the "off-by-one" variety. The code does one too few loop passes because a < condition was used in the Boolean expression when a <= condition should have been used, or it does one too many passes because <= was used when < should have been used. Perhaps a variable was initialized to 0 instead of 1 before a Do loop statement began, or vice versa, so that again the loop body gets executed one too many or one too few times. Perhaps a compound Boolean expression in a loop was expressed using And when Or should have been used; then the loop behaves improperly for some sets of data. To sum up:

Test carefully any code that uses loops.

The Visual Basic debugger, with its ability to trace through the loop and to watch variables during loop execution and after loop exit, is especially helpful when examining loops.

Name: _____ Date Due: _____

LAB 8.1

Potential off-by-one errors

LEARNING OBJECTIVES

- Detecting off-by-one loop errors
- Writing Do loops
- Writing For-Next loops

1. Here's a pencil-and-paper exercise on off-by-one errors. Each of the following code segments is supposed to add the integers from 1 to 5, so in each case the result should be 1 + 2 + 3 + 4 + 5. Assume that appropriate variable declarations have been made, and decide which of the following are correct and which have errors. In the case of an error, explain what goes wrong.

   a.
   ```
   sum = 0
   counter = 1
   Do While counter <= 5
       sum = sum + counter
       counter = counter + 1
   Loop
   Picture1.Print sum
   ```

   b.
   ```
   sum = 0
   counter = 1
   Do While counter <= 5
       counter = counter + 1
       sum = sum + counter
   Loop
   Picture1.Print sum
   ```

c. ```
   sum = 0
   counter = 0
   Do While counter < 5
      counter = counter + 1
      sum = sum + counter
   Loop
   Picture1.Print sum
   ```

d. ```
   sum = 0
   counter = 0
   Do While counter <= 5
      counter = counter + 1
      sum = sum + counter
   Loop
   Picture1.Print sum
   ```

e. ```
   sum = 0
   counter = 1
   Do While counter < 5
      sum = sum + counter
      counter = counter + 1
   Loop
   Picture1.Print sum
   ```
   ```

f. ```
    sum = 0
    counter = 1
    Do While Not (counter >= 5)
        sum = sum + counter
        counter = counter + 1
    Loop
    Picture1.Print sum
    ```

**2.** \_\_\_\_ Open a new Visual Basic project.

**Writing Do loops**

\_\_\_\_ Put a picture box on the form.

\_\_\_\_ Put five command buttons on the form, as follows

| Do-While-Loop | Do-Until-Loop | Do-Loop-While | Do-Loop-Until | For-Next |

\_\_\_\_ For the Do-While-Loop command button, put code in the click event procedure that brings up an input box, asks the user for a positive number, and prints

$n$
$n - 1$
$n - 2$
.
.
.
1

in the picture box, one number per line. For example, if the user enters 5, then the list

5
4
3
2
1

is printed in the picture box. Test that your procedure works properly.
    ```

3. ____ Now write code for the Do-Until-Loop, Do-Loop-While, and Do-Loop-Until buttons that produces the same effect as the button you already have. Use the Cls method to "erase" the picture box so that each button has a clean area to write to.

   ____ Test each case for $n = 5$.

   ____ Test each case for $n = 0$. What happens and why?

Writing For-Next loops

4. ____ Write code for the For-Next button that causes the even integers from 20 down to 0 to be written in the picture box, one per line. So the output reads

   20
   18
   16
   .
   .
   2
   0

5. ____ Save your files as *lab8–1.frm* and *lab8–1.mak*.

QuickCheck 8.1

1. What is the effect of applying a SetFocus method to a control object?
2. A sentinel value is used to _____.
3. Does a Do-While loop terminate when the Boolean expression becomes true or when it becomes false?
4. The loop body is executed at least once with either a _____ looping statement or a _____ looping statement.
5. In a For-Next statement, if the initial expression is larger than the final expression, then the Step increment should be _____.

8.2 Still more control objects: List boxes and combo boxes

When you choose the Search For Help On ... option from the Visual Basic Help menu, you see a screen that shows a list of words. You can scroll through this list to select one that interests you, or you can type a word in the text box at the top of the list (see Figure 8.11a). In either case, you then press the Show Topics button (or the Enter key). A list of topics is displayed (see Figure 8.11b). You may select a topic from this list and then press the Go To button. However, there is no text box to accept your suggestion for a topic. Many Windows applications use these same mechanisms—a list where the user can either select an item from the list or type in a choice, and a list where the user can select only from items in the list. Visual Basic provides controls that create these two types of list objects.

The Visual Basic **List Box** control object is used to display a list of string items from which the user selects one item by clicking on it. There is no provision for the user to type in a choice. If the list is longer than the display area, a vertical scroll bar allows the user to scroll through the rest of the list. The user can also navigate through the list items by using the up-arrow and down-arrow keys on the keyboard. By setting an appropriate property, the list box can be configured to allow the user to select several choices from the list. The default configuration, however, presents the user with a set of items from which he or she can select exactly one. In this configuration, the list box works exactly like a set of option buttons. But if the list of potential choices is long, say more than three or four, the list box is a much neater way to present these choices than littering the screen with many option buttons. The list box icon in the Visual Basic Toolbox is shown here.

Another Visual Basic control rather similar to the list box is the **Combo Box** control. The combo box icon in the Visual Basic Toolbox is shown here. The combo box combines (hence the name *combo* box) features of the text box and the list box. The user can

Figure 8.11
Topic lists in the Visual Basic Help system

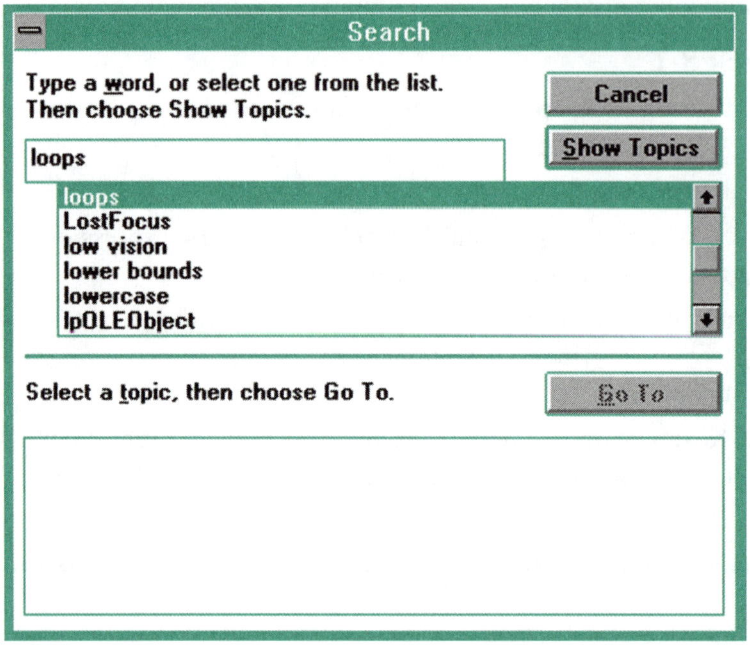

(a)

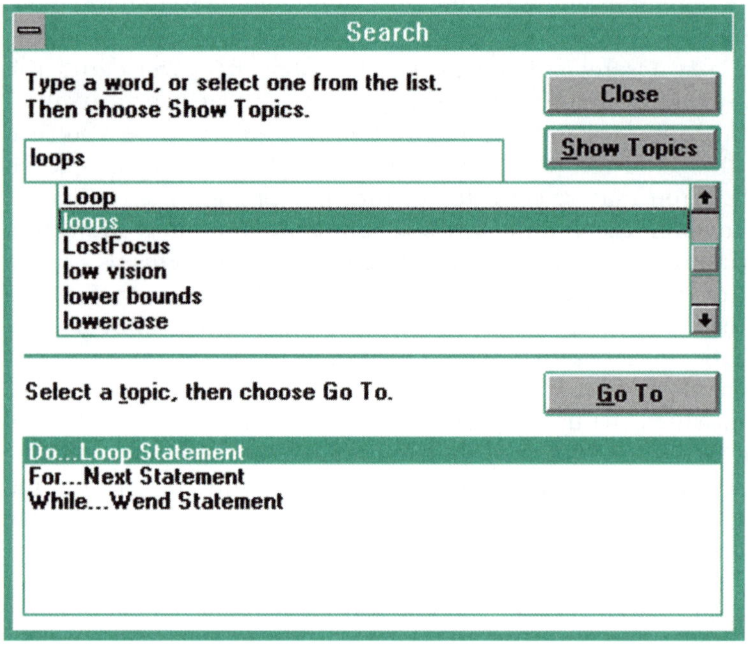

(b)

either enter text representing a choice (this is the text box feature) *or* make a choice from a list (this is the list box feature).

Figure 8.12a shows a list box where the first item, Sales, has been selected. Figure 8.12b shows a combo box where a new string, Marketing—not one of the original items—has been typed into the text box portion.

There are three variations of combo boxes, determined by the value of the combo box **Style property**. Here's the effect of the Style property value, which can be set in the Properties window at design time.

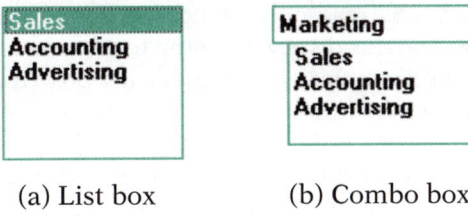

(a) List box (b) Combo box

Figure 8.12
List box and combo box examples

Style Property 0: Drop-down combo box   Only the text box portion of the combo box appears on the form (Figure 8.13a) until the user clicks the down arrow; then the list box portion drops down (Figure 8.13b). The initial value in the text box portion is supplied by the value of the combo box's Text property as set at design time. The user can leave what initially appears in the text box, click on one of the items from the list, or use the text box portion to type in a new choice. If an item is selected from the list (or typed by the user), it is displayed in the text box area. The drop-down combo box has the advantage of taking up little room on the form, at least until the user drops down the list box portion.

(a)   (b)

Figure 8.13
Drop-down combo box

Style Property 1: Simple combo box   There is no drop-down feature, and the text box portion and list box portion appear together on the form; Figure 8.12b shows a simple combo box. Again, the text initially shown in the text box portion comes from the Text property, but the user can type in something else or select an item from the list. The Height property of the control must be set large enough to display the entire list box portion.

Style Property 2: Drop-down list box   Only an empty text box area appears (Figure 8.14a) until the user clicks on the down arrow; then the list box portion drops down (Figure 8.14b). In this variation, however, the text box's editing capabilities are disabled so that the user cannot type in a choice. Nor can the Text property of the combo box be set at design time; trying to do so produces an error message that says

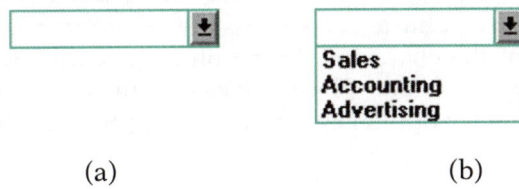

(a)   (b)

Figure 8.14
Drop-down list box

"'Text' property is read-only". Once an item is selected from the list, however, it is displayed in the text box area. This variation can be used in place of a regular list box when you need to save space on the form.

Given the similarities of list boxes and combo boxes, which do you use when? If you want the user to be able to type in a new selection, then you must provide a combo box. If you want to prevent the user from typing in a new selection and limit the choice to existing items, use a list box or, to save space, a drop-down list box (which is really a form of combo box).

List boxes and combo boxes share a number of properties. Of course, there are the usual ones like Name, Height, Width, Top, Left, TabIndex, and all the font properties. Both controls have a **Text property**, but it means something slightly different in each case. In the list box, the value of the Text property is the currently selected item. In the combo box, the value of the Text property is the string appearing in the text area; again, this string can be put into the text box by the Text property as set at design time, by the user's selecting an item from the list box portion, or by the user's typing into the text box. At any rate, it is through the Text property that the user's choices get into the program code, so these controls are additional input mechanisms. For example, the user could make a selection and click on some "OK, I'm finished" button, which could activate code like the following:

```
If List1.Text = "Marketing" Then
   Label1.caption = "Mail brochure"
ElseIf List1.Text = "Sales" Then
   Label1.caption = "Finish Sales report"
Else
   Label1.caption = "Set up meeting"
End If
```

Results of list box or combo box choices can also have an immediate effect, without waiting for a button click event. Both list boxes and combo boxes also recognize click events. Code like the preceding can be placed in the list box or combo box click event procedure. As soon as the user clicks on a list item to make a selection, the code is activated. However, this does not take care of the situation in which the user types a new choice in the text box portion of a combo box, because this does not constitute a click event. To have an immediate reaction here, code can be placed in the combo box's **Change event** procedure. Typing in the text box portion constitutes a change event for a combo box. (List boxes do not recognize a change event.)

A third alternative is to have the user make a selection by clicking, highlight an item by using the arrow keys, or—in the case of a combo box—typing in the text box, and then have nothing happen until the Enter key is pressed. Code here goes in the **KeyPress event** procedure, which occurs whenever a key on the keyboard is pressed. The **ANSI (American National Standards Institute) character set** assigns a positive integer between 0 and 256 to each of the characters found on a standard keyboard as well as additional special characters. The KeyPress event reads the integer associated with the character of the key that has been pressed. The integer associated with the Enter key is 13, so code in the KeyPress event can be written in the form

```
Sub Combo1_KeyPress (keyAscii As Integer)
   If keyAscii = 13 Then
           . . .
   End If
End Sub
```

One advantage to using the KeyPress event rather than the click event is that the same code can serve for both the text box portion and the list box portion of a combo box. Also, a click event in a list box or the list box portion of a combo box occurs not only when the user clicks on a selection but also when the up-arrow and down-arrow keys are used. So someone using the down-arrow key to get to a selection is generating a number of click events along the way, and it may not be appropriate for the program to respond to each of these.

The items in a list box or in the list box portion of a combo box are considered to be arranged in an array (like a control array). Each item has an index number, according to its position in the list. The index numbers begin at 0, however, so the first item in the list has an index number of 0, not 1. If there are three items in the list, their index values are 0, 1, and 2; the last index value is 1 less than the number of items in the list.

Several properties of list boxes and combo boxes relate to the index of the items in the list. For example, the value of the **ListIndex property** in a running program is the index of the selected item in a list or combo box if an item is selected, –1 if no item is selected (or if, in a combo box, the user has entered a new string). This property makes no sense at design time, so it isn't found in the Properties window for a list box or combo box. It is a run-time only property whose value can be examined in code. The **List property** is another run-time property. Given an index in a list, the List property's value is the string item found at that index. In Figure 8.12a, the value of

```
List1.ListIndex
```

is 0 because the first item in the list is selected. The value of

```
List1.List(1)
```

is "Accounting". The value of

```
List1.List(List1.ListIndex)
```

is "Sales". The value of the **ListCount property**, another run-time property, is the number of items in the list. If there are three items in the list, then ListCount has the value 3, but the items are indexed 0, 1, and 2. In other words, the highest index is 1 less than the value of ListCount. Finally, the **Sorted property**, which can be set to True at design time, arranges the list items in sorted (alphabetical) order.

How do items get into the list in a list box or a combo box in the first place? Some methods common to both list boxes and combo boxes manage list entries.

AddItem method: The syntax for the AddItem method is

> *objectname*.`AddItem` *string expression, index*

This adds a string expression to the list at position "index," with the indexes of previously existing items adjusted accordingly. The comma and index are optional; if they are omitted, the new item is added at the end of the list if the Sorted property for the list is false, or the new item is added at its correct sorted position if Sorted is true.

A list is built by starting with an empty list and repeatedly using the AddItem method. Items that are to appear in the list when the form is first displayed are added by using the AddItem method in the Form_Load event procedure. For example,

```
Sub Form_Load ()
   combo1.AddItem "Sales"
   combo1.AddItem "Accounting"
   combo1.AddItem "Advertising"
End Sub
```

sets up the list box portion of Figure 8.12b. The items to load can be obtained from an external file rather than being given explicitly in the code. Reading data from a file is discussed in Chapter 11.

RemoveItem method: The syntax for the RemoveItem method is

> *objectname*.`RemoveItem` *index*

This removes the item at position "index" from the list. The indexes of the remaining items are adjusted accordingly.

Clear method: The syntax is

> *objectname*.`Clear`

The result is to remove all items from the list.

8.3 Scroll bar

Scroll bars can appear on windows, text boxes, and list boxes when all of the contents cannot be shown within the display area. The Visual Basic **Scroll Bar** control is quite different. Both horizontal and vertical controls are found on the Visual Basic Toolbox, represented by the icons shown here. When pasted on the form, these controls look like Figure 8.15.

The purpose of a scroll bar is to allow the user to choose a value within some range of values; hence a scroll bar control serves as yet another

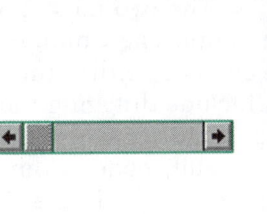

Figure 8.15
Horizontal and vertical scroll bar controls

input mechanism. The range of values a scroll bar can represent is determined by its **Min** and **Max properties**. These are integer quantities, and their default values are 0 and 32767. However, these properties can be set at design time in the Properties window. The Min value can never be less than –32768, and the Max value can never exceed 32767. In a horizontal scroll bar, the minimum value occurs at the left end and the maximum value at the right end; in a vertical scroll bar, the minimum value occurs at the top and the maximum value at the bottom.

The **Value property** reflects the position of the scroll box within the scroll bar, and thus represents a choice from within the range of values. When the scroll box is at the left end of a horizontal scroll bar, Value has the minimum value. When the scroll box is at the right end, Value has the maximum value. When the scroll box is halfway along the bar, Value has a value midway between the minimum and maximum values. The Value property can be set at design time; this determines the initial position of the scroll box. However, during execution, whenever the scroll box is moved, the Value property changes to reflect the new position. Thus in a horizontal scroll bar, moving the scroll box from the left end to the right end sends the Value property through the entire range of values from minimum to maximum. (The Min property can be set with a value larger than that of the Max property, in which case sliding from left to right "counts down" instead of "counting up.")

To move the scroll box, the user does any of the following:

OPTIONS

- Click one of the arrows at the ends of the scroll bar.
- Click within the scroll bar itself between the scroll box and an arrow.
- Drag the scroll box along the scroll bar.

Dragging the scroll box gives the impression of moving smoothly and continuously through the range of values. This can be considered an "analog" presentation of user choices, as opposed to the "discrete" selections the user must make from the list box or combo box. (Clocks give an analogy for the concepts of **discrete** and **analog**. A digital clock presents the time in a discrete fashion, jumping from one value to the next: 8:02, then 8:03, and so on. In a clock with hour, minute, and second hands, you can see the hands progressing smoothly and continuously around the face of the clock.)

The two other interesting properties of scroll bars are SmallChange and LargeChange. These act as increment steps for mouse clicks. The **SmallChange property** determines how much the Value property changes (and how much the scroll box moves) when the user clicks on one of the arrows at the end of the scroll bar. The **LargeChange property** determines how much the Value property changes (and how much the scroll box moves) when the user clicks on the scroll bar between the scroll box and an arrow. The default setting for these properties is 1.

The two most pertinent events for the scroll bar control are Change and Scroll. The **Change event** occurs when the Value property of the scroll bar changes, either through code or through user action. The user action can include dragging the scroll box, but the Change event checks the Value property to see whether it has changed only when the scroll box is released. As a result, code within the Change event procedure that uses the Value property sees only the final setting of Value after the scroll box is dragged, rather than a continuous reading of the Value property. The **Scroll event** occurs when the control box is dragged, but not when one of the arrows or the scroll bar is clicked. In order to know the current Value setting of a scroll bar at all times, a combination of the two events can be used. In the following code, the Change event invokes the Scroll event, so that the Scroll event occurs whenever the scroll box is moved by either clicking or dragging. Code within the Scroll event always has access to the current setting for the Value property, whether the user clicks or drags to move the scroll box.

```
Sub hscroll1_change ()
    hscroll1_scroll
End Sub

Sub hscroll1_scroll ()
    'Code here that references the Value property will see
    'the current setting no matter how the scroll box
    'is moved
End Sub
```

For allowing the user to input one integer value from a large numeric range, the scroll bar is the obvious choice. A final note about scroll bars is their appearance when they receive the focus—the scroll box flashes.

Name: _____ Date Due: _____

LAB 8.2

LEARNING OBJECTIVES

- Exploring combo box styles
- Writing code to react to selections made in a list box or combo box
- Investigating more list box and combo box properties
- Using list boxes and scroll bars

1. ____ Open the project **combo.mak**. The form has one list box and one drop-down combo box.

   ____ Run the program and make selections from each control, using both the mouse and the up-arrow and down-arrow keyboard keys.

   ____ Type a different selection in the text box portion of the combo box.

2. ____ Try running the program with the other two style property values for the combo box. In which of the three styles do you get to control the vertical dimension of the combo box at design time? Why do you not need to do this in the other two styles?

   Exploring combo box styles

3. ____ Add a label to the form.

   ____ Add a button to the form such that when this button is clicked, whatever is selected in the list box is written in the label. Test your program.

   Reacting to selections

4. ____ Set the combo box style to simple combo box (make sure the display area is big enough).
   ____ Write code so that whatever is selected in the combo box appears in the label immediately; this includes whatever is typed into the text box portion. Test.

5. ____ Add another simple combo box to your form.

   ____ Write the code to load four names into it when the program runs.

   ____ Now write code so that whatever is selected in this combo box appears in the label only when the Enter key is pressed. Test.

6. ____ Consider the list box in this example again. A shortcut for mouse users would be to double-click on the selection rather than press the command button. Use the Help system to find which events are recognized by list boxes. Which is the appropriate one to use?

____ Write the code to make this feature work.

7. ____ Set the Sorted property of Combo1 to true.

   ____ Add a last line of code to the Form_Load procedure to insert the name "Adam" in this combo box. Where does "Adam" appear in the list box portion when the program runs?

More list box and combo box properties

8. ____ Fill in Table 8.1 by consulting the Visual Basic Help system.

PROPERTY	EFFECT IN LIST BOX	EFFECT IN COMBO BOX
NewIndex		
Columns		
Multiselect		
Selected		

Table 8.1 List box and combo box properties

9. ____ Add a button to the form such that clicking this button changes the first name in the list box from "Joe" to "Joseph". (Hint: Use an assignment statement to change the value of the List property at the appropriate index.) Write the statement you used to make this work.

____ Save your files as **combo1.frm** and **combo1.mak**.

10. ____ Open the Visual Basic project *lister.mak* and run the program. The form contains two list boxes; the Form_Load procedure loads a list of customers into the first list box (see Figure 8.16). The scroll bar on the first list box indicates that there are more customers than can be displayed within this list box.

Using list boxes

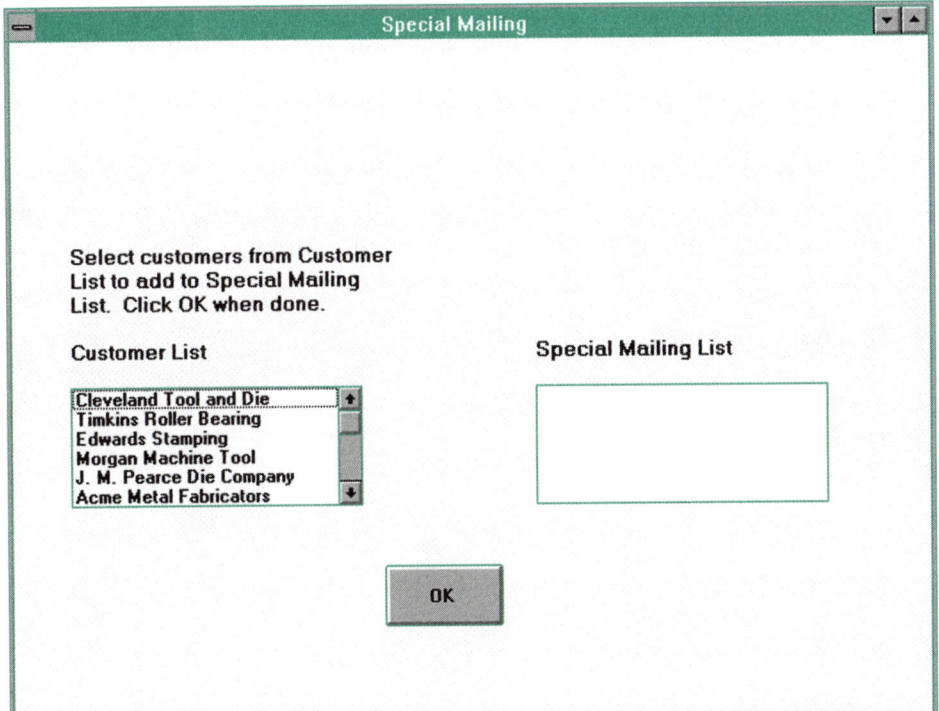

Figure 8.16
Form in project *lister.mak*

Following the instructions on the form, the user scrolls through the first list box and selects those customers to be sent a special mailing. (Note the setting of the MultiSelect property for the first list box.) At the click of the OK command button, those names are added to the second list box.

____ Add the appropriate code and test your program. (Hint: When the OK button is clicked, you want to process each item in the list to see whether it has been selected. You can use a For-Next loop to step through all the list items; the list indexes range from 0 to List1.ListCount – 1.)

____ Save your files as *lister1.frm* and *lister1.mak*.

11. ____ Put a frame at the top of the form with a horizontal scroll bar and two labels in it. This area of the form is to allow the user to estimate postal costs before selecting customers to receive the mailing. The scroll bar represents the potential number of customers to be added to the special mailing list, which can range from 0 to the total number in the first

Using a scroll bar

list box. The user chooses a number of customers by using the scroll bar. The first label in the frame shows the number of customers chosen, and the second label shows the postage cost for that number (at current first-class postage rates for a 1-ounce mailing). When the program runs, the scroll bar is initially set at 0 customers, with a corresponding postage cost.

_____ Give appropriate instructions in the caption of the frame.

_____ Add the necessary code and test thoroughly.

12. _____ Modify your program so that when the user clicks the OK button to put the selected customer names into the second list, the scroll bar reflects that number of customers and the corresponding postage is shown.

_____ Save your files.

QuickCheck 8.2

1. The type of combo box—simple, drop-down, and so on—is controlled by the _____ property.
2. If you want the user to be able to enter a new choice instead of choosing from the list, do you use a list box or a combo box?
3. If there are ListCount items in a list box, what is the index of the last item?
4. The position of the scroll box in a scroll bar is given by the _____ property.
5. What does the AddItem method do?

THOUGHTS ON PROGRAMMING

Prototyping

The dictionary definition of prototype is "an original model after which other similar things are patterned." New automobile designs are tested as prototypes, as are many other machines or devices. A prototype gives the manufacturer a chance to try out ideas and work out the kinks before gearing up to full-scale production.

In software, the product may not be mass-produced, but a prototype is still valuable. A **software prototype** is a program that presents the user with the essence of the user interface design, but with much of the program functionality missing or "faked." For a Visual Basic program, a prototype can include all the various forms and their control objects. The user can enter data in text boxes, click on command buttons, select option buttons, and so on. However, if clicking on a command button is supposed to, say, perform some computation and display the result in a label, the prototype button code can simply write a message like "results will be displayed here" in the label caption. Such code is often called a **stub**; it is code that is thrown away when the software is fully developed but is there in the prototype to show what the effect of clicking the button will eventually be. Or if the output is supposed to include a printed page using some particular layout, the page can be printed with the appropriate layout but only "dummy" output values.

If the prototype doesn't do any "real work," what is its value? Its value is to allow the user early involvement in program development as a check that the program requirements are being met. On trying out the prototype, the user may find that interacting with the program doesn't work at all the way he or she expected it would work or that the interaction can be improved by rearranging certain controls. Early involvement of the user, at the prototype stage, allows changes in the program to be made early on, before the investment of effort in writing much code.

The ability to develop prototypes quickly and easily is one of the strong points of the Visual Basic language.

8.4 Searching

One of the most common tasks performed by computers in the course of routine data processing is searching a list of items for a specific value, called the **target value**. Suppose someone hands you an unusual telephone book, one in which the names and corresponding telephone numbers are listed at random rather than alphabetically. If you are trying to find a name in this telephone directory, then your only option is to start at the beginning and look at every name until you find the one you want or exhaust the list.

This process describes the **sequential search algorithm**, which runs down the list and checks each item in turn until it finds the target value or runs out of list elements. If the items in the list are totally random, this is the only algorithm available to solve the search problem. One version of the sequential search algorithm is outlined in pseudocode in Figure 8.17.

Figure 8.17
First pass at sequential search algorithm

```
Compare the target value to the first list item
    If they match,
        write that the match occurred at position 1 and quit
Compare the target value to the second list item
    If they match,
        write that the match occurred at position 2 and quit
Compare the target value to the third list item
    If they match,
        write that the match occurred at position 3 and quit
                    •
                    •
                    •
Compare the target value to the last list item
    If they match,
        write that the match occurred at the last position and quit
    otherwise write that the target is not in the list
```

Figure 8.17 captures the idea of the algorithm, but it is clear that the same thing is being done over and over again. This calls for a loop. Figure 8.18 is an improved version of the sequential search algorithm using iteration (looping). In order to quit when the target value has been found, the algorithm uses something called *found*, which is either true or false.

> Set i = 1
> Set *found* = false
> Do while (*found* is false) and (i <= length of the list)
>   Compare the target value to list item i
>   If they match,
>   write that the match occurred at position i
>   set *found* to true
>   Increase i by 1
> If *found* is false, then write that the target is not in the list

Figure 8.18
Pseudocode for iterative sequential search algorithm

As in Figure 8.9, the condition for loop termination is a compound condition; the program exits the loop if the target value is found (*found* is not false) or if there are no more list elements (i becomes greater than the length of the list). Therefore the first thing to do right after the loop is figure out why the loop was exited. If *found* is still false, then the loop was exited because there were no more list items; an appropriate message is written.

Of course, when you look for a name in the telephone directory, you don't perform a sequential search. You can do less work because the telephone company has done some additional work first and sorted the names into alphabetical order. Searching and sorting will be discussed in more detail in Chapter 10.

Name: _____   Date Due: _____

LEARNING OBJECTIVES

- Using the Forms collection
- Applying sequential search

LAB 8.3

1. ____ Open the Visual Basic project *library.mak*.

    ____ Using the Project window, examine each of the six forms. The project is a "card catalog" for a (small) library, with a title page and five book pages. The only code at this point is the Form_Load code for the first form. What does it accomplish?

    Recall that the Load event for a form loads the form from storage (a disk or hard drive) into the computer's memory, but the form is not displayed. The reason we need to load all of the forms is explained next.

2. Visual Basic maintains something called a **Forms collection**. This is similar to a control array or an array of items in a list box or combo box, except it is for forms. It includes only the currently loaded forms, however, not all the forms in a project. This is why all the book forms are loaded along with the title page—so they are all part of the Forms collection. Like control arrays and list boxes, the Forms collection is indexed beginning with 0. Forms(0) refers to the first form loaded—in this case, the title page. Also like a list box, there is a **Count property**, so that Forms.Count returns the number of forms in the Forms collection. As usual, because of starting with index 0, the highest index is 1 less than Forms.Count.

    Using the Forms collection

    ____ Put a command button on the title page. For its Click event code, use

    ```
    Forms(1).Show
    ```

    What happens when you run the program and click the button?

Change the Form_Load code for the title page form to read

```
Load Form3
Load Form2
Load Form4
Load Form5
Load Form6
```

____ Now run the program. What happens when you click the button this time?

What determines the index ordering in the Forms collection?

(Note that if forms are dynamically unloaded and reloaded during program execution, their ordering in the Forms collection changes. In such a case—which will not happen here—it is not a good idea to count on forms being in some particular order. For this reason, the Forms collection is not a particularly useful construct. This program will later be modified to eliminate the Forms collection.)

____ Change the Form_Load code for the title page back to

```
Load Form2
Load Form3
Load Form4
Load Form5
Load Form6
```

____ Delete the code for the button on the title page; then make the button an Exit button that terminates the program.

3. ____ Add a command button to each form that lets the user browse through the book collection. Clicking this button on the title page causes the form for book 1 to be displayed, clicking this button on the book 1

page causes the form for book 2 to be displayed, and so on. Clicking this button on the book 5 page causes the form for book 1 to be displayed.

___ Add a command button to each book form that lets the user return to the title page.

___ Test and save your program.

4. ___ Now add another command button to the title page to allow the user to search the library. Clicking this button brings up a dialog box (another form) that:

Applying sequential search

> Requests the text string to search for.
> Gives the user the option of searching for title or for author.
> Provides a command button to start the search.

You need to implement a version of the sequential search algorithm to search the titles or authors of all books for the text string the user entered. If the search is successful, the appropriate book page is displayed. If the search is not successful, the dialog box remains in view but now displays a message about an unsuccessful search.

(Hints: In implementing the pseudocode of Figure 8.18, *found* can be an integer variable. A statement such as

```
found = False
```

is then legitimate because False is a Visual Basic constant whose value is 0. Likewise, True is a Visual Basic constant whose value is –1. Another alternative is to declare *found* as a string variable and do assignments such as

```
found = "False"
```

Make the sequential search a general procedure on the dialog box form with a single argument that is the target string. Use syntax such as

```
forms(i)!txtTitle.Text
```

to refer to the content of a text box on Form(i) of the Forms collection.)

___ Test your code.

___ Position the dialog box so that after an unsuccessful search, the user can click the search button on the title page to try again. Note that the text box in the dialog box should be fresh, and the message about the previous unsuccessful search should be gone.

5. Does the *user* of this application have any way to add additional books to the library? How?

Does the *programmer* have any way to add additional books to the library? How?

____ Save your work (call the new form *library7.frm*).

QuickCheck 8.3

1. True or false: A stub is any very short piece of code.
2. In performing a search, the item being searched for is called the _____.
3. Describe the two ways to exit the loop in a sequential search.
4. In order to be part of the Forms collection, a form must be _____.
5. The lowest index in the Forms collection is _____.

Review Questions

1. Why does code within the loop body of a Do-While-Loop statement need to affect the Boolean expression for the loop?
2. If the Boolean expression in a Do-While-Loop statement is initially false, what happens?
3. How is a sentinel value used in the Boolean expression for a loop that reads input data values?
4. What is the relationship between a Boolean expression in a Do-While-Loop statement and the expression in an equivalent Do-Until-Loop statement?
5. What is the difference between a Do-Until-Loop and a Do-Loop-Until?
6. To allow the possibility that a loop body is never executed, you use one of which two statements?
7. If the Boolean condition in a Do-While-Loop statement is a compound expression, what type of statement should immediately follow the loop statement?
8. Describe which circumstance must be true for a For-Next loop to be used.
9. What is the default if the Step increment in a For-Next loop is omitted?
10. Explain the difference between a drop-down list box and a drop-down combo box.
11. Explain the difference between a list box and a drop-down list box.
12. The Properties window for a list box control object does not include a Text property. Why not?
13. How is the Text property of a combo box set?
14. For the user to be able to select more than one item, do you use a list box or a combo box?
15. Describe how the ListCount property and For-Next loops are useful in processing list boxes or combo boxes.
16. Suppose that a Visual Basic program with a list box List1 is executing and that a single item in the list box has been selected. What is the effect of the following statement?

    ```
    Picture1.Print List1.List(List1.ListIndex)
    ```

17. What do the Min and Max properties of a scroll bar represent?
18. Why are the Change event and the Scroll event used together to determine the Value property of a scroll bar under all conditions?
19. What are the advantages to developing a software prototype?
20. In performing a sequential search, under which two conditions is every single item in the list examined?

Exercises
Reading code

1. What is printed in the picture box when the following code is executed?

    ```
    Dim n As Integer

    n = 10
    Do While n > 5
       Form1.Print 2 * n
       n = n - 2
    Loop
    ```

2. What is printed in the picture box when the following code is executed?

    ```
    Dim n As Integer

    n = 10
    Do
       Form1.Print n + 1
       n = n - 1
    Loop Until n < 5
    ```

3. How many times is the Print statement executed in the following code?

    ```
    Dim i As Integer
    Dim j As Integer

    For i = 1 To 5
       For j = 5 To i Step -1
          Picture1.Print j;
       Next j
    Next i
    ```

4. True or false: The following two sections of code produce the same result. Explain your answer.

    ```
    Dim i As Integer
    Dim found As Integer
    Dim Target As String

    Target = InputBox$("Enter your string")

    found = False
    i = 0
    ```

```
Do While i <= List1.ListCount - 1 And found = False
    If List1.List(i) = Target Then
        found = True
        Picture1.Print "Found at location " & i
    Else
        Picture1.Print "Not found yet "
    End If
    i = i + 1
Loop
```

```
Dim i As Integer
Dim found As Integer
Dim Target As String

Target = InputBox$("Enter your string")

found = False
i = 0

Do Until i > List1.ListCount - 1 And found <> False
    If List1.List(i) = Target Then
        found = True
        Picture1.Print "Found at location " & i
    Else
        Picture1.Print "Not found yet "
    End If
    i = i + 1
Loop
```

5. What is the effect of the following code?

```
Dim i As Integer

For i = List1.ListCount - 1 To 0 Step -1
    Picture1.Print List1.List(i)
Next i
```

Writing code

For exercises 6–9, assume the form contains a picture box Picture1 and a list box List1.

6. Write code to print in Picture1 the odd integers from 11 through 21 (inclusive).

7. Write code to print in Picture1 the first five items in List1 (assume there are at least five items in List1).

8. Write code to print in Picture1 all the selected items in List1 (there may be multiple items selected).

9. Write code to print in Picture1 the first item in List1 containing the string "Mrs."

10. The user types text into text box Text1 on a form and then clicks on a command button. The effect is to display in a label the number of

instances of the character "e" in the text. Write the necessary code for the Command1_Click event.

Exploring further

11. Visual Basic supports five different looping statements. If you had to choose only one to use at all times, which would you choose and why?

12. Figure 8.3 shows a form to total a series of prices terminating with 0. Figure 8.4 shows the relevant code, which uses a Do-While-Loop statement.

    a. Use the same form, but write code using a Do-Until-Loop statement. Save your files as *looper3.frm* and *looper3.mak*.

    b. Use the same form, but write code using a Do-Loop-While statement; assume that there is at least one legitimate price before the sentinel value. Save your files as *looper4.frm* and *looper4.mak*.

    c. Use the same form, but write code using a Do-Loop-Until statement; assume that there is at least one legitimate price before the sentinel value. Save your files as *looper5.frm* and *looper5.mak*.

13. In the *lister.mak* project of Lab 8.2, add a second command button to the form that prints (to the printer) all the selected customer names, along with some nice heading.

14. Open your *dive.mak* project from Chapter 7. Consider the FindMaxIndex and FindMinIndex procedures. Rewrite each of these procedures so that it uses a loop instead of six consecutive If statements.

15. Open your *calc.mak* project from Lab 5.2. Add an ON/OFF button that "toggles" the calculator on and off. When the calculator program begins, the calculator is off and all "keys" are disabled. The button displays the word ON. Clicking this button enables all the keys and changes the button display to the word OFF. Clicking again disables all keys and changes the button display to ON. And so on.

Projects

Do both high- and low-level designs before you write your programs.

1. A palindrome is a word or phrase that reads the same forward and backward (disregarding blanks). The following are palindrome examples:

    radar

    a toyota

    madam Im adam

    Write a program that collects a phrase from the user and tells whether the phrase is a palindrome.

2. The rules for converting English words to "pig Latin" are as follows:

    A word that begins with a vowel has "way" appended to the end of the word.

    A word that begins with a consonant has the consonant removed from the front of the word, added to the end of the word, and "ay" appended after the consonant.

The English phrase

> When in the course of human events

becomes, in pig Latin,

> Henway inway hetay oursecay ofway umanhay eventsway

Write a program to collect a phrase from the user and write out that phrase in pig Latin.

3. a. Create a prototype for a program that gives consumers information about loans. The program collects the loan amount, the annual interest rate, and the number of years of the loan. Assume that payments are made monthly at the beginning of each month of the loan. The user can:

   i. Click a button to find the amount of the monthly payment, which will be the same throughout the life of the loan.

   ii. Click a button to see an amortization table for a given year. The amortization table shows for each monthly payment in the year the amount of the payment attributable to interest, the amount attributable to principle, and the amount left on the loan balance after that payment.

   b. Write the complete program. (Hint: Consider some of the Visual Basic financial functions mentioned in Table 5.5.)

4. The local iguana population in your community is growing at the rate of 4 percent per year. Write a program that allows the user to enter the present year and the present iguana population. A list box showing the next 40 years is displayed; when the user selects a year, the corresponding iguana population for that year is shown.

5. Modify your *library.mak* program from Lab 8.3 to add an additional search option: the user can choose to enter a single word and search for a book that contains that word in its title.

CHAPTER 9

Menus; Graphics

KEY POINTS

- Creating menus is a snap with the Visual Basic Menu Design window.
- Picture file images can be displayed in picture boxes, image controls, or (seldom used) forms.
- Artwork consisting of lines and shapes can be placed in picture boxes or forms at design time by using graphic control objects or at run time by using graphics methods.
- Software reusability is a desirable goal but is often not achieved.
- Moving and changing graphic images in association with the Timer object can create simple animation effects.

9.1 Pull-down menus

Pull-down menus (also called **drop-down menus**) are a standard feature of windows programs. Visual Basic provides a really nifty tool called a **Menu Design window** that makes it simple to add menus to Visual Basic application programs.

Menus are another means for obtaining user input in the form of choices. The option button control serves the same purpose, but if there are many choices to be made, option buttons clutter up the form. Pull-down menus stay out of the way until they are wanted.

A menu is a control object that has a few properties and recognizes exactly one event, the click event. There is no "menu" icon in the Visual Basic Toolbox, however; menus must be created by using the Menu Design window.

If there are multiple forms in a project, first be sure the one to which you want to add menus is the active form. Then access the Visual Basic Menu Design window by doing any of the following:

- Pick Menu Design from the Visual Basic Window menu.
- Click the Menu Design button on the Visual Basic toolbar.
- Press Ctrl-M (hold down the Control key and press the M key).

The Menu Design window is shown in Figure 9.1. The top part consists of text boxes and check boxes for setting menu properties. Some menu properties are already familiar. **Caption** denotes the text the user will see on the menu, and **Name** determines how the menu control is referred to in program code. If the three-letter naming convention prefix is used, a menu control name begins with "mnu". As usual, giving a new menu control the same name as an existing menu control sets up a control array. If you are adding a menu control to a control array, for some reason its **Index property** is not automatically assigned, as happens for other control arrays. This property can be set (or changed) in the Index text box of the Menu Design window.

In Figure 9.1, only a caption and a name are required to create a menu control. Once these have been entered, the first main menu—one that appears at the top of the form—has been created. After a menu control has been created, it has a Properties window like any other control. Additional property settings or changes can be made either through the Properties window or through the Menu Design window.

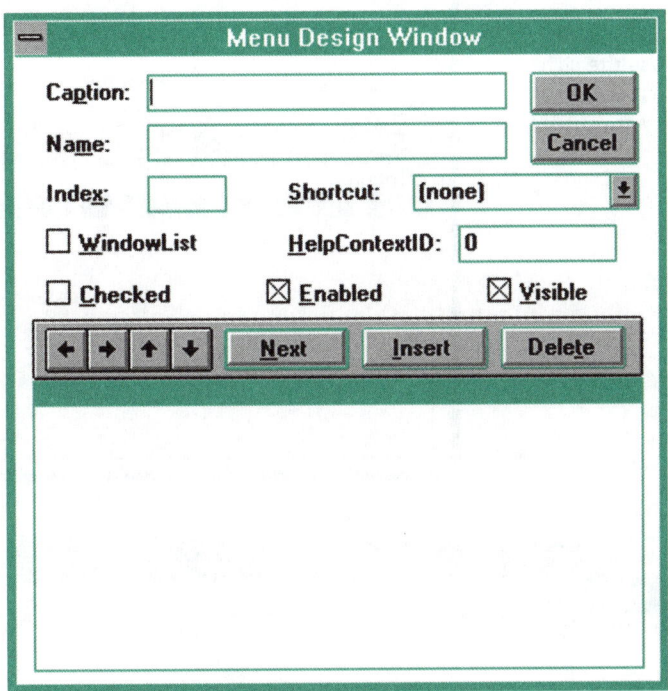

Figure 9.1
Visual Basic Menu Design window

There is an additional wrinkle to choosing a caption for a menu control. Many pull-down menus can be accessed in two ways: by clicking on the menu caption that appears on the form and by using a keyboard shortcut. If a menu caption has a letter underlined, then using the Alt key together with the underlined key pulls down the menu. (For example, in the Visual Basic File menu, the letter "F" is underlined. Holding down the Alt key and pressing F pulls down the File menu.) Such a keyboard shortcut is called an **access key**; access keys have been mentioned before in conjunction with Visual Basic menus.

You can set an access key for a pull-down menu in the Menu Design window. Just put the ampersand character & in the Caption property in front of the letter you want to use for the access key. If the caption

&Options

is entered in the Caption text box of Figure 9.1, then O is the access key, and the menu will appear on the form as shown in Figure 9.2. Pressing Alt-O pulls down this menu (once the submenus are added).

Indeed, once a main menu has been created, its submenus can be created. In Figure 9.1, clicking the Next button brings up a fresh copy of the Properties part of the Menu Design window so that a caption and name can

Figure 9.2
Options menu with access key O

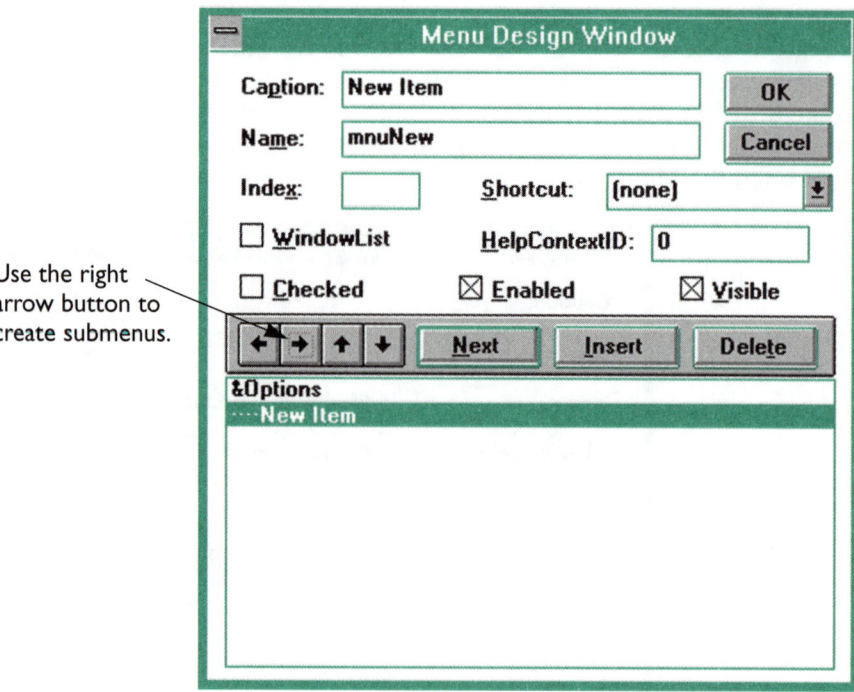

Figure 9.3
New Item submenu of the Options menu

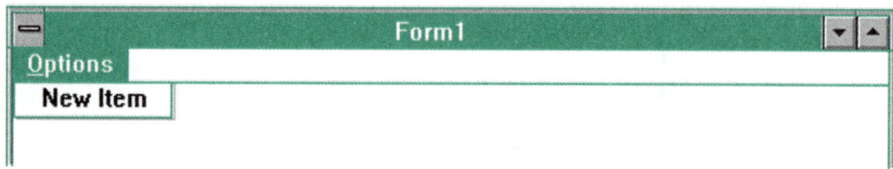

Figure 9.4
Options menu pulled down

be given to a new menu control. This new menu control is made a submenu of the previous menu by clicking on the right arrow of the Menu Design toolbar. Figure 9.3 shows the "indented" list of menus that indicates a submenu below a main menu, and Figure 9.4 shows the results when the user clicks on the main menu Options on the form.

The Delete and Insert buttons on the Menu Design window toolbar allow deletion of a selected menu control and insertion (above the selected menu control) of a new menu control. The left and right arrows determine the level of a menu (main menu, submenu, sub-submenu), and the up and down arrows rearrange the order of existing menus. These features allow you to come back later and add new menus, or rearrange or delete existing menus.

Once menu controls exist, they appear as objects in the Object box of the Code window. Selecting a menu object opens its Code window. Again, the only event recognized by a menu is the click event, so code can be written only for a Click event procedure.

Until such code is written, clicking on a main menu performs the action of dropping down its submenus but nothing else. Generally, this is all you want a main menu control to do, so there is usually no code associated with a main menu control. You do want some action to take place when you click on a submenu, however, so appropriate code must be written for the submenus.

One other property of menu controls is the **Shortcut property**. This property allows you to assign a shortcut keyboard combination, called a **hot key**, to a submenu control. What is the difference between an access key and a hot key? An access key is primarily used with a main menu to allow it to be pulled down by a keyboard action rather than by clicking on the menu caption. A hot key is used with a submenu to immediately execute its associated code without first having to pull down the menu and then click on the submenu. Hot keys should be assigned only to those menu controls that activate frequently used actions. Submenus can also be given access keys in the same manner as main menus, by using the & in the menu caption; once the main menu has been pulled down, using the access key for a submenu also activates its code. However, hot keys cannot be assigned to main menus. Attempting to do so will result in an error.

In Figure 9.3, you can see that the Shortcut text box is part of a drop-down combo box, which supplies a long list of potential hot-key combinations to use, such as Ctrl-A, F2, and so on. Unfortunately, by looking at this drop-down list, you have no way to see whether any of these hot keys is already in use by other menus, but if you do assign a duplicate, you will get an error message when you try to exit the Menu Design window.

9.2 Pop-up menus

Pull-down menus drop down from a menu bar that gives the main menu captions. Another form of menu is the **pop-up menu** or **floating menu**, which can appear ("pop up") anywhere on the form. To create a pop-up menu, use the Menu Design window in exactly the same way as for a pull-down menu, except uncheck the Visible property of the pop-up main menu. This prevents the main menu from being displayed on the form's menu bar.

A pop-up menu is displayed by applying the **PopupMenu method** to the form. The syntax is:

FormName.`PopupMenu` *MenuName, x, y*

Execution of a statement like this causes the named menu to be displayed on the form, provided no other pop-up menu is currently displayed and no pull-down menu is active. The *x* and *y* arguments are the left and top coordinates of the pop-up menu relative to the upper left corner of the form, as measured in the units determined by the ScaleMode property of the form. The *x* and *y* arguments are optional. If omitted, their default values are the current location of the mouse pointer.

For example, suppose a pop-up menu named mnuPopper has been created with two submenus, as shown in Figure 9.5 (note that the Visible check box is unchecked for the main menu). When the statement

```
Form1.PopupMenu mnuPopper, 500, 1000
```

is executed, the opened pop-up menu is displayed on the form at a fixed location, as shown in Figure 9.6. Execution of

```
Form1.PopupMenu mnuPopper
```

displays the same pop-up menu but at the current location of the mouse pointer.

The only remaining question is where to put the statement that invokes the PopupMenu method. It is customary for a pop-up menu to be displayed when the user clicks on the form using the *right* mouse button. Some test therefore needs to be done to determine whether the user clicked

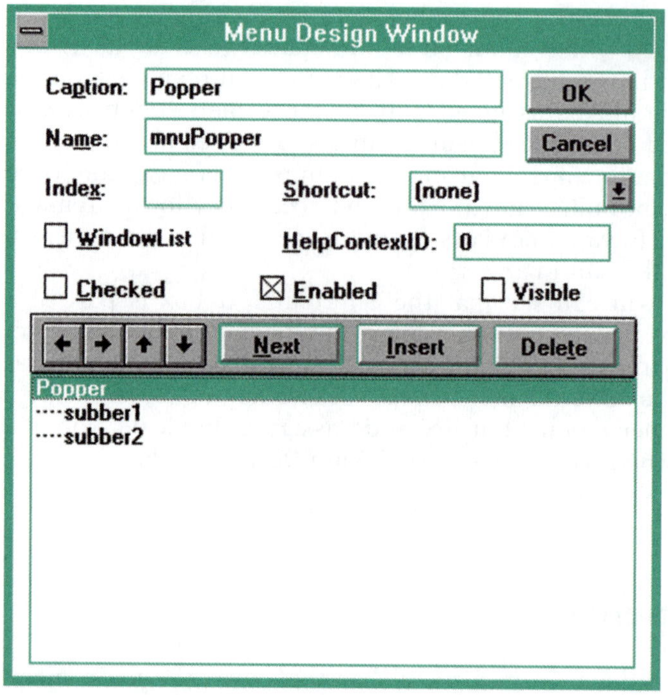

Figure 9.5
Menu design for a pop-up menu

Figure 9.6
Pop-up menu displayed on a form

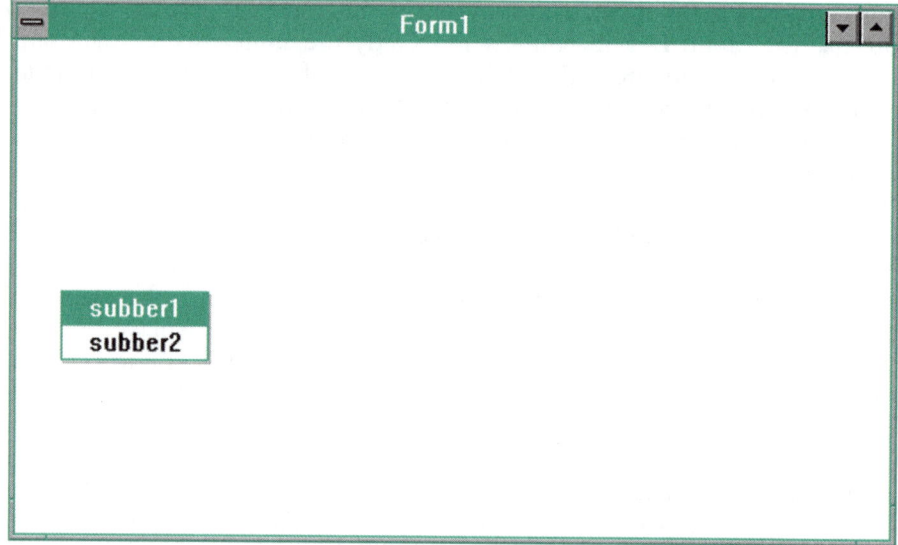

the left or the right mouse button. Instead of putting the code in the form's Click event procedure, put it in the form's MouseDown event procedure. The MouseDown event occurs whenever the user presses a mouse button; the Button argument in the MouseDown event procedure can be used to test which mouse button was pressed. The code for the right mouse button is 2. Therefore the complete code to control the pop-up menu is

```
Sub Form_MouseDown (button As Integer, Shift As Integer,
    X As Single, Y As Single)
    If button = 2 Then
        'optional x,y values omitted
        form1.PopupMenu mnuPopper
    End If
End Sub
```

Name: _____ Date Due: _____

LAB 9.1

LEARNING OBJECTIVES

- Creating drop-down menus
- Exploring menu control properties
- Creating pop-up menus

1. ____ Open a new Visual Basic project.

   ____ Put a picture box near the bottom of the form.

   ____ Using the Menu Design window, create the following menu structure consisting of two main menus, one with three submenus and one with two submenus:

One Menu	Two Menu
Sub 11	Sub 21
Sub 12	Sub 22
Sub 13	

   Creating drop-down menus

2. ____ Give One Menu an access key of O.

   ____ Give Two Menu an access key of T.

   ____ Run your program to be sure your access keys work.

3. ____ The action to be performed by submenu Sub 11 is to print "11" in the picture box. The action to be performed by submenu Sub 12 is to print "12" in the picture box, and so on. Write the necessary code so that all your menus work.

4. ____ Give a hot key of Ctrl-F to menu Sub 12.

   ____ Give a hot key of Ctrl-G to menu Sub 21.

   ____ Test your hot keys.

5. ____ Set the **Visible property** of Sub 11 to false, using either the Menu Design window or the Properties window. What is the effect when the program executes?

   Exploring menu control properties

___ Set the **Enabled property** of Sub 22 to false. What is the effect when the program executes?

6. The **Checked property**, also found in the Menu Design window, is peculiar to menus. It is used with menu controls that turn something on and off, that is, that act as toggle switches. When the program executes, a check mark is displayed next to the menu control. The user can select a checked menu control to toggle the check mark off or on, which also turns off or on the menu option.

___ Check the Checked property in the Menu Design window for menu Sub 22.

___ Change the code for menu Sub 22 so that when it is checked, the picture box on the form is visible and, when it is not checked, the picture box is not visible. Try your program to be sure it works.

Creating pop-up menus

7. Create a pop-up menu that appears wherever the user clicks the right mouse button. This menu has two submenus, Sub 31 and Sub 32, that print "31" and "32", respectively, in the picture box.

___ Test the new menu.

___ Save your files as *menu.frm* and *menu.mak*.

QuickCheck 9.1

1. Menus must be created using the Visual Basic _____.
2. How do you specify an access key for a menu?
3. Code is not usually written for _____ menu controls.
4. True or False: Only menu controls have a Checked property.
5. Code to display a pop-up menu should be placed in what form event procedure?

9.3 General information about graphics

Graphics, of course, implies "picture" or "visual material" instead of text. The term Visual Basic implies that graphics have been used in some sense all along. Both the Visual Basic environment and Visual Basic application programs are windows based, and so include the graphic effects of forms, title bars, command buttons, and so on. Now graphic effects that more specifically use artwork or pictures of some kind are considered.

Any graphic image must be placed in a container. Forms, picture boxes, and image controls are all legitimate **graphic containers**, although the graphic capabilities of image controls are quite limited. A graphic image is always confined within the boundaries of its container, and if the container moves, so does the graphic.

There are four kinds of graphic images.

1. Images from picture files that are loaded into graphic containers (these can be "fancy" pictures)
2. Artwork such as lines and circles that is placed in a graphic container at design time by the use of graphic control objects in the Toolbox
3. Artwork such as lines and circles that is placed in a graphic container dynamically during program execution through graphic methods written into program code
4. Text printed in a graphic container

Each kind in turn will be discussed. Image controls can contain only images from picture files, the first kind of graphic image described.

9.4 Picture file images

Picture files are graphic files obtained from some other source. For example, the Windows Paintbrush program can be used to create pictures and save them as "bitmapped" files with the file name extension .BMP. An icon file, usually with the file name extension .ICO, contains a small rectangular bitmapped picture. An icon library is supplied along with Visual Basic. The picture could be a Windows metafile format, with the file extension .WMF. A picture file can be created from a scanned photographic image or snipped from a video clip.

A picture file can be loaded into a container at design time through the container's Picture property. Double-clicking the Picture property in the Properties window brings up a dialog box that allows you to select the picture file you want to load. You loaded bitmapped files into image controls for the sandwich, drink, and gas pump of Auntie's Cash and Gas (Chapter 6) and for the peach, banana, and cherries of the slot machine (Chapter 7). Icon files were used for the flags of countries in the dive program (Chapter 7).

When a picture file is loaded into a container, the picture image is dropped into the upper left corner of the container. If the container is a form, this means there is no flexibility as to where on the form to put the picture. Therefore pictures are usually loaded into picture boxes or image controls so they can be positioned where desired on the form. Picture boxes and image controls differ in the sets of properties they have and in how they handle picture files. Again, the Toolbox icons for these two controls are:

Picture box   Image control

In addition to assigning a picture to a picture box or image control at design time, a picture can be dynamically assigned as the program is executing. This amounts to changing the Picture property of the picture box or image control in a Visual Basic statement, much like changing, say, a label Caption property. To load the picture file, the Visual Basic LoadPicture function is used. Its single argument is the name and location of the picture file. Thus the statement

```
Image1.Picture = LoadPicture("C:\WINDOWS\ARGYLE.BMP")
```

has the effect, when executed, of loading the **argyle.bmp** picture (a standard Windows "wallpaper" picture) into the Image1 control. Note that the path and file name for the picture file are given within quotes, as a string. To erase the picture from within code, use the LoadPicture function again and give the path and file name as the empty string:

```
Image1.Picture = LoadPicture("")
```

A container can also be loaded with the picture currently in another container by a statement such as

```
Picture2.Picture = Picture1.Picture
```

which loads whatever image is currently in Picture1 into Picture2.

9.5 Design-time artwork

The Visual Basic Toolbox contains two controls that allow you to draw in a graphic container (a form or a picture box but not an image control) at design time. These controls are the Line control and the Shape control. Their Toolbox icons are

Line   Shape

The **Line control** is for drawing straight lines. The line is placed in the container by the usual operation of selecting the control, then clicking and dragging it where you want it. In order to draw perfectly horizontal or perfectly vertical lines, hold down the Shift key while you drag.

Some lines may suffer from the "jaggies." Any image is obtained by coloring tiny areas of the screen, called **picture elements** or **pixels**, and the pixels are arranged in a square grid. Lines that are not horizontal, vertical, or at a 45° angle must select the best path of pixels possible to approximate a straight line. Figure 9.7 illustrates the problem for a not-quite-diagonal line. It shows a close-up view of the line at a pixel-by-pixel level. On a larger scale, the line appears jagged, as in Figure 9.8

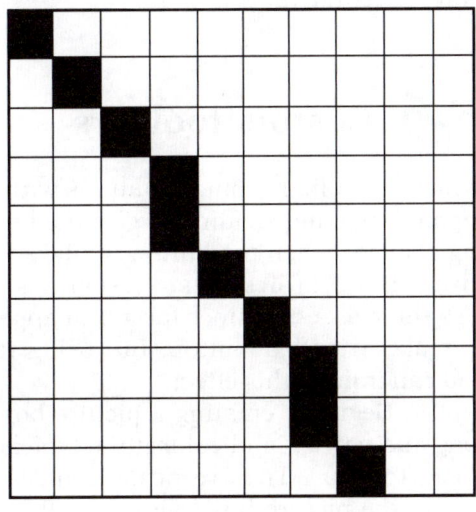

Figure 9.7
Pixel-level view

Figure 9.8
The "jaggies"

A line has properties of:

BorderColor (uses the Color Palette to set the color of the line)

BorderStyle (solid line, dashed line, dots and dashes, and so on)

BorderWidth (set the thickness of the line)

The location of a line is determined by its endpoints, and these are given as coordinates referenced from the top left corner of the container. The **X1 and Y1 properties** give the left and top position of the end of the line you started to drag from, and the **X2 and Y2 properties** give the left and top position of the end of the line where you stopped dragging. The units, of course, are those determined by the ScaleMode property of the container. Changing these coordinate properties changes the position of the line in the container. Likewise, moving the line changes these properties. A line lacks some of the properties of other controls; for example, there is a Name property so that the line can be referenced in code, but there is no Caption property because no text accompanies a line.

The **Shape control** has more properties than the Line control. The most important property is the **Shape property**. It selects the shape drawn in the container by the Shape control. The Shape control can draw rectangles, squares, circles, ovals, and rounded rectangles or squares, as determined by the Shape property setting. The Shape control also has a **FillStyle property**, which lets you select whether the enclosed Shape is to be filled in and, if so, with a solid color or with various patterns of lines.

Neither the Line nor the Shape control recognizes any events, so there can be no code associated with these control objects. Their purpose is purely decorative.

9.6 Custom toolbars

Windows toolbars contain buttons with icons that have a 3-D effect. There is highlighting and shading to give the button a 3-D appearance, and the shading changes when the button is clicked so that it appears to be "pressed in." Visual Basic Professional version has a 3-D push-button control that can also serve as a container for a bitmapped graphic image; that's the ideal way to make a toolbar button. But using the line control and a little patience, you can imitate this effect.

Begin by creating a picture box as the toolbar background; make it long and narrow and color it the typical gray background (look at the Visual Basic Toolbar). Then vertically center an image control with a fixed border within the picture box (see Figure 9.9). In order to position the image control properly, you need to turn off the Align-to-Grid setting in the Visual Basic Options/Environment menu.

Figure 9.9
Beginning of a custom toolbar

The image control supports graphics, so add a graphic image. Set the Stretch property of the image control to true. To get Figure 9.10, the image control's Picture property was used to load the file ARW06RT.ICO from the C:\VB\ICONS\ARROWS directory, but you can use a graphic image of your own created, for example, in Paintbrush.

Figure 9.10
Custom toolbar with a graphic image

Now comes the hard part. Using the line control, carefully place four lines around the border of the image control. Set the BorderColor property of the top and left lines to white and of the right and bottom lines to dark gray. Change the BorderWidth property to make the lines more pronounced. Figure 9.11 shows the result. The lines add a three-dimensional, shaded effect.

Figure 9.11
Toolbar "button" in the "up" position

The final part of the toolbar creation is to change the appearance of the image control when the user presses the mouse over the image control. To do this, put code into the MouseDown event procedure that changes the white lines to dark gray and makes the gray lines disappear. You can get the color code for gray by consulting the BorderColor property for the lines you already have. This code has the effect of giving the "button" a "pressed in" look, as in Figure 9.12. You write code to reverse this effect in the MouseUp event procedure.

Figure 9.12
Toolbar "button" in the "down" position

Finally, in the MouseUp procedure, you also put code for whatever is supposed to happen when the user clicks on the toolbar "button."

―――― THOUGHTS ON PROGRAMMING ――――

Reusability

Visual Basic programs are assemblages of bits and pieces of code—event procedures, form-level general procedures, and general procedures found in code modules. As indicated in Chapter 6, a procedure that does some particularly useful task can be written as a general procedure in a code module to make it easier to export it to another program. Code that is written for one program but is suitable for use in another program or programs is called **reusable code**. **Reusability** of software is one of the major themes in modern software development.

To understand the motivation for software reuse, consider the following analogy. Suppose you are putting together a stereo system for your room. You select speakers, a CD player, a tuner, and so on, perhaps from different manufacturers, and assemble the parts. You do not need to build the CD player from the ground up or manufacture the speaker parts. Each component of your system has already been manufactured and tested and is (supposedly) reliable. Your job is merely to wire the parts together properly, making sure that they can communicate.

What if, instead of building a program from ground zero, you could rummage around in a library of software components that have already been written and tested and are (supposedly) reliable? You select those components you need and merely "wire them together" so they can communicate (through argument passing). Wouldn't this be easier and more sensible than starting every program from scratch? Almost everyone would agree with this, so why is it that so much software is still built line by line as if no one had ever written a similar program before? What is necessary for software reusability to take place?

There are several answers to this, some of them technical and some "cultural." To further software reuse:

1. The programming language must make it easy to write code in separate modules. In some languages, a program is written as one complete piece of code with little or no separation into pieces. Although copying and pasting is always an option, it is much more difficult under these circumstances to know exactly what to copy and how to embed what you have copied into another program.

2. Along the same lines, if a code module is to to be reusable, it must perform a single, small, well-defined task. The technical term used to describe this is **cohesiveness**; a module should be highly **cohesive**, all its code focused on its one task. The more different things a module does, the less likely it is to be usable in a variety of situations.

3. There must be an easy way to **browse** (search and scan) the existing modules of code in order to know what is available and determine whether any of it is suitable for reuse in the current project. The importance of comments and other good documentation is certainly apparent here.

4. The philosophy of reuse must be accepted, both by those who may reuse code from another project in the current project and by those who write new code. Programmers need to be assured that using well-documented, well-tested code, when suitable, is not "cheating," assuming, of course, that they have legal access to this code. They need to familiarize themselves with available **code libraries** and tools for using those libraries effectively. Programmers writing new code need to plan for its possible reuse, which includes the issue of cohesion mentioned above, the use of generic names for parameters, excellent internal documentation, and so on.

Of course, resusable code does not always work as advertised. If the code module does not do exactly what you want and has to be modified to "fit" the new application, the time spent to understand and then modify the existing code may be almost as much as to write the code from scratch. In addition, the reliability of the modified code is immediately suspect. The code must be subjected to a new round of testing. All in all, the time saved by "reuse" in these circumstances may be little or none.

Reusable code is not a new concept. In engineering and scientific programming, libraries of code for certain mathematical computations have been available for years. Now, however, this idea has spread to other application areas and includes not only the code for procedures but also code for declarations of collections of related data called *data structures*.

You are already reusing code when you write Visual Basic programs. Visual Basic supplies intrinsic functions that you use. In addition, Visual Basic supplies the code that makes buttons click, list boxes pull down, forms have title bars, and so on. However, the term "software reuse" does not generally refer to commercial products, for which the programmer has no access to the underlying code.

The custom toolbar is one good candidate for reuse in Visual Basic. If you have created a custom toolbar that performs a collection of small subtasks relevant to many of your application programs and you've thoroughly tested the code for each of these subtasks and have high confidence in its reliability, then by all means "port it" to a number of applications.

Name: _____ Date Due: _____

LEARNING OBJECTIVES

- Exploring properties of picture boxes and image controls
- Building a custom toolbar
- Using the line and shape controls

LAB 9.2

1. Open a new Visual Basic project.

    ____ Put three picture boxes on the form. Make their dimensions

1700 × 1700	(Picture1—large)
300 × 300	(Picture2—small)
1200 × 1200	(Picture3—medium)

    Picture box properties

    ____ Note that the default value for the AutoSize property is false. Change the AutoSize property to true for Picture3 only.

    ____ Load the same picture file into each of the three picture boxes, say the paperclip icon found (usually) in C:\VB\ICONS\OFFICE\CLIP04.ICO. Describe the effect in each of the three cases.

What does the AutoSize property do?

____ Resize Picture3. What is the effect?

Image control properties

2. ___ Now put two image controls on the form. Make Image1's size large, and Image2's size small (using the dimensions of step 1). Note that image controls do not have an AutoSize property.

___ Load each image control with the same picture file as before. What happens?

___ The default value for the Stretch property is false. Resize Image1. What happens?

___ Set the Stretch property of Image2 to true.

___ Resize Image2. What is the effect of the Stretch property?

3. ___ Open a new Visual Basic project. You do not need to save the previous work. Save the new project files as *circles.frm* and *circles.mak*.

Building a custom toolbar

___ Create a custom toolbar on the bottom of the form using a picture box and two image controls.

Using the line control

___ Use the line controls and code discussed in this section to give the two "buttons" a 3-D effect that changes when the buttons are "pushed." (Save your work often!)

4. ____ Use Paintbrush (usually found in the Windows Accessories group) to create a green circle about the size of a quarter.

   ____ Using the Paintbrush scissors, "cut out" the circle and save it to a file (use the Copy To... command from the Edit pull-down menu).

   ____ Do the same thing with a blue circle.

   ____ Still in Paintbrush, create a tiny green circle on a gray background, "cut it out," and save it to a file.

   ____ Create a tiny blue circle on a gray background, "cut it out," and save it to a file. At this point you have four .BMP files.

   ____ Exit Paintbrush

5. ____ Load the graphic image of the tiny green circle into one image control on your toolbar.

   ____ Load the graphic image of the tiny blue circle into the other image control on your toolbar.

6. ____ Put one picture box (Picture1) on your form.

   ____ Now write code so that when the user clicks on the image control with the green circle, the large green circle is displayed in Picture1 and, when the user clicks on the image control with the blue circle, the large blue circle is displayed in Picture1.

7. ____ Use the shape control to decorate the form with five overlapping rings of five different colors.

   Using the shape control

   ____ Save your work.

> **QuickCheck 9.2**
>
> 1. The three types of objects that can serve as graphic containers are _____.
> 2. Images from picture files are usually not displayed on _____.
> 3. Which function is invoked to load a picture file into an image control while the program is executing?
> 4. What determines the shape drawn by the shape control?
> 5. True or false: The picture box AutoSize property accomplishes the same thing as the image control Stretch property.

9.7 Run-time artwork

In addition to artwork that is added through graphic controls at design time, graphic methods can be invoked while the program executes. Once again, forms and picture boxes can be acted on by graphic methods but image controls cannot.

The usual way to reference a method is

ObjectName. MethodName

but for graphic methods some additional information must often be provided in the form of arguments that specify the location or size of the desired graphic. The method reference then looks like

ObjectName.Method argument list

The ObjectName here is the name of the container object (form or picture box) that will hold the resulting artwork. The **DrawWidth property** of the container object controls the thickness of any graphics drawn in that container; think of the DrawWidth property as specifying the thickness of the pencil lead you use. The **ForeColor property** of the container object controls the color of the graphics drawn in that container.

Graphic methods exist that let your program draw dynamically during run time almost everything that can be drawn at design time with graphics controls. Of course since program code must execute to invoke these graphic methods, the resulting artwork only shows up when the program runs, not in design mode. Here are four graphic methods.

> *Line method:* The Line method draws a line determined by the coordinates of the two end points. These coordinates are similar to the X1, Y1 and X2, Y2 properties of a line you draw at design time. Execution of the statement
>
> ```
> Form1.Line (1000, 1500) – (3000, 3500)
> ```
>
> causes a line to be drawn on the form between the two points whose coordinates are given. One endpoint is 1000 units from the left edge of the form and 1500 units below the top edge of

the form; the other endpoint is 3000 units from the left edge and 3500 units below the top edge of the form. If the container is a picture box, then the coordinates of the line endpoints are given relative to the upper left corner of the picture box. (The Line method was used in the HORIZONTAL and VERTICAL procedures of the *jail.mak* project in Lab 6.2.)

Coordinates can also be given by variables or expressions, as in

```
Picture1.Line (3 * y, FirstTop) - (w, EndTop)
```

Other arguments can be used that cause the Line method to draw boxes or filled boxes.

Circle method: In order to draw a circle, this method needs to know the coordinates of the center of the circle and the size of the desired radius, so this information is given in the argument list for the method. The program statement

```
Picture1.Circle (Picture1.Width/2,
    Picture1.Height/2), 300
```

draws a circle with its center in the middle of the picture box and with a radius of 300 units.

Other arguments can be used that allow the Circle method to draw an arc (part of a circle) or an ellipse (a flattened circle).

Pset method: This method, given a set of coordinates as arguments, draws a single point at that location.

Cls method: This method erases all run-time graphics from the container.

Run-time graphic objects by default are **not persistent**. Suppose that code is executed that draws a run-time graphic on a form. Then a dialog box or a second form of some kind pops up, and partially obscures the first form. When the second form is removed, the first form must be redrawn. (Although it is convenient to think that the first form was underneath the second form the entire time, there is only one layer of pixels on the screen. If they are being used to represent a form, then they can't at the same time be used to represent an "underneath" form.) This redrawing, technically called a **refresh operation**, is done automatically *except for run-time graphic objects*. In order to have these automatically redrawn, the **AutoRedraw property** of the container, by default set to false, must be set to true. It turns out that setting this property to true taxes the memory requirements of your program, but it is the simplest way to ensure that your graphic objects persist. Again, nonpersistence applies only to run-time graphics, not to graphics you put on the form with the line or shape control.

At the beginning of this chapter, it was pointed out that text within a graphic container is considered to be a graphic image. Suppose your program applies a Print method to a picture box or to a form. Text is printed in the picture box or on the form. This text is treated as run-time graphics in that it is not persistent unless the AutoRedraw property of the picture box or form is set to true.

9.8 Simple animation

Any animation effect depends on the Timer control. As you remember, the Timer control recognizes only one event, the Timer event. A Timer event occurs every so often; the frequency is controlled by the Interval property of the timer.

Code for animation goes into the Timer1_Timer procedure. Then whenever a Timer event occurs, whatever change you have coded takes place. There are two types of changes you can use to create animation effects.

1. *Move a graphic.* Suppose you have some graphic image in a picture box or image control container. When the Timer event occurs, you can change the location of the container (and hence of the graphic image) on the form. To achieve an animation effect, you want successive changes in position to be small. You can set the new properties relative to the old ones by statements such as

```
Picture1.Left = Picture1.Left + 200
Picture.Top = Picture1.Top + 500
```

These statements, executed every time a Timer event occurs, have the effect of moving the picture box to the right and downward on the form. If the container is an image control and the Stretch property is set to true, you can also reset the Width and Height properties of the container, and thereby change the size of the graphic image.

Instead of having to write a statement for each property you want to change, you can apply a **Move method** to the container. The Move method can accept four arguments corresponding to Left, Top, Width, and Height (in that order) and has the effect of resetting those four properties in the object to which it is applied. You can't skip an argument, but you can leave off arguments at the end. For example, to move an image control to the left 200 twips and double its width, you can write

```
Image1.Move Image1.Left - 200, Image1.Top, Image1.Width * 2
```

Note that the argument for Top specifies that the Top property is to be unchanged, but that argument must be present before you can specify a new width. The fourth argument, for Height, has been omitted.

2. *Change a graphic.* If you have a repertoire of several picture files, you can change the graphic within a container by using the LoadPicture function. Suppose you want to repeatedly change back and forth between two graphic images contained in, say, files PIX1.BMP and PIX2.BMP. Then in the Timer event code you want to alternately execute the statements

```
Image1.Picture = LoadPicture("C:\MYSTUFF\PIX1.BMP")
Image1.Picture = LoadPicture("C:\MYSTUFF\PIX2.BMP")
```

In order to alternate between these two statements, use an If-Then-Else statement with some sort of condition that alternates between true and false. You can use a variable like the *found* variable used in implementing sequential search and set its value alternately to true and false.

Instead of actually loading the image from memory each time, you can speed up the process by loading the two image files into two other (invisible) containers, say Image2 and Image3, at design time. Then to change the image contained in Image1, write

```
Image1.Picture = Image2.Picture
Image1.Picture = Image3.Picture
```

These two techniques of moving a graphic or changing a graphic can be combined to create different effects. That is, you can write code to move a graphic container and change the graphic image it contains, both at the same time.

Name: _____   Date Due: _____

LAB 9.3

LEARNING OBJECTIVES

- Exploring graphic methods
- Creating simple animation

1. ____ Open a new Visual Basic project.

   ____ Put one command button near the bottom of the form and two picture boxes side by side on the form.

2. ____ Write code for the command button's click event to draw a blue horizontal line in one of the picture boxes somewhere near the bottom. Make use of the dimensions of the picture box to place the line. Also write text that says "This is a blue line" in the picture box.

   Line method

   ____ To the command button's click event code, add statements that draw a red circle near the bottom of the second picture box and write text that says "This is a red circle" in the second picture box.

   Circle method

   ____ Test your code to see that everything works properly.

   ____ Now use the line control (not the Line method) to draw a line on the form underneath the two picture boxes.

3. ____ Add a second command button to the form. When the user clicks on this button, a second form appears.

   ____ Set the properties of the second form so that when it appears, it covers half the leftmost picture box on Form1 and all the rightmost picture box.

   ____ Add a command button to the second form to hide the second form.

4. ____ Run your program. Draw the graphic images in the picture boxes. Then press the button to produce the second form. Finally press the button on the second form to make it disappear. What is the effect back on the first form?

Why is the line on the form unaffected?

5. ____ Set the AutoRedraw property of the rightmost picture box to true and repeat Step 4. What happens now?

6. ____ Put a third command button on your form. Clicking this button draws a "fan" of straight lines, as shown in Figure 9.13. (Hint: Use a loop to draw these lines; the lines have one common endpoint, and their other ends all have the same height.)

Figure 9.13
Fan button effect

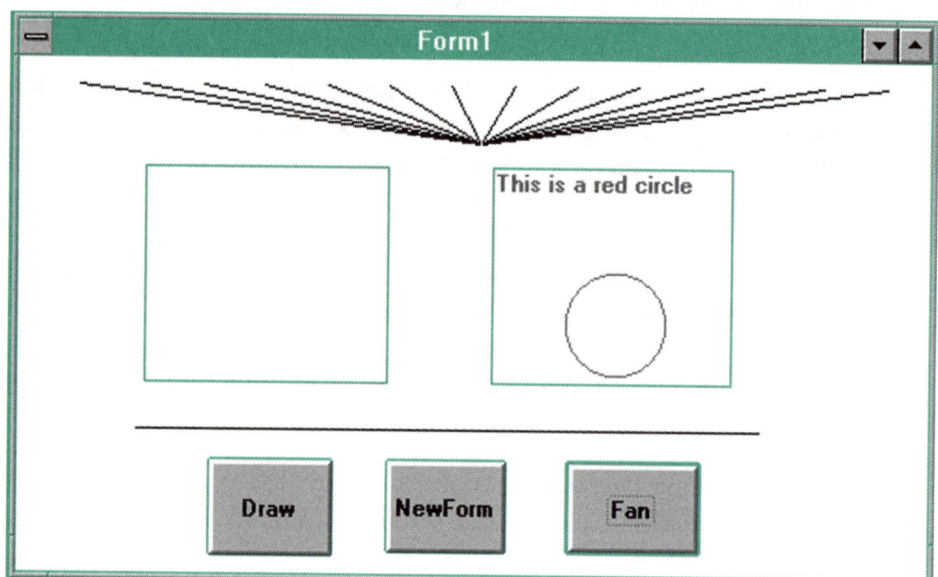

____ Finally, add code to the first command button to draw a small, green, filled box in the upper left corner of the form. (Hint: Look at the Help system information on the Line method to see the available arguments.)

____ Save your files as **Draw1.frm**, **Draw2.frm**, and **Draw.mak**.

Creating animation

7. ____ Open the project **chase.mak**.

____ Run the program and click on the Start button. What happens?

___ Examine the code in this project to be sure you understand how it works. Why is *switcher* declared using the keyword Static instead of Dim?

8. ___ Improve on this animation sequence by creating a mouse that the cat chases across the screen.

9. ___ Add a Speed menu with three submenus of Fast, Regular, and Slow that control the timing of the animation.

   ___ Add a Reset command button that sets the speed back to regular and "sets the stage" for the animation to begin again.

   ___ Save your files as *chase1.frm* and *chase1.mak*.

QuickCheck 9.3

1. Why are arguments needed with graphic methods?
2. What is a refresh operation?
3. A Move method can set which four graphic control properties?
4. Animation depends on the _____ control to change the scene.
5. How can the Line method be used to draw a box?

Review Questions

1. The "hierarchy" of menus is created through the use of _____ in the Menu Design window.
2. Explain the difference between access keys and hot keys.
3. Menu controls can only recognize the _____ event.
4. What action does the user perform to display a pop-up menu?
5. True or false: All graphic containers can hold all graphics created by the line and shape controls.
6. A file for a large image is loaded into a small picture box whose AutoSize property is set to false. What happens?
7. A file for a small image is loaded into a large picture box whose AutoSize property is set to false. What happens?
8. A file for an image is loaded into a picture box whose AutoSize property is set to true. What happens?
9. What is a pixel?
10. What are the "jaggies"?
11. The shape control is used to draw a square box on a form. Can you write code so that when the user clicks on the box, its color changes?
12. What technique is used to create the 3-D push-button effect on a custom toolbar?
13. What does it mean to say that a module of code is cohesive?
14. Explain some of the factors required for successful software reusability.
15. What are the parameters of the Line method?
16. What are the parameters of the Circle method?
17. The method that "erases" a graphic container is the _____ method.
18. What does it mean to say that run-time graphics are not persistent?
19. To have the Line method draw a heavy line, set the _____ property of the container.
20. Animation speed is controlled by the _____ property of the Timer control.

Exercises

Reading code

Describe the effect of each of the following program statements:

1. `Picture1.Picture = LoadPicture("C:\VB\ICONS` ↵
   ↳ `\ELEMENTS\SNOW.ICO")`

2. `Picture1.Line (0, 0)-(Picture1.ScaleWidth,` ↵
   ↳ `Picture1.ScaleHeight)`

3. `Form1.Circle (Form1.Width/2, Form1.Height/2),` ↵
   ↳ `Form1.Height/4`

4. `For i = 500 To 2500 Step 500`
      `Form1.Circle (Form1.Width/2, Form1.Height/2), i`
   `Next i`

5. `Image2.Move Image2.Left, Image2.Top – 500`

Writing code

Write code to perform the following tasks:

6. Change the appearance of a shape control on the form to a filled, rounded square.

7. Exchange the images in two picture boxes on the form. (You may assume that there is a third, invisible picture box on the form.)

8. Draw a diagonal line on the form from the top right corner to the lower left corner.

9. Somewhere on the form, draw a square 1000 twips by 1000 twips with a circle centered inside it, like

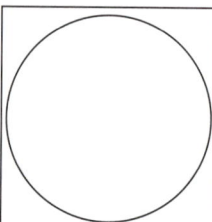

10. a. Move an image box gradually from the top left corner of the form to the top right corner.

    b. Where does this code go?

Exploring further

11. Access keys can be used with command buttons as well as with menus. The process for creating an access key is the same: use an ampersand in the button caption in front of the letter you want to use. Put a command button with the caption "Click me" on a form; clicking the button prints some message to the form. Make the C the access key and test your program to see that the access key works.

12. By convention, menu picks that result in a dialog box are indicated with captions that show trailing ellipses (as in Save Project As...). Create a menu on a form with two submenus, one of which brings up an input box.

13. Determine how to write code that generates a filled yellow circle on a form.

14. If a menu has many submenus, they can be grouped together visually by using a **separator bar**. Create a menu with three submenus and insert a separator bar between the second and third submenus. Hint: Consult the Help system.

15. Create a freehand drawing tool that, as long as the mouse button is held down, allows the cursor to act like a pencil point. Hints:

    a. The drawing tool draws all the time, but the effect is only seen when the mouse button is down. In the Properties window, set the foreground color of the form to be the same as the background color. When the mouse button is pressed, change the foreground color to black; when the mouse button is released, change it back.

    b. The Form_MouseDown, Form_MouseMove, and Form_MouseUp events have parameters that include X and Y, the current position coordinates of the mouse. In the Line method, the first pair of coordinates (giving the starting point of the line) can be omitted. When this happens, the starting point is the location of the last point drawn. The second pair of coordinates (giving the ending point of the line) can be the current mouse coordinates. Use this form of the Line method in the MouseMove event procedure so that as the mouse moves, the line continually "chases itself" across the form.

Projects

1. Create a bar graph application. The user enters five integers between 0 and 100 and sees the five values displayed in bar graph format in a picture box on the form.

2. Modify your **dive.mak** project from Chapter 7 by adding a "cover page" form with some appropriate animation.

3. Modify your **dive.mak** project from Chapter 7 by removing the two option buttons for the choice of report and using instead a pull-down Report menu.

4. Add a second animation scenario to the cat-and-mouse project of this chapter. In this scenario, the cat catches the mouse. Add a pull-down Scenario menu that lets the user choose which animation to see.

5. Create a complete animation application of your own design. (Note that in the cat-and-mouse project, an image control was used that filled the entire form.)

CHAPTER 10

Data Structures

KEY POINTS

- The array data structure organizes related items of data, all of the same data type, as an ordered list or as a table.
- For-Next loops are ideal for examining one-by-one all the elements in an array.
- The selection sort algorithm builds a sorted array from back to front in a series of passes through the data.
- Binary search is more efficient than sequential search on sorted data.
- Visual Basic allows a user-defined data type, which can accommodate components of different data types.

10.1 Arrays—something old, something new

An **array** is an ordered collection or list of similar items that all share a common name. Each individual item in the collection is identified by its index value, which gives its position in the list.

You have already used control arrays in some of your Visual Basic programs. Recall that a **control array** is a collection of similar control objects that all share the same name. Each individual object is identified by its index in the array. For example,

    cmdClickHere(0)   lblDisplay(0)
    cmdClickHere(1)   lblDisplay(1)
    cmdClickHere(2)   lblDisplay(2)

are two three-element arrays of command buttons and labels, respectively. There is a single Click event procedure for the buttons. It could look like

```
Sub cmdClickHere_Click (Index As Integer)
  lblDisplay(Index).Caption = "I clicked button" & Str$(Index)
End Sub
```

Clicking the button with index 0 puts "I clicked button 0" in lblDisplay(0), clicking the button with index 1 puts "I clicked button 1" in lblDisplay(1), and so on.

A control array thus acts as a whole, with a single name and single event procedures, yet also has individual elements that can be referenced by giving the appropriate Index values.

In the *library.mak* program of Chapter 8 you worked with the Forms collection, in which the loaded forms act like an array of forms that are referenced by Forms(0), Forms(1), and so on. The ordering of forms in the Forms collection can change if forms are unloaded and reloaded during program execution.

The items in a list box or a combo box are also treated as an array. Thus

```
Printer.Print Combo1.List(0)
```

prints the first item in the combo box list. Because the items in list boxes and combo boxes are strings, a list box or combo box can be thought of as an array of string data. So the arrays encountered so far are arrays of control objects, of form objects, and of string data.

The next move is to allow arrays of other data types, such as arrays of data of type Integer or arrays of data of type Single. In dealing with numeric data previously, a separate variable has been used to contain each piece of data. For example, three separate variables of type Integer are declared by

```
Dim Number1 As Integer
Dim Number2 As Integer
Dim Number3 As Integer
```

Assume an integer value has been assigned to each of these variables and you now want to print out the values. The three statements

```
Printer.Print Number1
Printer.Print Number2
Printer.Print Number3
```

certainly work. Now expand this situation to 100 integer variables. Do you want to do 100 declaration statements and 100 Print method statements? If there is an array of integers called *Number*, then the 100 integer variables share a common name and are referenced individually by their index values. The statement

```
For i = 1 To 100
    Printer.Print Number(i)
Next i
```

loops through the array and prints each of the 100 numbers in turn. This is a short, neat solution.

Visual Basic does allow arrays of any data type you choose. Such arrays are entities composed of ordered arrangements of individual data items. Presumably these data items are collected together because they are somehow logically related to one another. In the preceding example, you may want to print the 100 numbers because they represent the high temperatures for the first 100 days of the year or the quantities on hand of the best-selling 100 items in stock, and so on.

A **data structure** is a collection of related data items that are organized in some ordered or "structured" way. An array is thus an example of a data structure.

10.2 Array declarations

To use 100 individual integer data items, you have to declare 100 individual variables of type Integer. This sets aside 100 memory locations and assigns a variable name to each. An array of 100 integers like the *Number* array also requires 100 memory locations for storing integers, but this memory space is reserved by declaring the array as a whole.[1] There are three parts to an array declaration:

- Array name
- Data type of the elements the array will contain
- **Dimensions** of the array, that is, its size

The first two parts agree with what has to be done for any variable declaration (give its name and data type), but the third is new because now multiple memory locations are being requested. The array dimensions determine not only the size of the array, but also the range of index values used to identify the individual array elements. (By the way, array "dimensions" are the origin for the reserved word **Dim** used in Visual Basic declarations for other variables.)

To declare *Number*, the 100-element array of integers, either of the following declaration statements is acceptable:

```
Dim Number(100) As Integer
Dim Number(1 To 100) As Integer
```

Both declarations indicate that the array is to be named *Number* and is to contain data of type Integer. The first declaration, giving the single value 100, indicates that 100 is to be the upper limit of the index values. With this form of declaration, Visual Basic automatically supplies a lower limit of 0, just as the lowest index value for a control array or for a list box is automatically set to 0. So the array has been declared to hold 101 integer values:

Number(0), *Number*(1), *Number*(2), ... , *Number*(99), *Number*(100)

This is one more than is needed, but the *Number*(0) variable can simply be ignored. The second declaration explicitly declares the entire range of index values, from lower limit to upper limit, so the array elements for the second declaration are

Number(1), *Number*(2), ... , *Number*(99), *Number*(100)

Here a 100 element array has been declared.

The second declaration form is preferable because it indicates explicitly the range of index values. Also, it allows the creation of arrays with any range of index values you choose. For example,

```
Dim ThisArray(10 To 20)As Single
```

declares an 11-element array of type Single data items indexed from 10 to 20. A constant value can be used in the definition of the index range, as in

---

[1] Visual Basic requires that all arrays be declared, regardless of the Option Explicit setting; an attempt to reference an undeclared array results in an error message.

```
Const Upper = 20
Dim ThisArray(10 To Upper) As Single
```

Figure 10.1 illustrates *ThisArray*. It is a row of 11 elements with index values 10 to 20. The value of *ThisArray*(12) is the integer −43; that is, −43 is stored in the memory location referred to as *ThisArray*(12).

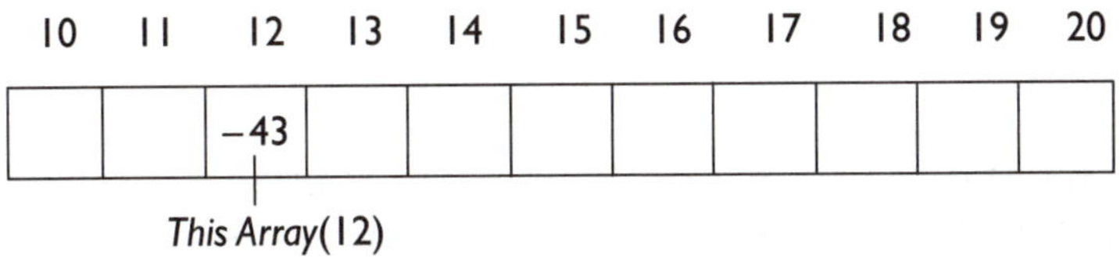

10	11	12	13	14	15	16	17	18	19	20
		−43								

This Array(12)

Figure 10.1
ThisArray

Declarations for arrays follow the usual rules of scope for variables:

- An array declared within a procedure (an event procedure, a general procedure in the general section of a form, or a general procedure in a code module—a .BAS file) is known only throughout that procedure.

- An array declared in the declarations section of a form is known throughout the form.

- An array declared in the declarations section of a code module with **Dim** is known throughout the module.

- An array declared in the declarations section of a code module with **Global** is known throughout the project.

However, there are some additional twists to array declarations. The arrays being considered here, in which the dimensions are known, are **fixed-sized arrays.** Because fixed-sized arrays can use a large amount of memory, it is inefficient to set aside memory every time the program invokes the procedure in which the array is declared. This is avoided by making the array a static array. Recall that a static variable is one that retains its values from one invocation of the procedure to the next; this is accomplished by retaining the memory location for that variable. A fixed-sized array declared within a procedure must be a static array. As a result, *you must use the reserved word* **Static** *instead of* **Dim** *when declaring a fixed-sized array within a procedure* (unless the entire procedure has been declared Static). Within a procedure, then, the declaration for the array *Number* is

```
Static Number(1 To 100) As Integer
```

How big should you declare an array to be? Suppose the user is going to supply some values to put in the array and you are not sure just how many values will be supplied. For a fixed-sized array, you must estimate the maximum number of elements and declare the array accordingly, so you have space to put everything. On the other hand, you don't want to waste memory space by declaring the array to be much bigger than needed. This requires a rather careful estimation.

Another option is to declare a **dynamic array**, for which the size is left unspecified at the time of declaration. To declare a dynamic array, simply use empty parentheses for the index range, as in

```
Static ThisArray( ) As Integer
Dim ThisArray( ) As Integer
Global ThisArray( ) As Integer
```

When the program executes and the number of elements to be stored has been determined and is contained, say, in the variable *HowMany*, then a **ReDim statement** sets aside exactly the amount of memory space needed:

```
ReDim ThisArray (1 to HowMany)
```

After this, the array is ready to use. The ReDim statement can be used in this way more than once, but each execution of such a statement destroys the previous array of that name and creates a new one of the size currently being requested.[2]

Figure 10.2 illustrates some of the options for array declarations.

Figure 10.2
Array declarations

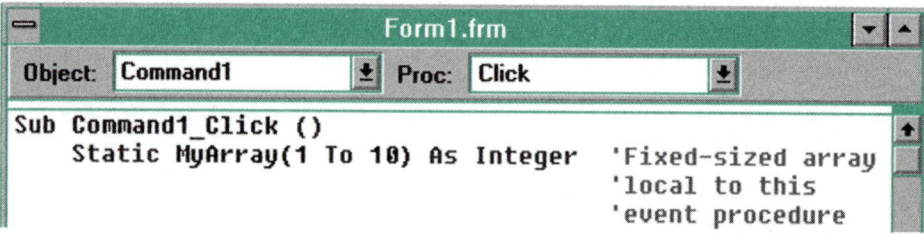

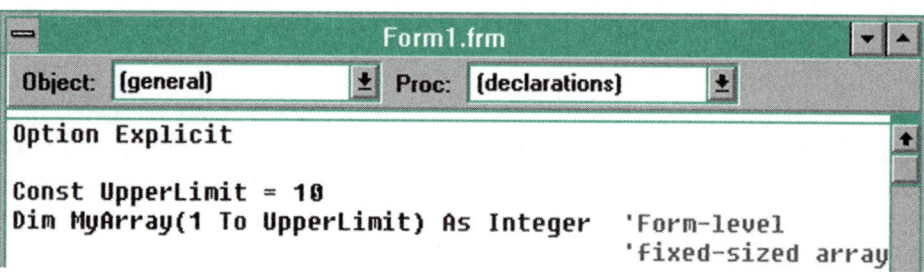

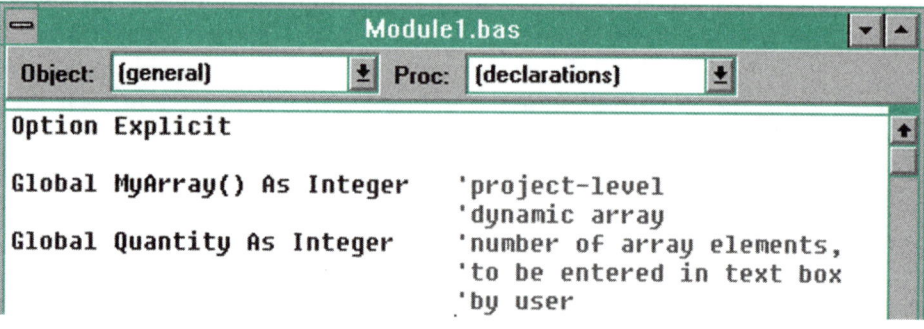

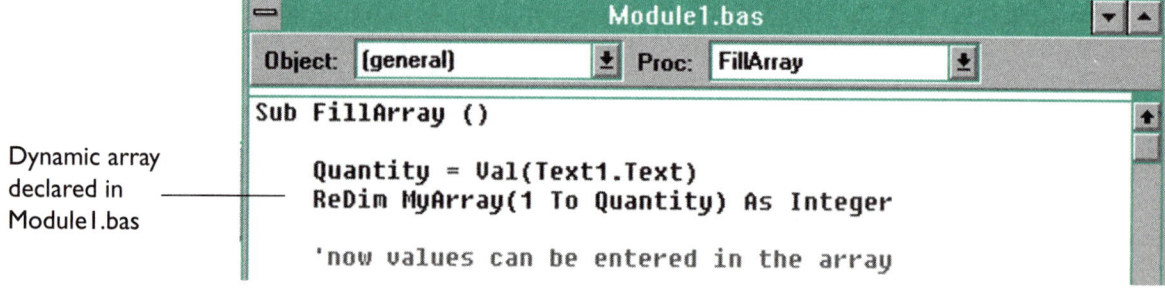

Dynamic array declared in Module1.bas

---

[2] A variation on the ReDim statement, `ReDIM Preserve ThisArray (1 to NewUpperIndex)`, extends the size of the array without destroying the current values in the array.

10.3 Array usage

There are several ways to get data into an array once it has been declared.

1. The user can enter all the data in a single text box. The data items are then part of one long string (the text of the text box). In order for the program to be able to separate the individual data items in the string, the user has to insert some special separation character, like a blank or a comma, between data values. Then the Visual Basic string manipulation functions can be employed to somewhat painstakingly pick through the string and get each data value in turn.

2. The user can enter data in a control array of text boxes. Then it is easy to loop through the text boxes and load the array. For example, if *TheArray* is declared by

```
Static TheArray(1 to 5) As Integer
```

and there is a control array of 5 text boxes on the form, then *TheArray* can be loaded by the For-Next statement

```
For i = 1 To 5
    TheArray(i) = Val(Text(i - 1).Text)
Next i
```

Note that the index for the text box is always one less than the index for the array position being filled. That's because the array indexes run from 1 to 5, while the control array indexes run from 0 to 4. At the start of the loop, when $i = 1$, the number entered in the text box with index 0 gets stored in *TheArray* at position 1. Then i is increased to 2, the number entered in the text box with index 1 gets stored in *TheArray* at position 2, and so on. Figure 10.3 illustrates the process. For small amounts of data, this does the job. If there is a large amount of data, however, the screen is littered with text boxes. Furthermore, only a fixed-sized array can be used because the number of text boxes to put on the form must be known at design time.

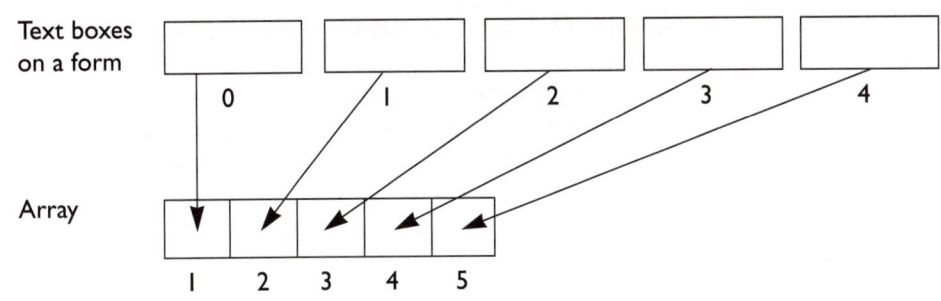

Figure 10.3
Filling an array from a control array of text boxes

3. The user can enter data in a series of input boxes. This avoids the littering-the-form problem of method 2. Also, you can ask the user for the number of data items, use ReDim to set the array size, and then execute a For-Next loop to invoke an input box the appropriate number of times.

4. For a large amount of data, none of these methods is particularly satisfactory. The user does not want to enter data every time the program executes, especially if most of the data is unchanged from one execution of the program to the next. Instead, the data should be entered in a permanent

external file that exists independently of the program; then any time the program executes, it simply reads data values from the file into the array. Use of data files is discussed in the next chapter.

In methods 2 and 3, a For-Next loop is used to load the array. In fact, For-Next loops are useful for almost all array operations that involve marching through the array elements one-by-one (just as they are useful for marching through the elements in a list box or combo box). Suppose, for example, that you want to double each of the 100 values in the array *Number* of integers. Easily done:

```
For i = 1 To 100
   Number(i) = 2 * Number(i)
Next i
```

Most of the time, program code refers to individual array elements, like *Number*(i). It is not possible, for example, to double all the array elements in one fell swoop by trying something like Number = 2 * Number, which produces an error about a duplicate definition because Visual Basic thinks you are using some new variable also named *Number*.

There are two occasions, however, when the array as a whole can be used in a Visual Basic statement (aside from the array declaration statement). One is the Visual Basic **Erase statement**.

```
Erase Number
```

sets each entry of the array *Number* back to a default value of 0. It has the same effect as

```
For i = 1 To 100
   Number(i) = 0
Next i
```

The Erase statement applied to a dynamic array releases the memory set aside for the array; a ReDim statement has to be executed before the array can be used again.

The second case in which just the array name can be used occurs when you want to pass an entire array as an argument to a procedure or function. In this case you can just pass the array name, but it must be followed by an empty set of parentheses. Suppose, for example, that you want to use a procedure *SumItUp* to add the 100 values in the array *Number* and display the total. Figure 10.4 shows such a procedure.

Figure 10.4
Procedure for adding array values

```
Sub SumItUp (A() As Integer)
Dim i As Integer
Dim Total As Integer

   Total = 0
   For i = LBound(A) To UBound(A)
      Total = Total + A(i)
   Next i
   Label1.Caption = "The total is " & Total
End Sub
```

There are several noteworthy points about Figure 10.4 First, the parameter in the procedure heading is denoted A(); the empty parentheses are required to alert Visual Basic that the corresponding argument will be an array. The "As Integer" in the procedure heading refers to the data type of the individual array elements. For this procedure to be as useful and reusable as possible, no assumptions have been made about the range of the array indices. Instead, the procedure makes use of two Visual Basic functions, *LBound* and *UBound*, that return, respectively, the lower index value and the upper index value for an array. Those functions are applied to the array that is passed into the procedure in order to get the bounds for the For-Next loop.

To invoke the *SumItUp* procedure, write

```
Call SumItUp(Number())
```

Here the argument is the name of the array, again with empty parentheses to match the form of the corresponding parameter.

10.4 Two-dimensional arrays

The arrays discussed so far have all been linear or **one-dimensional** (1-D) arrays. This means that the array elements can be pictured in a line, as in Figure 10.1. Sometimes it is useful to imagine data organized in two-dimensional form, as a table. This organization requires a **two-dimensional** (2-D) array. To declare such an array, two sets of dimensions must be given. For example,

```
Static Table(1 To 3, 1 To 4) As Integer
```

declares an array of integers with three rows and four columns. To identify an element of this array, a pair of index values, one for its row position and one for its column position, must be given. Figure 10.5 shows the array *Table*, where the value of *Table*(2,4) (the element in the second row, fourth column) is 15.

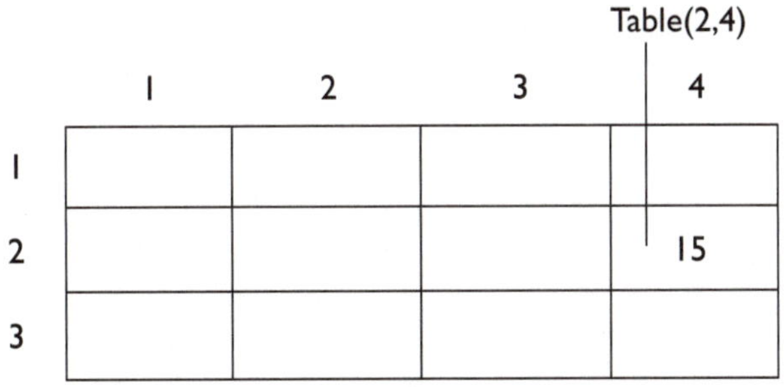

Figure 10.5
2-D array *Table*

To march through the elements of a two-dimensional array, nested For-Next loops are ideal. The following code prints the values of *Table* row by row.

```
For i = 1 To 3
   For j = 1 To 4
       Picture1.Print Table(i, j),
   Next j
   Picture1.Print 'this is to start a new row of output
Next i
```

The outer loop moves through the rows while the inner loop moves through the columns in a given row. At the beginning of the outer loop, i is set equal to 1. The inner loop then executes four times, setting the values of j from 1 to 4. The effect is to print the values of *Table*(1,1), *Table*(1,2), *Table*(1,3), and *Table*(1,4), which is the first row of *Table*. The outer loop then executes a second time, with i set to 2. The inner loop prints *Table*(2,j) as j changes from 1 to 4, which is the second row of *Table*. On the last pass through the outer loop, the third row of *Table* is printed.

Arrays of higher dimensions are possible in Visual Basic but seldom used.

LAB 10.1

Name: _____   Date Due: _____

LEARNING OBJECTIVES

- Using a 1-D array
- Exploring options for array data entry
- Using a 2-D array

1. ____ Open a new Visual Basic project.

   ____ Save the files as *grade.frm* and *grade.mak*.

   This project collects 5 quiz grades from the user and produces a summary report with the quiz average. The figure shows how the form looks after one set of user data is processed.

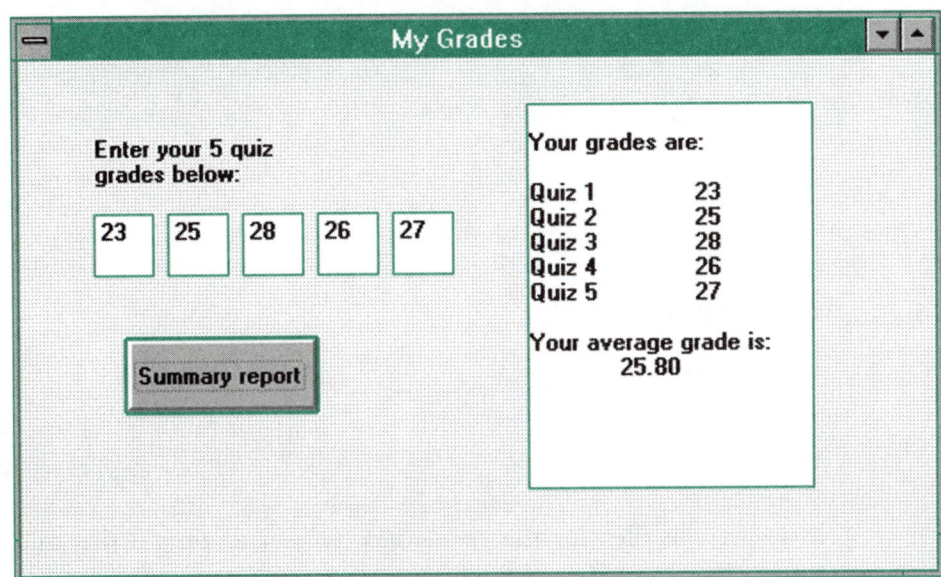

   ____ Design your form to include the necessary label (for the prompt), empty text boxes to collect data (make these a control array), command button, and picture box to display data.

2. ____ In the declarations section of the form, declare a fixed-sized array to store the five grades.

   Using a 1-D array

3. ____ There will be two form-level general procedures, *FillArray* and *DoReport*, each with a single parameter representing the array storing the grades. Write the headings for each of the two procedures.

   ____ The command button simply calls *FillArray* and *DoReport* and passes each a single argument that is the array storing the grades. Write the code for the command button.

At this point you can run your program and click the button, although nothing happens yet.

Array data from text boxes

4. ____ Write the *FillArray* procedure. Use a For-Next loop to load the items from the text boxes into the array.

5. ____ Do a pseudocode design for the *DoReport* algorithm. DoReport must both print the individual grades and add them up; try to loop through the array only once.

6. ____ Write the *DoReport* code.

____ Test your program.

____ Save your files.

Array data from input boxes

7. ____ Now save the files for the **grade.mak** project as **grade1.frm** and **grade1.mak.** In this version of the project, the number of quiz grades is not fixed. Instead, the user enters the number of quiz grades in a text box on the form. The appropriate number of input boxes pops up to collect user input.

____ Remove four of the text boxes from your form and, in the Properties window, delete the value of the Index property of the remaining text box so that it is not considered a 1-element control array.

____ Change the label to a user prompt to enter the number of quizzes in the one remaining text box.

____ Change the array declaration so that the array is dynamic rather than fixed sized, and declare a variable to represent the ultimate size of the array.

____ Add a statement within the command button code to collect the value of the array size.

8. Which of the two general procedures can be kept virtually unchanged from the previous version?

   ____ Modify the other procedure as necessary.

   ____ Test your program.

   ____ Save your files.

9. ____ Open the Visual Basic project *chick.mak*. This program gives information about the servings at a chicken fast-food restaurant. The user chooses one of three meals and can then inquire about the number of servings of any one or more of four food items. The number of servings of each item for each meal choice is contained in the following table.

   Using a 2-D array

Meal choice	Chicken pieces	Biscuits	Cole slaw	Drinks
Party Pack	20	10	4	5
Big Deal	8	4	2	2
Solo Splurge	3	2	1	1

   ____ This data is partially stored in an array called *Table* (declared in the general section of the form) when the form is loaded. Complete the Form_Load code so that it enters the rest of the Table data.

10. ____ Look through the project to observe the names of the various objects. In particular, what are the names (not the captions) of the objects that represent the meal choices?

   What are the names of the objects that represent the food items?

What are the names of the output labels?

11. ____ Write code for the check boxes so that (assuming the meal choice has been made) the number of servings is entered in the appropriate label.

____ Write code for the option buttons so that choosing a different meal clears out the text boxes and unchecks all the check boxes so the user can start again.

____ Test everything and save your work.

> **QuickCheck 10.1**
>
> Consider the declaration
>
> `Dim List(1 to 15) As Single`
>
> 1. How many elements are in *List*?
> 2. What kind of elements are they?
> 3. How would you refer to the third element in *List*?
> 4. What is *UBound(List)*?
> 5. In all likelihood, this declaration will *not* be found within _____. Explain your answer.

10.5 Sorting

One of the nice properties of a list box or a combo box is the Sorted property. Recall that the items in a list box are strings. When the Sorted property is set to true, every new item is added to the list box in alphabetical order, so that the entire list box ends up sorted alphabetically. As a generalization of the list box idea, an array can be sorted according to whatever data type it contains. If the array contains string data, then "sorted" means sorted in alphabetical order. If it contains numeric data, then "sorted" means sorted in numerical order. To achieve this effect, you have to do the work yourself because an array is a data structure in your program and not a control object whose properties you can set.

Sorting is a very common task in data processing. Think about such items as a mailing list of customers, a parts list for inventory, or a telephone book. Keeping such information in sorted order allows finding a particular item much more quickly than keeping it in random order. With items in random order, the only way to search for a target value is to use a sequential search (described in Chapter 8) and plod through the list (array), checking each value encountered against the target.

Because sorting is such an important task, many people have devised algorithms to sort data. You may wonder why more than one sorting algorithm exists; once one algorithm that works is devised, isn't that enough? Why look for others? Strictly speaking, the answer is yes, one algorithm is enough. However, again because this is a task that is frequently done—sometimes on very large sets of data—there is a question of how efficient an algorithm is. How quickly does it execute, and how much memory space does it require? Time and space are resources that are consumed when a program is executing. The reason that more than one sorting algorithm exists is that some algorithms work more efficiently when the input data are totally random, and some work more efficiently when the data are already close to being sorted. Some algorithms are easier to understand than others even though less efficient, so they may be suitable for sorting small amounts of data.

A sorting algorithm called **selection sort** is relatively easy to understand, and its efficiency does not depend on the arrangement of the initial data. It operates just as quickly (actually just as slowly, since it is not a very efficient algorithm) whether the data are completely random or almost in order to begin with.

Selection sort works by making multiple passes through the array of data. Assume you want to sort the data in increasing order. On each pass, one element of the array gets put into its proper position. On the first pass, the largest element in the array gets put into the last position, its proper place. On the second pass, the next-largest element gets put into the second-last position, its proper place. The "sorted" part of the array grows from back to front until it takes up the whole array, while the "unsorted" part of the array—the front part—gets smaller and smaller until it disappears.

For example, here's a small array of five integers.

Initial array | 6 | 4 | 8 | 3 | 5 |

The largest element in the unsorted section of the array (which is the whole array) is 8. The proper position for 8 is the last position in the unsorted section of the array (which is the last position in the whole array). In order to put 8 into the proper position, 8 gets swapped with the element currently in that position (which is 5).

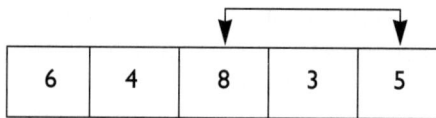

Here's the result after pass 1; the heavy black line divides the unsorted portion of the array (the front) from the sorted portion of the array (the back).

After pass 1 | 6 | 4 | 5 | 3 | 8 |

On the second pass, the algorithm again finds the maximum value in the unsorted section of the array (6) and swaps it with the value at the end of the unsorted section of the array (3). Here is the result after pass 2; note that the sorted section has grown to two elements.

After pass 2 | 3 | 4 | 5 | 6 | 8 |

On the next pass, the maximum value of the unsorted section (5) gets swapped with the element at the end of the unsorted section (5). The only effect is to move the sorted marker one cell farther to the left.

After pass 3 | 3 | 4 | 5 | 6 | 8 |

Pass 4 and pass 5 are similar.

After pass 4 | 3 | 4 | 5 | 6 | 8 |

After pass 5 | 3 | 4 | 5 | 6 | 8 |

The entire array has now been sorted.

Selection sort therefore involves repetitions of the following actions:

Find the maximum value in the unsorted section.

Swap the maximum value with the value at the end of the unsorted section.

In code to implement selection sort, these actions are the body of a loop statement. What controls the loop? The size of the unsorted section is initially the size of the whole array, and is reduced on each pass. Program code can accomplish this by keeping track of the array index marking the end of the unsorted section of the array. A pseudocode version of selection sort is shown in Figure 10.6.

> For i = upper array index down to lower array index
>   Find the maximum value in the array between lower
>   index and i
>   Swap the maximum value with the value at i
> Next i

Figure 10.6
Pseudocode for selection sort algorithm

The two subtasks making up the loop body consist of finding a maximum value—or rather, finding where the maximum value occurs—and swapping two elements in an array. These can be done as separate procedures. Figure 7.16 gives a pseudocode version of a FindMaxIndex algorithm for a control array of text boxes. However, that was written before looping mechanisms were discussed, so it needs to be modified now that more powerful Visual Basic programming constructs are at hand. And of course it also needs to be modified because the array is not a control array.

The swapping procedure has a little twist to it. Suppose the task is to swap the elements in position i and position j of array A. At first it might seem that this could be done by the two statements

```
A(i) = A(j)
A(j) = A(i)
```

But after the first statement has been executed, the value of $A(i)$ has been replaced by the value of $A(j)$ (and the value of $A(i)$ has been destroyed). Then the second statement just replaces the value of $A(j)$ with itself. What is needed is a temporary variable *temp* to store $A(i)$ before it is overwritten with $A(j)$. The three statements

```
temp = A(i)
A(i) = A(j)
A(j) = temp
```

accomplish the swapping.

10.6 Searching

Along with sorting, another frequently done task is searching a collection of values for some desired target value. Sequential search is one algorithm to accomplish this task. The sequential search algorithm starts at the first element in the list and marches through the list, comparing each value with the target value, until it either finds the target value or runs out of the list. Lab 8.3 called for a sequential search on book titles or book authors from a collection of forms. Sequential search can certainly be applied to data stored in an array. Figure 10.7 shows how the sequential search procedure can be invoked from some command button that passes to the procedure the name of the array, the name of the target value, a variable for the index where the value is found, and a *found* indicator. The array *A* has been declared as a form-level variable.

Figure 10.7
Sequential search on an array of integers invoked from a command button

```
Sub cmdSeqSearch_Click ()
Dim target As Integer
Dim index As Integer
Dim found As Integer

    target = Val(InputBox$("Value to search for:"))
    found = False
    Call seqsearch(A(), target, index, found)
    If found <> False Then
        Picture1.Print "value found at position " & Str$(index)
    Else
        Picture1.Print "value not found"
    End If
End Sub

Sub seqsearch (A() As Integer, ByVal target As Integer,
 n As Integer, found As Integer)
'does sequential search on array A for target value
'returns position n of index in A where found

Dim i As Integer

    i = LBound(A)
    Do While (found = False) And (i <= UBound(A))
        If A(i) = target Then
            n = i
            found = True
        Else
            i = i + 1
        End If
    Loop
End Sub
```

If the data are random, then sequential search is the only option. But if the data are sorted, then another search algorithm, called **binary search**, can be used. Binary search is more or less what you do to look for a name in the (alphabetically sorted) telephone directory. Suppose you are looking for the name Hirano. You open the book somewhere near the middle, say at the name Leonardo. Because Leonardo comes after your target value (Hirano), you know that you can confine your search to the pages before Leonardo. You repeat this process, looking somewhere in the middle of the pages between AAAA Radiator Service and Leonardo. You find the name Drover. Because Drover comes before your target value (Hirano), you know you can confine your search to the pages between Drover and Leonardo. And so on.

The binary search algorithm follows this idea of repeatedly looking at an item in the middle of the list and then, if that item is not the target value, searching on a smaller list. The list to search is repeatedly cut in half until either the target value is found, or the list shrinks to nothing. Figure 10.8 parallels Figure 10.7 in that a command button invokes the binary search procedure and passes it the necessary arguments. These include, as before, the name of the array to search, the name of the target value, a variable for the index where the value is found, and a *found* indicator. There are two additional arguments that represent the range of the array to search. Initially, the range is the whole array, so the command button passes *LBound(A)* and *UBound(A)* to the binary search procedure.

When the binary search procedure is initially invoked, the parameters *first* and *last* correspond to the arguments *LBound(A)* and *UBound(A)* in the command button's Call statement. Therefore *first* ≤ *last*. The midpoint is computed as (roughly) the average between *first* and *last*; that is, *middle* = (*first* + *last*)\2. For an odd number of elements, this formula turns out to give the middle position. For an even number of elements, where there is no middle position, this formula gives the position at the end of the left half of the list.

The target value is compared with the array value at this middle position. If they are equal, the target has been found and the procedure, after setting *n* and *found*, is done. If not, the search begins again on half of the list, either the half after the middle if the middle value is less than the target, or the half before the middle if the middle value is greater than the target. To begin the search again, the procedure *BinSearch* is invoked again—from within *BinSearch*. The process whereby a procedure can invoke itself is called **recursion** and is a powerful technique for solving certain kinds of problems. The new search is limited to half of the previous list by resetting the arguments for the *first* or *last* values. To search the half after the middle, *first* is increased to one more than the middle; to search the half before the middle, *last* is decreased to one less than the middle. If the target value is not in the list, then, since *first* keeps getting bigger and *last* keeps getting smaller, eventually it is no longer the case that *first* ≤ *last*, and the algorithm terminates with *found* still set to false.

Here's a simple illustration of binary search. Suppose the array A is indexed from 1 to 7 and contains sorted integer values as shown:

8	14	16	19	22	26	31
1	2	3	4	5	6	7

Figure 10.8
Binary search on a sorted array of integers invoked from a command button

```
Sub cmdBinSearch_Click ()
Dim target As Integer
Dim index As Integer
Dim found As Integer

   target = Val(InputBox$("Value to search for:"))
   found = False
   Call BinSearch(A(), target, index, found, LBound(A), UBound(A))
   If found <> False Then
      Picture1.Print "value found at position " & Str$(index)
   Else
      Picture1.Print "value not found"
   End If
End Sub

Sub BinSearch (A() As Integer, ByVal target As Integer,
    n As Integer, found As Integer, first As Integer,
    last As Integer)
'does binary search on sorted array A for target value
'returns position n of index in A where found

Dim middle As Integer

   If first <= last Then
      middle = (first + last)\2 'integer division to get midpoint
      If A(middle) = target Then
         n = middle
         found = True
      ElseIf A(middle) < target Then
         'search last half
         Call BinSearch(A(), target, n, found, middle + 1, last)
      Else
         'search first half
         Call BinSearch(A(), target, n, found, first, middle - 1)
      End If
   End If

End Sub
```

The target value is 22. Here's what happens. *First* and *last* are initially 1 and 7. *Middle* gets computed as (*first* + *last*)\2 = 4. The target value 22 gets compared with the $A(4) = 19$.

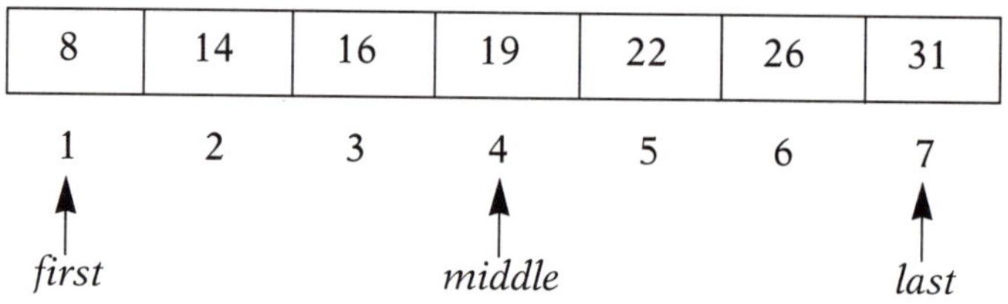

8	14	16	19	22	26	31
1	2	3	4	5	6	7

↑ *first*   ↑ *middle*   ↑ *last*

Because $A(4) < 22$, the argument corresponding to *first* gets set to *middle* + 1, so that on the next invocation of *BinSearch*, the picture is

8	14	16	19	22	26	31
1	2	3	4	5	6	7

                          ↑   ↑   ↑
                        first middle last

where $middle = (first + last)\backslash 2 = 6$. Now $A(6) > 22$, so the argument corresponding to *last* gets set to *middle* − 1 and *BinSearch* is invoked again. This time

8	14	16	19	22	26	31
1	2	3	4	5	6	7

                          ↑
                   first middle last

and the comparison $A(5) = 22$ is successful. The variable *found* is set to True and *n* is set to 5, the index where the target value was found.

If the target value is 25, then everything proceeds the same up to the point of comparing $A(5)$ against 25. Because $A(5) < 25$, the argument corresponding to *first* gets set to *middle* + 1 and *BinSearch* is invoked again.

8	14	16	19	22	26	31
1	2	3	4	5	6	7

                          ↑   ↑
                        last first

Now *first* has overtaken *last*, so the *BinSearch* procedure terminates with *found* still set to false.

To locate 22 in the above array, the target value had to be compared with $A(4)$, $A(6)$, and $A(5)$, a total of three comparisons. To locate 22 in the same array by using sequential search requires comparisons at $A(1)$, $A(2)$, $A(3)$, $A(4)$, and $A(5)$, a total of five comparisons. Binary search usually requires fewer comparisons than sequential search, and this difference is more pronounced the larger the array. Remember, however, that binary search does not apply unless the array is already sorted.

THOUGHTS ON PROGRAMMING

Algorithm Efficiency

The primary consideration when an algorithm is proposed as a solution to a problem is whether the algorithm correctly solves the problem. When the steps of the algorithm are carried out, will the algorithm behave properly for all possible input cases? For example, the problem of searching an array for a target value may be specified as follows:

> **1.** If the target value occurs within the array, the algorithm must return the index at which the target value occurs

If this is the only requirement in the problem, then an algorithm can behave in some ambiguous way for target values that are not in the array. But if a second requirement is added:

> **2.** If the target value does not occur, the algorithm must return some indication of this.

then to be sure the algorithm is correct, it is necessary to verify that it acts properly both for target values that are in the array and for target values that are not in the array.

So algorithm *correctness* is a primary concern. Suppose, however, that there are several correct algorithms for a given problem. Then algorithms are compared on the basis of other considerations such as their *efficiency*. "Efficiency" means what resources of time and space an algorithm consumes ("time" refers to how long the algorithm takes to execute, and "space" refers to how much memory is required to execute the algorithm).

Of the two algorithms that apply to the task of searching a sorted array, sequential search and binary search, it is claimed that binary search requires fewer comparisons than sequential search. Because comparison (of the target value against array values) is the major task done in searching, the number of comparisons required translates into an indication of an algorithm's time efficiency.

Suppose the array has n values in it. The number of comparisons required to search for a given target value is variable. The target value might be found in the first position searched. For either algorithm, this requires only one comparison and is a best-case scenario, one requiring the least amount of work. For either algorithm, a worst-case scenario occurs when the target value is not in the array at all, but the amount of work done for this scenario differs between the two algorithms.

For a sequential search the target value must be compared with every element in the list—A(1), A (2),..., A (n–1), A (n)—in order to conclude that the target value is not in the list. This requires n comparisons.

Now suppose the binary search algorithm is used. One comparison is done at the midpoint of the entire list, then one comparison is done at the midpoint of half of the list (either the front half or the back half), then one comparison at the midpoint of one quarter of the list. This process continues as long as the list can be cut in half. In the preceding example, in which the array had seven elements, the process was

7 elements (whole list)
7\2 = 3 elements (half list)
3\1 = 1 element (quarter list)

for a total of three comparisons. An eight-element list would require

8 elements (whole list)
8\2 = 4 elements (half list)
4\2 = 2 elements (quarter list)
2\2 = 1 element (eighth list)

for a total of four comparisons.

Now look at the worst case for a sorted array with 256 elements. Sequential search requires 256 comparisons to learn that the target is not in the array. Binary search requires working with successive lists of size.

256
128
64
32
16
8
4
2
1

for a total of 9 comparisons. Quite a significant difference. Hence in the worst case—and in many other cases—binary search is a more efficient algorithm than sequential search (provided, of course, that the data has been sorted).

Speaking of sorting, consider the only sorting algorithm that has been discussed, selection sort. What is its efficiency? Selection sort works by making a number of passes through the array, each time working with just the unsorted section. In the pseudocode of Figure 10.6, each iteration of the loop body represents a pass through the unsorted section of the array. If there are n elements in the array, then the loop executes n times (from the upper array index down to the lower array index). During each pass, two tasks are done:

Finding the maximum element in the unsorted section

Swapping it into its proper position

In discussing the work the algorithm does, these two tasks are considered separately. If a swap occurs on each pass and there are n passes, then a total of n swaps is done.

To find the maximum element in any one pass, the current maximum is set equal to the first element, and then every other element is compared with the current maximum. On the first pass, there are n elements in the unsorted section of the list; this requires $n-1$ comparisons with the current maximum to find the maximum. On the second pass, there are $n-1$ elements in the unsorted section; this requires $n-2$ comparisons to find the maximum. And so on. The number of comparisons on each pass gets smaller and smaller until it finally reaches 1. The total number of comparisons is

$n-1$
$n-2$
•
•
•
3
2
1

which turns out to add up to $n^2/2 + n/2$. What does this mean? On a 10-element array, selection sort requires $10^2/2 + 10/2 = 55$ comparisons and 10 swaps. On a 100-element array (10 times as large), selection sort requires 5050 comparisons and 100 swaps. This is much more than 10 times the work!

Other sorting algorithms require less work than selection sort, at least under certain circumstances, but are a little hard to understand.

Name: _____   Date Due: _____

LEARNING OBJECTIVES

- Using random numbers
- Using the Pset graphic method
- Implementing selection sort

LAB 10.2

1. ____ Open a new Visual Basic project.

   ____ Save the files as **sort.frm** and **sort.mak**.

2. This project does a visual animation of the selection sort algorithm at work. Overall, the plan is this: A large section of the form is set aside as a picture box. When the user clicks a button, an array is filled with random integer values, and these values are graphed as points in the picture box, where the height of the point represents its value. Clicking another button causes the selection sort algorithm to be implemented, and the progress of the algorithm is reflected in the position of the points in the picture box. The form layout is given here.

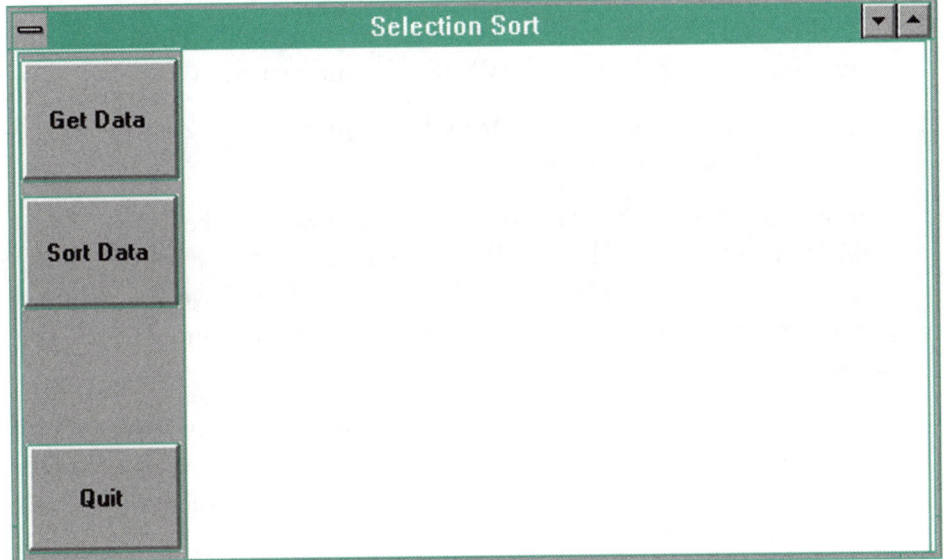

____ Change the caption of your form to "Selection Sort".

____ Put a picture box on the form of width 6000 twips and height 4000 twips (this picture box is the large blank area shown in the form layout).

____ Put a small picture box on the left of the form and make its background color gray.

___ Put three command buttons on this picture box and give them the captions shown.

___ Write the code for the Quit button, which exits the application program.

3. ___ In the declarations section of the form, declare a 100-element array of integers.

Using random numbers

___ Write the necessary code for the Get Data Click event procedure to fill the array with 100 random integers between 1 and 4000; remember that the picture box in which the data will be displayed is 4000 units high. (Check what the Help system has to say about the *Rnd* function in order to generate integer values in a certain range.) Remember to use the Randomize statement to get truly random values.

___ The last task of the Get Data button is to graph the random values in the picture box. This will be done by a form-level general procedure called *Grapher* that has an array as its one parameter. Make the last statement in the Get Data code a call to invoke *Grapher*, passing your array as the argument, then comment out this statement until the Grapher procedure is written. Run your program at this point. Use the Debug window to print one or two array values to make sure they all look correct.

4. ___ Now start on the code for the *Grapher* procedure. First, clear the picture box of any data. (Use the Cls method mentioned in Section 9.7.)

___ Next, set the picture box **DrawWidth property** to 2 so the points drawn can be seen more easily.

Using the Pset method

You have to give the (X, Y) coordinates of each point to be drawn. The X coordinate is the point's horizontal position relative to the left of the picture box. The picture box width is 6000 units, and you have 100 points to plot along the width. This means you plot the points 60 units apart, at X locations of 60, 120, 180, and so on.

The Y coordinate is the vertical position of the point relative to the top of the picture box. The Y distance is measured downward. As an example, suppose an array value of 3000 is to be drawn (see the following figure). What is the value of its Y coordinate?

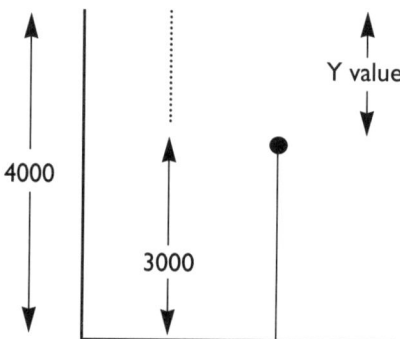

In general, given the array value, what do you do in order to find the Y coordinate?

___ What is the method to draw a single point? (See Section 9.7)

___ What is the object to which you want to apply this method?

___ Write code for the single For-Next loop that plots in the picture box all the points in the array. This completes the *Grapher* procedure.

___ Remove the comment from the call to the *Grapher* procedure in the Get Data command button and try your program. If all goes well, you see the initial data scattered in the picture box.

5. ___ Go to the Click event procedure for the Sort command button.

> **Implementing selection sort**

___ Declare a local variable *MaxPosition* to hold the maximum index value at each pass through the selection sort algorithm.

___ Declare a local variable *i* to be the array index marking the end of the unsorted section of the array.

___ Using the pseudocode of Figure 10.6 as a guide, write the loop for the body of the Sort Click procedure. Invoke a function *MaxIndex* (to be written later) to return the maximum index value, which is then assigned to *MaxPosition* The *MaxIndex* function has two arguments: the array and *i*. Use a procedure *Swap* (to be written later) to swap two elements in an array; this procedure has three arguments: the array, and the indices of the two array values to be swapped.

___ Add a third statement within the loop that invokes *Grapher*. This causes the data to be redrawn after every swap, so that the points represent the array as the sorted section grows from back to front.

6. ____ Write the *MaxIndex* function (see Figure 7.16 for ideas, but use a loop).

   ____ Write the *Swap* procedure.

   ____ Test your program. You can see the points representing the sorted section of the array as more and more of them accumulate from right to left until the array is completely sorted.

   ____ Try the Get Data button several times. It should produce a new set of data values each time.

   ____ Save your work.

7. (Extra credit)

   ____ Add another command button to the form with the caption "Step". The Step button does one pass through the selection sort algorithm each time it is clicked. (Hint: again use a local variable *i* as the array index marking the end of the unsorted section of the array. Declare *i* using the **Static** keyword; then *i* retains its value from one invocation to the next. By default, *i* is initially set to 0. Within the procedure, decide what to do on the basis of the value of *i*.

   ____ Test your code; if it is working property, each click of the Step button repaints the picture box with one more array value swapped into its correct position. You can anticipate before each click which (tallest) point will be moved to the right.

8. Save your work.

QuickCheck 10.2

Consider the following array, indexed from 1 to 5:

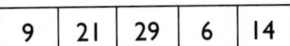

1. Describe the array after pass 1 of the selection sort.
2. Describe the array after pass 2 of the selection sort.
3. Altogether, how many comparisons are required to sort the entire array?

The sorted array is

| 6 | 9 | 14 | 21 | 29 |

4. If a binary search is done on this sorted array for a target value of 21, with which numbers is 21 compared?
5. If a binary search is done on this sorted array for a target value of 10, with which numbers is 10 compared?

10.7 Parallel arrays

Suppose your store sells a variety of products and you want to keep track of the dollar amount in sales per month for each product. You want to be able to see this data in two forms:

> Sorted alphabetically by product names, so that you can easily track how much each product is selling

> Sorted numerically by sales, so that you can easily see which products are selling well and which are generating less income for the store

And of course you want to know the total monthly sales. Figure 10.9 represents a small sample of typical data. Figure 10.10 shows the kind of output report you want for these data.

Espresso Italiani	1450.28
Kona Koffee Kup	1270.57
Café Au Lait Mix	890.37
Tea Totalers' Tonic	965.29
Juan Haldez Fresh Brewed	1672.84

Figure 10.9
Sample data for January store sales

It sounds like an array would be useful here; there is a collection of related items (various product names/sales), and you know how to sort an array. But if you try to view Figure 10.9 as an array with five elements, then how can you separate the product name and the sales amount? These are two different pieces of data; they must be treated separately because you

Figure 10.10
Output report for data in Figure 10.9

January Sales

Sales data sorted by product name

Café Au Lait Mix	$890.37
Espresso Italiani	$1450.28
Juan Haldez Fresh Brewed	$1672.84
Kona Koffee Kup	$1270.57
Tea Totalers' Tonic	$965.29

Sales data sorted by sales amount

Café Au Lait Mix	$890.37
Tea Totalers' Tonic	$965.29
Kona Koffee Kup	$1270.57
Espresso Italiani	$1450.28
Juan Haldez Fresh Brewed	$1672.84
Total Sales for the month	$6249.35

want to be able to sort on either one. Well, what if you view Figure 10.9 as a 2-D array with five rows and two columns? This won't work either. The product names are string data and the sales figures are numeric data. All the elements in an array must have the same data type. You can't treat the sales figures as strings that just happen to be numbers—unless you want to do a lot of work with the *Val* and *Str$* functions for the necessary conversions—because you have to do some arithmetic on those numbers in order to compute the total sales.

The solution is to use two 1-D arrays, a *Product* array containing string data (the product names) and a *Sales* array containing data of type Single (the sales figures). However, these two arrays cannot be treated as two completely independent arrays, or the connection between a product name and that product's sales is lost. A product name and that product's sales figures must always appear in the same relative locations in their respective arrays. Thus for any index *i*, *Sales(i)* always contains the sales figure for the *Product(i)* product. This relationship is expressed by saying that *Product* and *Sales* are **parallel arrays**.

When using parallel arrays, there is always a little extra work involved in preserving the relationship between the two arrays. For example, you sort the *Product* array in order to produce the output sorted by product name. Part of the sorting algorithm involves swapping elements within the *Product* array. If you swap elements 2 and 4 of the *Product* array, you need to swap elements 2 and 4 of the *Sales* array at the same time. Also, when you sort the *Sales* array to get the output sorted by sales, any rearranging of items in the *Sales* array must be reflected in the *Product* array.

Managing parallel arrays seems rather artificial, and all because of the restriction that arrays can contain only one data type. It would be nice if you could think of Figure 10.9 as a one-dimensional array of five items of "row" data type. Each item of "row" data type would contain two pieces of data (of different data types). Of course, you have to be able to access either piece of data in a row when needed. Fortunately, Visual Basic grants this wish by allowing you to define your own data types.

10.8 User-defined types

The standard data types in Visual Basic (Integer, Single, String, and so on) require no description within a Visual Basic program because the system already understands them. You can simply declare a variable to be type Single, and Visual Basic knows all about the kind of data that will be stored in that variable; you never have to say that data of type Single are decimal numbers falling within such and such a range. A **user-defined data type**, however, is a data type you are inventing. You must first describe the data type so that when you later declare a variable to be of that type, Visual Basic knows what kind of data will be stored there.

The description for a user-defined data type must be placed within a code module (a .BAS file), not within any form file. This gives the description global scope; a variable of that data type can then be declared anywhere in the program. A description for a user-defined data type that works for the product-sales example is

```
Type StoreData
    Product as String
    Sales as Single
End Type
```

This description alerts Visual Basic to the fact that any variable declared to be of type StoreData consists of two parts, a string part and a decimal numeric part. Be sure you understand that this code only describes the structure of potential variables; it does not declare any variables.

The general syntax for a **Type statement** is

> Type *Typename*
>   *ComponentName1* **As** *type*
>   *ComponentName2* **As** *type*
>   •
>   •
>   *ComponentNamek* **As** *type*
> End Type

The reserved words **Type** and **End Type** mark the beginning and end of the type description. The body of the type description consists of a list of component names and their data types. Any variable of a user-defined data type consists of multiple components that can be a variety of data types. Such a variable is another form of data structure, since the various components are presumably related and are organized as parts of a single whole.

Once the data type is described, variables of that type can be declared. For the StoreData data type, a variable declaration such as

```
Dim Store1 As StoreData
```

sets aside memory space for a string component and a numeric component making up the variable *Store1*. Values can then be assigned to these individual components by separate assignment statements:

```
Store1.Product = Espresso Italiani
Store1.Sales = 1450.28
```

Notice that a component of a user-defined variable is referenced by giving the variable name, a dot, then the component name.

Most of the time, you want to manipulate the separate components of a user-defined variable, to assign values to them (as with *Store1* above), print them out, or do calculations with them. Again, the way to reference an individual component is

VariableName.ComponentName

However, there are two occasions when you can use a user-defined variable as a whole. First, an assignment statement can be used to assign one user-defined variable to another. For example, you can do the following:

```
'Declare two variables of type StoreData
Dim Store1 As StoreData
Dim Store2 As StoreData

'Assign values to the components of one variable
Store1.Product = Espresso Italiani
Store1.Sales = 1450.28

'Assign the same values to the components of Store2
Store2 = Store1
```

After the last assignment statement, all the components of *Store2* have the same values as the corresponding components of *Store1*, so *Store2* has the same product name and sales figure. Each component value has been put into place by means of a single assignment statement.

Second, a variable of user-defined type can be passed as an argument to a procedure. Thus you can write a procedure called *PrintValues* as follows:

```
Sub PrintValues(Row As StoreData)
'prints the components of Row

    Picture1.Print = Row.Product
    Picture1.Print = Row.Sales

End Sub
```

and invoke it by

```
Call PrintValues(Store1)
```

The result is to print both the product name and the sales figure for *Store1*. Although the variable is passed in its entirety as a single argument, once inside the procedure you can access all the individual components.

Variables of a user-defined type are especially helpful when they are collected into an array. You can declare an array whose elements are of a user-defined data type, just as you declare arrays whose elements are any standard data type. Assuming that the data type StoreData has been declared, then the declaration

```
Static MonthData(1 to 5) As StoreData
```

declares an array of five rows. Each row could look like one of the rows in Figure 10.9. This would achieve the goal of representing this figure as a one-dimensional array of "rows" where the individual components of any row can be accessed. The value of the Sales component of the third row, for example, is represented by

`MonthData(3).Sales`

MonthData(3) is the name of a single element in the array, which is of type StoreData. *MonthData*(3).*Sales* picks out the Sales component of that array element.

To produce the desired output then requires sorting the array based on either the Product component or the Sales component. Array elements can be exchanged as part of the sorting process with no fear of a product name and its sales figure ever getting separated, as they are both components of a single array element.

The next lab implements these ideas. Because a sorting task is involved, you can modify much of the code developed in Lab 10.2 rather than having to write code entirely from scratch.

Name: _____   Date Due: _____

LAB 10.3

LEARNING OBJECTIVES

- Defining user-defined data types
- Using arrays of user-defined type
- Modifying existing code

1. ____ Open the Visual Basic project *sales.mak*. The form is filled with a picture box used to display output. In the Form_Load procedure, two arrays have been loaded with the data of Figure 10.9. (This is a somewhat artificial device to save you the work of doing data entry. The disadvantages of maintaining these data values in parallel arrays have been discussed.)

2. ____ Create a code module and save the file as *sales.bas*.

   ____ Within the code module, use the Type statement to describe an appropriate user-defined data type. **[Defining user-defined data type]**

   ____ In the declarations section of the form, declare an array of this user-defined type.

   ____ Add code at the end of the Form_Load procedure that fills this array with the given data. **[Array of user-defined type]**

3. ____ Write a general procedure *PictureHeader* that first clears the picture box, puts the title "January Sales" in the center near the top of the picture box in some large and fancy type font, and then resets the picture box font in preparation for the rest of the output. (Hint: If the first three lines of this procedure are

```
Picture1.Cls
Picture1.CurrentX = 2700
Picture1.CurrentY = 500
```

what is the effect?)

   ____ Finish the *PictureHeader* code. *PictureHeader* has no parameters.

   ____ Call the *PictureHeader* procedure from the Form_Load procedure.

_____ Test your code; what happens at this point when you run the program?

4. _____ Set up a menu structure on your form. A File menu has two submenus, Print Report and Exit. A Report Option menu has three submenus, Sort by Product, Sort by Sales, and Sales Total.

_____ Write the code for the Exit menu pick.

_____ Write the code for the Sales Total menu pick, which computes the total sales and displays it near the bottom of the picture box (see Figure 10.10).

Modifying existing code 1

5. In order to sort your array, you need a *Swap* procedure. Look at the *Swap* procedure you wrote for **sort.mak** in Lab 10.2. What changes are needed?

_____ Copy the code from **sort.mak** to the general section of your **sales.frm** file. While you are at it, copy the *MaxIndex* function also.

_____ Make the necessary changes in the *Swap* procedure.

Modifying existing code 2

6. You want the *MaxIndex* function to be able to do double duty and to find either the maximum index among the product names or the maximum index among the sales amounts. Explain how you can add another parameter to the function and then modify the body of the function so you can use the code for either purpose. (Hint: In the body of the function, a decision on one of two courses of action needs to be made.)

_____ Write the code for function *MaxIndex* using the extra parameter.

7. ___ Create a general procedure called *Sorter* that has two parameters, the array of user-defined type, and a second parameter that indicates which component is to be used for sorting.

   ___ Copy the body of your code for the Sort command button from Lab 10.2 into *Sorter*. Make the minor changes needed to accommodate your new *MaxIndex* function, the fact that you are working with a different array, and the fact that you are not using the *Grapher* procedure.

8. ___ The Sort-by-Product menu pick invokes your *Sorter* procedure and passes it appropriate arguments, calls *PictureHeader*, writes a heading for the data, and then uses a loop to write the output for data sorted by product. Write the code to accomplish this.

   ___ Test your program at this point.

9. What are the three changes needed to the Sort-by-Product code in order to sort by sales?

   ___ Write the code for the Sort-by-Sales menu pick.

   ___ Test your program.

10. The only remaining task is to implement the Print menu pick, which prints a hard copy report similar to Figure 10.10. Here is a rough pseudocode outline for the first half of the code.

    > print a fancy header
    > invoke the *Sorter* procedure to sort by product
    > print the header for the data sorted by product
    > print the data sorted by product

    Fill in the remaining pseudocode steps.

    ___ Write the code to print the hard-copy output. To test your program, be sure you have a printer on-line.

    ___ Save your work.

QuickCheck 10.3

1. True or false: Parallel arrays are two or more arrays that are both horizontal or both vertical.
2. True or false: The Type statement declares variables that have multiple components of different types.

Given the Type statement

```
Type MyType
    Title As String
    Quantity As Integer
End Type
```

3. Write the declaration for a variable *Stock* of type MyType.
4. If *Stock* is a variable of type MyType, write a statement to add 3 to the Quantity component of *Stock*.
5. Suppose *Portfolio* is an array declared by

    ```
    Dim Portfolio(10 to 20) As MyType
    ```

    Write a statement to assign "ATT" to the Title component of the third element in this array.

Review Questions

1. In what sense is an array a generalization of a list box?
2. An array declaration must include which three pieces of information?
3. The declaration for an array does not include a data type for the array itself, only for its elements. Explain why this is not a problem.
4. The declaration

    ```
    Dim Table(3,4) As Integer
    ```

    describes a two-dimensional array with how many elements?
5. The declaration of a fixed-sized array within a procedure requires the use of the _____ keyword.
6. Explain the advantage of a dynamic array.
7. What is the purpose of the ReDim statement?
8. List three options for getting data into an array.
9. To use a For-Next loop to process array elements, the counter variable in the For-Next loop should match the array _____ values.
10. Give the declaration for an array that can be used to contain the following set of data:

    ```
    3  5  2
    1  7  6
    ```

11. Two of the most common data processing tasks are _____ and _____.

12. What is true at the end of the first pass about an array being sorted by the selection sort algorithm?

13. Why does the data have to be sorted in order to use the binary search algorithm?

14. Explain, using Figure 10.8, why binary search is a recursive algorithm.

15. A sorted array contains the values

    34 37 42 48 51 62 75 83 95 103

    If a binary search is done on this array with a target value of 75, with which numbers is 75 compared?

16. For the values in the previous question, what is the maximum number of comparisons required to learn that a target value is not in the list?

17. Suppose the selection sort algorithm is run on an array of 20 items. How many swaps and how many comparisons are required to sort the array?

18. Suppose the selection sort algorithm is run on an array of 20 items that are already sorted. How many swaps and how many comparisons does the algorithm do?

19. The entries in an array of user-defined data type have both Double and String components. Explain why this does not violate the requirement that all array entries be the same data type.

20. You need to keep track of your employees' names, Social Security numbers, and hourly pay rates. Give a type statement for an appropriate user-defined data type.

Exercises

For these exercises, assume the following declarations have been made in appropriate places:

```
Type RowType
    Site As String
    Percent As Integer
    Date As String
End Type

Dim Stuff(1 To 10) As Integer
Dim Box(1 To 5, 1 To 5) As Double
Dim Row As RowType
Dim Rows(1 To 100) As RowType
Dim i As Integer
Dim j As Integer
Dim Temp As Integer
```

Reading code
1. What is the effect when the following code is executed?

   ```
   For j = 1 To 10
      Stuff(j) = Stuff(j) + 1
   Next j
   ```

2. What is the effect when the following code is executed?

   ```
   For j = 1 To 5
      Temp = Stuff(j)
      Stuff(j) = Stuff(10 - (j-1))
      Stuff(10 - (j-1)) = Temp
   Next j
   ```

3. Describe the array *Box* after execution of the following code:

   ```
   For i = 1 To 5
      For j = 1 To 5
         Box(i, j) = 1.0
      Next j
   Next i
   For i = 1 To 5
      Box(i, i) = 2.0
   Next i
   ```

4. What does the following statement do?

   ```
   Picture1.Print Row.Site
   ```

5. What is the result after execution of the following code?

   ```
   Temp = 0
   For i = 1 To 100
      Temp = Temp + Rows(i).Percent
   Next i
   Picture1.Print Temp / 100
   ```

Writing code
6. Write code to set every entry in array *Stuff* equal to 20.
7. Write code to put the following values in the array *Box*:

1.0	0.0	0.0	0.0	0.0
1.0	1.0	0.0	0.0	0.0
1.0	1.0	1.0	0.0	0.0
1.0	1.0	1.0	1.0	0.0
1.0	1.0	1.0	1.0	1.0

   (Hint: First initialize the entire array to 0.0 and then change some of the entries to 1.0; these two tasks can be accomplished with two sets of nested For-Next loops.)

8. Write statements that assign the values "North", 15, and "10/18/96" to the Site, Percent, and Date components, respectively, of the variable *Row*.

9. Write code that prints in a picture box the three components in the fifth element of the array *Rows*.

10. Write the declarations for an array of 50 entries indexed from 51 to 100, where each entry has an integer component called Number and a string component called Nickname.

Exploring further

11. The following array elements are to be sorted using the selection sort algorithm:

    17   5   24   2   51   33   9   47

    Write what the array looks like after each pass.

12. Rewrite the pseudocode of Figure 10.6 so that the array gets put into sorted order from front to back, rather than from back to front.

13. An array containing 1000 elements is sorted on a particular computer using an implementation of selection sort. The sort takes 1.5 minutes. On the same machine, using the same algorithm, you will sort an array containing 10,000 elements. What is your best estimate of how long it will take?

    a. 3 minutes
    b. 15 minutes
    c. 150 minutes

14. Is there any way to modify the selection sort algorithm so that it stops once the array is sorted? (Hint: Think about a way to modify the "find maximum" algorithm so that it counts how many times *CurrentMaxIndex* gets changed.)

15. If the following array elements are searched for the value "thyme" using binary search, with which strings is "thyme" compared?

    anise   basil   clove   ginger   mustard   nutmeg   saffron   thyme

Projects

1. Modify your ***sort.mak*** project from Lab 10.2 so that the numbers are sorted in decreasing order, with the sorted section growing from left to right.

2. Modify your ***grade.mak*** project from Lab 10.1. In this version, collect the user input for five grades as a string in a single text box (option 1 as described in Section 10.3). Be sure to prompt the user to separate the grades with blanks or commas so that your program can break the string down into the separate quiz grades.

3. This project maintains data on household expenditures for one month. The user can enter the following data about an expenditure: the amount, the date (1-31), and the category (food, rent, automobile, insurance, entertainment). The user can enter as many expenditures as desired, but not more than one for any given date-category combination. At any time, the user can ask to see:

Total expenses for any one date

Total expenses for any one category

Total expenses for the month

Do both high-level and low-level design, and then implement the program. (Hint: Think about the data structure to use; it seems natural to organize the expenditures in a table format.)

4. The output in project **sales.mak** from Lab 10.3 is displayed in a picture box on the form. The output for either the data sorted by product name or the data sorted by sales amount is basically tabular, as in Figure 10.10. Indeed, the data is stored as an array of user-defined type elements (the rows), each of which has two components (the columns).

The Visual Basic **grid control** can be used as a nice mechanism to display tabular data. Open your **sales.mak** project, and save the files as **sales2.frm** and **sales2.mak**. Add a grid control to the picture box on your form. The Toolbox icon for the grid control is shown here. (If you don't see this icon in your Toolbox, make sure that GRID.VBX is one of the files in your project. If not, use Add File from the Visual Basic File menu; the GRID.VBX file can probably be found in C:\WINDOWS\SYSTEM.) Set the following properties of the grid control:

BackColor	White	(use the color palette)
Cols	2	(number of columns)
FixedCols	0	(number of columns used to label rows)
FixedRows	1	(number of rows used to label columns)
Height	1605	
HighLight	0	(active cell is not highlighted)
Rows	6	(number of rows)
ScrollBars	0	(none)
Width	4050	

Add the following code, which sets up the grid control size and fixed headings, to the Form_Load procedure:

```
'adjust grid control
Grid1.ColWidth(0) = 3000
Grid1.ColWidth(1) = 1000

For i = 0 To 4
   Grid1.RowHeight(i) = 250
Next i

'enter fixed headings in grid control
Grid1.Row = 0
Grid1.Col = 0
Grid1.Text = "Product"
Grid1.Col = 1
Grid1.Text = "Sales"
Grid1.ColAlignment(1) = 1
```

Write a Grid Display procedure that loads the data from your sorted array into the grid cells. You assign a value to a cell by setting the Text property of the grid control to the desired value. Notice that this says nothing about which cell you want this value to appear in. Before you set the Text property, you must identify the cell by setting the grid's **Row** and **Col properties** (rows and columns in a grid are both numbered from 0). Invoke the GridDisplay procedure at the end of the code for both the product name sort and the sales amount sort (and of course get rid of the previous code that printed the output directly in the picture box). The total sales can still be written to the picture box.

5. Modify your *sales.mak* project from Lab 10.3 to include a stock number (a three-digit integer) for each product. Allow sorting by stock number. Also implement a binary search procedure that allows the user to search the data for a particular stock number; if found, the product name and sales amount are displayed. Add more data to the Form_Load procedure for a better test of your binary search procedure.

CHAPTER 11

Files; Message Boxes

KEY POINTS

- Files provide permanent storage for arbitrarily large quantities of data.
- Visual Basic supports both sequential and random-access files; each type of file is used in a particular way, and each has advantages and disadvantages.
- The Common Dialog control object provides an easy way for a program to let the user select a file name.
- A message box is a form of dialog box that gives the user information and provides for limited user input through clicking on a choice of command buttons.
- Anticipated run-time errors can be "trapped," and flow of control can be routed to error handling code.

11.1 Why use files?

So far, any data used by a Visual Basic program have been obtained entirely within the program. Data items have usually been collected by user input via text boxes or input boxes. When the program terminates, these data items are gone; they must be entered again when the program next executes. The aim is to find a way to create and use **persistent data**, data that "persist" from one execution of the program to the next so that they do not have to be entered at each execution.

In two projects, data persistence has been achieved, but only in a very inflexible way. In the case of the *library.mak* project of Lab 8.3, five separate forms are used to hold data about five books, and the data items are "hard coded" into the project by setting the Text property of text boxes on the book forms. The data items are persistent, but any changes to the data must be made by the programmer using the Properties window in Visual Basic design mode, not by the user. In the *sales.mak* project of Lab 10.3, the data items are "hard coded" into the project by the Form_Load procedure that enters product names and sales amounts into two arrays. Again, the data items are persistent but only the programmer can change them, in this case by changing the code.

What if you have a body of data that you want to be persistent from one execution to the next, yet you want to give the user the ability during program execution to change some portion of it? To solve this problem, keep the data in an **external data file**, a file that contains data but is separate from the Visual Basic files that are part of the project. The data file is stored on a hard drive or diskette. Then when the Visual Basic program executes, it reads data from the file into memory, that is, into variables or text boxes or list boxes or arrays. The program can be written to allow the user not only to process the existing data but also to modify the data, add new data, and so on, and save the resulting changes in the data file, where they are available for the next program execution.

So one reason to use external files is to achieve data persistence. Another is to deal with large amounts of data. The amount of memory available to a Visual Basic program is limited; hence there is a limit on the maximum size of an array or a list box. Suppose there are simply too many data items to read all of them into, say, an array. (The data file consists of all the names and addresses of General Motors stockholders, for example, or all the entries on Federal Form 1040 tax returns for 1996. These are huge files.) Then a program to process these data items must repeatedly access the file, bring some of the data into memory, process it, and put the result back out in the file.

In order to use files, you must know how Visual Basic reads data from files and writes data to files. If the file is small, the program can read all the data into memory at one time, process them, and then write all the data back to the file. If the file contains more data than can be stored in memory at one time, this reading, processing, and writing cycle takes place multiple times during program execution.

You also need to know how to create a data file in the first place. This can be done within a Visual Basic program or by a different piece of software, depending on the type of file.

11.2 Types of Visual Basic files

Visual Basic supports three types of files: *sequential*, *random-access*, and *binary*. In a **sequential file**, data values are read from the file one at a time in sequential order. This means that the program begins reading at the beginning of the file and at any time can read only the next item in the file. If you want the tenth data value in the file, you must first read (and ignore) the nine preceding values. This is similar to an audio cassette tape, which you must start at the beginning and fast-forward to some particular spot. Sequential files are text files, so they can be created by a text editor like Windows Notepad, as well as by a Visual Basic program. As an example, a sequential file containing the data for the *sales.mak* project looks like Figure 11.1 and could be created using Notepad.

Figure 11.1
Sequential file for *sales.mak* data

```
"Espresso Italiani", 1450.28
"Kona Koffee Kup", 1270.57
"Cafe Au Lait Mix", 890.37
"Tea Totalers' Tonic", 965.29
"Juan Haldez Fresh Brewed", 1672.84
```

In a **random-access file** (also known as a **relative file**), data can be accessed (read) from any point in the file. If your program wants the tenth data value, it can directly access that value without having to read the preceding nine values first. This is similar to an audio CD, on which you can pick out any particular song without having to fast-forward past anything.

This ease of access is possible only by requiring that data be stored in a rigid format. A random-access file is not simply a text file, and it can't be created by a text editor.

A **binary file** stores groups of bits that are just dumped out from memory. There is no organization imposed on them, and any meaning attached to them must be managed by the program that reads the file. Binary files won't be mentioned again in this book.

Whatever the file type, a file must be *opened* before it can be used, and it must be *closed* after it has been used. **Opening a file** identifies the file to be opened by specifying the file name and the path (that is, which drive and directory the file is in), indicates the type of file to be opened (sequential, random access, or binary), assigns an integer number by which the file is referenced throughout the rest of the program, and establishes a communication link between the program and the file. **Closing a file** closes that communication link. So the program closes the file only when it has no more use for the file.

11.3 Opening and closing sequential files

A sequential file is opened in one of three modes, Output, Append, or Input, depending on the intended use for the file. Opening the file in **Output mode** means that you intend to write data into the file. In fact, you will create the file from scratch, because if the file previously existed, all its data are destroyed when it is opened in Output mode. If the file did not previously exist, an empty file is created, ready to receive data.

Suppose, for example, that you are writing a Visual Basic program to create the data file shown in Figure 11.1, and you want the file to be called SALES.TXT and to be located on the C drive in the MYSTUFF subdirectory. An appropriate Open statement is

```
Open "C:\MYSTUFF\SALES.TXT" For Output As #1
```

This creates an empty file SALES.TXT (or empties an existing file of that name) and leaves it ready to receive values. The "As #1" associates the integer 1 with this file. When the program has no further use for the file, the statement

```
Close #1
```

closes the file.

An existing file to which more data are to be added is opened in **Append mode**. If the SALES.TXT file already exists and the program will add additional data, the appropriate Open statement is

```
Open "C:\MYSTUFF\SALES.TXT" For Append As #1
```

New data can be added only at the end of a sequential file; opening For Append opens the file and moves past existing data, so the file is ready for additional data to be added at its end. If the specified file does not exist, an empty file with that name is created; this is the same effect as using Output mode. Be careful, however, not to Open For Output a file with existing data to which you intend to append new data at the end; recall that opening For Output destroys the existing data.

An existing sequential file from which data values will be read must be opened in **Input mode**, as in

```
Open "C:\MYSTUFF\SALES.TXT" For Input As #1
```

This opens the file at the first data value so that values can be read sequentially from the file. Attempting to open a nonexistent file For Input results in a "File not found" error message.

Sequential files can be opened for only one purpose at a time. If you have opened a file to write to it (For Append or For Open), you cannot read from that file without first closing it and then opening it For Input.

11.4 Common Dialog control

In order to open a data file, the program must know the file name and path. If this is written directly in the code, as in the preceding examples, then there is a potential problem. Suppose the Visual Basic program with these Open statements was written on a machine with a subdirectory MYSTUFF because that's where the programmer kept all his or her files. Then the program and the data file get moved to another machine that doesn't have this subdirectory. A "Path not found" error occurs when the program executes. The user should always be given the option of saying where an existing data file resides and what the file name is, as well as where to put a new data file and what to name the new file.

The **file specification** (file name and path) is just a text string. The Visual Basic program can collect user input for the file specification in a text box, and then use the text of that text box in the Open statement. An Open statement of the form

```
Open txtGetFile.Text For Output As #1
```

is perfectly legal. But in the spirit of the GUI interface, Visual Basic allows the user to point and click rather than type the file name.

The file specification in the Open statement can be obtained by using a truly remarkable control from the Toolbox called the **Common Dialog** control, with the icon shown.[1] Like the Timer control, the Common Dialog control can be placed anywhere on the form at design time because it does not appear when the program is executing.

The Common Dialog control has a run-time-only property called Action that can be set to several different values. When code to set the value of the Action property is executed, any of several different dialog boxes appears, depending on the value that Action was given. These include dialog boxes for specifying the name and path to save a file, for defining a custom color, for selecting options for printing, and so on. Of interest here is that setting the Action property to 1 causes the Open dialog box to appear, as shown in Figure 11.2a. Notice that in Figure 11.2a, there is a "filter" set that says to list only files of type text, that is, files with extension .TXT. A .TXT

---

[1] If this icon does not appear in your Toolbox, make sure that the file CMDIALOG.VBX appears in your Project window. If it is missing, it can be added by using Add File from the Visual Basic File menu. The file can probably be found in C:\WINDOWS\SYSTEM. In addition, Visual Basic programs using the Common Dialog control need both the files CMDIALOG.VBX and COMMDLG.DLL from the WINDOWS\SYSTEM subdirectory, so include these files along with the .EXE file for your program.

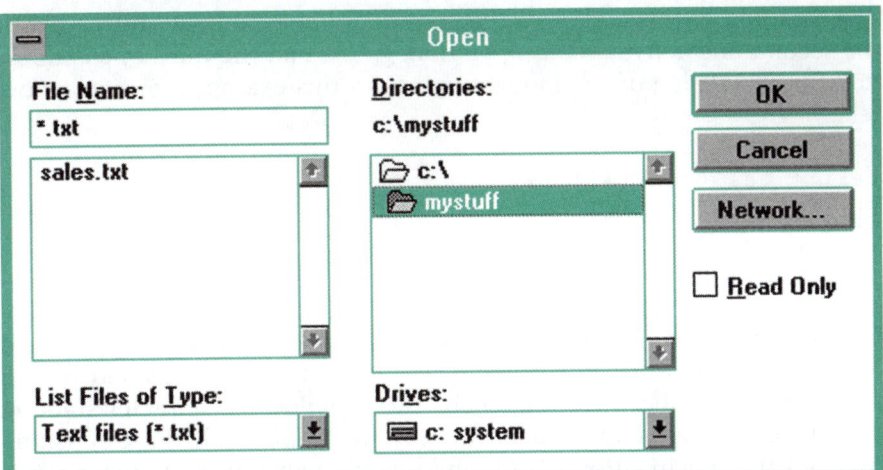

(a)

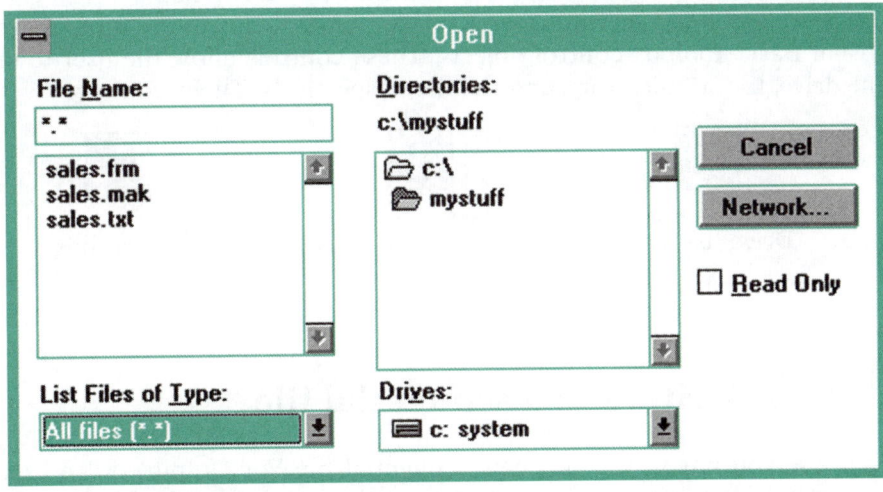

(b)

Figure 11.2
Open dialog box

extension is likely for a sequential file name, and narrowing the choices makes it easier for the user to find the appropriate file. The pull-down list under "List Files of Type:" allows the user to ask to see all files; choosing this option results in Figure 11.2b.

If an existing file is being opened, the user can select the file name (after perhaps changing the drive and directory through the dialog box). If a new file is being created, the user can enter the file name to be used. In either case, the user's choice becomes the value of the common dialog control's **Filename property**, and this property can be used as the file specification in the Open statement.

The following code fragment opens For Output whatever file the user specifies in the Open dialog box.

```
cmdialog1.Filter = "Text files (*.txt)|*.txt|
    All files(*.*)|*.*"
cmdialog1.Action = 1
Open cmdialog1.Filename For Output As #1
```

The first line of this code sets the common dialog control's **Filter property**, the second line activates the Open dialog box, and the third opens the specified file. The value of the Filter property in this example consists of two filters,

```
Text files (*.txt)|*.txt
All files (*.*)|*.*
```

separated by a vertical line. (The vertical line is probably shown on your keyboard as |.) Each filter comes in two parts, also separated by a vertical line. The first part of a filter is the text that appears in the dialog box's drop-down list box for the type of file (see Figure 11.2). The second part is the actual file name specification, where "*" is a wildcard character standing for any string of characters. Therefore any file name with the extension TXT matches the specification *.TXT, and any file name at all matches the specification *.*. The first filter listed is the default that appears when the dialog box opens, and the second is available on the pull-down list.

The Common Dialog control combines features of three separate Visual Basic Toolbox control objects. These controls allow the user to select the drive, the subdirectory, and the file, respectively. Their icons are

Drive list box   Directory list box   File list box

11.5 Writing to a sequential file

Suppose you have opened a new sequential file For Output, or an existing sequential file For Append, and you want to write data to the file. Recall that the only choice is to write new data at the end of the file, either after existing data in the case of Append mode or at the end of an empty file (after nothing) in the case of Output mode. The examples of this section write to new files using Open For Output; adding data to the end of an existing file using Open For Append works exactly the same way.

Data can be written to a sequential file using either the Write # statement or the Print # statement. The primary use for files is to store (possibly large) amounts of data that frequently are repetitive in nature. The file of Figure 11.1 is typical. Each line of the file is called a **record** and consists of related data items called **fields**. In Figure 11.1, each record contains two fields, a product name and the sales figure for that product. In that file, records are formatted by separating fields within a record by commas and enclosing string data within quotes. This common way to format data files is called **comma-delimited file format**. The advantage of storing data in a comma-delimited file is that many other applications, such as spreadsheets and database management software, can make use of data stored in such a format.

The **Write # statement** produces a comma-delimited file. Each Write # statement produces one line in the file, that is, one record. The general form of the Write # statement is

Write #*filenumber, expression list*

Here "filenumber" is the integer identification for the file that was assigned by the Open statement, and the expression list is the list of data for the record fields. The file of Figure 11.1 can be created by the following code:

```
cmdialog1.Filter = "Text files (*.txt)|*.txt| ↵
 ↳ All files (*.*)|*.*"

cmdialog1.Action = 1
Open cmdialog1.Filename For Output As #2

Write #2, "Espresso Italiani",1450.28
Write #2, "Kona Koffee Kup",1270.57
Write #2, "Cafe Au Lait Mix",890.37
Write #2, "Tea Totalers' Tonic",965.29
Write #2, "Juan Haldez Fresh Brewed",1672.84

Close #2
```

Of course, this "hard codes" the data and only creates this particular file. A more flexible approach uses the declarations

```
Dim ProductName As String
Dim SalesAmount As Single
Dim i As Integer
```

and then includes the following statements between the Open and Close statements:

```
For i = 1 To 5
   ProductName = InputBox$("Give the product name")
   SalesAmount = Val(InputBox$("Give the sales amount for ↵
    ↳ this product"))
   Write #2, ProductName, SalesAmount
Next i
```

When the record is written to the file, the Write # statement supplies the quote marks around the string quantity *ProductName*, the comma between the two fields, and the carriage return/line feed at the end of the record. The field values for the Write # statement can be obtained from text boxes as well as from input boxes.

A still more flexible approach is to obtain the number of products from the user and make the file an arbitrary size:

```
NumberOfProducts = Val(txtNumberProducts.Text)
For i = 1 To NumberOfProducts
   ProductName = InputBox$("Give the product name")
   SalesAmount = Val(InputBox$("Give the sales amount for ↵
    ↳ this product"))
   Write #2, ProductName, SalesAmount
Next i
```

As will be seen when how to read values from a file is discussed, it is convenient to know how many records are in the file. You can put a first record, called a **control record**, in the file that has a different format than all the others and contains just the number of other records in the file. To do this, insert the statement

```
Write #2, NumberOfProducts
```

just before the For-Next loop in the preceding section of code.

Again, sequential files are just text files and can be created using Notepad or some other text editor. Having a Visual Basic program create the file, however, ensures that the file format is correct.

Using the **Print # statement** to write to a file is rather like using the Print method to print to a picture box or to the printer. Whereas the Write # statement supplies comma-delimited formatting automatically, formatting with the Print # statement is controlled via Tabs, commas for zone printing, semicolons for concatenation, and so on, just as the Print method controls formatting in a picture box or on a printed page. The general form is

```
Print #filenumber, expression list
```

Notice the comma that must precede the expression list (the Print method has no such comma).

For example, suppose file #1 has been opened For Output. If *greeting* is a string variable containing the string "hello", txtUserName is a text box in which the user has entered the name "Milo", and *X* is an integer variable with the value 17, then

```
Print #1, Tab(18); greeting, txtUserName.Text; "The End"
Print #1,
Print #1; X + 2; "Really the end"
```

writes three lines of output to the file. The second Print # statement has an empty expression list and puts a blank line in the file; the comma must be present even though the expression list is empty.

After running the Visual Basic program containing this code, you can use Notepad to open the file that was created. Figure 11.3 shows what you see, with an extra "ruler line" added so you can check the spacing. The "hello" string begins in column 18 because of Tab(18), which says go to column 18, followed by the semicolon, which says to concatenate the next item. "Milo" begins in column 29 because the comma between *greeting* and txtUserName says to use zone printing. The next zone begins in column 29. The semicolon between txtUserName and "The End" again says to concatenate. In the third line, the space preceding 19 is for the (understood) positive sign, and the space behind 19 is the trailing space for numeric data. No quote marks have been supplied around the string data.

Figure 11.3
Contents of text file written with Print # statements

```
1234567890123456789012345678901234567890
                 hello          MiloThe End
 19 Really the end
```

In this example, the small string that was the Text property of a text box got written to the file as one of several pieces of output. However, the entire contents of a large, multiline text box, including any carriage returns, is contained in the Text property of the text box and is written to a file by the statement

```
Print #1, txtTextStuff.Text
```

The file now contains a duplicate of all the text in the text box, which may be a form letter or a memo—some body of text the user wants to keep and retrieve later.

11.6 Reading from a sequential file

Suppose a data file has been created, and a Visual Basic program needs to read data from the file. There are three different ways to read data from a sequential file that has been opened in Input mode, using the Input # or Line Input # statements, or the *Input$* function. Suppose the file is a comma-delimited file of records (created perhaps by using the Write # statement). The easiest way to read data from such a file is to use the **Input # statement**, probably within a loop to march through the records in the file. The syntax of the Input # statement is

```
Input #filenumber, variable list
```

The Input # statement goes through the file sequentially and matches the next data item in the file with the next variable in the variable list. String data in the file (recognizable by the double quotes) must match up with a string variable and numeric data in the file must match up with a numeric variable. Values in the data file can have been placed there directly from a control property (like the text of a text box) using the Write # statement, but values read from the data file by the Input # statement can only be read into variables and then, if desired, copied into control properties.

If the end of the file is reached while an Input # statement is executing and there are still unfilled variables in the variable list, an error message occurs. But if there are more data items left in the file after the variables in the list have all been filled, no error message occurs. Any subsequent reads from the file just pick up the next value and go on from there.

To read the data from a file that looks like Figure 11.1, do a series of Input # statements. In the original **sales.mak** program, the data were stored in two parallel arrays and then copied into an array of user-defined type. The parallel arrays can be skipped and the data just read directly into the components of the user-defined type array. Recall that the declarations were

```
'Declared in a module
Type StoreData
    Product As String
    Sales As Single
End Type

'Declared on the form
Dim MonthData(1 To 5) As StoreData
```

Now in the Form_Load procedure (after putting a Common Dialog control on the form), you can use

```
cmdialog1.Filter = "Text files (*.txt)|*.txt|
    All files (*.*)|*.*"
cmdialog1.Action = 1
Open cmdialog1.Filename For Input As #1
Dim i As Integer
For i = 1 To 5
    Input #1, MonthData(i).product, MonthData(i).sales
Next i
```

If the user, when creating the file, was allowed to enter an arbitrary number of records, then this code must be changed to accommodate an arbitrary-size file. (This is assuming the file is small enough to load into memory. Actually, **sales.mak** has other restrictions on the size of the file because the data were printed in a picture box on the form, so if the file is very big, the data don't fit.) It may be possible to learn how big the file is by asking the user, or, if the file was created with a control record, by doing one read from the input file. Then this information is used to redimension the array and set the upper limit on the For-Next loop.

If it is not possible to learn the number of records in the file, the Visual Basic *EOF* function can be used. This function returns True when the last data item in the file has been read (the *"End Of File"* has been reached). If there are more data items in the file, this function returns False; hence if there are more data items in the file, the expression Not EOF(1) is true. So the array size can be set to some *Limit* value, which, it is hoped, is big enough to accommodate the entire file. The file is then read using the following code, where *MaxSize* stores the number of records read into the array:

```
MaxSize = 1
Do While Not (EOF(1)) And (MaxSize <= Limit)
    Input #1, MonthData(MaxSize).product, MonthData
        (MaxSize).sales
    MaxSize = MaxSize + 1
Loop

MaxSize = MaxSize - 1
```

This says to keep reading values from the file as long as there are more values in the file, that is, as long as Not (EOF(1)), and as long as the array size hasn't been exceeded, that is, *MaxSize <= Limit*. *MaxSize* is increased within the loop body in anticipation of reading the next record, but if the next record is not read and the loop is exited, either because the file contains no more records or because *Limit* has been exceeded, the value of *MaxSize* must be reduced by 1.

In addition to the Input # statement, there are two other ways to read data from a sequential file. The **Line Input # statement** reads one line of a text file at a time (everything in the line up to, but not including, a carriage return) and stores it. The syntax is

`Line Input #`*filenumber, variable*

where "variable" is a string variable. A text file that was created with carriage returns can be reconstructed on a line-by-line basis, except that the carriage returns/line feeds have to be written into the code.

If an entire text box is written to a file using the

`Print #1, txtTextStuff.Text`

statement discussed in the previous section, it can be retrieved in its entirety by the *Input$* function. The *Input$* function has two arguments, the number of characters to be read from the file and the file number. The number of characters in an open file can be found by using the *LOF* (Length Of File) function, which has the file number as its single argument. Hence

`txtFileStuff.Text = Input$(LOF(1), 1)`

reads all characters in the file—including commas, carriage returns, line feeds, quotation marks, and assigns the resulting string to the text box txtFileStuff. The text box then contains an exact copy of what it originally contained.

You can now open and close, and write to and read from, sequential files. For a file of data records, you can add new records (at the end of the file), and read a data record (the next record in the file). What hasn't been discussed are two other likely operations: what if you want to modify (make a change in) an existing record? What if you want to delete an existing record? The sequential nature of the file precludes elegant answers. To do either task, you must use not only the original file (file A) but also a second file (file B). Read records from file A into memory and write them to file B until you read the data for the record to be modified or deleted. If the record is to be modified, make the changes, write the new record to file B and then continue copying records from A into B. If the record is to be deleted, then do not write it to file B but simply continue reading records from A and writing them to B. When you are done (and have closed the files), delete file A from within the program by the Visual Basic **Kill statement:**

`Kill` *filespecification for A*

and then rename file B as file A with

`Name` *filespecification for B As filespecification for A*

Obviously, the Kill statement is always to be used with caution. The very name suggests it is a dangerous tool.

This same approach can be used to insert a new record in the middle of file A:

> read records from A and write them to B until the point where
>   the new record is to be inserted
> write the new record to B
> read the rest of the records from A and write them to B
> kill A and rename B as A

Name: _____   Date Due: _____

LEARNING OBJECTIVES

- Reading from a sequential file
- Searching a sequential file
- Adding records to a sequential file

LAB 11.1

1. ____ Open your *library.mak* project from Chapter 8.

   ____ Run the program and examine the code to review how this program works.

   ____ Save each of the seven form files as *libfil.frm*, *libfil2.frm*, …, *libfil7.frm*. Save the project file as *libfil.mak*.

2. ____ For each of the five book forms, make the text of each of its text boxes blank. Now the data about books are not part of the program.

   ____ Run the program. What is the result?

   ____ Using Notepad, examine the sequential file *books.txt*. This contains the data for the five book forms. Note that all data items are string data, because the year of publication does not need to be treated as a number. The program will be changed so that it reads the data from the file into the book forms.

   ____ Add a common dialog control to the opening form.

3. In the existing Form_Load event procedure for the opening form, the five book forms are loaded, thus creating the Forms collection, which acts like an array of forms. After the code to load the forms, add code to:

   ____ Use the common dialog box to open a file For Input.

   ____ Do a loop five times to read the data from this file into the book pages of the Forms collection. The title page is *forms(0)*, so the book pages are *forms(1)* through *forms(5)*; you need to store the three data values for each record in variables first, and then move them into the form text boxes.

   ____ Close the file.

Reading from a sequential file

_____ Run your program, using **books.txt**; it should work exactly as the original version.

_____ Save your work.

4. The version of the library program you just completed works for any file of five books. It copies the file into a collection of forms. Each form is then a "window" into the file showing the contents of one record. To make this program more general, so it works with files of arbitrary size but does not load the whole file into a collection of forms, use only one form as a window into the file and "scroll" that window through the file by reading new values from the file into the form.

_____ Open your **libfil.mak** project. Save the title page form, one of the book forms, and the search form as **books.frm**, **books1.frm**, and **books2.frm**, respectively; remove the rest of the files from the project, and save the project as **books.mak**.

5. _____ In the Form_Load procedure for the opening form, load only the single book form and delete the remaining Load statements.

_____ Still in the Form_Load procedure, open the file and put the first record's data into the single book form.

_____ Move the statement that closes the file from the Form_Load procedure into the Exit button Click event code. (The program must continue to read values from the file long after the first book page has been loaded.)

6. _____ On the book form, the Browse command button should scroll your view through the book file much as it previously did. If the file is not empty at this point, what should happen when this button is clicked? (Hint: What happened in the old program?)

If the file is empty at this point, what should happen when this button is clicked? (Hint: What happened in the old program?)

In the code for the book form's Browse button, what kind of Visual Basic statement should you use to manage the flow of control?

____ Write the code for the Browse button's click event. If you want to read the first record from the file, you must first close the file and then reopen it in order to get back to the beginning of the file. But you don't need to ask the user the file name again because you already have that information in your program.

____ Test your program using the file **bigbooks.txt**. You should be able to browse through the entire file.

7. The last thing to modify is the code for the search by title or by author on the last form. Instead of searching through the Forms collection, you search through the records in the file. The following is a pseudocode version for a possible solution to searching by title. As long as the target is not found, the search proceeds from the current record to the end of the file and then back to the beginning of the file (after closing and reopening the file) until it comes back to the starting record. This is the sequential search algorithm again, except that it starts somewhere in the middle of the list (that is, in the middle of the file).

> **Searching a sequential file**

```
save the current record title
set found = false
if the current record title is the target, then
    show the book form—no need to search further
else
    Do while (not the end of the file) and (found is false)
        read the next record from the file
        if the title is the target, then
            fill in the book form and show it
            set found to true

    If found is false, then
        close and reopen the file
        Do
            read the next record from the file
            if the title is the target, then
                fill in the book form and show it
                set found to true
        Loop While (the title is not the saved title) and (found is false)

    If found is false, then bring up the error message
```

___ Implement this pseudocode, and similar code for searching by author.

___ Test your program thoroughly.

Adding records to a sequential file

8. ___ Add a command button to the title page that allows the user to add a new book to the file. The steps are:

    Close the file.
    Open the file for append.
    Collect data and write the record to the file.
    Close the file.
    Open the file for input (because that is the mode the file is assumed to be in for the other tasks, such as browsing and searching).

___ Run this program on the file **book.txt** and add two new records to the file. Exit your program and inspect the file using Notepad. What has changed?

___ Save your work.

> **QuickCheck 11.1**
>
> 1. Give two reasons for using files with Visual Basic programs.
> 2. State the three types of files that Visual Basic supports.
> 3. Writing to a sequential file using the Write # statement produces what sort of file?
> 4. Which statement is used to read values from a file that were written to the file using the Write # statement?
> 5. Explain the process of modifying one particular data record in a sequential file.

11.7 Random-access files

The major disadvantage of a sequential file of records is the sequential nature of the file access. To reach record 35 requires reading all the data in the first 34 records, whether you are interested in those data or not. In a random-access file you can retrieve record 35 directly. This is possible because records are stored in a particular way in random-access files.

In a sequential file, each record is stored as a set of individual items. Each field in the record (like the product name and the sales amount in the SALES.TXT file) is written to the file and read from the file separately. It is only within the program that you can, if you wish, associate these quantities as components of a user-defined type. In a random-access file, however, variables of user-defined type can get written to the file and read from the file as single entities. The internal concept of a user-defined variable translates directly to a data item in an external file.

However, there is a restriction on the user-defined data type. Each component must be of a fixed length, that is, take up a fixed amount of storage space. The standard numeric data types like Integer and Single are already fixed length. But the String data type is variable length, depending on how big the string is, unless a fixed length is specified in the declaration. For example,

```
Dim UserName As String
```

says "use as much space as you need to store the name," whereas

```
Dim UserName As String * 20
```

says "use 20 characters to store the name." In this case, 20 characters are used even if the name is very short (in which case the rest of the 20 characters are filled with blanks) or very long (in which case any characters in the name beyond 20 are lost). If the declaration is redone for the StoreData user-defined type using fixed-length components, it looks like

```
'Declared in a module
Type StoreDataFixed
    Product As String * 25
    Sales As Single
End Type
```

Now every variable of type StoreDataFixed takes exactly the same amount of storage space, say 29 units. Suppose many such variables are written as records in a random-access file. The first 34 records take 34 * 29 units of storage, so the 35th record begins at storage location 34 * 29 + 1. This gives the address of the 35th record directly, so Visual Basic can access that location and retrieve the 35th record. The fixed-length record requirement is how random-access files are able to provide random access.

A random-access file, then, is composed entirely of fixed-length records. Within the program, a user-defined type can be declared, with all the components either numeric or fixed-length string data types. To open a random-access file, the length of the records (which correspond to variables of the user-defined type) to be stored there must be given. Fortunately, the Visual Basic *Len* function returns the length of a variable.

Continuing the sales example, declare a variable of type StoreData-Fixed:

```
Dim OneRecord as StoreDataFixed
```

A random-access file to hold the data collected in *OneRecord* or in other variables of the same data type can be opened by the following statement (assuming a Common Dialog control is still being used to get the file specification):

```
Open cmdialog1.Filename For Random As #1 Len = Len(OneRecord)
```

Unlike a sequential file, there are not separate Open statements for reading from or writing to a random-access file. The file just gets opened, and the program can read from it or write to it as desired. If a file of that name already exists, it is opened (without being destroyed), and if a file of that name does not exist, an empty file is created.

A random-access file is closed in the usual way. The file opened as #1 is closed by the statement

```
Close #1
```

11.8 Writing to and reading from random-access files

Writing a record to a random-access file is done by a **Put statement**, and reading a record from the file is done by a **Get statement**. The syntax is

```
Put #filenumber, record number, variable
Get #filenumber, record number, variable
```

For example,

```
Put #1, 4, OneRecord
```

writes record number 4 to the file. This statement can be used to add a new record to the file or to overwrite an existing record 4. To read this record later, use

```
Get #1, 4, OneRecord
```

Notice that what gets written to the file and read from the file in this case is a variable of user-defined type, not the separate components of that variable.

You can write and read randomly to and from the file. For example, you can create record 4 without creating records 1, 2, and 3. If record 4 is the only record you have written to the file, then records 1, 2, and 3 do exist but contain garbage. You can use a Get statement to read record 2, for example, but the values are junk. So it is best to organize your use of records and not abuse the random capability.

In the sales application, the order of the records in the file is unimportant because the program is prepared to sort them internally on either field. So records can be added to the end of the file by maintaining a form-level variable *recordnumber* that gives the largest record number in the file. An "add record" button can then have the following Click event code:

```
recordnumber = recordnumber + 1
OneRecord.Product = InputBox$("Give product name")
OneRecord.Sales = Val(InputBox$("Give sales amount"))
Put #1, recordnumber, OneRecord
```

The variable *recordnumber* can also be used as a loop index in a loop that reads and processes all the records in a file. (Note that *recordnumber* is not necessarily used here to dimension an array in which to store the file.)

Although it is easy to add a record at the end of the file, it is not easy to insert a record in the middle of a file. Suppose records in the file are ordered in some way, records 1 to 5 already exist, and a new record needs to be added between records 2 and 3. This requires an entire shuffling operation: record 5 must be read from the file and written back as record 6, record 4 must be read from the file and written back as record 5, record 3 must be read from the file and written back as record 4, and finally the new record must be written as record 3 (Figure 11.4). If a variable *recordnumber* is used to keep track of the number of records in the file, then *recordnumber* needs to be increased by 1 as part of this process.

Original File	New File
Record 1 ⟶	Record 1
Record 2 ⟶	Record 2
Record 3 ⟶	Record 3 (new record)
Record 4 ⟶	Record 4
Record 5 ⟶	Record 5
	Record 6

Figure 11.4
Adding a new record in the middle of a random-access file

The opposite sort of shuffling is required to logically remove a record from a file. Records after the one to be deleted are each read from the file and then written back to the file using the previous record number. In Figure 11.4, if record 3 in the new file is to be deleted, then record 4 is read from the file and written back as record 3, record 5 is read and written back as record 4, and record 6 is read and written back as record 5. The file now contains only five **logical records**, that is, records that contain meaningful data. However, it still contains six **physical records** (actual records in the file). Record 6 is just a duplicate of what is now record 5; as data, it is meaningless and should be ignored. The process that has taken place, called a **logical delete**, creates a situation in which the number of physical records in the file does not matter. What matters is the number of logical records. The variable *recordnumber* should reflect the logical record count, not the physical record count. Therefore *recordnumber* is decreased by 1 whenever a record is logically deleted.

Now suppose you are opening a random-access data file. How can you determine the value for *recordnumber*, that is, how can you find the number of logical records in the file? A calculation like `LOF(1)/Len(OneRecord)` determines the number of physical records in the file but not the number of logical records. The solution is to maintain the value of *recordnumber* within the file itself. The first record in the file can be a special control record that always knows the number of logical records—including the control record—in the file. The control record is read when the file is opened to determine the value of *recordnumber*; when the file is closed, the control record is updated to contain the current value of *recordnumber*, which reflects record additions and logical deletions done while the file was open. The control record must be the same fixed length as every other record in the file.

If the number of meaningless physical records in the file is large, they can be eliminated by running a separate data compaction program that reads all records and writes all logical records into another file. The original file can then be killed and the new file renamed with the original file name. This is the same process used in sequential files to eliminate any record, but with random-access files it is necessary to do this only when the number of meaningless records gets large.

Modifying a record in a random-access file is easy, however, at least as long as that change does not affect its record number. Just read the record, change it, and put it back.

A random-access file is not a text file. Once the file has been created by a Visual Basic program, the data in it, particularly numeric data, can't be viewed in any reasonable way. This can generate some feeling of discomfort that you don't really know for sure what the data values are because you can't inspect them directly.

11.9 File type comparisons

What are the relative advantages and disadvantages of the two types of files, sequential and random access?

First, if a file is to contain unstructured text (like a paragraph) instead of records, there is no choice, you must use a sequential file. Assuming that the file is to be a file of records, there are trade-offs in the two file types related to how easy it is to create the file, disk space required to store the file, and ease of writing a record to the file, reading a record from the file, modifying a record, and deleting a record. Table 11.1 summarizes some of these points. As a general rule of thumb, the file type should reflect how the data will be used. If the application will typically process all the records in the file, say to update each employee's pay-to-date, then a sequential file may be most appropriate. If the application will typically process only some records in the file, say to change a given employee's number of dependents, then a random-access file may be more appropriate. However, the "employee file" may be used by several applications; this can muddy the water on the decision of which file type to use. The same things can be done with either sequential files or random-access files; it is just a question of the effort involved.

	SEQUENTIAL FILE	RANDOM-ACCESS FILE
Advantages	Can create and inspect with a simple text editor. Can handle any kind of text. Easy to add new records at end of file.	Can read or write any specific record. File records correspond directly to variables of user-defined type. Easy to modify a given record. Don't have to keep opening and closing the file to read and write.
Disadvantages	To read a record, must read all preceding records. To modify or delete or insert a record requires reading the entire file and writing to a temporary second file.	May waste storage space because of fixed-length records. Inserting or deleting records may require shuffling. Some means must be used to distinguish between logical and physical records in the file.

Table 11.1
Comparison of sequential and random-access files

Name: _____   Date Due: _____

LEARNING OBJECTIVES

- Writing to a random-access file
- Reading from a random-access file
- Deleting records from a random-access file

1. You will work with the library books again, but this time the data will be stored in a random-access file instead of a sequential file. There are enough changes that it is probably easier to start from scratch.

    ____ Open a new Visual Basic project. Save the files as *libran.frm* and *libran.mak*.

    ____ Records in the random-access file will correspond to variables of a user-defined data type, which can be defined only in a code module. Add a code module and save it as *libran.bas*.

    ____ In the code module, do a Type statement for a user-defined type to store book data. Remember that there are three strings, which must be fixed length: title, author, and publication date. Allow 20, 20, and 4 characters, respectively, for these strings.

    ____ Declare a Global variable *Book* of this user-defined type.

    ____ Declare a Global constant *BLANK* that is a literal string of 20 blanks. This will be used to create a phony book title.

2. ____ The random-access file will have a control record. The data records are all 44 characters, so the control record must be the same length. Put the following declaration in the general section of form *libran.frm*:

    ```
    Dim ControlRecord As String * 44
    ```

    Then you can read and write the *ControlRecord* variable the same as any other record in the file. The numeric value of the string is the number of logical records in the file.

    ____ In the general declarations of the form, declare a variable *recordnumber* of type Integer that represents the number of logical records in the file

3. ____ In the Form_Load procedure, open a random-access file in which book records will be stored. Use a Common Dialog control; you may wish to change the filter for the file extension to .DAT (for "data file") since the file will not be a text file.

When sequential files were used in Lab 11.1, it was assumed that a file containing book data had already been created by some text editor program; the Visual Basic program just used this file. Records in a random-access file must be written to the file in a particular way. The Visual Basic program you are now building will be able to create the data in a file (by adding records to an empty file) or work with data already existing in the file.

In the Form_Load procedure, the value of *recordnumber* needs to be set to the number of logical records already in the file. If the file is a new, empty file, it contains no records (and also no control record). If the file is nonempty, its first record is the control record giving the number of logical records in the file.

____ Fill in the pseudocode below to assign a value to *recordnumber*:

    If file is empty then
        set recordnumber to _____
    else
        get_____
        set record number to _____

____ In the Form_Load procedure, write code to implement this pseudocode. (Hint: to test whether a file is empty, look at its length; an empty file has length 0.)

____ Just as a quick test, use the Form_Click procedure to print *recordnumber* on the form; run the program and click on the form. What's the current value of *recordnumber*? Why?

____ Add a File menu with a submenu called Exit. Write code for the Exit menu to:

    Update the control record to the number of logical
        records currently in the file.
    Close the file.
    Terminate the program.

4. ____ Add a Record menu with submenus Add a Record and Delete a Record.

____ The Add-a-Record submenu collects input from the user about a book and adds that record to the end of the file. Instead of having three separate input boxes asking for the title, author, and date of publication, you will use a special dialog box with three text boxes to collect this information (see Section 4.10). Design another form for the dialog box. This form collects the necessary data for one book and has Cancel and OK command buttons. Save the form as *libran2.frm*.

____ Write code for the OK button on the dialog box that:

> Collects the data values for *Book*.
> Clears the text boxes so they are ready for the next book to be added.
> Hides the dialog box.

____ Write code for the Cancel button on the dialog box that:

> Sets the title component of Book to *BLANK* (this will be the test for whether valid book data was collected).
> Clears the text boxes.
> Hides the dialog box.

____ In the Form_Activate procedure for the dialog box form, apply the SetFocus method to the text box that collects the book title. Then this text box always has the focus when the dialog box appears.

The following is pseudocode for the Add-a-Record menu on form *libran.frm*:

Writing to a random-access file

> Bring up the dialog box
> If there is valid book data, then
> > If the file is empty, then
> > > adjust recordnumber
> > > write the control record to the file
> > Else
> > > adjust recordnumber
> > Write the book data to the file

____ Write the code for the Add-a-Record menu pick. Be sure to note that if the file is empty, you write two records to the file—the control record and the data record.

____ Run your program and add two book records to the file. Click on the form; what is the current value of *recordnumber*? Explain.

Reading from a random-access file

5. In this application, assume that the file is small enough that all records can be stored in memory. Actually, only part of each record is stored; this saves some space. A list box displays the titles of the books, sorted in alphabetical order. This is the "window" into the file. The string for each title is the same length. The list box also contains the record number for each title, but the width of the list box can be set so that the record number is not visible to the user.

   ____ Put a list box on the form. What can be done to make sure that each title takes the same amount of space when it is written in the list box?

   ____ Do this. What can be done to display the titles in the list box in alphabetical order?

   ____ Do this.

   ____ Add code in the Form_Load event procedure to load data (book title and record number) into the list box from the file.

   ____ Test your code.

   ____ Add a new record. Does it show up in the list box?

   ____ Modify the Add-a-Record code to take care of this.

6. ____ Put a command button on the form with a caption something like "Get Complete Book Data". The idea is that the user selects a title from the list box and then clicks this button to see the complete information about this book (title, author, publication date).

   ____ When the button is clicked, the complete data for the currently selected title in the list box is displayed in a form like the *books1.frm* from the *books.mak* project, except without the Browse button. Create this form and save it as *libran3.frm*.

___ Write the code for the button that returns to the title page.

___ On *libran.frm*, write the code for the "Get Complete Book Data" button that:

    Gets the record number from the list box.

    Gets the record from the file.

    Displays the data in the book form.

___ Test your program. What happens if the user clicks on this button before selecting a title?

___ If there was a problem, fix up your button Click event code. If the user clicks before selecting a title, display a previously hidden label reminding the user to select a title first.

7. The last menu pick to implement is for deleting a record. The user selects a title from the list box and then clicks on the Delete-a-Record menu pick. Things to think about:

    Deleting records from a random-access file

    Be sure the user has selected a title first.

    Logically delete the record from the file by shuffling forward the records after this one in the file.

    Adjust *recordnumber*.

    Adjust the list box display.

___ Write the code.

___ Test your program. Be sure that you can add and delete records and exit the program and that the changes are reflected in the list box when you run the program again.

A Search option has not been implemented for this version of the library. It is easy to search for a title because the titles are all displayed in the list box in alphabetical order. Searching for an author is more difficult because this information is not in the list box (see Project 5 at the end of this chapter).

___ Save your work.

QuickCheck 11.2

1. What must be true of all records stored on a random-access file?
2. True or false: A random-access file can be opened for both reading from and writing to at the same time.
3. The _____ statement is the "opposite" of the Put statement.
4. To write a record to a random-access file, you specify where you want to write it by giving the _____.
5. True or false: Random-access files can be created by any text editor.

11.10 Message boxes

A message box is a form of dialog box. Dialog boxes have been used before. The *InputBox$* function creates a dialog box whose main feature is a text box for collecting user input. Activating the Common Dialog control brings up a dialog box for, say, opening a file. Dialog boxes like the one to collect new book data in Lab 11.2 have been created by building custom forms.

The main purpose of the Visual Basic **message box**, as the name suggests, is to display a message to the user. Although a message box is a dialog box, the "dialog" part is limited because the user cannot type any input but can make a selection only from among command buttons.

You've already seen instances of Visual Basic message boxes (probably many times) because syntax and run-time errors generate message box alerts like the one shown in Figure 11.5.

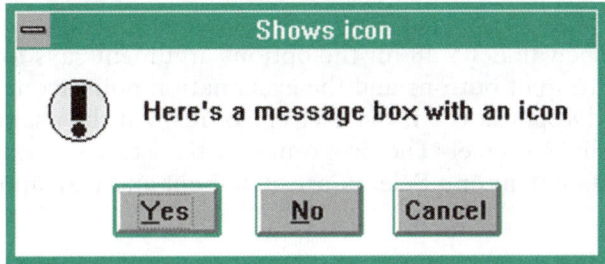

Figure 11.5
System-generated message box

But you can also write code to generate message boxes. The syntax for the message box function is

`MsgBox`(*message, options, title*)

where the parameters represent the following:

Message: String expression that is the displayed message

Options (optional): Integer expression that specifies features of the message box

Title (optional): String expression that appears in the title bar of the message box

The message box function returns a numeric value that is a code for the command button the user chose.

The following code uses the simplest form of the message box function; the required message argument is present and the two optional arguments are missing.

```
Dim response As Integer
response = MsgBox("Your computer will self-destruct in 3 minutes")
```

The message box displayed when this statement executes is shown in Figure 11.6. The absence of the options argument results in a single command button with the caption "OK", and the absence of a title string argument results in the title bar of the message box displaying the project name. The dialog box disappears when the user clicks on the OK button. The value returned by the function and assigned to the integer variable *response* is 1, which signifies that the user clicked on an OK button (the only choice for this hapless user).

Figure 11.6
Simple message box

Figure 11.7 shows another instance of a message box. It is produced by execution of the statement

```
response = MsgBox("Here's a message box with an icon",
    3 + 48, "Shows icon")
```

The value 3 + 48 for the options argument says to display the Yes-No-Cancel group of buttons and the exclamation point icon. The integer value assigned to *response* is 6 if the user clicks Yes, 7 if the user clicks No, and 2 if the user clicks Cancel. The program can then test the value of *response* using an If statement or a Select-Case statement and take appropriate action.

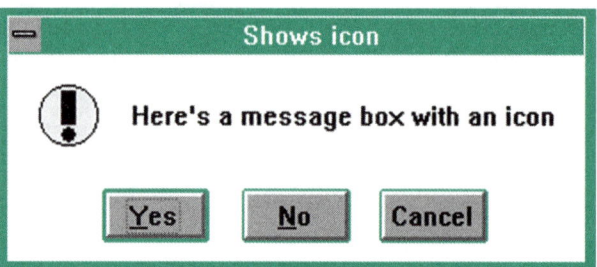

Figure 11.7
Message box with three buttons and an icon

The integer expression for the options argument in the *MsgBox* function controls which command button or buttons appear in the message box; which, if any, predefined icons appear; and several other features of the message box form. Each feature is assigned a particular integer "code," and the options argument is the sum of all the codes to be applied. In order to get an exclamation point icon, for example, you must use 48 as one of the terms in the sum. You could memorize all the different numeric codes, but an easier alternative is to use the CONSTANT.TXT file supplied with Visual Basic. (You may remember that this file was used to get the constant values for basic colors in the *jail.mak* project of Lab 6.2.) Two entries in the CONSTANT.TXT file are

```
'Yes, No, and Cancel buttons
Global Const MB_YESNOCANCEL = 3
'Warning message
Global Const MB_ICONEXCLAMATION = 48
```

You can therefore declare an integer variable called *Options* and set its value by

```
Options = MB_YESNOCANCEL + MB_ICONEXCLAMATION
```

and then invoke the *MsgBox* function by

```
response = MsgBox("Here's a message box with an icon",
    Options, "Shows icon")
```

Table 11.2 lists all the numeric code values for message boxes, together with the global constant equivalents from CONSTANT.TXT. The category "Default button" specifies which button in a group has its Default property set to true. The "Modality" category specifies whether the message box form is modal only to the Visual Basic application or to every loaded application. In the first case, which is the default, the user must click one of the buttons before doing anything else in the Visual Basic program but can click on a window for another application—like the Program Manager—and proceed to use that application normally. System modality freezes all loaded applications until the user clicks a button.

Table 11.2 also lists the numeric values for the user's responses; these are the values the *MsgBox* function will return.

It's possible to give conflicting instructions in the options expression, such as 32 + 48, which asks for two different icons to be displayed. The result is the default case: no icon is displayed. You are less likely to make this sort of error if you use the global constants supplied by CONSTANT.TXT.

The icons vary in their intended severity. The stop sign is used for critical error conditions.

The exclamation point and the question mark are used for warning messages or warning queries.

The information icon is intended just for informational messages.

A variation on the *MsgBox* function is the **message box statement**. The syntax is

`MsgBox` *message, options, title*

Table 11.2
Numeric codes for the *MsgBox* function

CATEGORY	INTEGER CODE	CONSTANT.TXT EQUIVALENT	MEANING
Button group to display	0	MB_OK	OK button only, the default.
	1	MB_OKCANCEL	OK, Cancel buttons.
	2	MB_ABORTRETRYIGNORE	Abort, Retry, Ignore buttons.
	3	MB_YESNOCANCEL	Yes, No, Cancel buttons.
	4	MB_YESNO	Yes, No buttons.
	5	MB_RETRYCANCEL	Retry, Cancel buttons.
Icon to display	0		No icon, the default.
	16	MB_ICONSTOP	Red STOP sign.
	32	MB_ICONQUESTION	Green question mark.
	48	MB_ICONEXCLAMATION	Yellow exclamation point.
	64	MB_ICONINFORMATION	Blue circle with an *i* inside.
Default button	0	MB_DEFBUTTON1	First button is the default.
	256	MB_DEFBUTTON2	Second button is the default.
	512	MB_DEFBUTTON3	Third button is the default.
Modality	0	MB_APPLMODAL	Modal to current application, the default.
	4096	MB_SYSTEMMODAL	Modal to all loaded applications.
Response	1	IDOK	User clicked OK.
	2	IDCANCEL	User clicked Cancel.
	3	IDABORT	User clicked Abort.
	4	IDRETRY	User clicked Retry.
	5	IDIGNORE	User clicked Ignore.
	6	IDYES	User clicked Yes.
	7	IDNO	User clicked No.

There are no parentheses, and, unlike the *MsgBox* function, this is a stand-alone statement. The MsgBox statement returns no value, so there is no point in putting any button except an OK button on the form. The purpose of the MsgBox statement is to display information to the user.

11.11 Error handling

Errors in Visual Basic programs fall into three categories: syntax errors, run-time errors, and logic errors. Assume that for any Visual Basic application you have already corrected all the syntax errors (a reasonable assumption because Visual Basic alerts you to syntax errors by way of message boxes) and all the logic errors (a far more risky assumption). Run-time errors occur during program execution because a particular set of data values, conditions, or user actions results in an attempt to perform an invalid operation. Examples are attempts to:

Divide by 0 due to a certain set of data values.

Open For Input a nonexistent sequential file.

Read data past the end of the file.

Remove a selected item from a list box when none has been selected.

Open a file on drive A when there is no disk in the drive.

Because the program cannot entirely control user input or other user actions, run-time errors may be unavoidable.

Run-time errors result in Visual Basic message boxes with OK buttons. If the Visual Basic program is running in the development environment, clicking the OK button on an error message dumps the program into break mode, opens the code window where the error occurred, and highlights the offending statement. But if the program is running from an .EXE file, then clicking on the OK button usually just terminates the program.

Because Visual Basic has sent an error message, it is well aware that an error has occurred. Such an error is called a **trappable error** because it is possible to "trap" it before it has a chance to display its message box and terminate execution. Instead, the Visual Basic program can direct the flow of control to a special section of code called an **error handler**. An error handler displays its own error message, gives the user a chance to correct the problem (enter some different input values or select an item in the list box or put a disk in the drive, for example), and then allows program execution to continue. If the error is such that the user can't fix it on the spot, the error handler provides as much information as possible about the error and terminates the program gracefully.

In order to use an error handler, you need a **line label**. A line label is any identifier that ends with a colon. It is a separate line of code. The line label works in conjunction with the **On-Err-GoTo statement**. The syntax of this statement is

```
On Error GoTo line label
```

Suppose this statement is present in procedure X (either an event procedure or a general procedure). If a trappable error occurs in any code within procedure X that follows this statement, then control is transferred to the next line after the line label. Here is where the error handler code goes. If the error is one that it is expected, the user can repair within the context of this procedure; then within the error handler there is a statement to return control back to the main part of procedure X. This is done with a **Resume statement**. The two common forms of the Resume statement are

```
Resume
Resume line label
```

Execution of the first form sends program control back to the statement that originally caused the error. Execution of the second form sends program control to the statement following the specified line label.

Suppose, for example, the user clicks a button designed to open For Input a sequential file on drive A. The file is explicitly specified in the Open statement:

```
Open "A:\data.txt" For Input As #1
```

However, there is no disk in drive A. Without error trapping, this results in the run-time error message shown in Figure 11.8, followed by program termination.

Figure 11.8
System-generated error message

Instead, you can trap this error, alert the user to the problem, and give him or her a chance to correct the problem and resume execution. The code of Figure 11.9 does the job. The On-Error-GoTo statement wakes up the error trapping mechanism. If no error occurs on execution of the Open statement, then a message box reports that the file open operation was successful (Figure 11.10). After the user clicks on the OK button, the **Exit Sub statement** is executed. This statement exits the procedure but not the program as a whole. Without this statement, execution proceeds right into the following error handler code even though no error has occurred.

Figure 11.9
Event procedure with an error handler

```
Sub cmdOpenFile_Click ()
Dim response As Integer
Dim Options As Integer
```

```
On Error GoTo ErrorHandler

    Open "A:\data.txt" For Input As #1
    MsgBox "input file successfully opened", , "File Project"
    Exit Sub

ErrorHandler:
    Options = MB_RETRYCANCEL + MB_ICONSTOP
    response = MsgBox("Check that there is a disk in
    ↳ drive A",Options, "Error message")
    If response = IDCANCEL Then
        MsgBox "Program will terminate", , "File Project"
        End
    Else
        Resume
    End If
End Sub
```

Figure 11.10
No error on opening the file

If, however, there is no disk in drive A, then Visual Basic generates an error. Because of the On-Error-GoTo statement, the error is trapped. Instead of displaying the message box of Figure 11.8, control is transferred to the error handler code, that is, the code right after the ErrorHandler label. Now a different message box is displayed (Figure 11.11). The error handler checks the user's response to the message box. If the user selected Cancel, presumably because the situation was not understood or for some reason is not correctable, then a final message box warns that the program will be terminated (Figure 11.12) and the End statement terminates the program. If the user selected Retry, presumably because the situation has been repaired, then the Resume statement sends the flow of control back to the Open statement to try again.

Figure 11.11
Message box generated by error handler

There are some 200 trappable errors in Visual Basic (search Help for "trappable errors"). Each has a unique integer associated with it. For example, the particular error that generated the message in Figure 11.8 is error 71. Another potential error is 53 ("File not found"). The *Err* function returns

Figure 11.12
Final message to user

a value that is the numeric code of the error that just occurred. One error handler in a procedure can thus take care of many problems by using a Select-Case statement to evaluate the error number and choose the appropriate action. Figure 11.13 contains a more extensive error handler, which addresses specifically errors 71 and 53, then includes an Else case for all other errors connected with trying to open the file.

Figure 11.13
More extensive error handler for opening an input file

```
ErrorHandler:
   Select Case Err
      Case 71
         Options = MB_RETRYCANCEL + MB_ICONSTOP
         response = MsgBox("Check that there is a disk
          in drive A",Options, "Error message")
         If response = IDCANCEL Then
            MsgBox "Program will terminate", , "File Project"
            End
         Else
            Resume
         End If
      Case 53
         MsgBox "No such file on the disk in drive A,
          program will terminate"
         End
      Case Else
         response = MsgBox ("An error occurred while
          opening this file. Choose to try again (OK) or
          terminate program (Cancel)", 1 + 48,
          "File Project")
         If response = IDOK Then
            Resume
         Else
            End
         End If
   End Select
```

It is difficult to test error handling code if it is necessary to create all of the different error conditions you want to handle. However, the Visual Basic *Error* statement can be used to generate fake errors in order to test error handlers. The statement

```
Error 71
```

when executed, causes Visual Basic to believe that the error condition associated with 71 has occurred. Control then transfers to the error handler just as if a real error 71 had been trapped.

In addition to the trappable errors that Visual Basic generates, there may be certain situations that should be considered error conditions for a particular application. There are some unused error numbers, and you can use them to create a trappable error of your own. For example, suppose that a value entered by the user in a text box is supposed to be numeric. Despite the program's prompt to that effect, the user has not complied, and you want to trap this as an error condition. Figure 11.14 shows the code for the text box's KeyPress event. The KeyPress event occurs whenever the text box has the focus and the user presses and releases a key on the keyboard. The KeyPress event has a parameter called KeyAscii, which contains the standard numeric code for that keyboard character. The *Chr$* function changes this numeric code into the character it represents, so that

```
Chr$(KeyAscii)
```

returns the keyboard character that the user entered. If this character is not between "0" and "9", then the user did not enter a numeric digit. Using the Error statement, this condition is assigned the unused error number 12 and becomes a trappable error. The error handler uses the **Beep statement** (which causes the computer to "beep") as well as a warning message box. When the user clicks the OK button, the statement

```
KeyAscii = 0
```

cancels the keystroke so that the offending character never reaches the text box. Then the event procedure terminates by the Exit Sub statement (which is necessary, even though the very next statement is an End Sub anyway). This event procedure is then executed again by the next keystroke of the user.

```
Sub Text1_KeyPress (KeyAscii As Integer)

Dim Key As String * 1
On Error GoTo ErrorHandler2

    Key = Chr$ (KeyAscii)
    If (Key < "0") Or (Key > "9") Then Error 12
    Exit Sub

ErrorHandler2:
    Beep
    MsgBox "You must enter a number", MB_ICONEXCLAMATION
    KeyAscii = 0
    Exit Sub

End Sub
```

Figure 11.14
Error handling for a non-numeric text box entry

THOUGHTS ON PROGRAMMING

Program Testing and Reliability

When the steps in the programming process were first outlined in Chapter 1, program testing was mentioned. All along the way, as you've written Visual Basic programs, you have tested them to be sure they run correctly.

At first, it seems that merely getting the program to produce an answer at all is a great achievement. Then the answer needs to be checked for correctness, perhaps by using a calculator if there is a numeric computation involved, or by checking to see that the correct items are added to a list box, that clicking a button produces the correct form, that an output file has been created, and so on.

However, getting the program to produce one correct set of behaviors and output values for one particular set of user actions and input data is not program testing. It can be compared to driving one particular make and model of automobile (say a sedan with an automatic transmission) down one street on one particular sunny day. It tells you that that particular model, under those conditions, can perform. But it tells you nothing about the performance of that vehicle on a completely different terrain, under different weather conditions. And it surely tells you nothing about how other vehicles—trucks, stick-shifts, sports cars, and so on—behave under the same conditions or other conditions. In other words, successfully completing one run of a program is a test drive. It gives you some confidence that the program is not a total disaster, but that's about it.

Of course it is usually not possible to go to the other extreme and test a program so thoroughly as to cover all possible cases because there are simply too many of them. Instead, test cases that are representative must be devised. (If you can't drive all the pickup trucks, then drive three or four that represent the various options available.)

There are two approaches to program testing. One approach looks at the program strictly from the performance viewpoint, apart from details of the code. This approach assumes that the tester does not even have access to the code. The tester treats the program as a "black box" that is given some input and produces some output, but whose inner workings (that is, the code) are not visible. This is called **black-box testing**. In black-box testing, the program specifications developed early on (and perhaps modified through user involvement in prototype demonstrations) are the standard against which testing is conducted. The program must behave as specified under all possible circumstances. This includes all the normal types of input values and user actions, as well as the unusual but possible cases, which also should be addressed in the problem specification.

Consider a trivially simple case. The program has two text boxes where the user enters integers; when the user clicks a command button, the larger of the two numbers is to be displayed in a label. The program should be tested for the following "typical" scenarios:

> User enters two positive numbers.
>> Larger number is in text box 1.
>>
>> Larger number is in text box 2.
>
> User enters one positive number and one negative number.
>> Positive number is in text box 1.
>>
>> Positive number is in text box 2.
>
> User enters two negative numbers.
>> Larger number is in text box 1.
>>
>> Larger number is in text box 2.

and for the more unusual but certainly possible cases:

> One of the values is 0.
>> Text box 1 value is 0.
>>
>> Text box 2 value is 0.
>
> Both numbers are the same.
>
> User neglects to enter a number in one or both of the text boxes before clicking the button.
>
> User enters a noninteger value in one or both of the text boxes.
>
> User enters a nonnumeric value in one or both of the text boxes.

The last three cases, which are based on user error in running the program, are prime candidates for error handling as discussed in Section 11.11.

Recall that the problem specification includes not only functional requirements for what the program should produce under various circumstances, but also performance requirements, how the program should behave. These requirements may be specified as "the program will run in less than _____KB of memory," "the program will produce complete results within _____ seconds," or "users with a high school education will be able to run the program with less than 2% error rate after 5 hours of training." Performance requirements also need to be tested.

Another approach to program testing is **white-box testing**. Here the tester has access to the program code. As with black-box testing, the white-box tester must devise test cases for all the typical and all the unusual situations, but now these situations are cast in terms of program code. Each branch of program logic should be tested. In an If-Else statement, there are two paths. One set of test data should ensure that the program takes path A and another set should ensure that the program takes path B. In an If-ElseIf or a Select-Case statement, there are multiple branches. A set of test data must be developed for each branch. In a loop, there can be multiple conditions under which looping terminates; each must be tested. When you consider that If statements can be nested within other If statements within loops, and so on, it is clear that white-box testing quickly leads to many, many cases. Also, it can be difficult to find a set of data that guarantees that way down inside the program code, one particular branch is taken.

The unusual cases in white-box testing again refer to the code. If a looping condition is

number >=3

then what happens when number = 3? What happens when number = 2? If an array is dimensioned to hold 10 values, does the program work when only 9 values are loaded? What happens when the user tries to enter 11 values (or a file contains 11 values)?

Testing is usually done with a combination of black-box and white-box testing. In large programming projects, a separate testing group is set up at the beginning of the project to begin to develop test cases for black-box testing from the program specifications. As code segments are completed by the programming group, the testing group also begins to generate data for white-box testing. The idea of a separate group for testing is much the same as having some disinterested party proofread your document. The testing group sees things with a fresh and unbiased eye, and also has no vested interest in the code as it stands. The separate testing group, which may involve users as well as technical personnel, is sometimes called a "tiger team"; its job is to use the program and try at all costs to make it crash, wringing out every error it can find.

Obviously, program testing is expensive in terms of human time and effort, which translate into dollar expenses in the program development budget. The amount of time and money to be devoted to testing is affected by the type of application being developed. If this program is a little application you are writing at home to keep track of your holiday card mailing list, then it is no big deal if the program fails, and it is not worth much testing time. If the program is one you are writing for a client to keep track of his or her employee payroll, then it is pretty important that the program work correctly; this justifies time and money spent on program testing. If the program is managing the aircraft control system at the Chicago airport and its failure would result in the potential loss of life, then this is a critical application for which the program can never be tested too thoroughly.

Critical applications are those for which failure threatens human safety or may result in disastrous economic consequences. Programs designed for critical applications must perform reliably. **Reliability** means the ability of the program to run without failure over a specified period of time. The higher the reliability requirement, the more testing is needed. In most critical applications, a certain amount of **fault tolerance** is built into the system, usually through having back-up hardware or back-up software that can take over when an error occurs and keep the application running smoothly until the error can be found and corrected.

Name: _____ Date Due: _____

LAB 11.3

LEARNING OBJECTIVES

- Writing a message box
- Using error trapping

1. ____ Open your *libran.mak* project from Lab 11.2.

   ____ Save all the project files as *liberr.frm*, *liberr2.frm*, *liberr3.frm*, and *liberr.bas*, respectively, and the project as *liberr.mak*.

2. ____ Go to the *liberr.bas* module.

   ____ Under the Visual Basic File menu, choose Load Text to load the file CONSTANT.TXT (usually found in the C:\VB directory). Because you already have code in this module, choose Merge from the dialog box to add this file to what you already have.

   ____ Scroll through this module and delete all the CONSTANT.TXT part except for the MsgBox parameters and the MsgBox return values.

3. Where in this application should the user be entering numerical digits?

   Writing a message box

   ____ Write the code to turn on error trapping and trap this condition. The corresponding error handler displays a message box that informs the user about the need to enter numeric digits. Your code can be identical to the body of Figure 11.14.

   ____ Test your program.

4. Two user actions on the opening form of this project require that a book title already be selected from the list box. Which two actions?

Using error trapping

5. ___ To handle these cases, your program may have displayed a previously hidden label with user instructions to select a title before attempting this action. These are good places to use a message box instead. Pick one of the two procedures in which this situation can occur. Insert a line label at the bottom of the procedure for the error handler. This error handler line label must have a different name than the one you used before.

___ Put an On-Error-GoTo statement at the top of the procedure to trap errors.

___ Set the condition where no title has been selected as error 15.

___ In the error handler code, write an appropriate message to the user and exit the procedure. Note that using a Resume statement doesn't work here because the message box is modal; the user can't select a title while the message box is present, and if the error handler returns control to earlier in the procedure, it is too late then to select a title.

___ Test your program thoroughly. If it doesn't seem to work properly, check to see that you included an Exit Sub statement above your error handler code.

6. ___ Add similar code to the other procedure.

___ Test your program.

___ If you used a warning label in the previous version of your program, delete the label and all the code associated with managing the label. Then test your program again.

7. ___ Try adding a new book to your library; use a valid publication date, but use the Enter key instead of the Tab key at the end of entering the publication date. What happens and why?

___ The value of KeyAscii is 13 when the Enter key is pressed. Add an additional statement in the text box code to trap this condition.

___ Add additional code in your error handler to display a message such as "Use Tab key, not Enter key" for this case.

___ Test your program and save your work.

QuickCheck 11.3

1. How does a message box differ from an input box?
2. Which Visual Basic statement "turns on" error trapping?
3. True or false: An error handler is a special Visual Basic intrinsic function.
4. If an Exit Sub statement is not placed before the error handler code in a procedure, what happens?
5. Explain the difference between black-box and white-box testing.

Review Questions

1. What are the first and the last operations to be done when using a file?
2. To read values from a sequential file, it is opened For _____.
3. What happens when an existing sequential file is opened For Output?
4. What does the Filter property of the Common Dialog control do?
5. Describe the format of a comma-delimited file of records.
6. To write a sequential file that is ordinary text, as opposed to a comma-delimited file of records, use the _____ statement.
7. What is the difference between the *EOF* function and the *LOF* function when applied to sequential files?
8. Explain the major difference between how a single record is accessed in a sequential file and how it is accessed in a random-access file.
9. True or false: A variable of user-defined type, even though it has multiple components, can be written as a record in a random-access file with a single Put statement.
10. Explain the process of inserting a record in the middle of a random-access file.
11. Explain the process of deleting a record from the middle of a random-access file.
12. Describe what random-access file logical and physical records are and explain under which conditions there may be more physical records than logical records.
13. What is a control record used for?
14. Why is the CONSTANT.TXT file useful when your code uses a message box?
15. What is the difference between a message box function and a message box statement? Why do you choose to use one as opposed to the other?
16. Why are message boxes useful in conjunction with error handling?
17. In an error handler, explain when to use a Resume statement, an Exit Sub statement, or an End statement.
18. Which Visual Basic statement allows you to create your own trappable errors?

19. Programs designed for the most _____ applications have the highest _____ requirements and require the most thorough _____.

20. Explain why an independent testing group is useful in a program development project.

Exercises

Reading Code
What is the effect or result of each of the following segments of code?

1. ```
   Dim i As Integer
   Open "C:\MYFILE.TXT" For Output As #1
   For i = 1 To 20
      Write #1, "i = ", i
   Next i
   Close #1
   ```

2. ```
   Dim i As Integer
   Open "C:\MYFILE.TXT" For Output As #1
   For i = 1 To 20
      Print #1, "i = ", i
   Next i
   Close #1
   ```

3. Assume that *OneRecord* is a variable that has been declared as some user-defined data type and that MYFILE.DAT contains records that correspond to data of this type.

   ```
   Dim i As Integer
   Dim j As Integer
   Open "C:\MYFILE.DAT" For Random As #1 Len = 44
   Open "C:\NEWFILE.DAT" For Random As #2 Len = 44
   i = 2
   j = 1
   Get #1, i, OneRecord
   Do While Not EOF(1)
      Put #2, j, OneRecord
      j = j + 1
      i = i + 2
      Get #1, i, OneRecord
   Loop
   Close #1
   Close #2
   ```

4. ```
   Dim response As Integer
   Dim Options As Integer
   Options = MB_ICONSTOP + MB_YESNOCANCEL
   response = MsgBox("This is your last chance",
      Options, "test case")
   ```
   ```

```
    Select Case response
      Case IDYES
         MsgBox "You've seen the error of your ways"
      Case IDNO, IDCANCEL
         MsgBox "That was your last warning"
         End
    End Select
```

5. Assume that the user enters "Roger" in text box txtName and then clicks the cmdDoIt command button.

```
   Sub cmdDoIt_Click ()
      On Error GoTo ErrorHandler
      If txtName.Text = "Roger" Then
         Error 12
      Else
         lblDisplay.Caption = txtName.Text & " is a nice name"
      End If
      Exit Sub
   ErrorHandler:
      MsgBox "'Roger' is illegal here"
      Resume
   End Sub
```

Writing Code

6. You want to add new records to an existing comma-delimited sequential file called MYDATA.TXT which is on the C drive. Write a Visual Basic statement to open the file.

7. Suppose the random-access file INSURE.DAT contains records corresponding to data of user-defined type, as follows:

```
   Type PolicyType
      Number As String * 10
      Premium As Single
      DueDate As String * 5
   End Type
```

Your program needs to read the third record from the file and change the *Premium* value to 587.90. Write the necessary code.

8. Write code to copy the entire contents of the INSURE.DAT file (Exercise 7) into a new random-access file EXPENS.DAT. Assume that the files have already been opened as 1 and 2, respectively, and that they will be closed somewhere else; also assume that there is no control record in the INSURE.DAT file.

9. Write code to display a message box with a question mark icon, the message "Do you want to delete this record?" and a choice of Yes or No command buttons. The user's response is collected in an integer variable *response*.

10. The following code for a command button collects user input on total sales in dollars and number of customers and then computes the average

dollar value of sales per customer. Write an error handler to manage division by zero (Visual Basic error 11); give the user the choice of correcting the error within this procedure (OK button) or exiting the procedure (Cancel button). Your error handler also has an Else case that gives a general message and terminates the application. (If you run this program, try using the Cancel button on both input boxes; this should activate the Else error case.)

```
Sub Command1_Click ()
    Dim sales As Single
    Dim number As Integer
    Dim average As Single

    sales = Val(InputBox$("Enter total sales amount"))
    number = Val(InputBox$("Enter number of customers"))
    average = sales / number
    label1.Caption = Format$(average, "currency")
End Sub
```

Exploring Further

11. Suppose the comma-delimited sequential file INSURE.DAT contains records with three fields: the policy number (a string), the premium due (a decimal value), and the due date (a string). A typical record might be

    "AF008P",427.80,"11/14"

    Your program needs to read the third record from the file INSURE.DAT and change the *Premium* value to 587.90. Write the necessary code. Compare the amount of work required with that for Exercise 7.

12. A random-access file contains records about insurance, as described in Exercise 7. A new record is to be inserted into the file, with record number 5. Comment on the following section of code that is written as part of the insertion task (you may assume that *Policy* has been declared As PolicyType, that data values for *Policy* have already been obtained, and that *recordnumber* holds the number of logical records currently in the file).

    ```
    Dim i As Integer
    For i = 5 To recordnumber
        Get #1, i, Policy
        Put #1, i + 1, Policy
    Next i
    Put #1, 5, Policy
    ```

13. In the ***books.mak*** project from Lab 11.1, add an error handler to take care of the situation in which the input file is empty.

14. In the following section of code from Section 11.6, values are read from a comma-delimited sequential file into an array. The array size is set to *Limit*.

```
MaxSize = 1
Do While Not (EOF(1)) And (MaxSize <= Limit)
   Input #1, MonthData(MaxSize).product, MonthData ↵
   ↳ (MaxSize).sales
   MaxSize = MaxSize + 1
Loop
```

Add code to bring up a message box if there are still values left in the file after the array is full.

15. Project 3 of Chapter 7 describes a program to be written for Puddlejump Airlines. From the problem description given there, describe a set of test data for black-box testing of this program.

Projects

1. A comma-delimited sequential file contains records about orders filled for one month. Each record has a string field for the customer name and a numeric field for the amount of that order. The following is a typical record:

   "Sam's Tire", 47.50

   A customer may make several orders during the month. Write a program to read the data file, compute the total dollar amount in orders for the month per customer, and print the results in a nicely formatted report.

2. Write a simple text editor application. In a text box, the user should be able to enter a memo, save it to a file, and bring up that file when the program next runs. Use menus for user choices. Also implement cut-and-paste operations on the text box. For help on how to implement cut and paste, read the Help system on the Clipboard object, and also Example 2 under the SelLength, SelStart, SelText properties in the Help system.

3. Write a program to merge two sorted, comma-delimited sequential files. Each file contains records with three string fields, and the records in each file are stored in alphabetical sorted order based on the first field. The program is to read through each file and form a third file that is sorted and contains all the records from the two original sorted files. (Hint: Do not read all of one file and then all of the other—read a record at a time from each file.)

4. In the dive program of Lab 7.3, you constructed a form to be displayed when the data entry for individual scores is not yet complete but the user asks for the final score to be computed. (See Figure 7.12.) Change the code to use the message box statement instead. Also use message boxes to verify the data entry for degree of difficulty of a dive and the dive scores (see Exercise 13 of Chapter 7).

5. (This is a very ambitious project.) In the *libran.mak* project, book information is kept in a random-access file called, say, A. When the program executes, book titles are displayed in alphabetical order in a list box. Scrolling through the list box provides a way for the user to search for a

particular book title. Selecting that title and clicking on a button displays a form with the complete book information. Unlike the earlier versions of the library program, this version does not allow searching for a book by author.

Suppose that a second random-access file B exists whose records contain two fields: the book author's last name and the record number in file A of the corresponding full book record. Suppose also that this file is maintained in alphabetical order by author's last name. Because file B is in alphabetical order, a search for the author's name can be done by a binary search algorithm. (Binary search cannot be applied to a sequential file, even if the file is in sorted order, because it is impossible to move back toward the front of the file.)

How can file B be maintained in sorted order? Each new record must be inserted in the proper place. The proper place can also be found by doing a binary search; binary search finds where the record is if it is present, and if it is not present, the search finds the place where it belongs.

Revise the *libran.mak* project so that as records are added to file A, they are also inserted in the correct location in file B. Add a button to the form that allows the user to search file B by author's last name and then displays the full book information if the name is found. Assume that there are no duplicate author last names in the data file.

A file that contains only partial fields from all the records of another data file, along with record numbers that "point to" that data file, is called an **index file**. So here B is an index file for file A. (The list box on the form also acts like an index file for file A, since the list box contains only title information, not the complete book record, but also contains record numbers for file A.)

CHAPTER 12

Communicating with Other Applications

KEY POINTS

- Visual Basic can exchange data with other Windows applications through the Clipboard and through Dynamic Data Exchange (DDE).
- Object Linking and Embedding (OLE) provides a more powerful way for Visual Basic to communicate with and make use of other applications.
- Visual Basic's ability to link with databases results in tremendous record-handling capabilities with little effort.
- Visual Basic can use Structured Query Language (SQL) to pose a query to a database.

12.1 Evolving communication

A Visual Basic application program can communicate with other application programs in various ways. In order of increasing power and flexibility, available techniques include use of

  Clipboard
  DDE (Dynamic Data Exchange)
  OLE (Object Linking and Embedding)

  Within Visual Basic, you have used the Clipboard in conjunction with the Edit menu to transfer information from one part of the program to another. Within the Code window, for example, you can select (highlight) a section of code and choose Copy from the Edit menu; this puts a copy of the selected text into the Clipboard. Then in another Code window, you can use the Edit menu and select Paste; this puts whatever is in the Clipboard—in this case, the code you just copied—into the Code window at the location of the insertion bar. The Clipboard serves as a bridge for text transfer from one part of the code to another. The Clipboard is not limited to transferring text information; you can also Copy/Cut and Paste to copy or move control objects from one form to another, or create multiple controls on a single form.
  In much the same way, the Clipboard functions as a bridge between Visual Basic and other Windows applications. The Clipboard is a Visual Basic object, and has its own collection of methods. Here's a simple example, using the Clipboard GetFormat method. Figure 12.1a shows a Visual Basic form with one command button and one text box. The code for the command button is

```
If Clipboard.GetFormat(1) = True Then
    Text1.Text = Clipboard.GetText()
Else
    MsgBox ("Clipboard does not contain text")
End If
```

The GetFormat method tests whether the item currently in the Clipboard object matches a specific format. Here the GetFormat method returns True if the item matches format 1, which indicates that this is a text item as

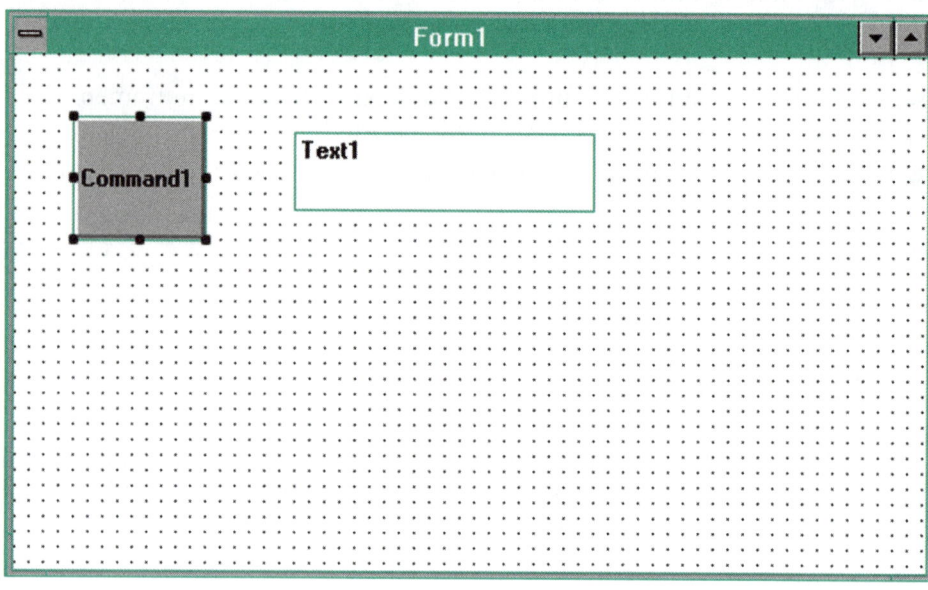

Figure 12.1
Using the Clipboard to copy text from another application

(a)

(b)

opposed to, say, a graphic file. If so, it makes that item the text of the text box, and if not, an error message is displayed. (The multiline property of the text box should be set to true because the amount of text to be copied is unknown.) Suppose you are running this Visual Basic program and, while it is running, you also run a word processor like Word for Windows, or even a simple text editor like Notepad, and open a file. You select a portion of text in this file, copy it to the Clipboard, return to the task that is your running Visual Basic application, and click on the command button. The text appears in the text box, as shown in Figure 12.1b.

This data transfer from the word processor to Visual Basic can be considered a one-way "conversation." Two way "conversations" can be established between applications by using the Windows **Dynamic Data Exchange (DDE)** feature. In DDE, one application acts as the **client**, who initiates the DDE, and the other acts as the **server**, who is contacted because the client application wants some service performed. In Visual Basic, text boxes, labels, and picture boxes can be clients, and initiate DDE and request services from other applications. Forms in Visual Basic (actually the objects on forms) can be servers that are contacted by other (client) applications.

The client can be made to "link to" another application that acts as the server, to send data to that application, to request information back from the application, and to close the link. As an example, suppose an Excel spreadsheet contains two cells; cell A1 contains a data value, and cell B1 applies a formula to that value, producing a result that is displayed in cell B1. Suppose a Visual Basic form contains two text boxes, A and B. By writing code to set various properties and apply certain methods, the following can be made to take place when the Visual Basic program executes (Figure 12.2 shows the sequence of important events):

Figure 12.2a
Excel is started.
The appropriate spreadsheet file is opened.

Figure 12.2b
Text box A is linked to cell A1 in the spreadsheet.
A number entered as text in text box A is sent to cell A1.

Figure 12.2c
The link between text box A and the spreadsheet is closed.
The spreadsheet applies the formula to the data in cell A1
   and displays the result in cell B1.

Figure 12.2d
Text box B is linked to cell B1 in the spreadsheet.
Text box B requests the result that is displayed in cell B1.

Figure 12.2e
The link between text box B and the spreadsheet is closed.

By this DDE process, a Visual Basic application has taken advantage of an Excel spreadsheet; in fact, it has made the spreadsheet perform some work for it and send it the results. DDE can be used to exchange graphic data as well as text data.

The code needed to perform the DDE described in the above example has not been presented. That's because there is an even more powerful technique than DDE to allow Visual Basic and other applications to communicate, and that is to use Object Linking and Embedding (OLE).

456 • CHAPTER 12 • COMMUNICATING WITH OTHER APPLICATIONS

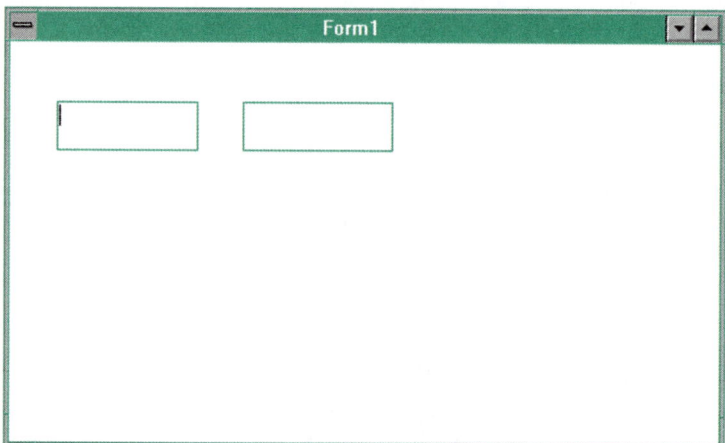
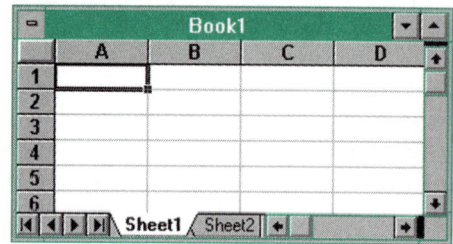

(a) Visual Basic form and Excel spreadsheet

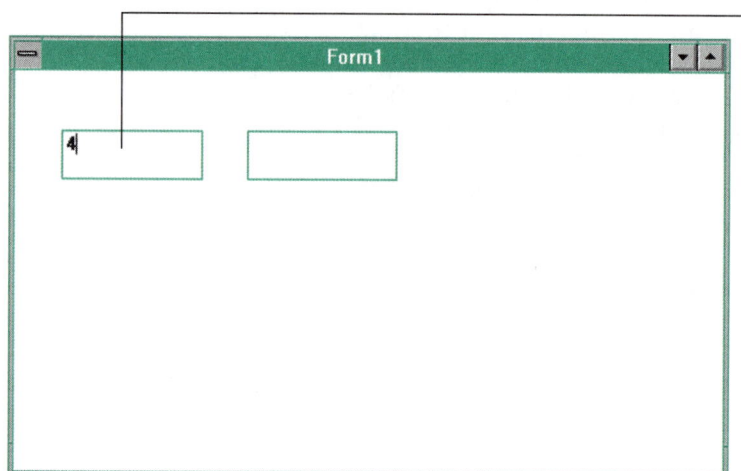
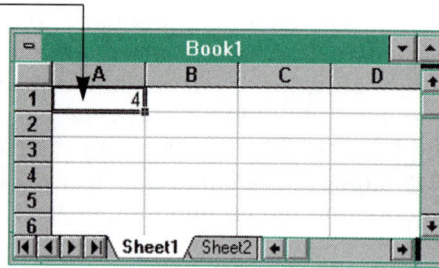

(b) Link established and data transferred

Value computed from formula in cell B1

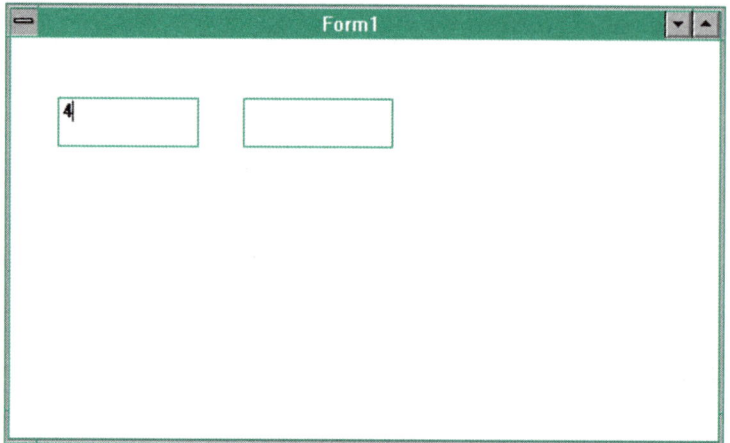

(c) Link broken, formula applied in spreadsheet

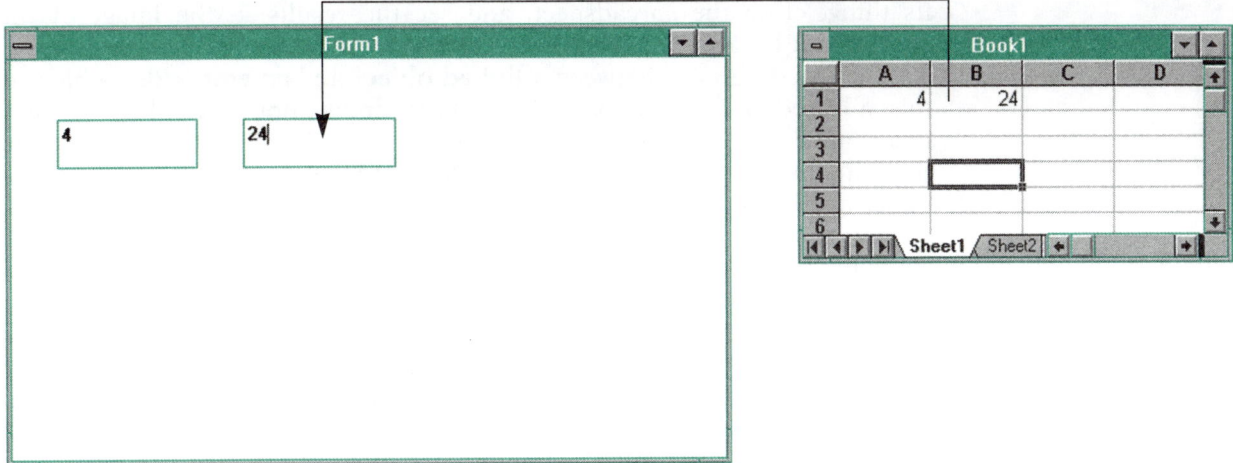

(d) Link established and result transferred back

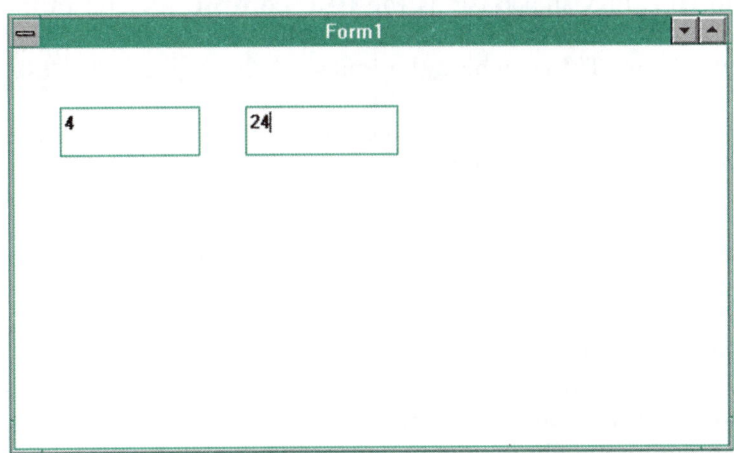

(e) Link broken

Figure 12.2 (a-e)
DDE exchange between a client Visual Basic application and a server Excel spreadsheet

12.2 Object linking and embedding

OLE (Object Linking and Embedding) is an extension of DDE. Instead of sending data from a client application to a server application and then asking for data back again, OLE allows a complete graphic image of the server application to appear within the client application. The client application is also called the **container application** because it contains this image. By double-clicking this image, the server application is invoked and used, and the results of that use become available within the container application. To be more specific, in the preceding example an image of the spreadsheet with cells A1 and B1 can be put on the Visual Basic form and then, while running the Visual Basic program, this image can be double-clicked on. Excel is then opened with this spreadsheet loaded; that is, *the image of the spreadsheet becomes the real thing.* You can put data in cell A1, watch the spreadsheet do its thing, close the spreadsheet, and see the results in the image of the spreadsheet back on the form.

The difference between a **linked object** and an **embedded object** is this: a linked object remains with the server application and only its graphic image appears in the container application. An embedded object is stored in the container application. For example, suppose Visual Basic is the container application and an Excel spreadsheet is the server application. If the spreadsheet is a linked object in the Visual Basic program, then the Visual Basic program contains a picture of part of the spreadsheet together with a link to the actual spreadsheet; double-clicking on this picture opens the actual spreadsheet. However, no data from the spreadsheet is part of the Visual Basic program, and to run the Visual Basic program and link to the spreadsheet, the spreadsheet has to be present on the system. If the spreadsheet is embedded in the Visual Basic program, then it is an actual copy of the spreadsheet, data and all. The original spreadsheet need not be present to run the Visual Basic version. One advantage to a linked object is that, because the object remains part of the server, it is available to any other applications that wish to establish a link to it.

The key to OLE in Visual Basic is the **OLE control**. Its icon in the Toolbox is shown here.[1] Using this icon, you can click and drag a large rectangle on a form. This is where the image of the application will appear.

Linking or embedding an object can be done at design time or at run time. Once the OLE control is on your form, you can use the right mouse button to bring up a pop-up menu that walks you through a series of choices about the server application, the particular object to be linked or embedded, and whether it is to be linked or embedded. The OLE control also has its own long list of properties that can be set.

The next lab illustrates one way to use OLE. Although there are many features and aspects of OLE that aren't covered, this gives you a flavor of what OLE is all about. It makes available an entire world of application software that you can reach and use from within your own Visual Basic applications.

---

[1] If this icon does not appear in your Toolbox, make sure that the file MSOLE2.VBX appears in your Project window. If it is missing, it can be added by using Add File from the Visual Basic File menu. The file can probably be found in C:\WINDOWS\SYSTEM.

Name: _____ Date Due: _____

LAB 12.1

LEARNING OBJECTIVES

- Using the OLE control
- Linking OLE objects into Visual Basic
- Changing chart formats in Excel

NOTE: In order to carry out this lab, you must have Microsoft Excel software available on your system.

1. ____ Open a new Visual Basic project. This project will show the results of sampling the levels of various contaminants at three different lakes.

   ____ Lay out the opening form with a title label and two command buttons, similar to the form shown here.

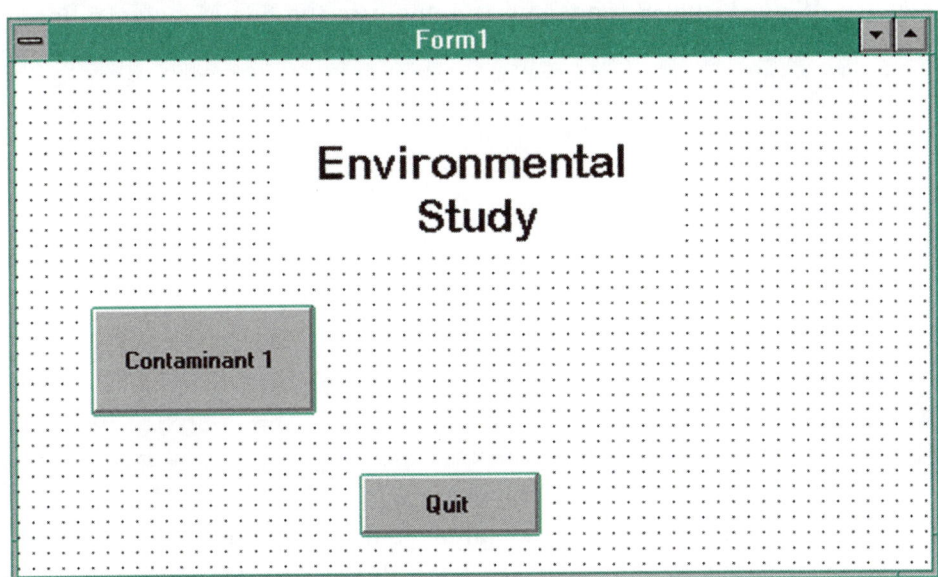

   ____ Write code for the click event for the Quit button.

2. ____ Create a second form, either by using the Toolbar icon or selecting New Form from the File menu.

   ____ Save your files as *environ1.frm, environ2.frm,* and *environ.mak*.

   ____ Write code for the click event for the Contaminant 1 button on the opening form that shows the second form. (The title form can have other command buttons that go to other forms to track the levels of other contaminants; this is just a demonstration.)

   ____ Put one command button on the second form that, when clicked, shows the title form again.

Using the OLE control

3. ___ Using the OLE icon, click and drag an OLE control to cover about half the second form. What happens next?

   ___ Select Cancel for this dialog box, as you are not going to insert an object yet.

   ___ Put a second OLE control on the other half of the second form, and select Cancel for its dialog box as well.

   ___ Save your work.

4. ___ While Visual Basic is still running, use the File Manager to locate the file *environ.xls*. Double-click on this file name. Describe what you see.

   This is an Excel spreadsheet containing data on parts per million of contaminant based on samples taken from three lake sites.[2] There is also a column graph of these data. The Visual Basic project you are building will serve as a "front end" to allow the user to easily work on this spreadsheet and similar spreadsheets that contain data for other contaminants.

   ___ Using the Excel cursor, which is shaped like a fat cross, click and drag to select (highlight) the data cells in the upper left corner of the spreadsheet. Select four rows and two columns.

   ___ Using the Excel Edit menu, select Copy, which places a copy of this section of the spreadsheet in the Clipboard.

Linking OLE objects

   ___ Return to the Visual Basic application; select the OLE1 control on Form 2.

---

[2] If you were unsuccessful in opening this file, check with your instructor about the Microsoft Excel software.

___ With the cursor inside the OLE1 control, click on the *right* mouse button. You see a pop-up menu. What are your choices?

___ Choose Paste Special. You see the following dialog box. The source (the server) has already been identified as a Microsoft Excel worksheet.

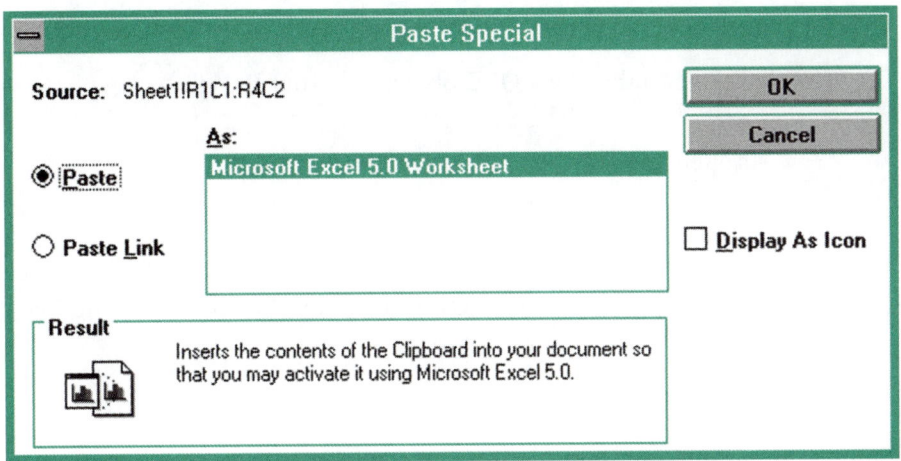

___ Choose the Paste Link option and then OK. What is the result?

5. ___ You have now created a linked OLE object in your Visual Basic form. Repeat this process to paste the chart portion of the spreadsheet as a linked OLE object in the OLE2 control on Form 2.

___ Resize and rearrange your OLE controls to provide the most pleasing display.

___ Go to the Excel spreadsheet and choose Exit from the File menu, which will close the spreadsheet and exit the Excel software.

6. ___ Run your Visual Basic program and double-click on the data OLE object in Form 2. What happens?

___ Change one of the data items by a large amount. What happens to the chart in the spreadsheet?

What happens to the chart OLE object in Visual Basic?

___ You can update the chart OLE object by double-clicking it. Try this. What happens?

___ Close Excel.

___ Go back to design mode in Visual Basic. Do the images in Form2 reflect the new values or the old values?

___ The linked objects in Visual Basic retain their original values; these values are updated the next time the link to the spreadsheet is activated. This means that the next time the Visual Basic program is executed, before the spreadsheet is activated, the values displayed are not the most current. To fix this, put the following code in the Form2_Load procedure:

```
OLE1.Action = 6
OLE2.Action = 6
```

This causes the images to be updated as the Visual Basic program is run, without having to activate the spreadsheet link.

7. ___ Run your Visual Basic program and activate the chart OLE object.

   ___ In the Excel spreadsheet, double-click on the chart object to activate it.

   ___ From the Excel Format menu, choose AutoFormat.

   ___ Change the chart to a pie chart, in which each sector has a different color and is labeled with the name of the site. What does the chart look like in Excel?

   Changing chart formats in Excel

   ___ Close Excel.

   ___ What does the chart look like in your running Visual Basic program?

   ___ Go to design mode. What does the chart look like on Form 2?

   ___ Run your Visual Basic program again. What does the chart look like on Form 2 when the program is running?

   ___ Close your Visual Basic program and save your work.

> **QuickCheck 12.1**
>
> 1. What does DDE stand for?
> 2. What does OLE stand for?
> 3. Who initiates a DDE "conversation," the client or the server?
> 4. When a Visual Basic program that contains an OLE object is running, how is the application software for that object accessed?
> 5. True or False: A linked OLE object includes the actual data associated with the object.

12.3 Interacting with databases

The library project has gone through a number of stages. In Chapter 8, the first version of the library project (*library.mak*) "hard-coded" data about five books into a collection of forms. In Chapter 11, that evolved into a program (*libfil.mak*) that could read data about any five books from a sequential file and display it in the Forms collection. A more general version (*books.mak*) used an arbitrary-size sequential file of book information and displayed the current record in a single form. These three versions all allow the user to browse the book collection and to search for a particular book title or author. The *books.mak* project also allows the user to add a new book to the file. Another version (*libran.mak*) in Chapter 11 stores the book data in a random-access file. A list box allows the user to scroll through the book titles, arranged in alphabetical order, and to get complete book information for any selected title. Options to add a record to the file and delete a record from the file are also available.

In all the work so far using files for the library data, the file has no intelligence about the kind of data stored there. In the sequential file, the data are merely comma-delimited strings (in the library application there is no numeric data). In the random-access file, although a record structure is written to the file, it is the Visual Basic program that understands the various fields of the record. Indeed, the first record in the file is a control record; the file doesn't know the difference, as long as the record is the correct length.

Instead of keeping the library data in a file, it can be kept in a relational database. A **relational database** is a collection of data organized into one or more tables of related data. A **table** contains a set of similar data records, that is, records that have the same fields. An individual data record is one row of the table. The table, however, also includes knowledge about the record fields. In creating the table, the name of each field and the type of data it contains is specified. Figure 12.3 shows part of the Books table for the library database. The record structure is similar to the record structure used before, except that two more fields have been added to each record, the author's country of origin and an image of that country's flag. (The description of the Flag field indicates that a binary object—a graphic file of the flag—is stored there. Databases can contain graphic data as well as text and numeric data.)

Figure 12.3
Part of the Books table in the library database

Title	Author	PubDate	Country	Flag
Leaves of Grass	Walt Whitman	1855	United States	Long binary
The Last of the Mohicans	James Fenimore Cooper	1826	United States	Long binary
The Scarlet Letter	Nathaniel Hawthorne	1850	United States	Long binary

This simple database has only one table, but the power of relational databases is their ability to link together related tables. For example, the library database can have another table that contains more details about a book title—its publication history, its ISBN number, how many copies of it the library carries, and so on. Still another table can contain more data about authors. Both these tables are related to the table of Figure 12.3 by a common field (book title in one case, author name in the other).

The library database can be constructed using database software such as Microsoft Access. Visual Basic also provides a program called the Database Manager that creates Access-format databases, although the Database Manager is a much weaker tool for creating databases than Access.[3] The Database Manager can be launched from the Windows menu of Visual Basic.

Assume that the database has been constructed. The aim is to do, from Visual Basic, the same things with the library database that can be done with data in a file: browse the data, search the data, add more books, and delete existing books. Visual Basic provides a **Data control** that links a Visual Basic application to a database and allows many of these tasks to be done with very little code. The icon for the data control is shown here.

The **DatabaseName property** of the data control connects the data control to a particular database. The **RecordSource property** connects the data control to a particular table within the database. Once these connections are established, the data control has the set of records from the table available to it and can scroll through the record set. Figure 12.4 shows the data control as it appears on a form. When the program executes, the first record in the record set automatically becomes the "current record." Scrolling through the records is done by using the arrow buttons on the data control, as shown in Figure 12.4. The rightmost arrow makes the last record the current record. The leftmost arrow makes the first record the current record. The inner arrows move to the previous record (left arrow) or the next record (right arrow).

Figure 12.4
Data control

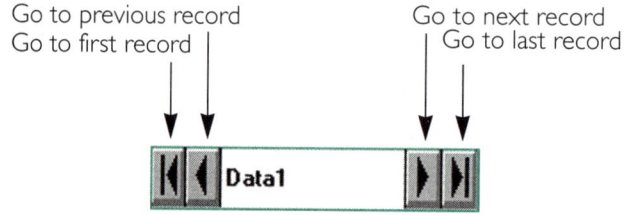

---

[3] The Database Manager in Visual Basic 3.0 produces a database in Access 1.1 format. If a database is created using Access 2.0, Visual Basic 3.0 will be unable to read it. This problem can be solved by installing additional software called the Microsoft Jet 2.0/Visual Basic 3.0 Compatibility Layer, available at no charge from Microsoft.

Although the data control provides the current record concept as a sliding "window" in the database table, this by itself does not make the current record visible on the Visual Basic form. The various fields of the current record are made visible by adding other control objects to the form and "binding" them to the data control. Each such **bound control** can be made to display the data from a specific field of the current record; because of this, bound controls are also called **data aware**. As the data control scrolls through the record set, the bound controls all change their display accordingly, so that they always present data from the current record. Furthermore, if the user changes the data in a bound control, those changes are saved in the data control's record set, that is, in the database table. Controls that can be made data aware are text boxes, labels, check boxes, image controls, and picture boxes.

Binding, say, a text box to the data control is done by setting the **DataSource property** of the text box to the name of the data control. The **DataField property** of the text box is set to the name of the field the text box is to display. When the program executes, this text box displays the value of that field for the current record.

The ability to browse the records in a database table is achieved without having to write a single line of code, thanks to the power of the Visual Basic data control. Moreover, modifying a record field is equally easy—just make the desired change in the control that is bound to that field. As soon as you move to a different current record, the change is incorporated into the database.

This operation is, in fact, a bit too easy. It may be appropriate to grant read-only access to the database. This gives users of the Visual Basic program the ability to browse all the records but prohibits them from changing the data in the database. The **ReadOnly property** of the data control, set by default to false, controls read-only versus read-write privileges.

When the data control is set as ReadOnly and the user changes a record field, there is no indication—other than coming back and looking at the record again—that the change didn't take effect in the database. It is nice to issue a message to the user that the database is set to read-only so that he or she doesn't bother with further attempts to change data. When the user changes the data in a bound control, a run-time property of that control called the **DataChanged property** gets set from false (the default) to true. When the data control is about to leave the existing current record (and before attempting to update the database), a **Validate event** takes place. The data control's Validate event is an appropriate place to put code that checks for any true DataChanged properties and writes a message about the read-only status.

12.4 Adding, deleting, and searching records

In order to add, delete, and search records, some code must be written. This code involves the **Recordset property** of the data control, a run-time-only property. Although technically a property, Recordset can be thought of as an object—the set of records available to the data control. Methods can be applied to the Recordset property, just as if it were an object.

Some methods that can be applied to the Recordset duplicate the effects of the arrows on the data control. For example, a command button on the form can be used to move to the next record by applying the **MoveNext method** to the Recordset. The Click event code for the button would be

```
Sub Command1_Click ()
    Data1.Recordset.MoveNext
End Sub
```

Clicking this button has the same effect as clicking one of the arrows on the data control. Notice the syntax of giving first the control object (Data1), then the read-only property (Recordset), then the method (MoveNext). The methods that duplicate the effects of the other three arrows on the data control are **MoveFirst, MoveLast,** and **MovePrevious**.

Adding a new record can be done by the **AddNew method** applied, as the MoveNext method, to the data control's Recordset property. The AddNew method creates a new, blank record as the last record and makes all the bound controls blank so that new data can be entered. Using the data control's arrows to move to a different record saves this new record in the database.

The **Delete method** deletes the current record. It's a good idea to use a message box to ask the user if he or she really wants to delete a record from the database before proceeding. Also, after the Delete method is applied, the data from the current record still remains on the screen, even though it is no longer a valid record. This can be confusing. Including a MoveNext method at the end of the delete procedure changes the screen display; this is probably more consistent with the user's idea of deleting a record.

Searching records can be done using the Recordset's **FindFirst method**. To use this method, specify the criterion you are trying to satisfy. This is not difficult, but the syntax is confusing (see Lab 12.2). Then the FindFirst method sets the current record equal to the first record in the Recordset that matches this criterion. If there is no match, the current record remains current, and the Recordset's **NoMatch property** is set from false (the default) to true.

With relatively little code, all the capabilities that had to be worked so hard for when using files—browsing, modifying, adding, deleting, and searching records—are accomplished.

Name: _____   Date Due: _____

LEARNING OBJECTIVES

- Linking a Visual Basic program to an Access database
- Modifying records in the database
- Adding new records to the database
- Deleting records from the database
- Searching the database

LAB 12.2

1. ____ Open a new Visual Basic project; save the files as *libdb.frm* and *libdb.mak*.

   Linking to a database

   ____ Place a Data control on the form.

   ____ In the Properties window, select the DatabaseName property and open the Settings box. This opens a dialog box similar to the one shown here, although you may have to change the drive and directory to locate the file *lib.mdb*. Select this file, which is a Microsoft Access database containing a Books table similar to that shown in Figure 12.3.

   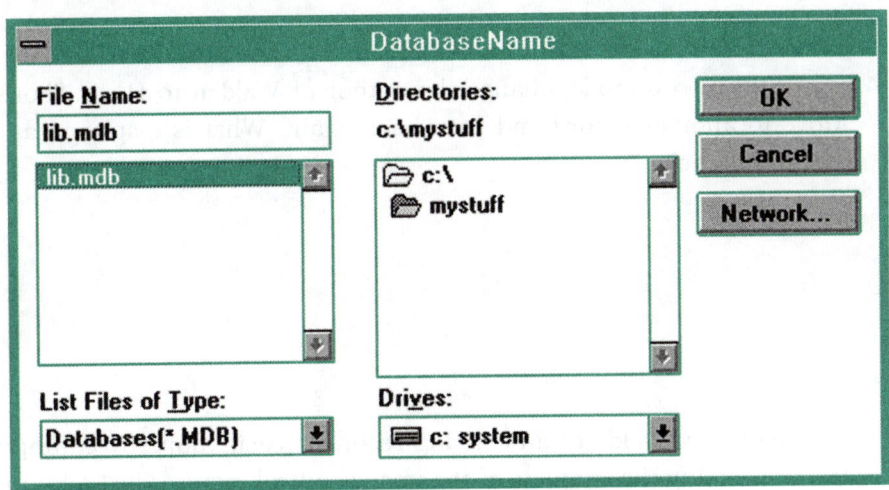

   ____ The Visual Basic program is now connected to the database, but the database can contain multiple tables. Use the RecordSource property to select the only table in this database, namely Books. (If there are other tables, clicking the Settings box produces a pull-down list.)

2. ____ Place four text boxes and one image control on your form to correspond to the five fields of the database. Set their DataSource properties. (The data source is Data1 for each control. You can set this property for all controls at the same time by using the selector arrow to group the controls in an elastic selector box. Then open the Properties window and double-click on DataSource to set this property to Data1—the only option

for this form. This will set the DataSource properties of all five controls to Data1.)

_____ Set the five DataField properties.

_____ Add descriptive labels for each of these controls.

3. _____ Run the Visual Basic program. Describe the data for the last record in the record set.

Give the country of origin of the author of the seventh book in the record set.

Modifying records in the database

4. _____ Still in run mode, change the author of Walden to H. D. Thoreau. Move to another record and then back again. What is displayed as the author's name?

Modifying text fields of an existing record is easily done by editing the text. Modifying the contents of the image control requires just a bit more work (see Project 2 at the end of this chapter).

5. _____ Set up a menu structure on your form as follows:

> Files
>> Exit
>
> Records
>> Add a Record
>> Delete a Record
>
> Search
>> On Title
>> On Author

_____ Write code for the Exit menu pick.

6. ____ Write code for the Add-a-Record menu pick. As part of this code, apply the **SetFocus method** to the text box where you expect the user will first want to enter data, probably the text box for the Title field. This ensures that this text box is the one that has the focus.

Adding new records to the database

____ Run the program and add text data for two new books. What about the image control for these new records? (Adding data for the image control is discussed in Project 3 at the end of this chapter.)

7. ____ Write code for the Delete-a-Record menu pick.

Deleting records from the database

____ Delete the first record in the file. What happens to the screen display?

____ Delete the last record in the file. What happens to the screen display?

____ Test to see that your program works correctly when the user cancels a delete operation.

Searching the database

8. ____ Use the following code to implement the Search-by-Title menu.

```
Dim Target As String

Target = InputBox$("Enter the title you are searching
 for", "Library database")
If Target <> "" Then
    Data1.Recordset.FindFirst "Title = '" & Target & "'"
    If Data1.Recordset.NoMatch = True Then
        MsgBox "No record with this title was found",
         "Search Result"
    End If
End If
```

Be particularly careful of the punctuation; in the following code single quotes and double quotes are separated so you can see the order in which they appear, but these spaces should not be in your code.

```
"Title = ' " & Target & " ' "
```

____ Try your code for both successful and unsuccessful searches.

____ Add code to implement the Search-by-Author menu.

____ Test your program thoroughly and save your work.

> **QuickCheck 12.2**
>
> 1. What is a table in a relational database?
> 2. A data control is connected to a database by setting the _____ property.
> 3. A data control is connected to a particular table in a database by setting the _____ property.
> 4. What is a bound control?
> 5. Records in a database table are manipulated by applying methods to a data control's _____ property.

12.5 Querying a database

The search of the library database for a specific book title or a specific author is a particular form of **query**. The result is to show the first record that fits a specified criterion. One of the principal advantages of using database software is to be able to perform complex queries on the data. In the library database, for example, you may want to see all the records for books by British authors or all the records for books published in the 1800s. If the database consists of multiple tables, queries can be done that involve data from more than one table. For example, if the library database contains a second table with data about book titles that include the title, publication history, ISBN number, and number of copies in the library, you may want to see all the ISBN numbers (data from table 2) for books with British authors (data from table 1).

Different database software packages feature different ways for the user to pose a query. Behind the scenes, however, almost all systems translate the user's query into **Structured Query Language**, or **SQL**. SQL is an international standard query language for relational databases.

When a Visual Basic program is linked to a database, queries can be formulated in SQL and run against the database. For example, the search for a particular title in the library database, rephrased as an SQL query, is

```
SELECT * FROM Books WHERE Title = 'Walden'
```

"SELECT *" says to pick all records from the record set that satisfy the criterion that follows. In this case, the criterion is a specific value for the title, so only one record in the database satisfies the criterion.

When a search by title was done using the FindFirst method, the single matching record was displayed as the current record, but the data control's record set remained unchanged; that is, it was still possible to scroll through all the records in the table. However, when an SQL query is executed, the set of records displayed by the data control is reduced to just the set of records satisfying the query. This new set of records associated with the data control is called a **Dynaset** because it can be dynamically changed while the program is running by performing different queries. The code temporarily changes the data control's RecordSource property from the whole table (the design-time value) to the Dynaset represented by the query. The entire query is carried out by the two lines of code

```
Data1.RecordSource = "SELECT * FROM Books WHERE title = 'Walden'"
Data1.Refresh
```

The first line describes the Dynaset and assigns it to the data control's RecordSource property. (Note that the query is in quotes.) The second line of code actually reopens the database so that the appropriate records can be loaded into the Dynaset.

Multiple criteria can be applied as part of a Select statement, for example,

```
SELECT * FROM Books WHERE PubDate > '1800' and PubDate < '1900'
```

creates a Dynaset containing only the books with a publication date within the specified range.

An ordering can be imposed on the Dynaset by using the SQL ORDER BY command. Thus

```
SELECT * FROM Books WHERE PubDate < '1800' ORDER BY Title
```

arranges the Dynaset of all books published before 1800 in order alphabetically by title.

12.6 A disclaimer

The capabilities of Visual Basic to interact with a database have barely been touched on; they could be the subject of another entire book! In fact, as the end of your adventure with Visual Basic nears, there's a lot that hasn't been covered, but you have enough of a start to use the Help system, read the manuals, and explore on your own.

THOUGHTS ON PROGRAMMING

System Integration

A Visual Basic program may not be a stand-alone affair. Instead it may interact with other applications in the user's computing environment. The DDE, OLE, and database capabilities of Visual Basic enhance this integration so that the user has not just a collection of applications, but an integrated suite of communicating, cooperating applications. Also, in this era of networking and distributed computing, the user's "computing environment" may no longer mean just his or her desktop machine but all machines to which the desktop machine is networked.

The implications for testing a Visual Basic application are significant. If the application is supposed to interact with version A of software package B, then it needs to be tested in that environment, Don't assume, for example, because you have version A1 of software package B and have tested the Visual Basic application in that environment, that it will work in the user's environment. Experienced developers allow plenty of time for testing in the user's environment to make sure that their application integrates seamlessly with the rest of the user's world.

The implications for program maintenance are also significant. The more other applications your Visual Basic application "talks to," the more you are at risk for updated versions of those other applications. Software developers attempt to keep new versions "downward compatible" with previous versions, meaning that what ran under a previous version still runs under the new version. If your Visual Basic program worked with version 4.0 of some other application, it is likely—*but not guaranteed*—to work with version 4.5. What is likely, however, is that version 4.5 introduces some new feature that your user wants your Visual Basic program to take advantage of. This sends you back to your documentation (Thoughts on Programming, Chapter 4), and perhaps requires a renegotiation of the program requirements and specifications (Thoughts on Programming, Chapter 5), a modification of your original top-down design (Chapter 6) and representations of your new design (Chapter 7), and a new prototype to show your user for early feedback to see if you are on the right track (Chapter 8). You may be able to reuse code modules from other projects (Chapter 9), but you are alert to the issue of algorithm efficiency in any code you decide to reuse (Chapter 10). Of course, you'll have to test everything again (Chapter 11), and make sure it integrates into the user's computing environment (Chapter 12). By that time there may be another version of . . .

Name: _____   Date Due: _____

LAB 12.3

LEARNING OBJECTIVES

- Building an SQL query in Visual Basic
- Using simple SQL queries

1. ____ Open your *libdb.mak* project from Lab 12.2.

   ____ Save the files as *libSQL.frm* and *libSQL.mak*.

   ____ Delete the code for the two Search menu choices.

   ____ Using the Menu Design window, delete the Search menu and its submenus. Replace them with

   Query
     Compose Query
     Ordered By
     Reset Display

2. ____ The Ordered By is a checked menu item. When checked, it means that the query has an ORDER BY component; when unchecked, there is no ORDER BY in the query. A checked menu item is a toggle switch. Write code for the Ordered By menu click event that turns the checked property on if it is off, and off if it is on.

3. ____ Add one long label to your form that is used to display the query the user made. Add another label that identifies what is in this long label.

   ____ Set the Visible property of both labels to false.

4. The Compose Query menu pick does all the work for a query. The query, which is a string, is built by concatenating up to three parts.

   ____ In the Compose Query click event, declare four string variables: *FirstPart*, *SecondPart*, *ThirdPart*, and *SQL* (which is the final query string).

   ____ *FirstPart* is the same string in any query. Assign the string

   `"SELECT * FROM Books WHERE "`

   to *FirstPart*.

   ____ Make *SecondPart* the value returned by an *InputBox$* function that collects the user's criterion for the search. (Remind the user that strings are placed in single quotes.)

   ____ Concatenate *FirstPart* and *SecondPart* to get *SQL*.

Building an SQL query in Visual Basic

___ Write code so that if the Ordered By menu is checked, *ThirdPart* is assigned the value of an *InputBox$* function that asks the user what to order by, and then *SQL* is assigned the value

```
SQL & " ORDER BY " & ThirdPart
```

___ Write code to assign the *SQL* string to the data control's RecordSource property and refresh the data control.

___ To finish up, write the *SQL* string in the query label's caption (after making it and its identifying label visible, of course).

5. ___ Run your program. Try a query that asks for all records for title = 'Walden'. Scroll the data control. What happens and why?

___ Run your program, try a query, and select Cancel at the input box. What happens?

___ Fix the Compose Query code to handle this situation.

___ Run your program, check the Ordered By menu pick, and select Cancel at the input box that asks how to order. What happens?

___ Fix the Compose Query code to handle this situation.

6. ___ The Reset Display menu pick is used after a query has been made. It should set the Dynaset back to the original set of records. This can be done by using a SELECT query with no criteria and then refreshing the data control. Write the two lines of code needed in the Reset Display menu click event.

____ Run your program, make a query, and then try the Reset Display menu pick. What problem do you see on the form?

____ Add two more lines of code to the Reset Display menu code to solve this problem.

7. Try your program on the following queries and write the titles of the records returned by each query:

Using simple SQL queries

____ All records for books whose author comes from Great Britain. Titles:

____ All records for books published between 1800 and 1900. Titles:

____ All records for books published before 1850, ordered by publication date. Titles:

___ All records for books published by U.S. authors, ordered by title. Titles:

___ All records for books with the title 'The White Cat'. There is no such record in the database; what happens as a result of this query?

8. ___ Save your work. And congratulations on finishing the last lab!

QuickCheck 12.3

1. SQL stands for _____.
2. What is the meaning of "SELECT *" in an SQL query?
3. What is the difference between searching for a title with the FindFirst method and doing an SQL query?
4. What is the Dynaset for a query for which no records satisfy the criterion?
5. What is meant by "system integration"?

Review Questions

1. The ability to send data to another application and request services from that application best describes DDE or OLE?
2. The ability to launch another application directly from a graphic image within a Visual Basic program best describes DDE or OLE?
3. Explain the difference between a linked OLE object and an embedded OLE object.
4. What is the advantage in a multiuser environment of a linked OLE object as opposed to an embedded OLE object?
5. Starting with a new Visual Basic form, describe the steps needed to link a text box control to a field in a database table.
6. What control objects can serve as bound controls?
7. Why are bound controls called "data aware"?
8. Describe how to browse the records in a database table.
9. Describe how to modify a record in a database table.
10. Suppose you want a user of your Visual Basic program to be able to browse a database but not make any changes in it. What property should be set?
11. Name the four Recordset methods that simulate the actions of the data control's four arrows.
12. When the AddNew method is applied to a data control's record set, where does the new record go in the table?
13. Almost all database systems use _____ as the underlying language for queries.
14. The string that is the SQL query is assigned to what property of the data control?
15. What is the difference between a Dynaset and a Recordset?
16. What is the purpose of the Data1.Refresh statement after a query?
17. A SELECT query that asked for the records resulting from the query to be arranged in a certain way would use the _____ command.

18. What is the SELECT query to retrieve all records from the Books table?
19. What does it mean when a new version of a software package claims to be downward compatible with a previous version?
20. What are the implications of system integration for testing a Visual Basic program?

Exercises

Reading code

1. What is the effect of the statement

   `Data1.Recordset.MoveLast`

2. The condition

   `Data1.Recordset.NoMatch = True`

   is tested under what circumstances?

   Describe the results of each of the following SQL queries against the library database.

3. `SELECT * FROM Books WHERE Country = 'Russia'`
4. `SELECT * FROM Books WHERE Country = 'Great Britain' and PubDate > '1900'`
5. `SELECT * FROM Books WHERE PubDate > '1850' ORDER BY Country`

Writing code

6. Write a statement to make the first record in the record set the current record.
7. Write two statements that delete the last record in a database table.
8. Write three statements that delete the second record in a database table.
9. Write an SQL query for the set of records in the Books table for books that were published in 1850.
10. Write the two Visual Basic statements that result in a Dynaset of all the records in the library database for books with British authors ordered by publication date.

Exploring further

Note: In order to do Exercises 11 and 12 below, you must have Microsoft Excel software available on your system.

11. In the *environ.mak* project of Lab 12.1, change the chart to a line chart.
12. Using Excel, set up a spreadsheet with data similar to those of the *environ.mak* project of Lab 12.1, together with a chart. Then on the title form of the *environ.mak* project, create another command button for a second contaminant that has linked objects consisting of the data and a chart from this new spreadsheet.

13. Using the Visual Basic Data Manager, modify the *lib.mdb* database by adding an additional record field called Type (poetry, essay, novel, and so on). Fill in the value of this data field for each of the existing records.
14. Using your *libSQL.mak* project from Lab 12.3, include another text box (and label) for Type (see Exercise 13).
15. Perform several queries, such as asking for all the records for books of British poetry, or for U.S. novels.

Projects

1. In the *libdb.mak* project, set the data control's ReadOnly property to true. As noted, changes made to a record appear successful, unless you later scroll back to the record and find it to be unchanged. Add code to the data control's Validate event that checks each of the text box controls for any changes and issues a message that the data base has been set to read-only mode.

   An attempt to add a record or delete a record in read-only mode generates an error message, after which the system crashes. You could use error trapping to solve this problem, but for the delete, the error handler takes effect only after the user has already been asked to confirm that he or she wants to delete the record. It is annoying to answer this question, only to then see a message about the inability to delete due to the read-only status. So instead, handle this problem with an If-Then-Else statement, for both adding a record and deleting a record.

2. In the *libdb.mak* project, the picture shown in the image control is obtained from a file (one of the icon files supplied by Visual Basic, usually stored in C:\VB\ICONS\FLAGS). Modifying the image control means using a different icon file for the picture property.

   Add a Common Dialog control to the form. The image control is modified by clicking on it, so for the image control's Click event, write code to:

   Set the Filter property of the Common Dialog control to show icon files (*.ICO) as a first choice, then all files as a second choice.

   Set the **DialogTitle property** (which controls the title bar of the dialog window) of the Common Dialog control to something like "Choose a flag icon".

   Set the Common Dialog control Action property to 1 (an Open dialog box).

   Apply the **LoadPicture** function to the Filename property of the Common Dialog control and assign the result to the image control's Picture property (this is all one statement).

   Run your program (with ReadOnly set to false) and change the flag for Walt Whitman, author of the first book, to the Mexican flag. Go to another record and back to see that the change was permanent.

3. In the *libdb.mak* project, when adding a new record, the data for the image control must be added. Assuming the code written for Project 2 is in place, clicking on the image control allows the icon file to be selected. However, the image control is not visible, so it is difficult to click on it. This problem can be solved by having the text box for the Country field, as it loses the focus, invoke a click event for the image control. Add the necessary code and test your program.

4. Using the Visual Basic Data Manager, set up a database consisting of a single table with information about employee Social Security numbers, first names, last names, job classifications (salaried, hourly), and years of employment. Create a Visual Basic program linked to this database, with the ability to display the record fields. Add menu choices to add a record or delete a record.

5. In the program from Project 4, add the ability to do queries on the table, such as selecting all records with a given employee last name, all salaried employees, all hourly employees with more than five years' service, and so on.

APPENDIX A

Windows—Once Over Lightly

To bring up the Windows operating system on your computer, you probably need to type "win" (for Windows, of course) at the DOS (Disk Operating System) prompt, which looks like

```
C:\>
```

The only thing (promise!) this book says about DOS is that in order to give an instruction to DOS, you have to type a specific command, like "win", which of course you have to remember. In Windows, you can often issue commands by selecting a small pictorial representation, called an **icon**, of the task you want performed. Because of this pictorial or graphical approach, most people consider Windows much easier to use than DOS, with its command-line approach.

Once you have brought up Windows, what do you see? One of the features of Windows is the way it can easily be configured to the personal desires of each user, so what you see on your system may differ somewhat from what is described here. There is likely, however, to be an assortment of **windows**—that is, rectangular panes enclosed within a frame. One window may be the central or "parent" window, which may contain one or more "child" windows that group related items together. In Figure A.1, for example, the parent window is the Program Manager window, which contains three child windows: Main, Visual Basic 3.0, and Accessories. The child windows each contain several icons.

The usual way to interact with a windows system is to use a pointing device like a **mouse** or a **trackball**; moving the mouse or rolling the ball controls the movement of a **cursor** on the screen. You can think of the cursor as a finger that marks your current "place" on the screen. In the Program Manager window, the cursor usually looks like an arrow. However, the shape of the cursor changes on various parts of the screen and in response to various actions. For example, the arrow shape becomes a two-headed arrow when it is over the edge of a window. It becomes an **hourglass** when you must wait for the completion of some action that is taking place.

Each window has a **title bar** at the top describing the window (Program Manager, etc.). A window can be moved about by placing the cursor anywhere in the title bar, holding down the left mouse button, and rolling the mouse. This operation, called **dragging**, is a common way to move things about on the screen. When the item is in the position you want, you drop it there by letting go of the mouse button. The entire operation of dragging an item to a new position and dropping it there is called a **drag-and-drop** operation. Icons can be dragged and dropped within the child window in which they appear or from one child window to another.

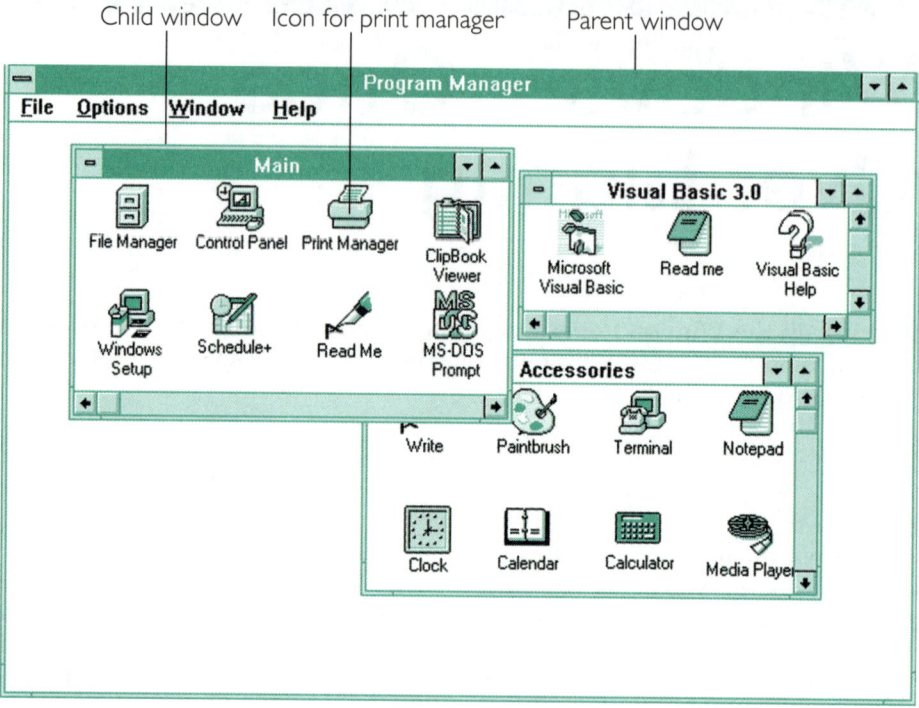

Figure A.1
A Windows screen

Only one child window at a time can be the **active window** or the window that **has the focus**. In Figure A.1, the Main window has the focus; its title bar is highlighted with the color used for the active window, and it overlaps the Accessories window. To give a different window the focus, move the cursor to anywhere within that window and give one rapid "click" (press down/release action) on the left mouse button—in other words, **click** on the window. In Figure A.1, if we click on the Accessories window, it becomes the active window (**gets the focus**). It moves to the foreground, overlapping the Main window, and its title bar is highlighted in the active window color while the Main title bar loses highlighting. The screen now looks like Figure A.2.

A window can be **resized** by moving the cursor to the window's edge until it assumes a double-arrow shape and then dragging the edge to make the window larger or smaller. Some windows may display a horizontal or vertical **scroll bar**. In Figure A.3, the Visual Basic window has both. The presence of a horizontal scroll bar indicates that there are more icons to the side that can't be displayed in the current window size. The presence of a vertical scroll bar indicates that there are more icons above or below that can't be displayed in the current window size. To see these additional icons by "scrolling" them through the window, do one of the following three steps:

OPTIONS
- Drag the little square scroll box along the scroll bar.
- Click one of the arrows at the end of the scroll bar.
- Click in the scroll bar between the scroll box and an arrow.

(When working with windows, there are often multiple ways to do the same task. The icon above is used in this book whenever alternate ways to do the same thing are presented. No one method is better than another; just pick one and use it.)

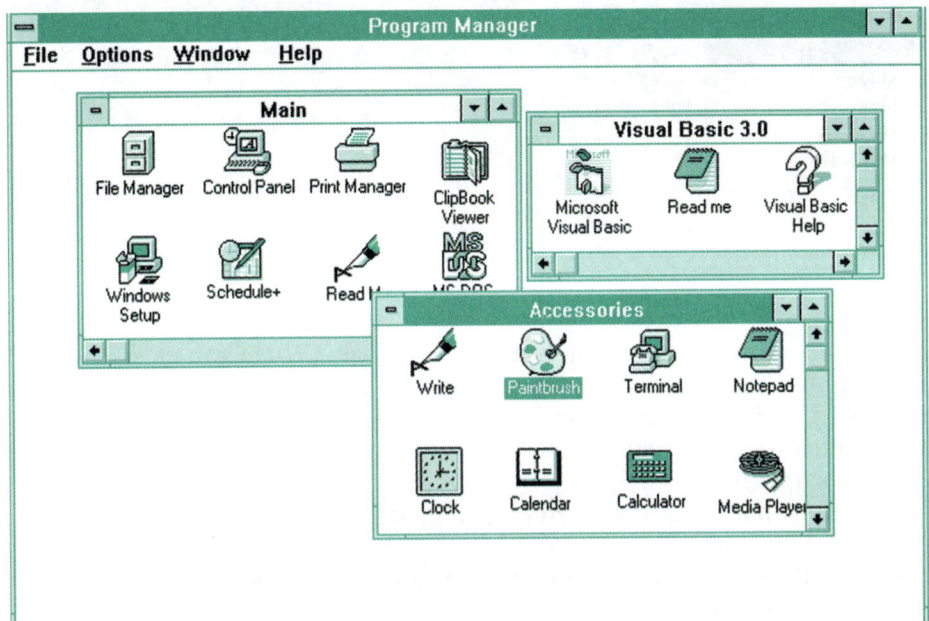

Figure A.2
The Accessories window has the focus

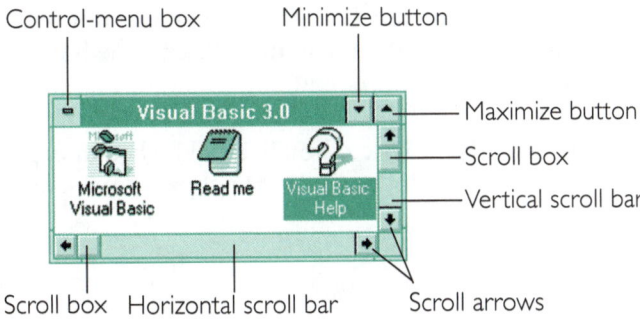

Figure A.3
Additional parts of a window

Figure A.3 also shows a control-menu box, a maximize button, and a minimize button. Clicking on the **maximize button** causes the window to enlarge to fill the size of the parent window or the entire screen. When the window is maximized, a button with a double-headed arrow appears in place of the maximize button; clicking on this button reduces the window to its former size. Clicking on the **minimize button** reduces the window to an icon at the bottom of the screen. To restore the icon to a window, do one of the following:

OPTIONS
- Click once on the icon, which produces a **pop-up menu** (a menu of choices that "pops up" somewhere on the screen); select the Restore option by either pressing the Enter key or by clicking on Restore.
- Double-click (two quick clicks in succession) on the icon.

Still another way to do some of these same windows housekeeping tasks is to use the **control-menu box** at the left end of the title bar. Clicking this box produces a **pull-down menu** (a menu that drops down below the item clicked; see Figure A.4). This menu has choices (also called **menu**

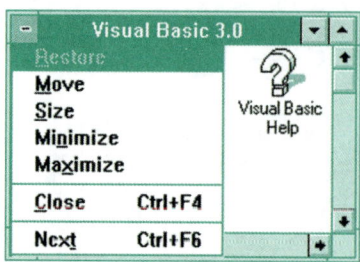

Figure A.4
A pull-down menu

picks) including maximize, minimize, and **close**. (When you close a window for a running program, you are quitting the program.) Double-clicking this box reduces the window to an icon or closes a program. Using the control-menu box in the program manager title bar is also a way to exit the Windows operating system.

To run a windows-based program, again there are some choices.

OPTIONS
- If the program is represented by an icon, double-click on its icon.
- Double-click on the File Manager icon, find the appropriate file name representing the program (you have to know both the file name and where the file is stored), and double-click on the file name.

With a little practice, you'll quickly become proficient at opening, closing, and resizing windows, double-clicking on icons, and dragging-and-dropping.

APPENDIX B

Managing Files

Every Visual Basic program is stored on the computer in several files. Data used by programs can also be stored in files. Eventually, you will have saved quite a number of files on your computer's hard drive or on diskettes, which you may want to delete, copy, or move somewhere else.

To help you with these file management tasks, Windows provides a **File Manager**. The icon for the File Manager, almost always found in the Main window, is shown here. Double-clicking on this icon opens the File Manager application, which provides you with a view of the files on your hard drive or diskette. These storage areas are organized into **directories**; each directory can hold multiple files. Figure A.5 shows the sort of lists you see in the File Manager. The central window is divided into two sections. On the left is a listing of the various directories to be found on hard drive C of one particular machine. The directory *msoffice* is highlighted. The right pane shows the subdirectories of *msoffice* (*access*, *clipart*, etc.) as well as files in this directory (*msoffice.exe*, etc.).

Using the View pull-down menu lets you select All File Details, which gives you information about the date and time each file was created or last changed. This information is helpful when you want to know how long a file has been around or when you last changed it.

New directories can be created by choosing Create Directory... from the File pull-down menu in the File Manager. You are asked to name the new directory before it is created. Highlighting a file name or directory name and choosing Delete from the File menu deletes the file or the entire directory, including all the files it contains. Because this is a rather drastic action, Windows asks you to confirm that this is really what you want to do before blowing your files away.

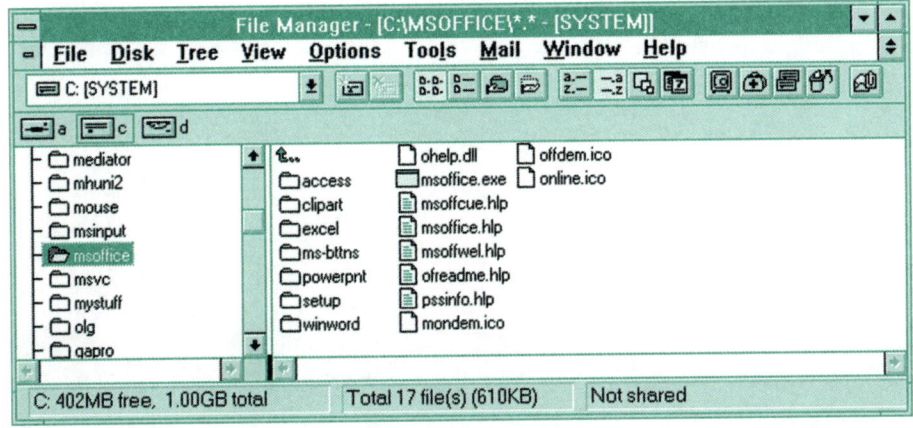

Figure A.5
File Manager window

A highlighted file or directory can be moved or copied to another directory by choosing **Move (Copy)** from the File pull-down menu in the File Manager. Or you can simply drag-and-drop the file name to the new directory. In this case, the status bar at the bottom of the File Manager window tells you whether the file is being moved or copied. If you want to copy instead of move, use the Ctrl key when you drag the file. If a file of the same name already exists in the destination directory, Windows asks you to confirm that you want to overwrite that file.

After a bit of practice, you'll feel comfortable using the File Manager. Just remember to exercise caution; you should make back-up copies of all important files, and you should delete with forethought.

APPENDIX C

Windows 95

If your computer is configured with the Windows 95 operating system (Win95), the operating system comes up automatically when you turn on your computer. One of the features of Windows 95 is the way it can easily be configured to the personal desires of each user, so what you see on your system may differ somewhat from what is described. Figure A.6 shows a typical opening configuration. Several small pictorial representations, called **icons**, appear on the screen. The icons represent pathways to further programs that can be run from the operating system or to other information.

Figure A.6
Windows 95 desktop

The usual way to interact with Win95 is to use a pointing device like a **mouse** or a **trackball**; moving the mouse or rolling the ball controls the movement of a **cursor** on the screen. You can think of the cursor as a finger that marks your current "place" on the screen. The cursor usually looks like an arrow, as in Figure A.6. However, the shape of the cursor changes to signify different things. For example, it becomes an **hourglass** when you must wait for the completion of some action that is taking place.

The mouse is used to "navigate" through the various options available. If you want to see what an icon represents, move the cursor over the icon and **double-click** on that icon (do two quick press down/release actions with the left mouse button). For example, the bottom icon on the "desktop" shown in Figure A.6 represents the Visual Basic program. Double-clicking on that icon opens Visual Basic. Other icons represent not a single program but groups of programs, or **folders**. For example, double-clicking on the

Microsoft Office folder in Figure A.6 opens the window shown in Figure A.7. A **window** is a rectangular pane enclosed within a frame. The window in Figure A.7 contains other icons, and double-clicking on them opens other programs.

Every window has a **title bar** at the top describing the window (Microsoft Office in Figure A.7). A window can be moved by placing the cursor anywhere in the title bar, holding down the left mouse button, and rolling the mouse. This operation, called **dragging**, is a common way to move things about on the screen. When the item is in the position you want, you drop it there by letting go of the mouse button. The entire operation of dragging an item to a new position and dropping it there is called a **drag-and-drop** operation. Icons can be dragged and dropped within the window in which they appear or from one window to another or from a window onto the desktop.

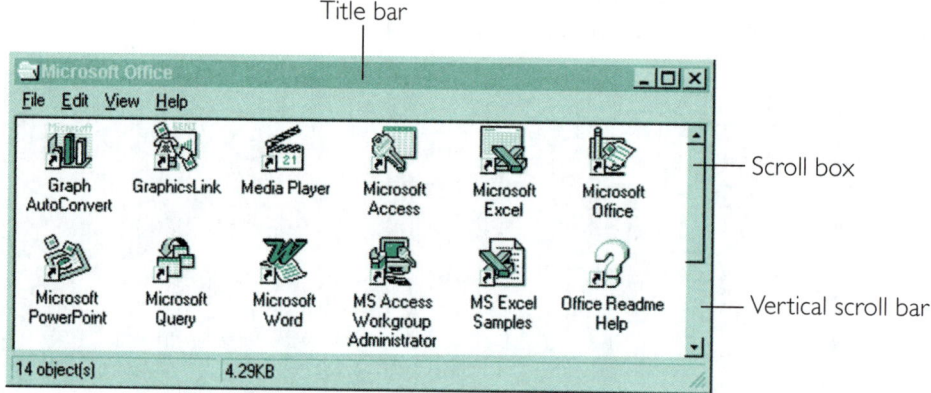

Figure A.7 The Microsoft Office window

A window can be **resized** by moving the cursor to the window's edge until it assumes a double-arrow shape and then dragging the edge to make the window larger or smaller.

Some windows may display a horizontal or vertical **scroll bar**. In Figure A.7, the Microsoft Office window has a vertical scrollbar. This indicates that there are more icons above or below that can't be displayed in the current window size. To see these additional icons by "scrolling" them through the window, do one of the following steps:

- Drag the scroll box along the scroll bar.
- **Click** (press and release the left mouse button) one of the arrows at the end of the scroll bar.
- Click in the scroll bar between the scroll box and an arrow.

(When working with windows, there are often multiple ways to do the same task. The icon above is used in this book whenever alternate ways to do the same thing are presented. No one method is better than another; just pick one and use it.)

It is possible to have multiple windows open at one time. Figure A.8 shows a desktop with three open windows. Only one window at a time can be the **active window** or the window that **has the focus**. In Figure A.8, the Microsoft Office window has the focus; its title bar is highlighted with the color used for the active window, and it overlaps the other windows. To give a different window the focus, move the cursor to anywhere within that window and click the left mouse button. In Figure A.8, if you click on the Control Panel window, it becomes the active window. It moves to the foreground, overlapping the other windows, and its title bar is highlighted in the active window color, while the title bar of the previous active window loses highlighting (Figure A.9) When multiple windows are open, the **taskbar** at

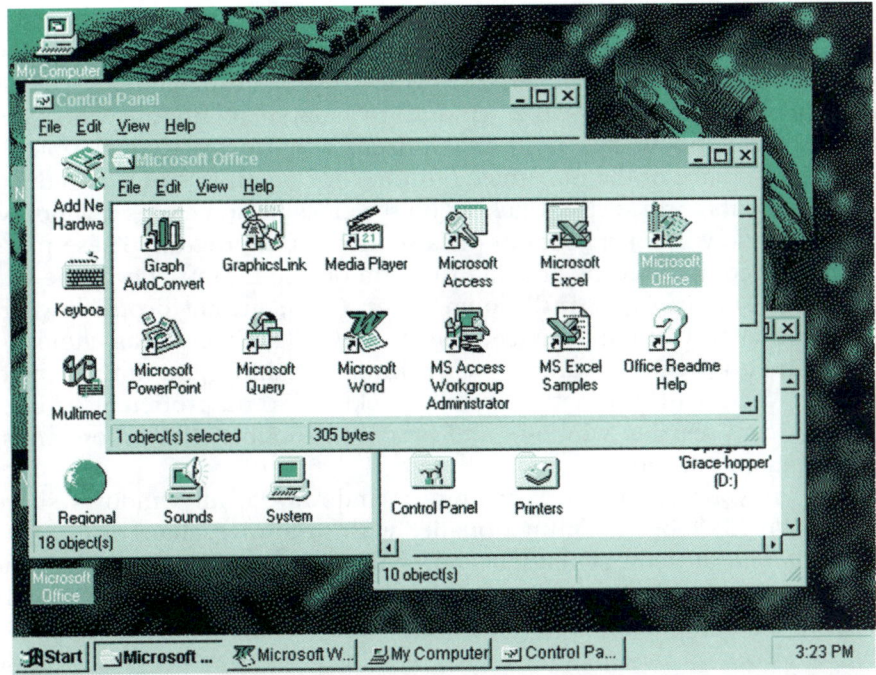

Figure A.8
Microsoft Office is the active window

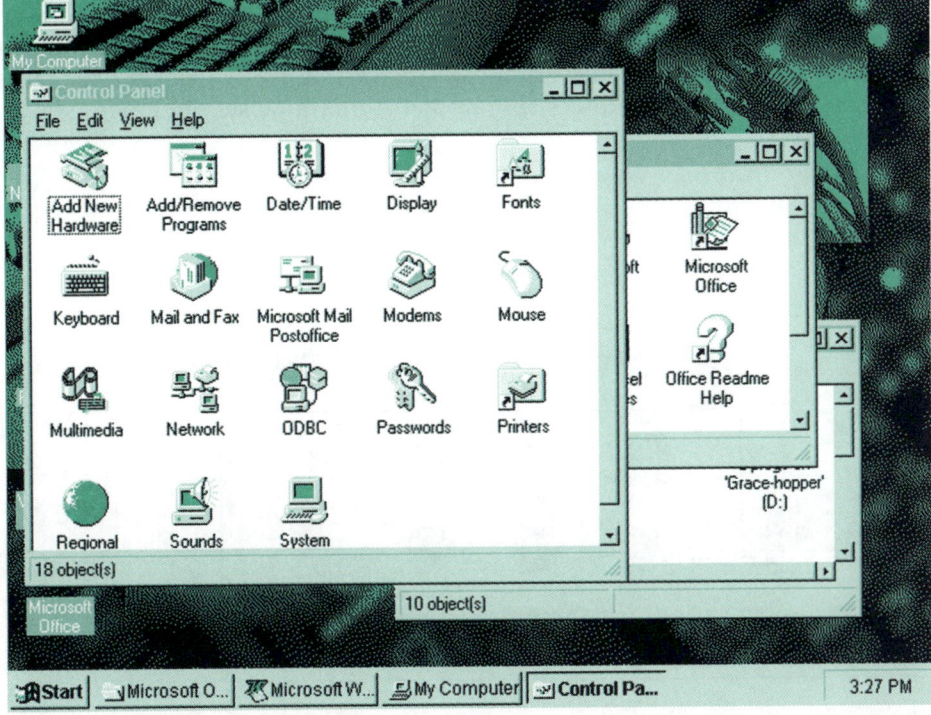

Figure A.9
Control Panel is the active window

the bottom of the screen shows a button for each window (again see Figure A.9), including windows that are folders and windows that are programs. Clicking on one of these buttons is another way to select a window to be the active window. In this way it is possible to switch back and forth between a number of programs that may be running simultaneously. The ability to have more than one application running at one time is a strong point of Windows 95.

Figure A.10 shows the three buttons that appear on the right end of the title bar of every window. These are the **minimize button**, the **maximize button**, and the **close button**. Clicking on the minimize button reduces a window to a button on the taskbar at the bottom of the screen. If the window represents a program, the program is still available. Clicking on the maximize button causes the window to enlarge to fill the whole screen. When the window has been maximized, a button with a double image appears in place of the maximize button; clicking on this button reduces the window to its former size. Clicking on the close button closes a window and, if the window is for a program, it also closes the program These tasks can also be accomplished by clicking the icon on the far left end of the window title bar. This causes a **pull-down menu** (a menu that drops down below the item clicked) to appear (see Figure A.10). This menu has choices—also called **menu picks**—to, among other things, maximize, minimize, and close.

With a little practice, you'll quickly become proficient at opening, closing, and resizing windows and programs, double-clicking on icons, and dragging-and-dropping.

If your computer is running Windows 95, all windows share the same Win95 "look" and functionality with minimize, maximize, and close buttons and an icon at the left end of the title bar. This includes windows you see in Visual Basic and in the programs you create in Visual Basic. Figure A.11 shows the Win95 version of the Visual Basic Form window.

Back on the opening screen of Win95, if programs you want do not have icons on the desktop, you can locate them through a series of menus at the bottom of the screen. Click on the **Start** button on the taskbar. This produces a **pop-up menu** of choices (Figure A.12); one of these is Shut Down, to turn off your computer. Another choice is Programs. Selecting Programs pops up a second, "floating" menu (Figure A.13), and selecting Microsoft Office here produces (Figure A.14) the same set of choices shown in Figure A.7.

Figure A.10
A pull-down menu

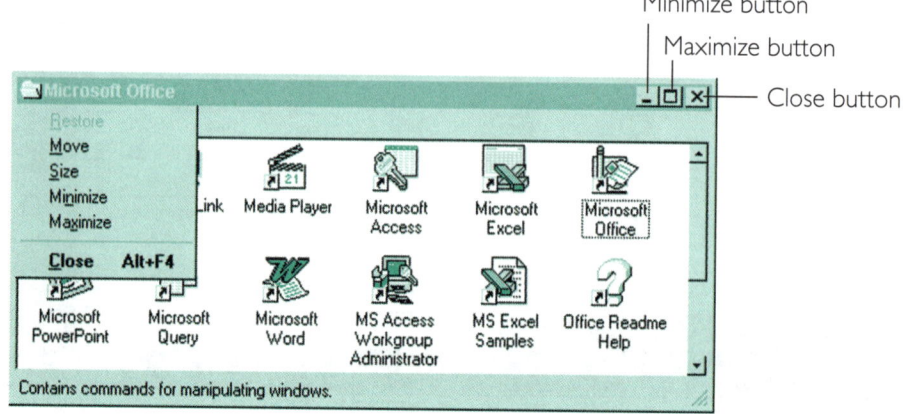

Figure A.11
The Visual Basic Form window in Windows 95

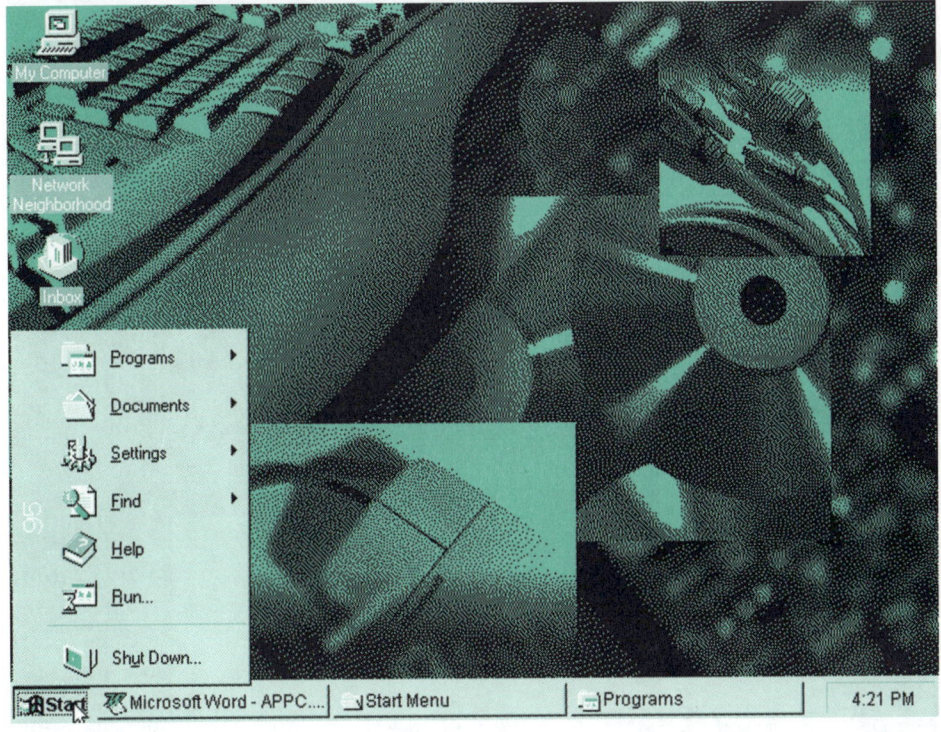

Figure A.12
Pop-up menu

With a little practice, you'll quickly become proficient at opening, closing, and resizing windows and programs, double-clicking on icons, and dragging-and-dropping.

Every Visual Basic program is stored on the computer in several files. Data used by programs can also be stored in files. Eventually, you will have saved quite a number of files on your computer's hard drive or on diskettes, which you may want to delete, copy, or move somewhere else.

To help you with these file management tasks, Windows 95 provides the **Windows Explorer**. The quickest way to bring up Windows Explorer is to click on the Start button on the taskbar using the *right* mouse button,

Figure A.13
Floating menu

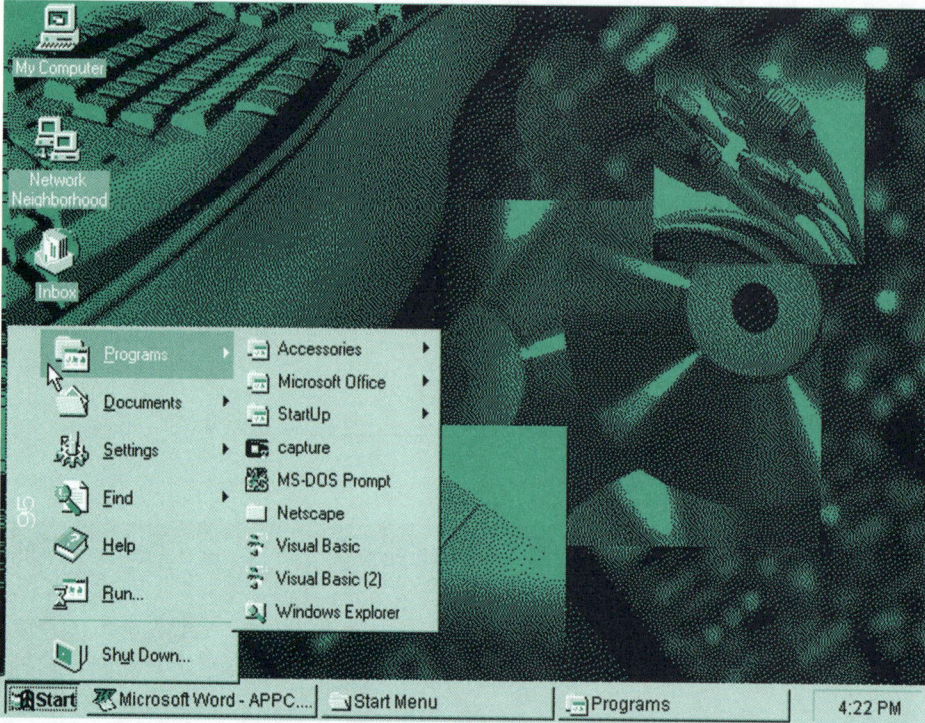

Figure A.14
Third-level menu for Microsoft Office

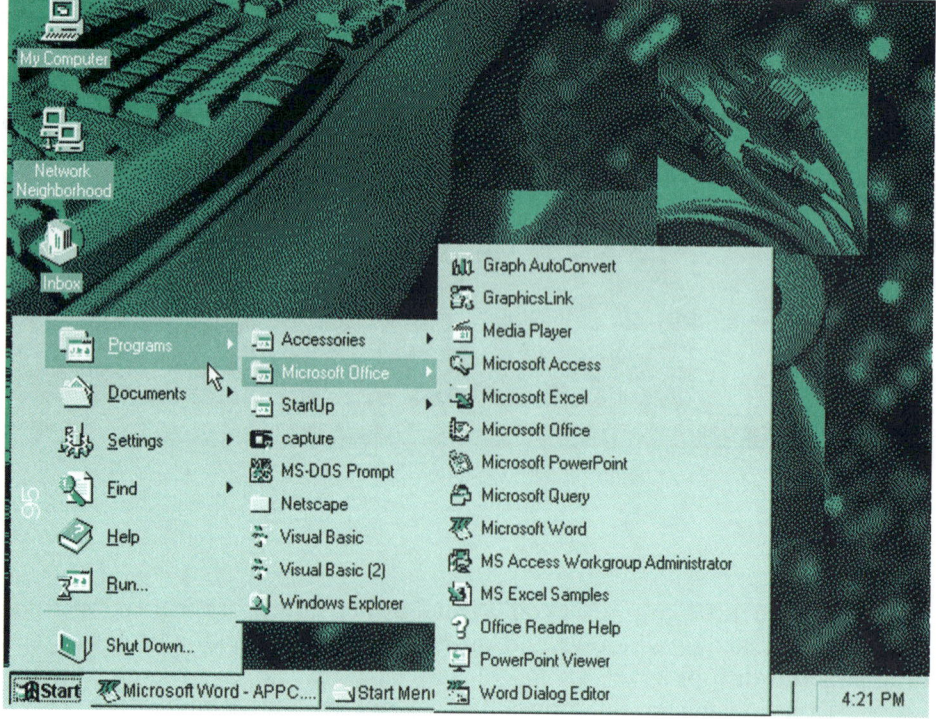

then choose Explore from the pop-up menu. Figure A.15 shows a portion of the Explorer window. It is divided into two sections. On the left is a listing of various folders. The folder *mystuff* is highlighted. The right side shows the files in this folder. Using the View menu, you can select Details, which gives

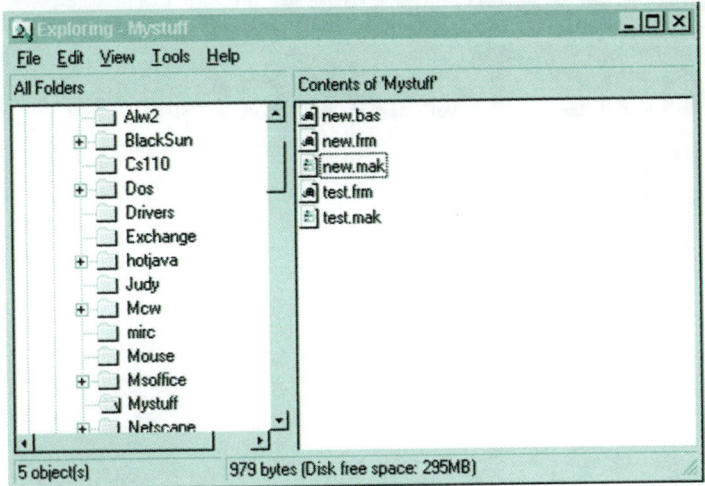

Figure A.15
Windows Explorer

you information about the size of the files and the date and time each was created or last changed. This information is helpful when you want to know how long a file has been around or when you last changed it.

New folders can be created by choosing New and then Folder from the File pull-down menu in Explorer. You are asked to name the new folder before it is created. Highlighting a file name or a folder name and choosing Delete from the File menu removes the file or the entire folder, including all the files it contains. Because this is a rather drastic action, Windows 95 asks you to confirm that you really want to move your files to the **Recycle bin**. The Recycle bin is accessible from its desktop icon (see Figure A.6). As a further protection for the user, Windows 95 stores files in the Recycle bin and does not actually delete them until the user specifically asks (from the File menu of the Recycle window) to empty the Recycle bin. Selecting a file in the Recycle bin and choosing Restore from the File menu replaces the file or folder in its original location.

A highlighted file or folder in the Explore window can be moved (or copied) to another folder by choosing Cut (or Copy) from the Edit menu, going to the destination folder, and choosing Paste from the Edit menu. Or you can simply drag-and-drop the file name to the new folder to move it or drag-and-drop while holding down the Ctrl key to copy it. If a file of the same name already exists in the destination folder, Windows 95 asks you to confirm that you want to overwrite that file.

After a bit of practice, you'll feel comfortable using Windows Explorer. Just remember to exercise caution; you should make back-up copies of all important files, and you should delete with forethought.

Visual Basic Toolbar and Toolbox

APPENDIX

New Form
New Module
Open Project
Save Project
Menu Design Window
Properties Window
Run
Break
Stop
Breakpoint
Instant Watch
Calls
Single Step
Procedure Step

Figure A.16
Visual Basic Toolbox

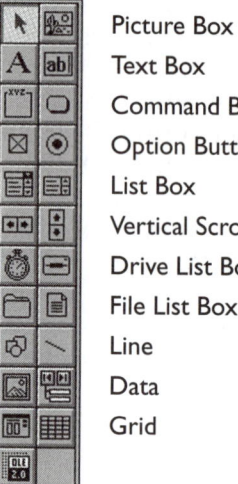

Pointer — Picture Box
Label — Text Box
Frame — Command Button
Check Box — Option Button
Combo Box — List Box
Horizontal Scroll Bar — Vertical Scroll Bar
Timer — Drive List Box
Directory List Box — File List Box
Shape — Line
Image — Data
Common Dialog — Grid
OLE

Figure A.17
Visual Basic Toolbox

APPENDIX E

Visual Basic Version 4.0

Visual Basic 4.0 has a number of changes and new features from version 3.0. This appendix discusses those that most directly affect what you see as you work through this textbook.

The general layout of the Visual Basic environment is roughly the same—there is a main window with a menu bar and toolbar, there is a Form window, a Project window, a Properties window, and a Toolbox. The Form window and Project window are relatively unchanged in version 4.0. The default background color for the Form window is now "standard gray" rather than white. The Project window no longer lists files for custom controls.

The toolbar and menu bar are shown in Figure A.18. The Debug, Options, and Window menus from Visual Basic 3.0 are gone, and there are new menu choices of Insert, Tools, and Add-Ins. Even for menus with the same names as in version 3.0, menu choices have changed. The File menu (Figure A.19) has been rearranged so that options for saving files and saving projects are now together. Existing files can still be added to or removed from a project, but to create a new form or module in a project, you use the Insert menu.

Figure A.18
Visual Basic 4.0 toolbar and menu bar

Figure A.19
File pull-down menu

The Edit menu (Figure A.20) has the usual Undo, Cut, Copy, Paste, Delete, and Find/Replace options. Two new choices are the Indent and Outdent (Tab and Shift+Tab) to control indenting in the Code window. These options were available in version 3.0, but not as menu picks. The Code window itself can be configured to show either one procedure at a time (as in

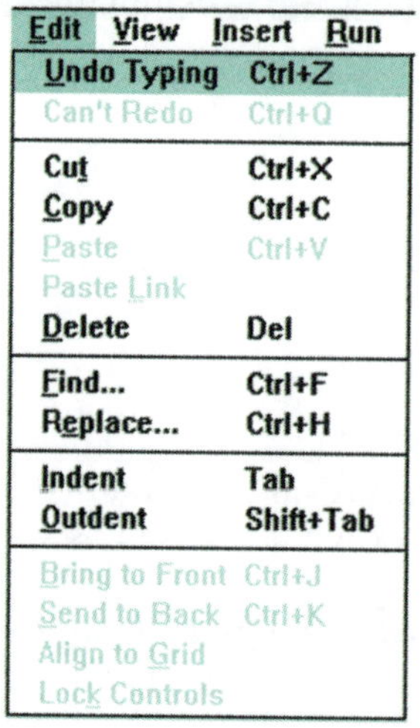

Figure A.20
Edit menu in version 4.0

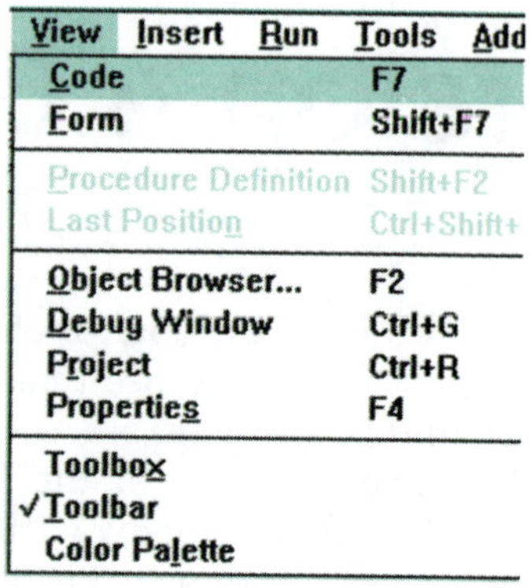

Figure A.21
View menu in version 4.0

version 3.0) or all the procedures in the current module. You can also set the font and font size for the Code window.

The View menu (Figure A.21) allows you to toggle back and forth between the form and the code for a selected object. As before, it provides some ways to move from one procedure to another within the project. A more powerful choice is the Object Browser, which lets you scroll through a list of all of your objects, procedures, and available methods. The new View menu also takes over some of the tasks of the old Window menu, letting you bring to the fore the Toolbox, Debug, Project, or Properties windows.

The new Run menu incorporates some of the old Debug menu tasks, such as single-stepping and setting and clearing breakpoints. Other Debug tasks having to do with the Watch window are now controlled from the Tools menu. The Tools menu also has a pick for the Menu Design window, now called the Menu Editor, and a Custom Controls pick to allow addition or removal of custom controls from the Toolbox. The Tools menu also contains an Options pick, replacing the old Options menu. The Add-Ins menu need not concern you; the Help menu works as before.

The toolbar again incorporates buttons for frequently used menu picks. New choices here are shown in Figure A.22. Locking a control locks its position on the form; a locked control cannot be moved. The step into and step over buttons are the old single step and procedure step but without the cute footprints! With the new toolbar, however, you don't have to memorize which buttons do which. If you hesitate for a moment with the cursor over an icon on the toolbar, a small yellow text box—a Tool Tip—appears to tell you what the icon represents.

The Toolbox (Figure A.23) also supports Tool Tips. All the controls from Visual Basic 3.0 are in the new Toolbox, although their icons have changed slightly. A few additional custom controls have also been added. (The Professional version has even more controls.) The Properties window (Figure A.24) is more convenient to use than in version 3.0. Gone is the separate single text box in which you type a new value for any property. Instead,

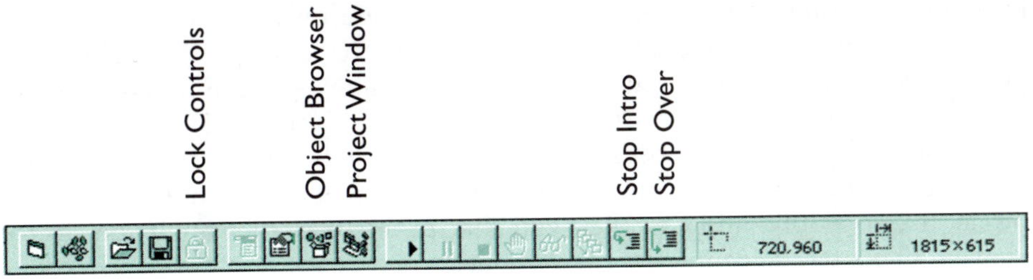

APPENDIX E • 501

Figure A.22
New toolbar choices

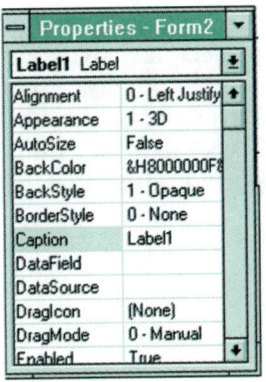

Figure A.23
Visual Basic Toolbox

Figure A.24
Properties window

you edit a property value by double-clicking on the property itself. In addition, most control objects have more properties than previously.

All the programs for this textbook, developed in Visual Basic 3.0, execute under Visual Basic 4.0. However, the process is not reversible. Once brought into Visual Basic 4.0, the project files are reformatted so that they no longer execute under Visual Basic 3.0.

Event procedures that used to look like

```
Sub Command1_Click()

     'body of procedure here
End Sub
```

look like

```
Private Sub Command1_Click()

     'body of procedure here
End Sub
```

under version 4.0. The keywords **Public** and **Private** determine the scope of procedures. Event procedures are by default Private, other procedures are by default Public. Private procedures have scope only within the form or module in which they occur. Public procedures have scope throughout the project. So form-level general procedures, which are private in Visual Basic 3.0, are by default public in 4.0. However, unlike version 3.0, you control the scope of procedures because you can change Public to Private and vice versa. For example, you can change the keyword Private in an event procedure to Public and can then call that procedure from anywhere in the project. (This has a big impact on the work in Lab 6.1).

Similarly, you have more control over the scope of variables. Variables within procedures are still declared with Dim and are still local. Variables declared in the declarations sections of either forms or modules are declared using either Private (available only within the form or module) or Public (available throughout the project). Thus a Public variable in either a form or a module is equivalent to a module variable declared as Global in Visual Basic 3.0.

The version 4.0 version of the .MAK file, the file that coordinates the project, has an extension of .VBP, which stands for Visual Basic Project.

Finally, although this does not impact anything in this book, Visual Basic has become a true object-oriented language. You can define reusable class modules as object data types. Inheritance and polymorphism are supported; Visual Basic 3.0 already supported the idea of encapsulation.

APPENDIX

Hot Keys

SHORTCUT KEY	ACTION
F1	Activates context-sensitive help
F2	When the Code window is open, brings up the View Procedures window
F3	When using the Find command on the Edit window, goes to next instance of word being searched for in code
Shift F3	When using the Find command on the Edit window, goes to previous instance of word being searched for in code
F4	Brings up Properties window for the active object Also drops down choice list for certain properties in the Properties window
F5	Runs a Visual Basic program from design mode or resumes execution from break mode
Shift F5	Restarts execution from break mode
F6	Toggles between panes in a split Code window
F7	Brings up the Code window for the active object
F8	In Break mode, single-steps the program
Shift F8	In Break mode, procedure-steps the program
F9	In the Code window, toggles breakpoints on and off
Shift F9	In Break mode, performs an Instant Watch for a selected variable

APPENDIX G

Alternate Type Declarations

Under the Option Explicit switch, all variables are declared by using one of the statements

```
Dim VariableName As datatype
Static VariableName As datatype
Global VariableName As datatype
```

In case you are reading code where this convention is not followed, you should be aware of other conventions about declaring variables. One method is to use a set of suffixes on the variable name. The following rules apply:

SUFFIX SYMBOL	DATA TYPE	EXAMPLE
%	Integer	number%
&	Long	GrainsOfSand&
!	Single	Rate!
#	Double	LightYears#
@	Currency	NationalDebt@
$	String	UserName$

Another method is to use Deftype statements. These statements specify all variables with identifiers that start with particular letters to be of one type. For example:

```
DefInt I-N
```

says that all variable whose names begin with I through N, inclusive, are Integer data type.

```
DefSng D
```

declares all variables whose names begin with D as type Single.

Another method is to make no type declarations at all but simply use a variable name when needed. Such a variable is generated as a Variant data type.

APPENDIX H

Project Files

Here is a list of all project files needed for the labs. These can be found on the disk at the back of this book.

Chapter 1
chap1.frm, chap1.mak, hello.frm, hello.mak, lab1.bas, lab1.exe, lab1.frm, lab1.mak, lab1a.frm, lab1b.frm

Chapter 2
flags.frm, flags.mak

Chapter 3
colors.frm, colors.mak

Chapter 4
adder.frm, adder.mak, prac.frm, prac.mak

Chapter 5
mycalc.exe

Chapter 6
ave.frm, ave.mak, drink.bmp, gas.bmp, jail.frm, jail.mak, sand.bmp

Chapter 7
banana.bmp, cherry.bmp, fence.frm, fence.mak, peach.bmp

Chapter 8
combo.frm, combo.mak, library.frm, library.mak, library2.frm, library3.frm, library4.frm, library5.frm, library6.frm, lister.frm, lister.mak

Chapter 9
chase.frm, chase.mak

Chapter 10
chick.frm. chick.mak, sales.frm, sales.mak

Chapter 11
bigbooks.txt, books.txt

Chapter 12
environ.xls, lib.mdb

INDEX

Abs function, 168, 169
Access key, 12, 331
Activate event, 50, 85, 86, 146
Adder program, 128–129
AddItem method, 310
AddNew method, 468
Algorithm, 106
  efficiency of, 380–382
  implementation of, 128–129
  pseudocode, 106, 107–108
Analog, 311
Animation, 351–352
Annuity, 169–170
ANSI (American National Standards Institute) character set, 308
Append mode, 405–406
Application program, 1, 4, 5
Argument, 125
  passed by reference, 214–215
  passed by value, 214–215
Argument passing, 211–216
Arithmetic expressions, 157–161
  mixed data types in, 160
  precedence of, 158–160
  variables in, 160–161
Arithmetic operations, 157, 158
Arrays, 360–361
  data entry into, 365–367, 370–371
  declarations for, 362–364
  dynamic, 363–364
  fixed-sized, 363
  For-Next loop for, 366–367
  parallel, 387–388
  two-dimensional, 367–368, 371–372
Artwork
  design-time, 338–340
  run-time, 349–350
As Integer statement, 119
Assembler, 3
Assembly language programming, 2, 4
Assignment statement, 107, 111–112, 113–114

AutoRedraw property, 350
AutoSize property, 71–72

BackColor property, 33, 34, 219
BAS file, 78–79
BASIC, 3, 4
Beep statement, 439
Binary operator, 239–240
Binary representation, 106
Binary search, 377–379, 381
Black-box testing, 440–441
Boolean algebra, 237
Boolean expressions, 237–240
Bound control, 467
Browse, 343
Button(s), 5–6
  command, 8, 26–27, 30–31, 32, 33, 64–65, 66, 71
  Fan, 354
  Option, 253–255
  toolbar, 14
ByVal, 214–215

Calculator program, 98–99, 173–177
Call statement, 197, 211
Cancel property, 278
Caption property, 66, 330–331
  vs. name property, 66–67
Cash register program, 224–228
Change event, 69, 308, 312
Change event procedure, 308
Check box, 253–255
Checked property, 336
Chr$ function, 439
Circle method, 353–355
Click event, 39–43
Client, 455
Clipboard, 83, 89–90, 453–455
Cls method, 145
COBOL, 3, 4
Code, 11
Code generators, 262
Code library, 343
Code module, 50–51

Code window, 41–42, 44–45
  editing, 49–52
  navigating, 48–49
  splitting of, 177–178
  starting up, 47–48
Coding, 22–23
Columns property, 314
Combo box control object, 306–310, 313–314
  drop-down, 307
Comma-delimited file format, 408
Command button, 8, 26–27, 30–31, 32, 33, 64–65, 66, 71
Comments, 43, 141
Common Dialog control, 406–408
Compiler, 3
Computer program, 1
Concatenation operation, 161
Concatenation operator, 98
Conditional processing, 107, 108, 236–288
  Boolean expressions in, 237–240
  control objects for, 253–255
  if-then-else statement in, 240–243
  logical operators in, 239–240
  relational operators in, 238–239
  select-case statement in, 243–245
  for slot machine program, 250–251
Conditional statement, 114
Constants
  declaration of, 124
  scope of, 203
Container application, 457
Control array, 91, 95–96, 360
Control objects, 32
  for conditional processing, 253–255
  scope of, 202–203
Control record, 409
Control structures, 236–237
Count property, 321

Currency data type, 119–120
Current X property, 183–184
Current Y property, 183–184
Custom controls, 78
Custom toolbars, 340–341, 346–347

Data aware, 467
Data control, 466
Data flow diagram, 263
Data structures, 360–402
  arrays as, 360–372
  definition of, 361
Data types, 119–123, 155–156, 163–166
  for decimal numbers, 119, 120, 155–156
  user-defined, 389–391, 393–394
Database
  querying of, 473–474, 479–480
  relational, 465–467
  searching of, 472
DatabaseName property, 466
DataChanged property, 467
DataField property, 467
DataSource property, 467
Date functions, 171
Date$ function, 171
Day function, 171
Debug, 11
Debug menu, 13
Debug window, 274–276
Debugger, 272–277
Decimal numbers
  data types for, 119, 120, 155–156
Declarations, 119–123
  for arrays, 362–364
  for constants, 124
  for variables, 50–51, 119–123, 199–202
Default property, 278
Delete method, 468
Design mode, 17
Design-time artwork, 338–340
Dialog box, 15–16
Digital clock program, 258–259

Dim statement, 119–122
Disabled menu item, 14
Discrete, 311
Diving competition
   program, 267–271,
   282
DoAverage procedure,
   211–215
Documentation, 22,
   140–143
   technical, 140–143
   user, 149–141, 143
   readability of, 142
Do-Loop-Until, 295–297
Do-Loop-While, 295
Double data type, 119,
   120, 121, 122
Do-Until-Loop, 294
Do-While-Loop, 292–293
DrawWidth property, 349
Dummy variables, 213
Dynamic data exchange
   (DDE), 455–457
Dynaset, 473–474

Edit, 89–90
Edit menu, 13, 89–90
ElseIf, 242–243
Empty else situation,
   241–242
Enabled menu item, 14
Enabled property, 67, 279,
   336
EndIf, 240–242
EndDoc method, 185
Erase statement, 366
Error(s), 435–439
   debugger for, 271–277
   logic, 273
   run-time, 273, 435
   syntax, 272–273
   trappable, 435–439,
   446
   user-defined, 439
Error handler, 435–439
Event(s), 39–45, 81
   Activate, 50, 85, 86,
   146
   Change, 69, 312
   Click, 39–43
   DblClick, 39
   GotFocus, 69, 279
   Load, 47–48, 50, 85–86
   LostFocus, 69, 279
   MouseMove, 39
   notation for, 67
   Timer, 87, 88, 351
   Validate, 467
Event procedures, 41–43,
   45, 197–199
   parameters of, 215
Excel spreadsheet,
   455–457, 463
EXE file, 79
Exit Sub statement,
   436–437
Exp function, 168

Exponentiation operation,
   157

Fan button, 354
Fault tolerance, 443
Field, 408
File(s), 77, 403–404
   BAS, 78–79
   binary, 405
   closing of, 405
   Common Dialog
      control for, 406–408
   external, 403–404
   FRM, 78–79
   index, 452
   MAK, 78–79, 83–84
   opening of, 405
   Picture, 337–338
   random-access,
      404–405, 419–420,
      422–429
      deleting from, 429
      reading from,
         420–422,
         428–429
      writing to, 420–422,
         427
   sequential, 404,
      422–423
      closing of, 405–406
      opening of, 405–406
      reading from,
         411–413,
         415–417
      record addition to, 418
      searching, 417
      writing to, 408–411
File extension, 77
File menu, 12–14, 15–16
File specification, 406
Filename property, 407
FillStyle property, 340
Filter property, 408
Financial functions, 171
Find dialog box, 90
FindFirst method, 468
FindMaxIndex procedure,
   272, 275–276
Flow of control, 236
Flowchart, 265–266
Font, 182–183
Font properties, 67
ForeColor property, 220,
   349
Form design, 25, 54–56
Form window, 7, 14
Format$ function,
   148–149, 184–185
Forms collection,
   321–322, 361
For-Next loop, 297–298,
   366
FORTRAN, 3, 4
Frame control object, 229,
   257–258
FRM file, 78–79
Function(s), 125

Abs, 168–169
Chr$, 439
Date, 171
Date$, 171
Day, 171
Exp, 168
financial, 169–171
Format$, 148–149,
   184–185
Hour, 171
InputBox$, 135–138
InStr, 172
intrinsic, 167–172
invocation of, 222
Ipmt, 170
LCase$, 172
Left$, 172
Len, 172
Log, 168
LTrim$, 172
Mid$, 172
Now, 171
Pmt, 170
   vs. procedure, 222
Right$, 172
Rnd, 168, 169
RTrim$, 172
Sgn, 168
Sin, 168
SLN, 170, 171
Space$, 172
Sqr, 168
Str$, 124–128
string, 172
Time, 171
Time$, 171
UCase$, 172
user-defined, 221–222
Val, 124–128
VarType, 163–164
Weekday, 171
Functional requirements,
   181

General procedures, 45,
   174, 197–199
Get statement, 420–422
GetFormat method,
   454–455
Getname procedure, 49,
   55
GotFocus event, 69, 279
Grade averaging program,
   211–213
Graphic containers, 337
Graphical user interface
   (GUI), 3
Graphics, 337
   animation of, 351–352

Hardware, 1
Height property, 66,
   67–68
Help menu, 13–14
Help system, 13–14,
   19–21, 26–27

context-sensitivity of,
   21
menu bar of, 20–21
toolbar of, 20–21
Hide method, 80–82
Hot key, 17, 332, 333
Hour function, 171
Hypertext, 19–20

Identifiers, 110–111
   case insensitivity of,
   111
If-Then-Else statement,
   240–243, 248–249
Immediate pane
   of Debug window,
   275–276
Imperative languages,
   40
Index as Integer, 91
Index file, 452
Index property, 330
Infinite loop, 117, 293
Input, 106
Input # statement,
   411–412
Input box, 135–138, 145
Input$ function, 413
InputBox$ function,
   136–138
Instant Watch dialog box,
   277
InStr function, 172
Integer data type, 120
Integer quotient
   operation, 157
Integer remainder
   operation, 157
Integrated development
   environment (IDE),
   11
Interface
   procedure, 214
   user, 63–64, 92–93
Interpreter, 3
Interval property, 87
Ipmt function, 170

KeyPress event procedure,
   308
Keywords, 43. *See also*
   Reserved word.
Kill statement, 413

Label, 65
Label caption, 57
Label icon, 8
Label properties, 71–72
Language
   imperative, 40
   procedural, 40
LargeChange property,
   311–312
LBound function, 367
LCase$ function, 172

Left$ function, 172
Left property, 65, 67
Len function, 172
Line control, 339
Line input # statement, 412–413
Line label, 435–436
Line method, 217–219, 349–350, 353
List box control object, 306–310, 314–316
   drop-down, 307
List property, 309
ListCount property, 309
ListIndex property, 309
Listing, 84
Load event, 47–48, 50, 85–86
LOF function, 413
Log function, 168
Logic errors, 273
Logical delete, 422
Logical operators, 239–240, 247–248
Logical record, 422
Long data type, 120
Loop
   infinite, 117, 293
   Wait, 53, 54
Loop body, 292, 293
Loop statement, 115–117
Looping, 54, 108, 289–329
   Do-Loop-Until, 295–296
   Do-Loop-While, 295
   Do-Until-Loop, 294
   Do-While-Loop, 292–293
   logic errors of, 299
   off-by-one errors in, 299–303
LostFocus event, 69, 279
LTrim$ function, 172

Machine language programming, 2, 4
MAK file, 78–79
   editing of, 83–84
Mathematical functions, 168
Max property, 311
MaxLength property, 69, 74, 76
Menu, 12–15
   pop-up (floating), 333–334, 336
   pull-down (drop-down), 6, 330–333, 335
Menu bar, 12–15
Menu Design window, 330–334
Menu pick, 9
Message box, 431–435, 445
   numerical codes for, 434

Message box statement, 433, 435
Method(s), 80–82
   AddItem, 310
   AddNew, 468
   Circle, 353–355
   Cls, 145
   Delete, 468
   EndDoc, 185
   FindFirst, 468
   GetFormat, 454–455
   Hide, 80
   Move, 351
   MoveFirst, 468
   MoveLast, 468
   MoveNext, 468
   MovePrevious, 468
   NewPage, 185
   notation for, 82
   PopupMenu, 333–334
   Print, 112, 179, 183–184, 189–190
   PrintForm, 88
   Pset, 384–385
   RemoveItem, 310
   SetFocus, 146, 279, 471
   Show, 80
Mid$ function, 172
Min property, 311
Modal forms, 138–139
Modal window, 138
Module, 50, 77
Monospace font, 182
MouseDown event procedure, 334
MouseMove event, 39
Move method, 351
MoveFirst method, 468
MoveLast method, 468
MoveNext method, 468
MovePrevious method, 468
MultiLine property, 69, 74–75, 76
Multiselect property, 314

Name
   prefix convention for, 66
Name property, 66, 330
   vs. caption property, 66–67
Nested If statement, 241
NewIndex property, 314
NewPage method, 185
NoMatch property, 468
Notation
   for event, 67
   for methods, 82
   for property, 67
Now function, 171
Null string, 161–162

Object(s), 32–34
   active, 8, 14, 55
   control, 32
   embedded, 458
   events of, 40–42, 81
   linked, 458
   methods of, 80–82
   passive, 55
   properties of, 33–34, 81
Object linking and embedding (OLE), 457–458, 460–462
Object linking and embedding (OLE) control, 458, 460
Object task card (OTC), 54–56, 105
   for addition program, 128–129
   for calculator program, 98–99
   for new program, 57–58
Off-by-one errors
   in looping, 299–303
On-Err-GoTo statement, 436
On-line help, 13–14
Operating system, 1
Option button, 253–255
Options menu, 13
Output, 106
Output mode, 405, 406
Overflow error, 121

Parallel arrays, 387–388
Parameter list, 211, 213, 215
PasswordChar property, 76
Performance requirements, 181
Persistent data, 403
Physical record, 422
Picture box, 112, 345
Picture elements, 339
Picture files, 337–338
Picture property, 229
Pixels, 339
Pmt function, 170
Point, 14
Pointer, 65
PopupMenu method, 333–334
Precedence rules, 158–160
Prefix
   for names, 66
Print # statement, 410–411
Print method, 112, 179, 189–190
   spacing control mechanisms for, 184
PrintForm method, 80, 88
Printing, 79–80, 84–88

Problem specification, 180–181
Problem-solving, 21–22
Procedure(s), 196–235
   DoAverage, 211–213
   error message for, 198, 199
   event, 41–43, 45, 197–199, 215
   FindMaxIndex, 272, 275–276
   vs. function, 222
   general, 45, 174, 197–199
   Getname, 49, 55
   scope of, 197–199, 203, 205–210
   SumItUp, 366–367
Procedure body, 43
Procedure interface, 214
Process Item command button, 289–291
Process Prices command button, 291–292
Program code, 11
Programming
   black-box testing of, 440–441
   design representation in, 261–266
   data flow diagram for, 263
   flowchart for, 265–266
   Object Task Card for, 54–56, 262
   state transition diagram for, 264
   storyboard for, 265
   structure chart for, 262–263
   design step of, 22, 23, 54–56, 105–110, 131–133, 223–225
   for cash register operation, 224–228
   for diving competition, 267–271
   documentation step of, 22, 140–143
   event-driven, 40, 53–54
   implementation step of, 22, 23, 105
   object-oriented, 40
   problem-solving steps in, 21–22
   requirements analysis and specifications step of, 22, 180–185
   reusability of, 342–343
   testing step of, 22, 440–443, 475
   top-down design in, 223–225

white-box testing of,
442–443
Programming
environment, 6, 11
Programming language,
2–4
Project, 13
adder.mak, 128–129,
131
ave.mak, 217
birth.mak, 131–134,
145–146
calc.mak, 98–99,
173–174
carpet.mak, 146–149
cash.mak, 229–230
chase.mak, 354–355
chick.mak, 371–372
circles.mak, 353–354
clock.mak, 257–259
combo.mak, 313–315
dive.mak, 267–271
draw.mak, 353–354
environ.mak, 459–463
files of, 77–79
jail.mak, 217–220
lab1.mak, 15–16, 78
editing of, 83–84
event procedures of,
41–43
events of, 39–45
printing of, 84–85
properties window
of, 33–34, 35
startup form of,
55–56, 85
libdb.mak, 469–472,
477–480
libran.mak, 425–429,
445–446
library.mak, 321–324,
415–416
lister.mak, 315–316
management of, 77–79
menu.mak, 335–336
message.mak, 26
movie.mak, 57–58
namer.mak, 97
newmovie.mak, 95–96
printing of, 79–80
sales.mak, 393–396
slot.mak, 249–252
sort.mak, 383–386,
394
Project window, 15–17
Prompt, 68
Properties window,
33–34, 35, 65–68
Property (properties),
65–68, 81
AutoRedraw, 350
AutoSize, 71–72
BackColor, 33, 34,
219
Cancel, 278
Caption, 66–67, 330
changes to, 35–37,
97

Checked, 336
Columns, 314
Count, 321
Current X, 183–184
Current Y, 183–184
DatabaseName, 466
DataChanged, 467
DataField, 467
DataSource, 467
DrawWidth, 349
Enabled, 67, 279, 336
Filename, 407
FillStyle, 340
Filter, 408
Font, 67
ForeColor, 220, 349
Height, 66, 67–68
Index, 330–331
Interval, 87
Label, 71–72
LargeChange, 311–312
Left, 65, 67
List, 309
ListCount, 309
ListIndex, 309
Max, 311
MaxLength, 69, 74,
76
Min, 311
MultiLine, 69, 74, 75,
76
Multiselect, 314
Name, 66–67, 330
NewIndex, 314
NoMatch, 468
notation for, 67
of objects, 33–34
PasswordChar, 76
Picture, 229
ReadOnly, 467
Recordset, 467–468
RecordSource, 466
ScaleHeight, 184
ScaleMode, 65, 183
ScaleWidth, 184
ScrollBars, 69, 74–75
Selected, 314
setting code for, 73–74
Shape, 340
Shortcut, 332–333
SmallChange, 311–312
Sorted, 309
Style, 306–307
TabIndex, 277–278
TabStop, 278
Text, 68, 307–308
Top, 65, 67
Value, 254–255, 311
Visible, 67, 335
Width, 66, 67
WordWrap, 71, 72
X1, 340
X2, 340
Y1, 340
Y2, 340
Proportional spaced font,
182
Prototype, 317–318

Pset method, 384–385
Pseudocode, 106
Pseudorandom, 169
Put statement, 420–422

Quantity
data types for,
119–123, 155–156
Query, 473–474

Radio buttons, 253–255
Random numbers, 384
Randomize statement,
169
ReadOnly property, 467
Record(s), 408
addition of, 418
logical, 422
modification of,
467–468, 470–471
physical, 422
Recordnumber variable,
421–422
Recordset property,
467–468
RecordSource property,
466
Recursion, 377
ReDim statement, 364
Refresh operation, 350
Relational database,
465–467
Relational operators,
238–239, 247
Reliability, 443
RemoveItem method,
310
Replace dialog box, 90
Require variable
declaration switch,
123
Requirements analysis,
180–181
Reserved word, 43, 110.
See also Keywords.
Call, 197
Dim, 119
End Type, 389
Global, 200, 202
Static, 200, 363
Sub, 43
Type, 389
Resume statement, 436
Reusable code, 342–343
Reverse Polish notation
(RPN), 173
Right$ function, 172
Rnd function, 168, 169
Round-off errors, 156
RTrim$ function, 172
Run menu, 13, 17
Run mode, 17
Run time, 33
Run-time artwork,
349–350
Run-time errors, 273,
435

Safety-critical system, 64,
443
Save, 25–26, 79
ScaleHeight property, 184
ScaleMode property, 65,
183
ScaleWidth property, 184
Scope, 197
of constants, 203
of control objects,
202–203
of procedures,
197–199, 203,
205–210
of variables, 199–203
Scroll bar, 315–316
Scroll bar control object,
310–312
Scroll event, 312
ScrollBars property, 69,
74–75
Searching, 318–319,
376–379
binary, 377–379, 381
Select-case statement,
243–245, 249
Selected property, 314
Selection sort, 373–376,
382, 385–386
visual animation of,
383–384
Semantics, 109
Sentinel value, 291
Sequential processing,
107, 108
Sequential search,
318–319, 323–324,
376, 381
Server, 455
SetFocus method, 146,
279, 471
Sgn function, 168
Shape control, 339, 340,
347
Shape property, 340
Shortcut property,
332–333
Show method, 80
Side effects, 216
Sin function, 168
Single data type, 120, 121
Single stepping, 114–115
Sizing handles, 8
SLN function, 170, 171
Slot machine program,
250–251
SmallChange property,
311–312
Software, 1
prototype of, 317–318
reusability of, 342–343
Sorted property, 309
Sorter procedure, 395
Sorting, 373–376
Space$ function, 172
Sqr function, 168
Startup form, 53, 85
OTC design for, 55–56

State transition diagram, 264
Storyboard, 265
Str$ function, 124–128
String data type, 120
String expressions, 161–162
String functions, 172
String variable, 162, 187–188
String*n data type, 120
Structure chart, 262–263
Structured Query Language (SQL), 473, 477–479
Stub, 317
Style property, 306–307
SumItUp procedure, 366–367
Syntax, 43, 109
Syntax errors, 272–273
Systems analyst, 181

TabIndex property, 277–278
Table, 465–466
TabStop property, 278
Target value, 318
Technical documentation, 140–143
  external, 143
  internal, 140–143

Technical reference manual, 143
Text box, 68–69, 96–98
  properties of, 69, 74–76
Text box control, 69
Text property, 68, 307–308
Time functions, 171
Time$ function, 171
Timer control, 351–352
Timer event, 87, 88, 351–352
Toolbar, 12–15
  custom, 340–341, 346–347
Toolbox, 64–65
Toolbox window, 8
Top property, 65, 67
Trace, 85
Twip, 14
Type statement, 389

UBound function, 367
UCase$ function, 172
Unary operator, 239, 240
Unintentional side effects, 216
User documentation, 140–141
  external, 140–141, 143
  internal, 140–141, 143
User interface
  definition of, 63–64

  design of, 92–93
  flexible, 93
  internal consistency of, 93
  protectiveness of, 93
  transparency of, 93
User-defined functions, 221–222
User-defined variables, 389–391

Val function, 124–128
Validate event, 467
Value property, 254–255, 311
Variable(s), 110
  in arithmetic operations, 160–161
  declaration of, 50–51, 119–123, 200–202
  dummy, 213
  global scope of, 200–202
  initialization of, 161
  local scope of, 200–202
  scope of, 199–203
  string, 162, 187–188
  user-defined, 389–391
Variable name, 111
Variable value, 111

Variant data type, 120, 121–123
VarType function, 163–164
View menu, 13
Visible property, 67, 335

Wait loop, 53, 54
Watch expression, 275–276
Weekday function, 171
White-box testing, 442–443
Width property, 66, 67
Window(s), 1–2
  identification of, 6–8
  modal, 138
  pop-up, 15–16
Window menu, 13
Windows operating system, 1
WordWrap property, 71, 72
Write # statement, 408–409

X1 property, 340
X2 property, 340

Y1 property, 340
Y2 property, 340